THE TSARINA'S LOST TREASURE

Catherine the Great,
a Golden Age Masterpiece, and
a Legendary Shipwreck

GERALD EASTER
and MARA VORHEES

PEGASUS BOOKS
NEW YORK LONDON

THE TSARINA'S LOST TREASURE

Pegasus Books, Ltd.
148 West 37th Street, 13th Floor
New York, NY 10018

Copyright © 2020 by Gerald Easter and Mara Vorhees

First Pegasus Books paperback edition Jamuary 2022
First Pegasus Books cloth edition September 2020

Interior design by Maria Fernandez

Library of Congress Cataloging-in-Publication Data is available.

ISBN: 978-1-64313-942-5

10 9 8 7 6 5 4 3 2 1

Printed in the United States of America
Distributed by Simon & Schuster
www.pegasusbooks.com

For our Finnish family
Outi & Kauko Ojala

"The world is full of great and wonderful things for those who are ready for them."

—Tove Jansson, *Moominpappa at Sea*

CONTENTS

PART THREE

Prologue

THE WRECK

The approaching vessel struck sail before the bronze battery, reminding all captains that further passage required payment to the Danish king. Through sallow mist the towers of Castle Kronborg loomed. The citadel of Elsinore, home to Hamlet's ghosts, and gateway to the Baltic Sea.

The young skipper deliberately maneuvered his brig past Kronborg's steep sandstone walls and brawny earthen ramparts, mindful of his secret cargo. Beyond the fortress, the town's cascading red-tiled roofs and jabbing rust-green spires came into sight. The cramped harbor swayed and rattled with the spars and rigging of two dozen jostling merchant ships. English and Dutch colors snapped in the breeze. The captain secured an outlying berth and set down a launch in the direction of Tollbooth Quay, the central dock leading to the Customs House.

From King Eric's time, in the 15th century, all ships passing through the Sound—the narrow strait separating Scania, the southern tip of Sweden, from Zealand, the central isle of Denmark—were required to stop and pay an entry fee, the Sound Dues, or risk the wrath of Kronborg's gunners. Fixed between 1 and 2 percent of the value of a ship's cargo, this royal protection racket was the main source of wealth of the Danish state for four centuries. The two-hundred-foot walk down Tollbooth Quay presented its own challenges as dues-paying shipmasters navigated a human surge of longshoremen at work, sailors at liberty, and thieves on the prowl. Approaching the dock, the captain clutched a leather satchel; his demeanor stiffened.

The anxious skipper was fortunate to catch the attention of one of the uniformed customs officers patrolling Tollbooth Quay, and was hurriedly escorted past the touts and thugs. Elsinore was in good form, decorated with half-timbered row houses, cobblestoned alleyways, and a newly renovated harbor front. The centerpiece was the new mansard-capped Customs House, delivered in a restrained rococo style that suited Lutheran sensibility. The captain entered and declared his business.

He was Reynoud Lourens, master of the *Vrouw Maria*, a merchant vessel out of Amsterdam, en route to Saint Petersburg. The ship was an eighty-five-foot snow-brig, double-masted and square-rigged. Sturdy, steerable, and spacious, the snow-brig was a favored craft among Baltic traders. A customs officer drew up a new document: Dutch ship, no. 508; September 23, 1771. From his satchel, Lourens produced an itemized cargo list and a stack of letters embossed with diplomatic stamps. Lourens was impatient to expedite the transaction. He was already a week behind schedule because of late summer winds in the Atlantic. Lourens was more so anxious about the prize hidden in the ship's hold, the property of Russian empress Catherine the Great.

The officer looked down at the authoritative documents and up at the awkward captain. It was an exotic and expensive list of goods, intended to affirm the elite status of Russian high society. Sugar and coffee, indigo and brazilwood from the Americas; fine linen and woven fabric from the Low Countries; silver, zinc, and mercury for Saint Petersburg's master craftsmen; but that was not all. The officer readily surmised there was additional cargo of special interest. His inquiry met brusque resistance. It was the business of monarchs only. The Danish king was zealous about collecting the Sound Dues, except from fellow sovereigns, who were extended the courtesy of a royal exemption. Dropping the matter, the officer wrote "and assorted merchandise" into the ledger, then returned his attention to the cargo list. The *Vrouw Maria* was assessed a hefty passage bill of nearly four hundred

Danish rigsdalers for the items declared. Lourens paid without protest and departed with haste.

Returning to the vessel, Captain Lourens was accompanied by a navigation pilot provided by the Customs House, a standard procedure. The crew rowed the ship away from its harbor mooring until, catching a breeze, the *Vrouw Maria* gained momentum. Starboard, Lourens admired the hillside rising over the town, where bursting late summer flora embraced the neoclassical Marienlyst Palace. Portside, he glimpsed a Danish Man-of-War, a fierce sixty-gun ship of the line deterrent to would-be toll evaders. The channel through the southern Sound was tapered and twisted; the pilot stayed aboard for two days until the ship reached the safety of deep water and the Baltic Sea. Lourens scrutinized the pilot as he rowed back to shore, satisfied that his secret cargo was not betrayed.

To the unsuspecting, the *Vrouw Maria* was an ordinary trader, hauling barrels of rye grain or salted herring. In fact, she was a treasure ship. Concealed in the hold was a cache of more than a dozen masterpiece paintings, destined for the collection of Catherine the Great. The Russian empress was unrestrained when indulging her favorite passions, one of which was art. The *Vrouw Maria*'s secret cargo was the tsarina's most recent splurge: the highest-priced items from the estate sale of renowned Amsterdam wine merchant and art collector Gerrit Braamcamp. It was the most dazzling assemblage of Flemish and Dutch Old Masters ever to reach the auctioneer's block. Included in Catherine's treasure trove was the auction's biggest prize, Gerrit Dou's oak-panel triptych, *The Nursery*. Dou was Rembrandt's student, who surpassed his master to become the premier artist of his time. And Dou's triptych was the most admired and coveted artwork produced during the Dutch Golden Age.

Shipmaster Reynoud Lourens was only twenty-four years old. He had commanded the "Russia Run" three times previously, twice at the helm of the *Vrouw Maria*. For Dutch investors in the Saint Petersburg trade route, Lourens was valued for his experience with unpredictable Baltic tempests and petulant Russian princes. His business at the Customs House concluded, Reynoud stood braced against the laurel-carved oak rail and surveyed the stark shoreline. Along the water's edge, a clattering of jackdaws quarreled, swirled, and settled, then quarreled, swirled, and settled again as they came together for a winter roost. It was a reminder that the *Vrouw Maria* still had eight hundred miles to go.

The ship exited the Sound and entered the lower Baltic Proper. Lourens set a course north by northeast. To portside, the *Vrouw Maria* would follow Sweden's fir-clad eastern shore, home of legendary ogre-slayer Beowulf; then past the island of Gotland, from whence Viking longboats embarked on expeditions of discovery and demolition. To starboard, the ship would sail by prosperous Danzig, central granary of the old Hansa trading league; then along the famed Amber Coast, a sandy stretch of East Prussia and Poland; next came the western shores of Livonia, where five hundred years earlier Europe's defiant pagan tribes made their last stand in the Northern Crusades. With luck, fair winds from the south could help the *Vrouw Maria* make up lost time along this stretch.

Moving into the upper Baltic Proper, the voyage became trickier. With the outer islands of Stockholm distant in the west, the ship would be exposed to the whims of the sea. Here three colliding currents from the Bay of Riga, the Gulf of Finland, and the Bay of Bothnia caused unpredictable surface conditions. In this part of the Baltic, sudden storm surges peaked in the autumn months. The captain would need to turn due east into the Gulf of Finland and locate "the fairway," a narrow current that ran along the southern Finnish coast, and perilously close to the Archipelago Sea. The siren-like Archipelago was beguiling and deadly, where lay tens of thousands of rocky islets and hidden boulders. Known to sailors as the graveyard of the Baltic, the archipelago was the resting spot of countless wrecks. Once the *Vrouw Maria* was safely inside the fairway, Lourens had a two-hundred-mile final leg through the Gulf of Finland into shallow Neva Bay and the Baltic's easternmost anchorage, Saint Petersburg, where Empress Catherine awaited her prize.

Sober and devout, Lourens mustered a crew that was likewise; not an easy task, even in Calvinist Amsterdam. Steadfast faith was the young captain's ally against the capricious sea. As shipmaster, he felt a moral obligation to reinforce Christian dutifulness in his crew. And so, on the night of October 3rd, following supper, Lourens was as usual below deck leading evening prayers. Only two crewmen were left on the main deck to operate the vessel as she made for the fairway. The assembled sailors were likely distracted from their spiritual communion by a relentless assault of wind and waves.

From the start, the voyage had encountered adverse weather, which now turned ominous. All day dark low-lying clouds blotted out the land and sky, making it impossible to get an accurate bearing on the ship's location. In the aft a helmsman wrestled the ship's wheel, while in the fore a rigger trimmed the sails. The pair struggled to tack eastward in the face of an onrushing gale. The *Vrouw Maria* was caught in an Arctic rager, an autumn hurricane, which struck without warning in the upper Baltic when Icelandic lows clashed with Siberian highs.

The praying below became more earnest, the voices more urgent. The heaving ship was jolted by a crash from underneath and abruptly stopped rolling. Captain and crew dreaded the meaning. They rushed up to the main deck to confirm that their boat was grounded on a rocky outcrop. The storm had pushed them off course to the northwest. The *Vrouw Maria* was stranded in the Archipelago Sea.

The thick oak hull took the blow without breaking, the hold remained dry. Lourens knew the ship was more vulnerable aground than adrift, and considered his options. Suddenly an immense wave lifted the vessel off the rock and tossed it back into the sea. The helmsman instinctively resumed his fight against the storm for control of the ship. The prow climbed the cresting whitecaps, teetered for a moment at the peak, then crashed down the backside into the swirling trough. Each frigid splashdown left the crew gasping and stinging. In the tumbling blackness the correct course was indiscernible. No one yet knew how far leeway the *Vrouw Maria* was off course, or how at this moment she was surrounded by the archipelago's menacing boulders.

The hull cracked hard when it struck the rocks, ripping the rudder from the keel. The wounded vessel foundered; seawater rushed in. A combination blast of wind and wave knocked the *Vrouw Maria* onto her side, sending barrels and men sprawling. Lourens staggered to his feet, and barked commands to take in the mainsheets and to drop anchor starboard side. The ship lurched back upright. Two men were sent below to assess the damage. They reported that the sternpost was smashed and that the rear hold was already three feet underwater. The ship carpenter hastily went to work on a makeshift patch and the men began pumping and bailing. The crew labored through the night without pause, as the ship thrashed about. By morning, the brig was finally holding up. But prevailing winds and precarious mooring made it dangerous to stay on board. Lourens gave the order to abandon ship.

The weary crew loaded a few provisions and personal belonging into two skiffs, and slogged through the surf toward a fog-shrouded skerry, eerily appearing for a moment and then vanishing on the horizon. A base camp was organized on this grim granite slab. Lourens sent a boat out to look for help.

In the afternoon his men returned, accompanied by a second boat with five fishermen, speaking an obscure Swedish dialect. The men had rowed about five miles from their island village on Jurmo, at the outer edge of the Archipelago Sea. Lourens was dismayed to learn his location. The captain reported his situation, and the men left, promising to return with reinforcements next day. Their readiness to help was motivated in part by the universal code of seamen to come to one another's aid, and in part by the unique chance for poor fishermen to enhance their meager existence. That evening the storm broke. The *Vrouw Maria* emerged through the parting cloud cover, an oscillating silhouette against a slate- and rose-streaked sky.

The next morning was clear and calm. Lourens was hopeful that the islanders would bring sufficient manpower to rescue the crippled vessel. Without a rudder, he would not dare to sail in the archipelago, but the ship could be towed to a safe port and the keel repaired. The cargo, meanwhile, could be conveyed by longboat to shore, where arrangements could be made for overland transport along the Kungsvagen, the King's Road. The old post road was the central land artery of Sweden's northern empire. The eastern branch ran from Turku, Finland to Vyborg, Russia, swooshing through pine and birch forests. The overland route was preferred in winter months, when carriage sleds could travel directly over frozen rivers and wetlands. The *Vrouw Maria*'s secret cargo, reasoned Lourens, could still reach Saint Petersburg and Empress Catherine by year's end.

The captain's contemplations were cut short by a loud call—boat ahoy. A small craft with nine noisy islanders arrived in camp, who together with the crew headed out to the brig. As they rowed closer, Lourens could see that the stern was sitting conspicuously low in the swell. Climbing aboard several men hurried below to discover that the rear hold was submersed in eight feet of seawater. The battered hull could not be mended, and the leaking ship was weighed down and listing.

Lourens acted first to steady the wobbly vessel. Ten barrels were removed from the flooded aft, placed in the small boats and rowed back to their camp. The captain next ordered all unnecessary weight on the main deck or in the rigging above to be jettisoned. With a belly full of pitching seawater, a top-heavy ship was in danger of capsizing. Finally, all hands were directed to commence pumping and bailing. The men toiled through the morning to remove water from the rear hold and prevent it from penetrating the fore section. At midday, they paused briefly to devour a meal of black bread and lutefisk, chunks of lye-cured cod, a Scandinavian seafaring staple.

Progress was slow. The ship had two manually operated bilge pumps, but these provided only half the force capacity needed for a vessel of this size. The overworked pumps could barely keep ahead of the leaking. The fishermen departed in the late afternoon, vowing to come back next day with more men. When the crew finally climbed down into the rowboats to return to camp, they had managed to reduce the water level inside the hull by just one foot. Lourens was devastated. The *Vrouw Maria* was slowly sinking.

The captain was determined not to surrender his ship to the archipelago. But to save the *Vrouw Maria*, he needed to get the water out of the hold, and to do that he needed more hands. Early next morning Lourens sent two skiffs out to the islands to round up additional help. Twenty-six volunteers eventually joined the rescue effort, though some were surely more interested in scavenging than salvaging. Meanwhile, high winds roused hostile waves, making it unsafe to be aboard, and another day was lost.

On Monday, October 7, Lourens led a mixed company of crew and fishermen back to the *Vrouw Maria*, where his worst fears were realized: the rear hold was completely flooded. And there was more. As the ship rolled in the waves on the outside, the seawater sloshed about on the inside, forcibly dislodging the cargo. Broken barrels and floating debris littered the hold.

The crew's attempts to bail and siphon were frustrated by the discovery that the water had become sweet and sludgy. The ship was carrying forty tons of sugar, which had spilled open, turning the hold into a vast tureen of cold syrupy soup. Two crewmen cranked the bilge pumps to life, and with a whir and a gurgle, water began flowing out of the ship. But the pumps faltered in the sugary muck, and then stopped completely. They were clogged with coffee beans. Hundreds of pounds of coffee beans from torn gunny sacks had become part of the deluge. When the pumps were turned on, the beans were sucked through the filters, and clogged up the cylinders. The bilge system was disabled. There was no saving the ship now.

Lourens redirected his attention to salvaging the cargo. He ordered open the forward hatch. To the captain's dismay, the inner compartment seals had cracked and the front storage was under more than four feet of water. Taking a few accessible barrels with them, the crew retreated back to the skerry for the night.

The next day, Lourens organized a major salvage operation with thirty-four men. The captain assigned one team the task of stripping the ship bare, collecting and packing up all the sails, rigging, and navigation instruments. These items, Lourens knew, could be quickly resold in nearby Turku, Finland's main harbor town, earning at least partial compensation for his losses. A second team went to work in the fore hold, removing the crates and barrels nearest to the hatch. And a third team continued the arduous task of bailing and siphoning trying to delay the inevitable.

When the operation got underway in the morning, the sea was calm, but by early afternoon, the wind shifted to the south and whitecaps rocked the hull. Lourens was again forced to curtail activity on the unstable craft. Before departing, it was noticed that the anchor cable was badly frayed from the constant push of wind and surf, and two crewmen cut and retied the mooring line. A small flotilla of rowboats, packed high with gear and goods, careened back to camp through pelting rain and plunging spray.

On Wednesday morning, October 9, Lourens rose early. The storm had passed. The sea was tranquil, lavender, and empty. The captain stared at the horizon for a long time. His ship was nowhere in sight. The men were roused and sent back out in rowboats to search, perhaps the storm had severed the worn anchor line and the vessel was adrift. Meanwhile, a jolly boat commanded by a Swedish customs official arrived on the skerry.

Appraising the camp, he inquired about the craft and the cargo. Lourens could only sigh: his ship was missing, its cargo a secret. Before casting off, the officer instructed him that a formal declaration on the wreck must be made to the maritime court in Turku.

Later in the afternoon, the skiffs returned to camp and a crewman reported to the captain. The *Vrouw Maria* was lost. And with the ship, her priceless cargo.

PART ONE

1

REMBRANDT'S APPRENTICE

The New Student

A medley of redbrick, white-trimmed townhouses crammed the perimeter of Kort Rapenburg. The vibrant Rapenburg was an upscale neighborhood in the low-lying township of Leiden. Through the doorway at Kort Rapenburg no. 12, on the east side of the square, a father and son emerged into the squinting February cold.

The pair strode alongside a frozen canal, where wool-bundled skaters skimmed past cargo-hauling sleds. They passed beneath the thumping Weddesteeg windmill, making barley malt for Leiden's master brewers. Nearing the Galgewater drawbridge, the father tugged the teen into a twisting alley leading to a compact courtyard and their destination—the house of the miller's son. The father gazed up at the dwelling's high-reaching north-facing windows. A young man in a frizzy auburn mane and flowing blue smock appeared at the threshold. He welcomed the pair inside. It was Rembrandt van Rijn.

A native Leidener, Rembrandt had only recently moved back home from Amsterdam to open a studio and make a reputation. The ninth of

Harman van Rijn's ten children, Rembrandt had passed through Leiden's elite grooming academies, the Latin School and Leiden University. But unlike his classmates, he showed no interest in commerce or law. Rembrandt ditched his lectures to draw, paint, and etch, and excelled at each. At age eighteen, the prodigy moved to Amsterdam to work in the studio of Holland's premier historical painter, Pieter Lastman, whose robust compositions of popular bible and mythology tales were all the rage on the northern European art market. Lastman studied in Italy for five years, and was an early devotee of Caravaggio. He showed Rembrandt how the inherent tension between light and dark could be expressed on canvas through the haunting chiaroscuro effect (developed by Caravaggio in the 16th century, perfected by Rembrandt in the 17th century). To become a virtuoso, Lastman implored his apprentice, you must go to Rome, Florence, and Venice; you must engage Renaissance brilliance firsthand. But Rembrandt was in a hurry. He had no time to traipse around Italy copying what others had already accomplished. He went home instead.

The trio settled in a cozy reception room, decorated with a dozen paintings, mostly portraits and several bible scenes. The guests introduced themselves—Douwe Jansz, a local glassmaker, and his son, Gerrit.* It was a polite formality. Rembrandt already knew his visitors, or at least knew of them. The two families were neighbors in the Rapenburg, both of a similar middling social standing, headed by an artisan and a miller. For an aspiring artist in Leiden, Douwe Jansz was a valuable contact. He operated a profitable workshop, owned several houses in the Rapenburg, headed the local glassmakers' guild, and sat on the town council. He was calling this day to discuss the possibility of an apprenticeship for his boy Gerrit. As they talked, Douwe Jansz recognized Rembrandt's father and mother as models in the pictures on display. They were for sale.

The proud father listed Gerrit's credentials. From an early age, the lad showed a talent for drawing. When he turned nine, the boy was sent to study with Leiden's elder draftsman Bartholomeus Dolendo, former student of the renowned Northern Baroque master Hendrick Goltzius. After this, Gerrit began a two and half year apprenticeship with the town's leading

---

* The father's full name was Douwe Janszoon, meaning Douwe son of Jan, while Gerrit's full name was Gerrit Douweszoon, meaning Gerrit son of Douwe.

glazier Pieter Couwenhorn, whose stained glass creations adorned Leiden's handsome public halls and its Gothic grandiosity, the Pieterskerk. In Couwenhorn's busy workshop, young Dou perfected the patient craft of glass engraving. By age twelve, Gerrit was a registered member of the glassmakers' guild and actively employed in Douwe's family business. The boy has a precise and firm hand, the father assured. Rembrandt nodded, it was an impressive resume for a fourteen-year-old.

But why was the youth not continuing his training and following his father's trade? Douwe Jansz explained that his oldest son, Jan, was also a glassmaker and, God willing, would take over the family workshop one day. Moreover, Gerrit's recklessness fitting glass panels into snug wood frames high atop rickety scaffolding caused his parents anxious fits. Mostly, Douwe Jansz had come to accept that the boy's passion was drawing and painting, not glassmaking. Rembrandt was persuaded. He agreed to make Gerrit his new student. Besides, Rembrandt couldn't say no; he needed the money.

Rembrandt, as yet, had no well-to-do patrons, no workshop to speak of, and barely a wisp of facial hair. He was just twenty-one years old. Douwe Jansz could have chosen a teacher from Leiden's established masters, Jan van Goyen, the prolific landscape artist, or David Bailly, the popular portrait painter. But the elder craftsman wanted to meet the brash newcomer that Leideners were beginning to notice. From the pictures exhibited in the front room, Douwe Jansz was convinced that Rembrandt could instruct his son in portraiture, which in a town brimming with wealthy image-conscious merchants should provide steady income. They discussed terms of a contract. Since Gerrit lived nearby, he did not require room and board. Rembrandt suggested 100 guilders annually to cover lessons and materials. It was more than the master glassmaker wanted to pay the novice art instructor. Still, there was something special about the miller's son.

Inside the Master's Studio

Leiden, in the early 17th century, was a showcase of industry and culture. Its busy workshops fronting the Old Rhine put out the finest cambric and woolen cloths in northern Europe. Amid the handsome step-gabled homes were three impressive churches, a grand town hall, a high-tech municipal waterworks, a sprawling liberal arts university and medical center, and a flourishing book printing industry. A dedicated pursuit of profit sustained local prosperity. It was too much commercialism for the modest English Pilgrims, who after a brief stay departed Leiden for America in 1620. Indeed, greed could dull the faculties of even the shrewdest Dutch trader. Leiden was the epicenter of Tulipmania, Holland's infamous flower bulb market crash in 1637. When Rembrandt opened his studio, in 1625, Leiden was approaching 50,000 residents, making it the second largest Dutch city after Amsterdam. Prospects were promising.

Gerrit arrived early to Rembrandt's home. His new teacher instructed the boy to prepare the studio for a lesson in portrait painting. He slipped through the active kitchen area and ascended a steep narrow staircase. Because property taxes were assessed by frontage, domestic life in Leiden, as in most Dutch cities, was organized vertically. On the dimly lit first-floor landing, the teen clutched at a black iron knob and heaved open a stout oak door. He pulled back the heavy drapes, and morning entered the studio, casting a soft yellow light across the stucco walls and wooden floor.

To make a workspace, Gerrit cleared away his master's favorite props—a gold-plated helmet, sword and shield, and human skull. Against a stacked collection of drawings and prints by Italian masters, Gerrit steadied a heavy framed mirror should Rembrandt want to work on another self-portrait. His teacher was obsessed with painting himself. But it was a practical habit more than a narcissistic one. The best model for learning to paint facial features and human expression, Rembrandt liked to remind Gerrit, was oneself. Also, it saved the expense of a sitter. Artists were businessmen, and portraits were a dependable source of income, especially small-scale headshots, or *tronies*, which even modest-income households splurged on.

Now to make paint. Gerrit lugged onto the worktable a cumbersome drawer, partitioned with tight cubbyholes cradling chunks of rock, bits of clay, and packets of powder. Rembrandt preferred a sparing palette. He did not make full use of the array of colors available to 17th-century Dutch artists, instead relying mostly on white and black, earthy browns and yellows, and dusky red. While some pigments were expensive, especially blues,

Rembrandt's color choices had less to do with cost and more with style. He preferred warm tones and glowing accents, applied with lively broad strokes.

Rembrandt's ambition was not to replicate the outer physical likeness of his subjects, but to penetrate their inner personal character. Rather than vibrant bouquets of color, he worked out evocative arrangements of light and shadow to reveal the hidden self—swagger or reserve, comfort or hardship, pride or humility. It was this introspective quality that made Rembrandt a transcendent artist, appreciated by a post-Freudian world as the most modern of the Old Masters. At the time, however, Rembrandt's sitters were more often incensed than enthralled by his discerning brushwork.

Gerrit removed a satchel from the pigment drawer and scooped out a small heap of white granules. Rembrandt, like most Old Masters, concocted his own color recipes, a trade secret. Some pigments, however, were procured through the local apothecary. Rembrandt ran simultaneous tabs with several Leiden pharmacies, and was usually overextended. White lead was the most common paint pigment used by Rembrandt, but it was not so easy to make at home. It came from a razor-thin band of lead, coiled and packed into a ceramic pot, with a douse of vinegar. The pot was then immersed for a fortnight in a heaping pile of fresh horse excrement, where the vaporous comingling of acetic acid and warm manure caused the lead surface to oxidize in white blemishes. These toxic lead flakes were scraped off, boiled clean, and ground into a snowy white powdery pigment.

Gerrit arranged the mound of white lead next to a jug of linseed oil and a quartz muller on a granite slab. The oil acted as a binder for the pigment particles. He gripped the handle in his right hand and clenched his left palm over the top, and massaged the pile in circular figure eights. He added a splash of linseed oil, coaxing the granules and liquid together. The boy paused to stretch his sore hand muscles and expel a whiff of noxious fumes. Gradually the white mixture became smooth and spreadable. With a palette knife, he scooped the thick paste into a pliable walnut-sized sack—a pig's bladder, the preferred paint tube of the day. He tied the squishy bulge tightly so its contents would stay soft and moist. When Rembrandt was ready to paint, he would puncture a small hole in the membrane and squeeze out a dab of white lead onto a palette.

Gerrit repeated the mulling process with more colors. Rembrandt liked fast drying, easy to build up, low cost, opaque paints. His blacks came from charred animal bones, retrieved from the kitchen garbage. He frequently worked with ochre, a yellowish brown iron ore. To make red, Gerrit used a mortar and pestle to crush a flake of Spanish cinnabar, producing a mercury-laced pigment called vermillion. Rembrandt enhanced his reds with carmine, an acid secreted by Mexican cochineal beetles, which added a transparent crimson luster. Rembrandt's blues came from azurite mines in Hungary, until Ottoman Turks laid siege to Budapest. Reluctantly, he switched to Saxony cobalt, made from tiny shards of broken glass. To adjust the gloss and texture, Rembrandt taught Gerrit to use egg yolk for thickening and urine for thinning, as oil-based paints are not water soluble.

After securing the last of the bladder tubes, Gerrit turned his attention to preparing the supports. Wooden panels were the traditional support in European art. Canvas was a more recent innovation, favored by Venetian painters. Rembrandt preferred thin-sliced, bevel-edged oak panels. But the demand for oak from Dutch shipbuilders depleted local stocks, forcing Dutch painters to resort to canvas, readily available from sailcloth makers. Rembrandt taught Gerrit how to make a canvas support, stretching the fabric taut as a drum skin, and smearing a layer of glue across the surface to seal the fabric's natural pores. For today's lesson, however, they would be working with oak panels imported from Poland.

Gerrit propped a twelve-stiver panel on the cross post of a tri-legged easel. He took from the stove a pot of warm glue, made from melted-down rabbit skin. He sized the surface with a smooth coating, so that the paint would not touch the oak fibers. When it dried, Gerrit applied the first grounding. He built up a base layer of paint with a ten-inch curved priming knife, slopping on, pressing into, and flattening over, creating a thick foundation of earthy reddish brown pigment. Waiting for the first grounding to dry, Gerrit mixed lead white and bone black to make a murky gray color. Rembrandt favored dark-hued groundings to enhance a moody shadow effect in his paintings. The apprentice applied the second grounding, spreading and swirling the paint until the surface was mirror smooth. The studio was almost ready.

Rembrandt always painted from real life models. Gerrit set a wooden chair in the center of the room. Around it, he made a semicircle with four tri-legged easels, each cradling a primed panel. For today's sitting, they would be joined by Rembrandt's friend, Jan Lievens, and another pupil, Isaac de Joudreville.

The morning calm was broken by a rising fuss on the stairwell. Gerrit turned to see Rembrandt enter the studio, escorting today's model—his mother, Neeltgen Willemsdochter. Her furrowed skin, sunken eyes, and pointy chin were familiar features in Rembrandt's early paintings, appearing sometimes as a humble servant and sometimes as the Holy Mother. Today, Neeltgen was garbed in a flowing kerchief and fur-collared cloak. Gerrit stuck his thumb through the palette and dabbed his brush in a dollop of paint, as Rembrandt positioned his mother's chair slightly away from the outside light. The old woman hunched forward and opened a book of scripture in her lap. The lesson began.

A Visitor from the Royal Court

About a year into his apprenticeship, Gerrit arrived one morning to find the studio in a commotion. Rembrandt did not see his pupil, instead he was conversing excitedly with Jan Lievens. Both young artists were rifling through stacks of painted panels, holding different pictures up to the wall, and discussing how to best display them. Rembrandt was eager to pick a conspicuous spot for a recently completed historical painting, *Judas Returning the Thirty Pieces of Silver*, a visual narrative of the guilt-ridden disciple seeking redemption after his act of betrayal. Rembrandt noticed Gerrit, and directed him to help tidy up the studio. An important visitor from The Hague was expected.

Constantijn Huygens was royal secretary to the stadtholder, the Dutch head of state, Prince Frederik of Orange. More importantly for Rembrandt, Huygens acted as cultural standard-bearer of the realm. He was well suited to the role—a child prodigy, steeped in the arts, with a talent for music, poetry, and language. Constantijn was friends with Galileo and Descartes, and private tutor to young Prince William, the future king of Holland and

England. The Huygens family was accomplished in both art and science. Contantijn's great uncle, Joris Hoefnagel of Antwerp, was a successful landscape painter and naturalist illustrator. Constantijn's son, Christiaan Huygens, was a major figure in Europe's Age of Science who discovered Saturn's largest moon with a homemade telescope. Constantijn was in Leiden on court business, but the royal secretary always found time for the latest gossip on the local art scene.

Prince Frederik entrusted Huygens to assemble a grand art collection in The Hague, as a fitting display of the Republic's prosperity and independence. Constantijn's discerning eye recognized the technical and emotive elements of a masterpiece. He was not only official connoisseur for the prince, but a prominent art dealer in his own right. Constantijn procured an inspiring set of Flemish masters for the royal gallery—Rubens, van Dyck, Bruegel, and Teniers. These acquisitions were the foundation of Holland's world-class Mauritshuis art museum, housed in the palace of Count Johan Maurits of Nassau, Constantijn's neighbor in The Hague.

By 1629, the young lions, Rembrandt and Lievens, were the talk of Leiden. Constantijn's interest was no doubt sparked by the teasing reviews of the precocious Rembrandt. Only a few months earlier, the Utrecht lawyer and art aficionado Aernout van Buchel wrote: "The Leiden miller's son is highly, if prematurely, esteemed." Huygens had already met Lievens on a previous trip to Leiden, and commissioned a portrait from him. On this day, Rembrandt was giddy with anticipation. The royal secretary's visit could be the big break the young artist dreamed of.

"All honor to thee, my Rembrandt!" Constantijn wrote afterward in his diary. The encounter could not have gone better. Huygens was at once an admirer of "the noble pair of youths from Leiden." He gushed over the talents of both Rembrandt and Lievens: "Were I to say that they alone can vie with the greatest, I would still be underestimating the merits of these two; were I to say that they will soon surpass them, I would merely be expressing what their astonishing beginnings have led connoisseurs to expect."

Just as Rembrandt had hoped, Constantijn was most taken by his painting of Judas returning the pieces of silver. "Compare this with all Italy, indeed, with everything beautiful and admirable that has been preserved from the earliest antiquity," Huygens marveled. "The singular gesture of the despairing Judas, howling, praying for mercy, but devoid of hope, all traces of hope erased from his countenance, his appearance frightening, his hair torn, his garment rent, his limbs twisted, his hands clenched bloodlessly tight, fallen prostrate on his knees on a blind impulse, his whole body contorted in wretched hideousness. Such I place against all the elegance that has been produced throughout the ages. I am amazed that a youth, a Dutchman, a beardless miller, could bring together so much in one human figure and express what is universal." This work alone, Huygens asserted, reveals a latent genius in the youthful artist. Beaming with national pride, he saluted Rembrandt for having "brought the laurels of Greece and Italy to Holland."

In this encounter, Gerrit saw firsthand the effect that one influential patron could have on the fortunes of a struggling painter. Constantijn's lavish praise of his latest protégé brought Rembrandt wide notice, critical acclaim, and new commissions. Rembrandt conscientiously tended this relationship, writing letters from "your obliging and devoted servant" and offering gifts of artwork. Rembrandt painted a 8 x 10-foot Old Testament drama of the *Blinding of Samson*, which he bestowed on Huygens: "to do honor to my lord in his house."

Rembrandt, indeed, had much to be thankful for. Constantijn was captivated by the portraits displayed in the studio. He arranged for the artist to travel to The Hague to paint his older brother Maurits Huygens, a high official on the state council, and Jacob de Gheyn, a fellow artist and family friend. More requests from elite patrons to sit for Rembrandt followed, including Princess Amalia van Solms, First Lady of the Republic. Prodded by his secretary, the prince of Orange agreed to sponsor the young Leidener. He commissioned for the royal gallery a five-part series depicting the Passion of Christ, inspired by the famed Rubens altarpiece in the Cathedral of Our Lady at Antwerp. Though painted on a smaller scale, Rembrandt strove to surpass the Flemish virtuoso with his own Passion of Christ, as he explained to Huygens: "I have put great pleasure and devotion into these pieces, so that the most natural movement can be observed." Fetching six hundred guilders per painting, it was the most lucrative commission to date for the young artist.

Not long after Constantijn's fateful visit, Rembrandt's studio was again set astir by another distinguished guest. On a tip from Huygens, the English ambassador to the Netherlands, Sir Robert Kerr, journeyed to Leiden to meet Rembrandt. The ambassador purchased one of the artist's attention-grabbing self-portraits as a gift for King Charles I, which he sent with a note: "a picture of Rembrandt, being his own picture and done by himself." The English sovereign was an enthusiastic patron of Dutch art. And, at Huygens's urging, King Charles enticed Jan Lievens to quit Holland and relocate to London as his personal court painter.

The royal secretary's visit vaulted Rembrandt into the upper echelon of Dutch artists. The artist craved more than what Leiden could offer. Rembrandt was ready for a bigger stage. He was ready to return to Amsterdam.

The Mystery of *Anna and the Blind Tobit*

According to an old Aramaic tale, Tobit was an Israelite forced into exile in Nineveh, along the banks of the Tigris River. Charitable and devout, Tobit remained true to the traditions of his outcast Jewish community. One ill-fated night, while sleeping in his garden, Tobit was blinded by a sparrow. More misfortune followed. Tobit fell into poverty, forced to get by on the meager earnings of his spinster wife Anna. He sent his only son, Tobias, to faraway Media to collect an old family debt, while he waited at home, despairing and praying for death to relieve his suffering. On the journey to Media, Tobias was befriended by an archangel, assaulted by a giant fish, and seduced by a demon-possessed maiden. Taking the advice of the archangel, Tobias killed the big fish and boiled its guts, causing the demon to flee to Egypt. Tobias married Sarah, collected the debt, and returned home. Cooked fish innards, so it turned out, was just the cure for biblical blindness as well. Tobit regained his eyesight, rejoiced at his good fortune, and departed to a peaceful hereafter.

The Book of Tobit is an ancient text included in the Apocrypha, a compilation of biblical stories fixed between the Old and New Testaments. Largely forgotten in early modern Europe, the Book of Tobit enjoyed a popular revival in 17th-century Calvinist Holland. Tobit's plight resonated in the newly independent Dutch Republic. Pitted against superpower Catholic Spain, the enduring Dutch never betrayed their faith, and ultimately prevailed in triumph and prosperity. Dutch artists discovered that Tobit's ordeal had commercial appeal. Rembrandt's teacher, Pieter Lastman, had a knack for anticipating market demand for obscure historical narratives and embraced Tobit in a series of popular paintings. His apprentice Rembrandt also showed a fondness for the Tobit legend.

Tobit played muse to Rembrandt throughout his career, but especially in his Leiden years. One of his earliest historical paintings, in 1626, at just twenty years old, was *Tobit and Anna with a Goat,* which today hangs in the Rijksmuseum. There are more than fifty known Rembrandt paintings and drawings depicting the Book of Tobit. Art historians have debated the artist's Tobit fixation: perhaps he feared losing his creative vision or perhaps he saw a parallel with his own aged father. Rembrandt also used Blind Tobit to teach.

Gerrit was a quick study. In little more than a year, the young apprentice was an adept portrait artist. By age seventeen, Gerrit had produced high-quality portraits of Rembrandt's father as an astronomer and his mother reading the bible, which today hang in the Hermitage and Rijksmuseum respectively. One of Gerrit's first attempts at historical painting was *Blind Tobit Greeting His Son.* This painting found its way into the collection of the baron of Arundell, and is displayed at Wardour Castle in Wiltshire, England. In this early work, the student tried to emulate the teacher. Gerrit became so good at copying Rembrandt that experts later had difficulty agreeing on who painted what.

Rembrandt showed confidence in his young apprentice. Gerrit was invited to set up an easel and sit next to Rembrandt while he worked on his paintings. Rembrandt would peer over Gerrit's shoulder, and make suggestions, or take the brush to show him how to achieve a desired visual effect. Likewise, Rembrandt allowed Gerrit to fill out the details of the background and accoutrement objects in his paintings. Just because Rembrandt's signature was on a painting did not necessarily mean that he painted it. Rather it indicated that the piece was made in his workshop, either by his hand or under his supervision. Therein arose the mystery of *Anna and the Blind Tobit.*

In 1926, the London National Gallery on Trafalgar Square purchased a Gerrit Dou painting of Blind Tobit, sitting in contemplation in front of an open window with his wife Anna by his side. The 24 x 18-inch oak panel painting was dated around 1630, and likely created in Rembrandt's studio. Its provenance, passing through the households of two wealthy Glaswegian industrialists, John Bell and Sir Renny Watson, traced back to 1881. Before that, ownership was uncertain. Some speculated that it was the same *Blind Tobit and Anna* listed in a 1786 inventory of the Carmelite nunnery of San Hermenegildo in Madrid—except that the inventory identified the painting as a Rembrandt. In the early 1800s, Napoleon's army occupied Madrid in the Peninsula War. In the ensuing plunder, the San Hermenegildo Tobit was lost.

The National Gallery's *Anna and the Blind Tobit* was an indisputable masterwork. For decades, the painting was proudly featured in the museum's renowned Northern Baroque collection. What some disputed, however, was that it was painted by a seventeen-year-old apprentice. Perhaps it was the discerning portrait of Tobit's inner suffering, or the scene's dramatic chiaroscuro light and shadow effect, which caused doubts about the attribution. Experts and connoisseurs identified stylistic elements of both Rembrandt and Dou in the brushwork. Then came a breakthrough. While researching the nunnery's collection, an art historian uncovered a letter, written in 1804 by the sculptor José Foch y Costa, who had observed the Tobit painting firsthand. The detailed description of the image confirmed that the National Gallery's Dou and the Carmelite Convent's Rembrandt were the same painting.

The controversy was not ended. Was the painting a Dou, upon which Rembrandt added flourishing retouches; or a Rembrandt, upon which Dou filled in the details? The meticulously painted copper pot placed in the foreground and the exquisite attention paid to Anna's headdress were certainly Dou-like features; yet, the large-scale seated figures, rendered with self-assured spontaneous brushstrokes, were characteristic of Rembrandt. The National Gallery did not indulge the debate for long. It was more prestigious—and more lucrative—to own a Rembrandt than a Dou. The museum re-attributed the painting from the pupil to the master. Scholarly consensus, meanwhile, settled on an opinion that the painting was a collaborative effort; though the extent of each artist's contribution was disputed.

And so the mystery of *Anna and the Blind Tobit* remains unsolved. Yet the controversy provides insight into Rembrandt's Leiden studio circa 1630. It reveals the rapid maturation of young Gerrit, whose raw talent was fashioned into masterful craftsmanship in just a few years under Rembrandt's guidance. The distinctive styles cohabitating the panel in *Anna and the Blind Tobit* also indicate the diverging artistic paths that teacher and pupil were following. Rembrandt's paintings became bigger, his brushwork more instinctive and bold, and his subjects rendered in more impressionistic fashion. By contrast, Dou's paintings became smaller in scale, his brushwork more deliberate and fine, and his subjects as realistic as real life itself.

Rembrandt's ambition could not be suppressed. In a year's time, he would move to Amsterdam, marry upward into the family of a prosperous art dealer, cultivate the image of celebrity artist, and indulge a lifestyle beyond his means. Dou, on the other hand, stayed home in Leiden near his family, remained a bachelor, and preferred a comfortably modest lifestyle. The irony is that during their respective careers, it was Dou, not Rembrandt, whose paintings were most sought after and commanded the highest prices. In their time, and for more than a century after, by virtually all standards of comparison, the apprentice had surpassed the master. The first international superstar of the Dutch Golden Age was not Rembrandt, but his pupil, Gerrit Dou.

2

THE PRINCE'S BRIDE

Unexpected Invitation

On New Year's Day, 1744, the family of Prince Christian August, lord governor of the minor Prussian principality of Anhalt-Zerbst, sat down for a holiday dinner, after having spent all morning in chapel observing the Feast of the Circumcision of Jesus. Christian's wife, Johanna, prattled on about the slow pace of renovations to their crumbling castle, while Prince Christian and their fourteen-year-old daughter, Sophie, pretended to listen.

Austere and bland, Christian August was a soldier and proud servant to the king of Prussia. He had plodded through the ranks of the Prussian officer corps on a record of undistinguished competence. In 1720, already in his late thirties, Christian was appointed commander of a small garrison outpost in the town of Stettin, near the Baltic coast. He received no new assignment for the next twenty years. Professional prospects at last improved, in 1740, when a new Prussian king, Frederick II, came to the throne. Christian was promoted to field marshal and was conferred lordship over Anhalt-Zerbst, an insignificant patch of a principality near Saxony. The job came with a dilapidated castle, where, in 1742, the field marshal moved his family.

The sad-eyed jowly junker had done well in marrying Princess Johanna Elizabeth. She was a daughter of the ruling dynasty in the Duchy of Holstein-Gottorp, just below the Danish peninsula. Besides its bountiful black-and-white dairy cows, the duchy was home base to one of northern Europe's best-connected noble clans, the Holstein-Gottorps. Johanna's elder brothers and sisters were found in the upper echelon of the royal courts of Sweden, Denmark, and Russia. A less glamorous position was arranged for Johanna.

At the age of fifteen, she was betrothed to Prince Christian, then thirty-seven and stationed in Stettin, to bolster the Holstein-Gottorp presence in Prussia. It was a dreary fate for the fetching teen, jolted from a life of entitled indulgence to one of regimental frugality. Johanna eventually came to admire her husband's sense of duty and piety, and despise his lack of pomp and passion. Though she occupied a lesser branch of the Holstein-Gottorp family tree, the princess never stopped reaching for the higher boughs. But if Johanna's lofty ambitions were ever to be attained, it would have to be through her daughter, not her husband.

Sophie Fredericke Auguste was born in April 1729, in the white-walled, high-towered Ducal Palace of Stettin. Sophie's childhood was typical for her aristocratic status. She was raised a German Lutheran and received a French education. Tall, athletic, and strong, she was a fearless equestrian. She enjoyed organizing the local Stettin kids in rough-and-tumble sports. The precocious princess picked things up quickly, from reading and observing. Her fast wit was recognized and appreciated, at least by most of her elders. Sadly, young Sophie's smarts and confidence were not welcomed by the jealous Johanna. Her frustrated mother was forever upbraiding the girl for her supposed insolence.

Johanna's disappointment with Sophie was chronic, beginning when the bitter sixteen-year-old mother learned that her newborn was a girl, instead of the boy she hoped would carry on Prince Christian's legacy. Baby Sophie was abandoned to wet nurses, and raised by a French nanny, the kind and caring Babette. Two years later, an ecstatic Johanna delivered a male heir, Wilhelm Christian, who turned out to be a weakling, inflicted at birth with an undiagnosed dislocated hip. He died at age twelve. While Johanna doted on her physically distressed son, she heaped mental anguish on her daughter. The emotional wounds of maternal rejection never fully healed.

Johanna's interest in her daughter was as social commodity. She desperately wanted to marry off Sophie to improve her own aristocratic standing. By the time Sophie was eight-years old, Johanna was parading her through palaces and castles across northern Germany in hope of arousing matrimonial interest. The child was wise to the routine. Having been told by her mother from an early age that she was unappealing and plain, Sophie worked on perfecting a pleasing personality. The youngster showed a knack for finding the right mix of playfulness and poise to delight an audience. Sophie reveled in the attention of others, the attention that her aloof father and self-absorbed mother were incapable of giving.

Dinner was served. The clinking patter of silver on china was disrupted by excited voices in the outer foyer. An important message had arrived. A uniformed attendant, waving a large envelope ceremoniously tied with silk ribbon, appeared under the arched threshold. Prince Christian snapped upright in his chair and summoned him in. But the courier brushed past the baffled prince. The letter was for Her Lady the princess. Johanna snatched the parcel from the messenger's hand, tore it open and read silently; her eyes widened.

Sophie eased her chair back to steal a glimpse at the contents. Johanna pressed the letter into her supple bosom, and scolded the girl to look away and mind her business. Sophie leaned in to the table and suppressed a smile, certain that the message was about her. She had managed to see that the letter carried a stamp with a double-headed eagle, the official seal of the Russian Imperial court in Saint Petersburg.

King of Prussia

Johanna gaped at the regal dispatch. It was from Count Brummer, official guardian of the Russian grand duke Peter. The letter contained a list of special requests, which the count conveyed on behalf of Her Majesty, Empress Elizabeth of Russia. First, make immediate preparations for an extended visit to the Russian Imperial court, accompanied by your eldest daughter, the "lovely Sophie." Second, travel via the overland route from Berlin to Riga, and take care to conceal your identity and destination along the way. Third, under no circumstances shall Prince Christian be represented in your entourage. Finally, to cover expenses find enclosed a bank check for ten thousand rubles, redeemable in Berlin. In closing, the count teased that any intelligent woman will surely comprehend the true meaning of Her Royal Highness's invitation.

Johanna's matchmaking perseverance was at last rewarded. When Johanna had learned that the tsarina was bride shopping, she had immediately made Sophie sit for a new portrait, which was sent as a "gift" to the Russian court. Johanna was already on good terms with the empress. She had made certain to ingratiate herself to Elizabeth, with a congratulatory note on the success of the armed coup that placed her on the throne, and for good measure declaring she would name her next daughter Elizabeth in honor of Her Highness. It helped too that Elizabeth was particularly fond of the Holstein-Gottorp clan. As a young princess, Elizabeth was briefly engaged to Johanna's older brother Charles, who succumbed to smallpox before the wedding. Elizabeth never got over the tragedy. Meanwhile, Elizabeth's beloved older sister Anna was married to a Holstein prince, who was a cousin of her late fiancé. Thus, on the list of candidates to be the Russian prince's bride, Sophie's name stood out as a sentimental favorite. Empress Elizabeth invited mother and daughter to Saint Petersburg to visit with her and her adopted heir, Grand Duke Peter, who, when all the family relations were sorted out, was Sophie's second cousin.

For young Sophie, the unexpected invitation arrived in the nick of time. So despairing was Johanna about Sophie's prospects that she was considering a marriage proposal from her younger brother George. And while Johanna was fond of her brother, she hesitated because of the complications involving special approval from the Church for a conjugal union between uncle and niece. Now as Johanna's spirits soared, Prince Christian's were dashed. The father feared for his child. Russia was an untamed and far-off land, with an alien faith. What was the meaning of this confounding proposal? And why was he, the head of the household, not notified first? It was an indignity on multiple levels, and he shuddered in disapproval. But the prince's protests were muted when later that day a second letter arrived from his Liege, the king of Prussia.

King Frederick II wrote to confirm that the summons to Saint Petersburg concerned the betrothal of the Holstein teens. The Prussian ruler took credit for persuading the Russian empress of the merits of young Sophie as life companion for the grand duke. Just thirty years old, Frederick's interest in the union suited his ambitions to redraw the map of Central Europe and remake Prussia as a Great Power. Toward this end, Frederick thought it useful to have allies in the Russian court. The king requested mother and daughter to call on him before setting off to Saint Petersburg. Prince Christian cringed. Loyal and passive, he could not go against the will of his lord patron, let alone that of a foreign empress. He would escort wife and daughter as far as Berlin, where fate would take charge of his kin.

Anxious to claim her role on a bigger stage, Johanna oversaw every detail of the journey. "If only I had wings," she wrote back to Count Brummer, "I would fly to Russia." Ten days after receiving the invitation, Prince Christian's loaded-down coach wobbled into the Prussian capital. The ensemble passed through the gates of Charlottenburg Palace, the baroque showcase of German royalty. When the time came for an audience with Frederick, Johanna went alone, much to the king's dismay. And, she did so again the next day. The begrudging mother could not accept that her so obviously ordinary daughter was the star attraction. She feigned excuses for why Sophie had yet to meet the king. The child is fatigued; the child is ill; she lacks a proper dress. Frederick was annoyed at the charade. On the third day at Charlottenburg, the king demanded that Sophie—and only Sophie—join him for dinner. Johanna was devastated.

That evening, Frederick and Sophie, the two sovereigns who would shape the epoch of enlightened despotism and share the moniker of "Great," became personally acquainted during several hours of fine food and pleasant conversation about music, poetry, and philosophy. Sophie was at first flustered to be directed to the chair next to the king, but the apprehensive adolescent was put at ease by her flattering host. In turn, she impressed the table with her rounded intellect, gracious manner, and good humor. Sophie returned to her room glowing with satisfaction that the dinner had been a success. Indeed, Frederick reported on the occasion in a letter to Empress Elizabeth, expressing his warm approval for "the little princess from Zerbst."

Much to her relief, Johanna was not excluded from the king's attention. Before departing Berlin, she met several times with Frederick to discuss the volatile situation at the Russian court. A powerful faction therein was hostile to the rise of Prussia in Central Europe. High-ranking ministers and devious confidantes of Her Majesty were against the marriage, pushing their own contenders as consort. Chief among them was Elizabeth's talented and trusted chancellor, Count Bestuzhev. Frederick warned that Bestuzhev and his allies would seek to undermine Sophie before the empress. Should they succeed, the engagement would be ended, and her daughter endangered. To thwart their efforts, Frederick suggested that Johanna might act as informant, relating the latest gossip and rumors overheard in the Russian court, and keeping watch on the crafty count. Johanna tingled at the task; she was now officially a spy.

Prince Christian was gutted to see his family broken by scheming sovereigns. The stoic soldier used his time in Berlin to compose a set of directions to help his women navigate the treacherous shoals of high court intrigue. Be always courteous and respectful to your hostess, do not meddle in state policy or palace politics, and do not relinquish affection for your family, homeland, and religion. Johanna and Sophie politely agreed, and then immediately discarded the advice. The prince held on to his family until the eastern border town of Schwedt on the Oder River. There Sophie bade a tearful goodbye to her devoted father, the good Prince Christian, whom she never saw again.

Secret Journey

On January 16, mother and daughter began their adventure. The overland route from Berlin to Saint Petersburg was more than one thousand miles, running along the southern and eastern Baltic coast. The road was especially grueling in winter. Because of the political importance of their visit, Empress Elizabeth insisted that Johanna and Sophie keep their true identities and intentions secret.

King Frederick organized the first leg of the journey. At the empress's request, the entourage should appear as ordinary as possible. Four modest-sized coaches conveyed the women and their possessions. Johanna was permitted to bring along four personal servants and one cook. A junior military officer accompanied the party to deter would-be interceptors and highwaymen. Frederick devised *noms de voyage* for the women: Countess Rheinbeck and daughter. He made arrangements for their reception and good care in the German merchant towns of Danzig and Konigsberg, though in rural and wooded stretches the incognito caravan was on its own.

The troupe followed the script, keeping a low profile on the road. In the shortened winter daylight, they drove the horses without rest; in the evening, they took shelter in bare wayside inns, whose rustic charms were lost on Johanna. Meals were simple, but there was plenty of beer, which both Johanna and Sophie often drank too much of, making the next day's bumpy coach ride even more tortuous. As they made their way deeper into the Kingdom of Poland, travel conditions worsened. Chilling winds blew through the poorly insulated coach, while deep frozen ruts made the road nearly impassable. Sophie developed frostbite. So bad was the swelling and burning ache in her feet that she had to be carried in and out of the carriage.

Sophie could no longer endure the physical torment of the ordeal. Just when her stamina and spirit were at the breaking point, a bright omen appeared in the evening sky as the carriage passed into the pagan woodlands of the eastern Baltic. A magnificent fallen star, the passengers guessed. But rather than burning out, the brilliant celestial orb followed the coach, and could even be seen in daylight. It was the Great Comet of 1744, among the closest cosmic ice balls ever to streak past the Earth, at one point displaying a dazzling six-rayed tail. In her memoirs, Sophie marveled that she "never had seen anything so glorious." It was an auspicious sign, she thought, boding well for the rest of the road trip.

A few days later the carriage reached the eastern border of Poland, and crossed into Courland (today's Latvia). The small Baltic duchy was at this time contested between Poland and Russia, and hosted two rival dukes claiming to be in charge. It was not the safest corner of the empire. Outside the women heard a bellowing command to halt, followed by clopping hooves. Mother and daughter sat still and listened. The rider inquired as to the occupants. It is the carriage of Countess Reinbeck. Welcome to the countess and her daughter the princess came the reply. Johanna thrust her head through the curtain to see who would know this. She was looking up at a colonel in the Russian Imperial border guards. The officer signaled ahead, and a second horseman, elegantly dressed atop a muscular steed, joined the party on the road. He was Prince Naryshkin, officer at the court of Her Majesty, Empress Elizabeth. He handed Johanna a letter from Count Brummer. We have been expecting you.

The nightmarish trek turned into a fairy tale. Fur-capped horsemen led the coach to where the Courland woods opened up to a view of the spires of Riga, rising above a snowy white embankment and old town wall. Sophie took in her first glimpse of the Russian Empire. They entered the city to blaring trumpets and booming cannons. From Riga to Saint Petersburg, Sophie and Johanna rode in a luxurious imperial coach pulled by ten horses, warmly snuggled in soft sable blankets behind thick velvet drapes. Curious peasants came out to the road to gawk at the royal procession. The caravan included a fully decorated cavalry escort, a company of local officialdom, and a host of servants, including a team of chefs, a sommelier, a coffee maker, and a jam specialist. The empress liked to impress.

Five days later, they climbed out of their carriage to a sumptuous Saint Petersburg reception, with ceremonial marching guards, rousing musical tributes, an ensemble cast of counts and countesses, and a dozen dancing elephants. The suddenly reticent Sophie was taken aback, while her triumphant mother sparkled. Princess Johanna had at last arrived.

But Saint Petersburg was not the last stop of the long journey. The empress was in Moscow. Johanna was told to make haste to get there in time for the celebration of the grand duke's sixteenth birthday. Three days later, the Prussian princesses climbed into a deluxe sleigh coach for the four-day, four-hundred-mile dash along the smooth snow-packed road to Moscow. No one at court wanted to miss the festivities, so they traveled in a column of thirty coaches. It was late evening when they drew up to the glittering Golovin Palace, where Johanna and Sophie were met by Count Brummer, who instructed them in the etiquette of meeting Her Majesty. Sophie was listening to Brummer in the entrance hall when Grand Duke

Peter bounded down the sweeping staircase, and blushed, "I just couldn't wait any longer to meet you."

Audition for an Empress

The audition for role of royal consort was demanding. A retinue of ladies of court, both steely chaperones and saucy sorority sisters, were assigned to track Sophie's every move. She was liberated from her monitors only to be drilled by tutors in Russian language and Orthodox religion. And, she was on call at any moment at the empress's whim to appear at court. Sophie memorized scores of Russian aristocrats and foreign envoys by noble rank, family pedigree, political leanings, and personality quirks. Her practiced social skills served her well. Sophie consistently delighted the empress with her charm and wit. It was a nice start for a French-tutored fräulein from Stettin.

As much as Elizabeth found Sophie endearing, she found her mother grating. Poor Johanna could not conceal her obnoxious character, and fell into disfavor with the empress. When Sophie was bedridden with a high fever, her attendants noted Johanna's indifference to the girl's condition, and were aghast by Johanna's furious protests when an Orthodox priest, instead of a Lutheran, was called to her daughter's bedside. Elizabeth's ever-watchful courtiers further deduced that Johanna was in the habit of making Sophie hand over any valuable gifts she received.

One incident in particular damaged Johanna's position with the empress. While Sophie was still in bed recovering from illness, Johanna sent a chambermaid to claim a luxurious blue and silver-lined fabric from her daughter. "I liked it very much," Sophie recalled, "because my uncle, my father's brother, had given it to me." Sophie was dismayed, but dutifully gave up the cloth without protest. She described in her memoir what happened next: "The incident was recounted to her Majesty, who immediately sent me several superb pieces of rich cloth, including a blue and silver one. My mother was accused of having neither tenderness nor concern for me." Johanna blamed Sophie when the empress acted coolly toward her.

Besides having to restrain her meddlesome mother, Sophie also worked to gain approval from her fiancé, the grand duke. Sophie had first met her future husband several years earlier at a Holstein family event, at which they got along well. They both had miserable childhoods. Like Sophie, Peter received no affection growing up. His mother died only three months after giving birth, and his father, who was not around much anyway, died when he was eleven years old. With neither family nor friends, Peter was raised by exacting Prussian tutors. Unlike Sophie, he appeared awkward and wan, defeated by his loveless childhood. When he wasn't sick, he pretended to be, to avoid his lessons and obligations. By the time he was twelve, he found escape from the rigorous routine in alcohol, drinking himself into babbling oblivion during evening affairs. Yet, politically speaking, Peter was a good catch. He was a scion of one of the most powerful families in northern Europe, and the front-running successor to the Swedish throne, which is why Empress Elizabeth, unmarried and childless, chose the brittle blueblood as her heir apparent.

Peter was eager to befriend his bride-to-be cousin. They had much in common—youth and innocence, German language, and Holstein heritage, and both were political pawns; or so he thought. In the weeks following Sophie's arrival, the grand duke spent much time at her side. "Because we are cousins," he told Sophie, "I can talk to you with an open heart." And talk he did. He confided that he loved another, Mademoiselle Lopukhina, a former maid of honor at the court, who because of her family's transgressions against the empress was now exiled in Siberia. He made clear that he detested Russia and Russians, and would much prefer to live in Holstein, or Sweden, or anyplace more civilized. He yammered on and on about his insufferable tutors and sadistic overseers. Sophie listened in quiet astonishment; discretion was not the grand duke's strong point.

Sophie took the young prince's confessions in stride. Though only fourteen, she understood that this audition was a once-in-a-lifetime opportunity and she would not forfeit the prize on account of sentiment. "I saw clearly his feelings and that he would leave me without regret," Sophie surmised. "As for me, I was more or less indifferent to him, but not to the Russian Crown." The royal court was a den of intrigue, in which survival demanded constant vigilance. Sophie proved adept at building alliances and disarming foes. Her mother, by contrast, followed one faux pas with another; and in the end nearly wrecked the audition.

"My mother," Sophie observed, "saw with displeasure that I now preceded her in public." Johanna reflexively tried to redirect attention back to herself. And she succeeded. Johanna was a reliably brow-raising topic of gossip and disapproval. While Elizabeth's court was anything but prudish, Johanna tested the limits by wearing scoop-necked dresses, proudly displaying her generous cleavage. She was indiscreet about a romantic dalliance with the court chamberlain assigned to manage her entourage. But Johanna's biggest gaffe was not personal immodesty, but political imprudence.

Johanna took seriously her assignment to gather intelligence for King Frederick. She became complicit in a cabal with the Prussian and French envoys to weaken the influence of Vice Chancellor Bestuzhev. The count was wise to the plot. His agents intercepted their diplomatic dispatches and decoded their secret messages. They exposed Johanna as Frederick's spy. Bestuzhev patiently collected the details of their covert scheme, as well as a list of the snide insults made at Her Majesty's expense. Finally, the count revealed the incriminating evidence.

Sophie recalled the episode in her memoir. She and Peter were chatting idly in her apartment, when the empress, the chief conspirator French count Lestoq, and Johanna hurried past into the inner chamber. Lestoq exited first, and passing the giggling teenagers, paused to threaten Sophie: good times were over and soon you will be packing. Johanna next rushed out of the room, red-faced, and sobbing hysterically. Sophie was trembling; what had her mother done now? Finally, the empress emerged and noticed the shaken teens. Sophie knelt to kiss her hand, and Elizabeth returned a soothing smile. Sophie was safe. The Prussian and French envoys were expelled, while Johanna received a temporary reprieve.

Although Saint Petersburg was the political capital of Russia, Moscow was still its ceremonial center. In June, the empress gathered her court at the Kremlin for a grand display of pageantry in celebration of her succession plan. It began with Sophie's conversion to Orthodoxy. Wearing matching scarlet and silver laced gowns, Elizabeth led Sophie by the hand on a processional strut through the great hall of the royal palace to the chapel. Sophie's outfit was heavy and stifling. The frail teen was faint from three days of fasting. Still she never faltered. Even Johanna admitted in a letter to Prince Christian "that our daughter was the image of nobility and grace."

Sophie knelt at the center of the crowded sanctuary, where the Archbishop of Novgorod anointed the girl with holy oils. She recited her profession of faith in perfect Russian. "I learned it all by heart, like a parrot," she said. She took the name of Catherine to honor Elizabeth's mother, the adored second wife of Peter the Great. The empress wept.

The next day came the consecration of the engagement of Grand Duke Peter and soon-to-be Grand Duchess Catherine. The day began with a magnificent procession from the royal palace, down the famed Red Staircase, across the Kremlin courtyard, to the Assumption Cathedral, the most sacred shrine of Russia's tsars. Led by the empress clad in full regal attire, the chosen couple walked close behind, followed by a solemn parade of titled nobles, high priests, and royal regiments. The blessing of the betrothed was a four-hour marathon of religious and political ritual. The session concluded with the reading of a royal proclamation, which bestowed on the Grand Duchess Catherine the title "Imperial Highness."

Sophie held up well; her mother did not. Johanna was unable to step aside graciously for her daughter. She was visibly agitated during the long church service. "My back was numb from all the bowing required," she complained. And when the guests assembled later for the engagement feast, Johanna was infuriated by the seating arrangement, which placed her at a table with "mere ladies of the court." She insisted on sitting at the head table, even though her rank did not permit such. As a compromise, a separate table was set up for Johanna alone in a nook to the side of the main table. Elizabeth suppressed her scorn, while Sophie concealed her embarrassment.

The program concluded with a grand ball in the Kremlin's spectacular Hall of Facets. Bedecked in diamonds and rubies, the newly blessed fifteen-year-old Grand Duchess was radiant. Sophie had passed the audition.

3

FROM PUPIL TO MASTER

On His Own

Gerrit's apprenticeship was near its end. For three years, he had been part of something special, a new wave in Dutch painting, as Rembrandt and Jan Lievens shook up the local art scene. But the young Leiden upstarts were ready for bigger challenges in the world beyond.

With a promise of wealth and fame, art impresario Hendrik van Uylenburgh lured Rembrandt to join his stable of talent in Amsterdam. Rembrandt resettled in a four-story townhouse along the swanky Zwanenburgwal Canal. He was appointed master of Uylenburgh's workshop, mingled with his literati neighbors, and fell in love with his well-bred and independent-minded niece Saskia. Jan Lievens also departed Leiden at this time for the court of King Charles in London. Rembrandt's once bustling studio was disbanded. Gerrit and fellow apprentice Isaac de Jouderville continued to work for a while, mostly unsupervised, on paintings they had begun under their mentor's direction. Isaac agreed to continue as Rembrandt's assistant in Amsterdam. But not Gerrit. His final assignment was to help Rembrandt pack up his tools and supplies and a stack of unfinished paintings for transport thirty miles north. He covered the panels with straw and fitted them into wooden crates, pausing to admire his own hand on several pieces. Just eighteen years old, Gerrit was on his own.

Dou did not lament his situation; instead he saw opportunity. Rembrandt's studio had successfully staked out a corner of the local art market, and Gerrit was determined to claim it for himself. But first he needed to find a workspace. A property was available in a row house along the Galgewater canal, a branch of the Old Rhine, just around the corner from his childhood home on Kort Rapenburg.

Gerrit's clopping soles hurried across the cobblestones. He surveyed the brick facades lining the Galgewater, snug two-storied dwellings with tapered attics. Next to an arched portico, he located no. 3 Galgewater. Upstairs, he passed into a spacious room with a high ceiling framed by thick timber crossbeams. A spiral staircase wound its way to the upper level, while a snug side chamber off the main room provided a place to sleep. The artist was especially pleased by the unobstructed northern light, gleaming through tall leaded-glass windows. He sprung open the casement and looked down on a procession of freight barges plying the Galgewater. Gazing over the red rooftops on the opposite bank, he saw the sloping tower of the Blauwpoort city gate and the whirring blades of the De Valk gristmill. It was perfect. Better still, he could have the whole house for 2,000 florins.

Gerrit stocked his new workspace with a few pieces of furniture and studio props, mostly acquired from Rembrandt. These accessories made recurring appearances in Dou's early paintings—a wooden Savonarola armchair, a small roundtable, a lush green tapestry, a human skull, a cradled globe, a pewter ewer, a wooden birdcage, a Chinese parasol, a Greek theater mask, an ornately carved violin, and a lute with bent back pegbox. Gerrit set up a heavy three-legged wooden easel against the far wall, basking in the window light. He would fix a hook to the wall for his long russet-brown smock.

Gerrit had learned much from Rembrandt. Not just technique, but the business of painting as well. To prosper an artist must establish a reputation for portraiture. Gerrit would need to practice and produce samples of his work. It was not easy, however, for a start-up artist to hire models. Dou's parents agreed to sit for him, but they were more sparing with their time than Rembrandt's. So Gerrit made self-portraits. It became an obsession, creating a life-spanning visual record of himself, from floppy attired red-headed youth to stoutly tailored dignified old age, and always proudly brandishing the tools of his trade—a brush and palette.

Even before Rembrandt left for Amsterdam, Gerrit was getting noticed as "an excellent master." Requests for portraits trickled in to the Galgewater studio. Gerrit valued his time and skill, and charged a pricey six guilders per hour for his work. Despite the cost, he kept busy with new commissions. Gerrit's early portrait work showed Rembrandt's influence, particularly in rendering light and shade. But in one area, Gerrit was very different from his master. It was not the quality of his work—his portraits bore uncanny likeness to his sitters. It was the style of his work—his manner was meticulous, exacting, and unhurried. Gerrit gave as much attention to the buttons on a sleeve as he gave to the eyes on a face. Dou was not just fussy, he was a perfectionist in the extreme.

Sitting for a portrait with Dou became a test of endurance, in which the artist inevitably wore down the physical strength and good humor of his client. His friend and admirer Joachim von Sandrart enjoyed telling fellow painters the story of the sitter who posed for five straight days while Gerrit worked and reworked the under-painting for a single hand. "This tediousness," Sandrart sniped, "spoiled all the pleasure in sitting for Dou," and explained why even the most amiable countenance descended into "melancholy or displeasure" in his portraits. Nor did it help that sitters were paying by the hour. This was a problem. If Gerrit was going to survive as a painter, he would need to do more than portraits.

The Guild of Saint Luke

During the Dutch Golden Age, each town's artists were organized into guilds, named in honor of their holy protector, Luke the Evangelist, Christendom's original iconographer. Membership in the Guild of Saint Luke confirmed an artist's social rank as a skilled craftsman. The guilds determined levels of competence and compensation, conducted auctions, and licensed dealers. To organize a guild, local artists were obliged to petition the town council to grant a charter. The first officially recognized Guild of Saint Luke was in Antwerp, in 1442. Amsterdam's charter was reissued following its break from Spain in 1579; meanwhile, new or revised charters were enacted for Delft in 1609, Utrecht in 1611, and Haarlem in 1631. Leiden, however, had no guild, though not for lack of trying. City magistrates kept rejecting artist petitions, unconvinced that painting was an expert craft or lucrative trade.

On October 18, 1641, the guildless artists of Leiden gathered to celebrate their patron saint's feast day. One of their company, Philips Angel, read a short treatise penned for the occasion, "In Praise of the Art of Painting." His comments were mostly meant to persuade town fathers that "the painter's art is the most profitable and useful of any other." His remarks extolled the skill and ingenuity of one particular Leiden-born painter—and it was not Rembrandt. When considering the world's "great minds," Angel opined, one needn't "roam too far afield, aye, within our own city walls, we find the perfect and excellent Gerrit Dou." He implored aspiring artists to follow the example of Dou, "to whom no praise is sufficient for his meticulous ease, and sure and reliable drawing hand." In the same year, town mayor and book printer Jan Orlers included Gerrit's biography in his anthology of famous Leideners. The burgomaster wrote that Dou's work was "highly valued by art lovers and expensively sold. Everyone viewing his paintings is amazed at their highly finished neatness."

Ten years had passed since Rembrandt bolted to Amsterdam and Gerrit launched the Galgewater studio. The introverted glazier's son was now as widely famed as his attention-seeking former master. The Dutch were avid and savvy art consumers, across social classes, similar to modern society's consumption of popular music and film. Dou rose to the top of the Leiden art scene, and his reputation spread throughout Holland. He earned plentiful commissions so he was able to paint whatever he pleased. He attracted a following of young devotees, who tended his busy workshop. But most inspiring to fellow artists, Gerrit found a rich patron.

Pieter Spiering came from Delft, where his father operated a thriving tapestry business. The workshop was more fashion house than textile factory, producing intricate one-of-a-kind patterns. Like so many Dutch capitalists, the elder Spiering was also an art collector. Young Pieter grew up surrounded by Italian and Dutch masters. Eager to see the world, Pieter chose diplomacy over business as a career. He entered the Dutch foreign service and was appointed emissary to Sweden. Pieter's reputation as "an unparalleled art lover" was noticed by Sweden's Queen Christina, who was determined to make Stockholm a center of style and culture. The free-thinking Swedish sovereign hired Spiering to procure works of fine art for her court.

In keeping with 17th-century aristocratic tastes, the Scandinavian bluestocking was partial to Italian Renaissance works, riveting dramas of scripture and myth, and the sweeping sensuality of Botticelli and Raphael. The queen's new agent had decidedly different tastes. Spiering was an unabashed enthusiast of Dutch depictions of common people in everyday settings, displaying humanity's endearments and imperfections. And Pieter's favorite Dutch painter was Gerrit Dou. The entire Spiering family sat for portraits in the Galgewater studio. So enthralled was Spiering by Dou's nimble brushwork that he made the artist a sensational offer. He paid Gerrit one thousand florins annually for the right of first refusal on any of the artist's noncommissioned paintings. And, Pieter rarely refused. Herr Spiering ultimately acquired nearly two dozen Dous for Her Highness and for himself, making extravagant bids from 600 to 1,000 florins per piece.

Queen Christina gazed around the Great Hall of Tre Kronor, her castle home. Upon the soaring walls, she envisioned larger-than-life scenes of mighty Hercules slaying the lion of Nemea or Venus and Mars reclining with a party of frisky satyrs. She looked down at the two small panels before her: *A Man Playing a Violin* and *A Woman Peeling Potatoes*. This was not what the queen had in mind when she bankrolled the Dutch diplomat to find her some masterpieces. The eccentric Swedish noblewoman simply did not connect with the Dutch celebration of middle-class ordinariness. After Pieter left the queen's service, in 1652, she catalogued and returned to him ten Dou paintings. The venturesome Christina then grew bored with playing monarch, ready to live out her fantasies. She abdicated the throne and moved to Rome, where the Pope came to know her as the "queen without a realm and woman without shame."

As it turned out, Queen Christina's opinions about Dutch art were in the minority. Dou's small panels were in big demand. Now entering midlife, Gerrit's reputation and remuneration were on the rise. He remained on a steady course, painting away his days in the Galgewater row house, where he lived as a bachelor with his housekeeper niece, Anthonia van Tol, and his apprentice nephew Dominicus van Tol. But the artist was also undergoing a personal transformation, revealed in his self-portraits. As a young artist, Gerrit presented himself in a plain painter's smock, curly reddish locks flowing out of a cloth beret, looking earnest, but unimposing. Now his self-depictions showed the mature artist in brocaded academic robes and velvet cap, showing off a well-fed frame, and air of self-importance. Around him, the Galgewater studio was cluttered with new acquisitions—a handsome oak chest, an elegant copper chandelier, a luxurious ruby-red tapestry, a collection of leather-bound volumes. He assimilated into Leiden's patrician class. He even began to refer to himself as Gerard and Monsieur Dou, in the parlance of the aristocracy.

Gerrit's image makeover was not self-deception. He belonged to Leiden's in-crowd, the scientific-cultural intelligentsia in one of Europe's most cosmopolitan cities. Gerrit used his newfound status to further the cause of Leiden's painters. In 1648, Dou endorsed a new petition to the town council to charter an artist guild. The appeal stressed that the lack of economic protection was forcing local talent to leave town "which was regrettable as Leiden has long been celebrated for its excellent masters." This time the request was granted. In March, Gerrit signed the charter as a founding member of the Leiden Guild of Saint Luke. In October, seven years after Philips Angel delivered his famous treatise, Leiden's artists gathered to celebrate the feast of their patron saint and inaugurate their new guild. At the head table were Golden Age luminaries Jan Steen, Gabriel Metsu, and David Bailly. In the center, appropriately, was Gerrit Dou, founder of the Leiden School.

The Leiden School

Gerrit woke early and found breakfast on the table—a plate of soused herring, a slice of cumin-seasoned cheese, a loaf of *roggebrood* or dark grainy rye bread, and a mug of weak beer drawn from the kitchen keg. He stepped outside to check the sky over the Galgewater. Dou's work habits were legendary. If the sun was shining, Gerrit was painting. On gloomy days, he bundled up and went for long walks around the canals, socialized a bit, and took care of business. Today the weather was fair.

Gerrit was as devout in his studio routine as a priest in his sacramental ritual. He began by preparing his colors, just as Rembrandt had taught, but on a pristine glass surface rather than stone. He was fanatical about dirt getting into his paints. After maneuvering his easel and worktable into position and before opening his toolbox and uncovering his colors, Gerrit sat motionless for at least ten minutes, waiting for every last dust particle to settle back down to the floor. He propped a Chinese parasol atop the easel to catch any floating specks yet to alight. Gerrit then carefully removed a protective cloth from the panel he was working on, and took up his palette, brush, and knife. The session could finally get underway. When Gerrit was done for the day, he put everything away with the same measured vigilance. It was necessary, he believed, to attain the highly polished surfaces that made his paintings so renowned.

The Dutch Golden Age marked a new era in European art, in which patronage shifted from the Church and high aristocracy to the merchants and middle class. The change in patronage brought change in subject and style. Still, Dutch painters needed to make a living; thus, prevailing market tastes dictated choices about what to paint. Thanks to the indulgence of his patron, Gerrit was the exception. He took advantage of this freedom. While Rembrandt's influence was always discernible in Dou's work, the pupil defined a distinctive painting style, known as the Leiden School. It embodied an innovative mix of realism, storytelling, and symbolism, which captivated the European art world for two centuries.

Dou was a realist's realist. He perfected the technique of "fine painting," or *fijnschilder* as the Dutch called it. Before the invention of photography, fine painting was as close to real life as existed in Western art. This was the standard of the day: "art should come as close as possible to life," Philips Angel declared. In this regard, Gerrit was unsurpassed. Dou's paintings were so true to life that they were said to fool the viewer. Don't get too near the *Sleeping Dog Beside a Terracotta Jug*, lest you rouse the mutt.

Gerrit imparted a smooth enamel-like gloss to the surface of his pictures. With maximum precision, he removed all traces of brushwork. To accomplish this effect required special tools, technique, and temperament. Gerrit's work kit included state-of-the-art magnifying glasses and microscope lenses, which were all the rage at Leiden University. Gerrit made his own brushes, including some with just one or two bristles to be ultra-precise.

Gerrit was a master of simulating light and depth to create the illusion of reality for the viewer. His scenes employed exquisite one-point perspective, using interior framing to accentuate the feeling of three-dimensional depth. Gerrit portrayed his subjects in doorways and windows, not in a sneaky voyeuristic way, but as if the viewer had just arrived. Sometimes the subjects look up from their work making direct eye contact with the viewer; and, sometimes they remain engrossed in their task, yet to notice that the viewer has entered. With this technique, the viewer becomes part of the scene. Gerrit was able to perfect this effect because he had near infinite patience. His friend Sandrart again related an anecdote that when he complimented the artist on the realistic straws drawn on a broom no larger than a fingernail, Gerrit replied that "it still needs three more days of work."

Gerrit used his brush and palette to tell stories. Not grand narratives or heroic epics, but vignettes about people who lived in his community. He painted shopkeepers, housemaids, mothers, teachers, scholars, doctors, and dentists. He situated his subjects in cozy spots inside their homes or work places. The viewer mentally experiences walking into a kitchen as the cook chops a cabbage head, or gripping an armchair as a dentist extracts a rotten tooth, or peeping into a poultry shop as the proprietress plucks a fat duck. The expressions, gestures, and props relate an anecdote: the cook is flirtatious and probably available; the dentist is determined and his patient in pain; the proprietress is chatty and the young lad is fetching the family supper. Gerrit's pictures were snapshots of real life in progress.

Known as "genre" painting, these pieces were more than portraits but less than historical works. Gerrit's subjects were not valiant, self-righteous, or smug; they were regular people going about their regular business. In art history, the Dutch appreciation of the ordinary is lauded as a momentous advance for humanism and a democratic triumph, with Steen's raucous tavern-goers, Hals's earthy revelers, and Vermeer's solitary milkmaids exemplifying the trend. And in the vanguard of the Golden Age cultural revolution were the genre paintings of Gerrit Dou.

Gerrit's fine paintings were rich with symbols, referencing the social mores and cultural quirks of the day. An old woman reading the bible implied piety and devotion; a mother cutting bread for her children—frugality and caregiving; a hermit huddled in deep prayer—spirituality and contemplation; a doctor studying a vial—healing and science. These were straightforward personal qualities and social values admired and espoused by middle-class Dutch Calvinists. But Gerrit also liked to insert more subtle messages, side comments, and not-so-subtle jokes into his paintings. To do this, he imparted meaning to the props in his genre scenes. A human skull, for example, reminded the viewer of the vanity of the living and inevitability of death. Fresh carrots splayed across the table, alongside a buxom chef clutching a milk jug, suggested the strong possibility of extra-culinary activity. It was a highlight for art lovers to scrutinize a Dou painting, and uncover and debate the symbolic intentions of the scene.

The public was mesmerized by Dou's fijnschilder panels. The market demand led to a teaching demand, and young artists flocked to Leiden to learn fine painting from the unrivaled master of illusion. Gerrit employed a similar training regimen as Rembrandt, more practical than theoretical, painting side-by-side from real life. His services were not cheap, costing apprentices an annual fee of a hundred guilders (the same as Rembrandt charged). Several of Gerrit's students also reached the upper echelon of Golden Age fame, notably Frans van Mieris the Elder and Godfried Schalcken, whose works today hang in the world's leading art museums.

Golden Age Superstar

"Be it known to all gentlemen and amateurs, that in the house of Monsieur Hannot, opposite the Raethuys in the town of Leyden, every day, except Sundays, from 11 to 12, should there be no compulsory hindrances, 29 pieces may be seen most admirably painted and wonderfully finished by the skilled and renowned Mr. Gerard Dou," read the advertisement in the

September 26, 1665, edition of the *Haarlemsche Courant*, placed by Leiden art dealer Johan de Bye.

On the day of the premiere, a throng of connoisseurs and curious, garbed in black and mulberry coats, topped in broad-brimmed hats, with white lace bursting from collar and sleeve, gathered beneath the monumental facade of the Leiden Town Hall. The modish entourage crossed Leiden's main thoroughfare, the Breestraat, arriving at no. 117, a three-story townhouse with twin turrets and castle-like crenellations. The local landmark belonged to Johannes Hannot, a wine merchant and capable painter. Combining both pursuits, Hannot mainly painted still-life fruit plates, inevitably featuring a bunch of fat grapes and a half-filled stemmed glass. For forty guilders a year, Hannot rented out his front room to Johan de Bye, who needed extra space to house his burgeoning art collection. Johan hit upon the idea to use Hannot's parlor to show off the pride of his collection—more than two dozen paintings by Gerrit Dou. It was the first documented "one-man show" in Western art history.

The burghers entered the street-front apartment, illuminated in diffused northern light, which de Bye made certain to check before signing the lease. This way the paintings would capture the precise hue and tone the artist intended. Twenty-nine paintings bedecked the walls, but entering guests could not see which works they were. The paintings were concealed in a chasis, a decorated wooden box with a hinged door or sliding lid. Gerrit placed almost all of his panels inside a chasis for function and fun. The box protected the smooth-polished surface from dirt or damage during shipping. He also enjoyed knowing that the small act of opening the cover added a touch of suspense to the viewing experience.

The wool-and-silk-clad spectators paused at the first painting, hidden inside an ebony chasis, a pitcher and silver bowl painted on the cover. A hand dripping white lace fingered the lid open. Collective murmurs went around, thumbs and forefingers caressed trim goatees, pudgy faces moved closer to peer at the panel inside. It was a genre scene set in a prosperous home, where a languishing old woman in white cap and sleeping gown is propped in a chair. She is surrounded by three figures: a matronly attendant offering food, a kneeling daughter looking distraught, and a doctor in academic robes studying a vial of urine. There was much to take in. She will not survive. The clock on the mantle faces an open bible, surely her time is up. Well, the crone must know; see how she ignores everyone and stares upward into the light. And look there, that wine jug in a cooler, perhaps the old hag brought it on herself. Let's have a look at the lid again? A water pitcher. Yes, she must have the dropsy.

Most of the assembled had probably never seen the image before, but they must have known of it. *The Dropsical Woman* was a recently completed painting, which Gerrit had been working on for quite a while. It would rank as one of his most acclaimed. Shortly after Dou's death, the Elector Palatine of the German Rhineland paid an astonishing sum for *The Dropsical Woman*, and then gifted it to Prince Eugene of Savoy. The painting left Turin for Paris in the early 19th century, when the Louvre acquired and restored *The Dropsical Woman* for its showcase gallery, the *Salon Carré*, where it hung next to da Vinci's *Mona Lisa*.

The group moved to the next chasis, where they found *A Woman Playing the Clavichord*. Music making was a popular genre theme associated with courtship. Gerrit's image draws the viewer into an intimate space, again framed by a stylish tapestry and studio window. An alluring blonde presses a keyboard while looking directly into the eyes of the viewer, who stands at the threshold. A wine jug chills in a basket on the floor, with a nearly empty glass on the round table. A curvaceous viola and bow lean back against the table, waiting to be played. What is this? A birdcage suspended from the ceiling. Ah, the door is shut, the bird has not flown—a fair maiden yet. The lass may be looking for love, but a secure and faithful kind. It was agreed: Look, but don't touch. The painting eventually found a permanent home in the incomparable collection of Baroque Masters at the Dulwich Picture Gallery in London.

The chortling group moved on to a set of three small panels. A nude—this was unexpected. No, three nudes, bathing: a woman completely bare, her back to the viewer and one leg comfortably raised against a tree; a second woman turning her torso back with a cool gaze at the viewer; a fit man in naked repose against a tree, his soldier's garments strewn on the ground. The Dutch Golden Age was not averse to the frolicsome and bawdy; neither was it short on innuendo, but it usually remained clothed. (The main exception to this trend was Gerrit's former master Rembrandt.) In these risqué scenes,

Gerrit showed off his skill at the classical form. The companion set was later broken up by de Bye, but eventually reunited by Dutch dealer Willem Lormier, who sold the works to the Marquis d'Argenson in Paris. In 1768, Catherine the Great acquired the set of rare nudes for the very high price of 13,205 livres. They still reside in the Hermitage in Russia.

Given the prices that Dou's paintings sold for at this time, the value of the art on display was extraordinary. The collection eventually generated nearly 100,000 guilders, when de Bye finally parted with it. By comparison, one could buy a comfortable house in Leiden for a thousand guilders. Johan was understandably concerned about security. His lease agreement included a signed note by the landlord, promising "to take good care of the pieces as though they were my own." The lease also stipulated that there could be just one other key for the room, which only Hannot could possess, and could only be used with Johan's prior consent. Johan did not charge the public a fee to view Gerrit's pictures, but he did ask two things: first, "as you leave do not neglect to remember the extreme need of the poor, by making a liberal gift to the chest hanging in the room"; and, second, "if any one finds pleasure in the art displayed will he please speak of it to the owner."

Dou's one-man show was must-see entertainment for Leideners. The town burgomasters felt compelled to pitch the artist for a special commission. "Mr. Gerard Dou, picture painter, made his appearance being notified by the Burgomasters that, in consideration of his art being very famous and in great esteem, they are of a mind to have a piece by him here, and discussed whether he would feel disposed to make a handsome artistic piece of painting for the town." Gerrit was gracious, saying he was honored by the request and would come up with "an idea for the picture." But that was as far as it got. There were no Leiden counterparts to Rembrandt's *Nightwatch* or Vermeer's *View of Delft*. The Burgomasters expected Gerrit to accept the commission for the sake of honor, and offered a token silver pitcher as payment. Instead, the artist gave the burgomasters an itemized estimate, based on the number of hours it would take to complete the project. The city fathers took pride in the frugal management of public resources: if they paid Gerrit his asking rate, the town budget would go broke. The Burgomasters reconsidered their request, and quietly agreed "to put him off as cleverly as may be with an excuse."

Beyond Leiden, Gerrit's ultrarealistic paintings generated great interest, as genre painting became the rage of the Dutch art market. Between 1650 and 1700, the average price of a genre painting increased fourfold, surpassing both history and religion as the highest valued painting subject. And genre painting in the Leiden School's fijnschilder style was the most coveted of all. After Gerrit, the next leading practitioner of fine painting was Frans van Mieris the Elder, Gerrit's former apprentice. Frans, like Gerrit, had earlier trained as a glass engraver. Whereas Rembrandt was like an older brother to Gerrit, at seven years apart; Gerrit was more of a father figure to Frans, at twenty-two years apart. Frans studied in the Galgewater studio for three years, before certification as a "master" by the Guild of Saint Luke in 1658. Gerrit with pride referred to Frans as his "prince of pupils." Throughout the second half of the 17th century, Gerrit's paintings regularly topped the list of highest prices paid for Dutch artworks, with Frans's paintings coming in a close second. Gerrit's domestic life genre paintings continued to claim the top spot on the Dutch art market until the early 18th century, when finally challenged by Rotterdam's Adriaen van der Werff's erotic bible scenes.

The Leiden School transcended national boundaries, becoming the sensation of the 17th century European art market, with Gerrit Dou being the preferred painter among Europe's ruling class. Louis XIV of France owned several Dous, as did the king of Saxony. The archduke of Austria, Leopold Wilhelm, was also passionate about Dou. The former governor of Habsburg Netherlands, in Brussels, was an active player in the Dutch art market, employing David Teniers the Younger as an agent-consultant. Leopold went so far as to try to lure Gerrit to Vienna to serve as his court painter. When Gerrit turned him down, the archduke extended the offer to Frans van Mieris, who also declined.

Meanwhile, in the south, the grand duke of Tuscany, Cosimo III de Medici proved an incompetent ruler but a keen art collector. In 1669, Cosimo decided to embark on a tour of northern Europe to check out the Dutch art scene and to take his mind off Marguerite Louise, his scandal-prone French wife. Cosimo cruised the Rhine all the way to the Netherlands, where he visited both Rembrandt in Amsterdam and Gerrit in Leiden. After his visit, the duke ordered his secretary "to move heaven and Earth" to acquire a Dou miniature and a Dou self-portrait, to add to his family's special collection of self-portraits. The Medicis ended up acquiring a 1658 chiaroscuro-styled self-portrait of Dou standing at an open window in an elegant robe, arm resting on a human skull. The self-portrait still hangs in the Uffizi Gallery in Florence.

Perhaps Gerrit's most devoted international patron was located just across the North Sea. The Dutch Golden Age coincided with a historical period in which England and Holland were at odds over whose traders should reign over the high seas. No less than three Anglo-Dutch Wars were waged during the 17th century. In 1660, King Charles II of England was restored to the throne after more than a decade of Cromwellian civil strife. In May, Charles stopped over in The Hague on his way home from political exile. To curry favor and secure peace, the Dutch States-General promised Charles a present of "fine pictures by the most famous painters, both old and new, from Italy and from this country." A committee was formed to compile the extravagant gift. By October, the diplomatic offering was ready. It included twenty-four Italian Old Masters procured from the private collections of Holland's rich merchants. When the committee considered which Dutch artist to include in the package, they did not choose Rembrandt, Hals, or Vermeer; they chose Gerrit Dou.

"It will be necessary," the States-General informed Gerrit on October 18, "that the three paintings bought from you in our name should be transported to Rotterdam on Wednesday or Thursday next at the latest; and that you should pack the pictures well and securely." The Dutch gift to the English king contained one of Gerrit's most cherished paintings, *The Young Mother*. Staged at the Galgewater studio with Gerrit's favorite blond and blue-eyed model, it depicts an interior scene in which a confident mother pauses from her sewing to look up at the viewer, while her child plays with an infant sibling bundled in a bassinet. It is a tender rendition of the Dutch middle-class ideal of a comfortable and orderly household, accentuated by Gerrit's natural colors, soft tones, and intricate details. The States-General paid Gerrit a generous sum of 4,000 guilders for this painting alone. The Dutch envoy, on hand when the gift was bestowed, said that the paintings that "most pleased His Majesty were Titian's *Virgin and Child* and those of Dou." The delighted King Charles displayed Gerrit's paintings in the Great Hall of Whitehall Palace, the royal residence.

One day while working in his Galgewater studio Gerrit was interrupted by a messenger, who delivered a regal invitation to the artist to come to London and serve as court painter. Gerrit was flattered by the offer. But now in his late forties, he was wedded to his routine and content in his hometown. Gerrit politely turned down His Majesty. As the gossip spread, the story of the king's request and the artist's rebuff filled Leideners with pride. Popular local poet Dirk Traudenius immortalized the event in verse: "To Mr. Gerard Dou, who, by the king's command, was invited to go and paint in England." While he did not get the painter, King Charles did at least acquire two more Dou paintings. When Charles II's successor James II was forced to abdicate in 1688, the English throne passed to Holland's William III of Orange, who, over the strong objections of the English court, brought *The Young Mother* home to The Hague, where it still resides at Mauritshuis.

The Nursery

Gerrit secured an oak panel in the cradle of a solid tripod easel. It was larger than his signature small pieces. He ran his fingers over the surface, testing the smoothness of the nearly black grounding. Rembrandt taught him long ago that a dark-toned base creates a more profound rendering of shadow and light. Gerrit gazed into the empty square, envisioning the scene that he would bring to life. He was fifty-eight years old, widely acclaimed, and well-off. Life was satisfying. But he sought a new challenge. This piece must do something more. Many weeks later when he finally finished, he had not just one painting, but three in one: a triptych. *The Nursery* (*de Kraamkamer*) was Gerrit's crowning achievement. In his lifetime and for more than a century after, Dou's triptych ranked among the most venerated and highest valued paintings of the Dutch Golden Age, rivaled, perhaps, only by Rembrandt's monumental *Nightwatch*.

The piece brought together in fijnschilder style the genre themes that had made Gerrit famous, arranged here as a tribute to artistic endeavor. Gerrit's life work embraced ideals about art and beauty, which were rooted in the ancient classical age and which resonated in the early modern Golden Age. Making art was considered a special talent, reserved for a special few.

The artist must cultivate this talent through innate ability, expert instruction, and diligent exercise. Hence, the three panels in Gerrit's triptych were dedicated to nature, education, and practice.

The center panel represented "nature." Gerrit framed the scene in familiar fashion—a heavy tapestry pulled open wide to reveal an interior room with the studio's lead-glass window on the back left providing the source of light. The room is a nursery, which gives the triptych its title. In the rear left, Gerrit placed an antechamber with secondary figures preoccupied in a task, while in the foreground he positioned his old Savonarola armchair, partly obscured in shadow. The setup created the perception of depth, drawing the viewer into the scene, as if standing at the threshold and gazing into the nursery, unconsciously reaching out for the back of the armchair. It was an illusory technique perfected by Gerrit and emulated by his contemporaries.

Gerrit placed his main subject in the center right. A doting mother in a white bonnet is seated next to a sewing basket and bassinet. She is looking directly into the eyes of the viewer at the threshold. The mother cradles a newborn in her left arm, and with her right hand lifts a full breast from her blouse. She presses two fingers into the soft flesh, offering a nipple to the babe. The image recalls Dou's *The Young Mother*, the gift to the king of England. In this piece, however, the nursing mother emphasizes the living connectedness between parents and children. Her nourishing body feeds the next generation. The child will develop strengths and weaknesses, talents and flaws, by inheritance. That is, by nature.

Besides innate ability, an aspiring artist needed training. Formal education was valued among the urban middle-class in 17th-century Holland, and was especially esteemed in the university town of Leiden. Teaching and learning were recurring themes in Gerrit's genre paintings. In the left panel of the triptych, Gerrit recreated a scene he painted before, *The Night School*. A group of adolescents are huddled around a candlelit table. The older lad is teaching a teenaged girl and boy to write, while a fourth youngster looks on. The painting shows off Gerrit's impressive skill at recreating the delicate glow of candlelight. It also serves as a metaphor in which the candle illuminates the darkness, just as education reveals the unknown. A celebrated earlier version of *The Night School* was included in Johan de Bye's 1665 one-man show in Leiden and still hangs in the Rijksmuseum in Amsterdam. Other Dou paintings on the theme reside today in the Uffizi in Florence and the Met in New York.

On the right side of the triptych, Gerrit painted a solitary scholar absorbed in his work—another one of his signature themes. A man in academic robes is up late at night sharpening quills. Consistent with Gerrit's later work, the scene is draped in shadow, the colors are muted, and detail is obscured, except for the immediate area of the glimmering candlelight. The man is preparing the tools of his craft for the next day, perhaps to write a manuscript or to perform an equation. He is not unlike Gerrit, conscientiously preparing his brushes and palette for a painting session.

For Gerrit, the triptych was a compilation of his greatest pieces and summation of his life's achievement. His contemporary Arnold Houbraken, a painter and writer from Dordrecht, viewed *The Nursery* firsthand and marveled that it was: "a capital work of exceptional skill, and Dou's best known." Not long after Gerrit finished the triptych, it ended up in the private collection of Mennonite wool merchant Isaac Rooleeuw in Amsterdam. In the main hall of Rooleeuw's large house at 35 Nieuwe Dijk, Dou's *The Nursery* hung next to Vermeer's *The Milkmaid*. There is no question as to which was deemed more valuable at the time. Rooleeuw bought *The Milkmaid* together with a companion Vermeer for the dear sum of 330 guilders. By comparison, *The Nursery* cost Rooleeuw the staggering amount of 4,025 guilders. Indeed, for more than a century after his death, Gerrit's triptych was the most celebrated and most coveted piece of art produced in the Dutch Golden Age.

Gerrit patiently worked away at the crimson folds in the bed curtain. Toward the end of the afternoon, the light was waning. He pushed his fading red tresses back off his face to scrutinize the brushwork. Skies permitting, tomorrow he would start on the central panel's background scene of a man having a tooth extracted. He was pleased with this ploy to insert a mini-genre scene within a larger genre painting. Later in the evening, if he was not too tired, he would step out for a few hours. Jan Steen was back in Leiden, after nearly a decade in Haarlem. Steen never acquired a wealthy patron. He returned to Leiden to open a tavern, an occupation he learned from his father. The tavern would supplement Steen's meager income as an artist and provide material for his tippling-themed genre paintings. Gerrit had heard that his old acquaintance from Rembrandt's studio, Jan Lievens, was also back in town. Lievens would no doubt be visiting Steen, his nephew by marriage, and would likely spin a good yarn about his service in the royal court in London. And certainly Gerrit's former pupil, Frans van Mieris, would be found at Steen's tavern, that is, as long as the ale did not run out. Gerrit wanted to know if Frans had been offered any new commissions since last they met.

Gerrit pulled a cover over the panel of the healthy nursing mother staring back at the fatigued aging artist. Perhaps he and Lievens would reminisce about their youth and the times they shared together in Rembrandt's studio. It was now close to two years since their friend and teacher had died, alone in Amsterdam, a picture of *Simeon with the Christ Child in the Temple* unfinished on his easel.

4

FROM FRÄULEIN
TO EMPRESS

Transvestite Tsarina

I t was Tuesday in Saint Petersburg and the tsarina's court was in session. Catherine smiled. Tuesday nights were reserved for royal balls. Right after breakfast, Catherine summoned Monsieur Lande, the court violinist and dance master, to teach her the steps to the latest minuets and quadrilles. She won favor with Empress Elizabeth with her nimble footwork around the palace ballroom. Catherine would call Lande back in the afternoon to make sure she had mastered this evening's choreography.

Empress Elizabeth loved the pomp as much as the power. Her twenty-year reign was a nonstop aristocratic cabaret. She enjoyed a hedonistic lifestyle that revolved around hunting, drinking, and dancing. Most of all, she loved masquerade balls. Every Tuesday, the empress hosted a party where guests were required to come garbed in the clothing of the opposite sex. Her haughty courtiers cringed at the cross-dressing mandate. Catherine, still a teen and a bit of tomboy, could not have been tickled more by the farce. "I must say," she wrote, "there was nothing more hideous or humorous than to see the men dressed as women, and nothing more woeful than to see the women dressed as men." Elizabeth's exhibitionist urges could not be contained. She performed countless costume changes during the festivities, and always ended the night in drag. The masquerade charade was the only way Elizabeth could show off her long, lithe legs and voluptuous breasts, without violating royal standards of dress. She was, after all, the empress of the realm, a position that was not easy to come by.

Leadership succession has never been a routine affair in Russia, where political power is more personal than institutional. Even when the heir apparent is clearly designated, once the throne is vacant the sable gloves are off. Stakes are high in the succession game. For winners, there is influence and prosperity; for losers, exile and expropriation—or worse. This was the path to power of Empress Elizabeth.

In 1740, Russian empress Anna I died after a ten-year reign. Anna was the niece of Peter the Great, and the daughter of Peter's disabled half brother, Ivan V. Russia's old family boyar elites still despised Peter the Great, who had so thoroughly upset their world. The boyars preferred a weak monarch, and they schemed to replace Anna with her infant nephew Ivan VI. But Anna's cousin, Elizabeth Petrovna, disputed the choice. The last surviving child of Peter the Great, Elizabeth believed that she was the true legatee.

Elizabeth was the child of Peter and his second wife, Ekaterina, a household servant whom Peter married for love instead of status. As a young teen, Elizabeth was the gem of her father's court, "the finest beauty in all of Russia," as she was known across Europe. But being blond, blue-eyed, and fair did not shield Elizabeth from indignity and disappointment. Peter first tried to arrange a marriage for Elizabeth with the future King Louis XV. But the French court rejected the proposal because of her mother's Polish peasant past and whispers that Peter's princess was illegitimate. Elizabeth never forgot the insult delivered to her and her family by French Bourbon snobs. Later, young Elizabeth suffered the premature death from smallpox of her dear Holstein fiancé, Johanna's older brother Karl.

Elizabeth was just sixteen when her doting father died, but she was soon shoved into obscurity with the rise of the descendants of Ivan V. Empress Anna made certain that Elizabeth remained unmarried and childless. She even banished one of Elizabeth's suitors to Siberia, though not before cutting out his tongue. Anna's aim was to eliminate the emergence of future rivals to the throne.

Elizabeth managed to avoid Anna's wrath and bided her time. She quietly built useful alliances. An accomplished equestrian, Elizabeth became a favorite of the Imperial cavaliers. She acted as godmother to the Preobrazhensky Regiment, an elite military unit that was first organized by Peter with his childhood friends, and was still fiercely loyal to their founder's memory. When the boyars handed the throne to a newborn baby, the brazen *blondinka* appealed to the Preobrazhensky guardsmen in the name of Peter the Great. They rallied to his daughter's side and vowed to contest the succession, with swords if necessary. Showing early on her flair for the dramatic, Elizabeth donned a leather cuirass, raised a holy icon, and led the regiment in a mounted charge on the royal palace. Baby Ivan was deposed in a bloodless coup.

Elizabeth understood that image mattered in great power politics. Thus, she created the most dazzling court in Europe. Her court was renowned for its glamour as well as its promiscuity. And bawdy though she was, Elizabeth also got the Russian elite hooked on high culture. It was the Age of Enlightenment. For the first time, the Russian court was graced by poets, painters, and philosophers. Her reign saw the foundation of the Academy of Fine Arts and Moscow University. French became the language of the Russian aristocracy. A stage was erected in the palace, which hosted weekly performances of French plays and Italian operas. She took for her lover one of the court musicians, Alexei Razumovsky, a talented singer and bandura player.

Elizabeth presided over the transformation of Saint Petersburg into a city of resplendence. She persuaded the famed French-Italian architect Bartolomeo Rastrelli to fashion an appropriate style for her empire. Rastrelli swirled a vision of reckless rococo upon scores of palaces and churches. Elizabeth relocated the seat of power across the river from the redbrick Peter Paul Fortress to the Winter Palace. She forbade any building from rising higher than her new 1,000-room, 2,000-window, multi-columned mansion. The adjacent Palace Square could host as many as fifty parading infantry battalions at once. Its august archways led out to a beaming boulevard, which became the city's central artery, the Nevsky Prospekt. Elizabeth lovingly fulfilled her father's dream to make Saint Petersburg a grand Western-facing capital. And now, with Catherine's nuptials, she had the chance to show off her glittering city to the world.

The Wedding

For Empress Elizabeth, the royal wedding was the most important event of her twenty-year reign. To mark the occasion, she was determined to throw the splashiest party that European high society had ever seen, a display of refinement and riches that even Versailles would envy.

The empress had an imperial-sized ego to match her title, but the showy celebration had a political motive, too. Elizabeth was obsessed with her succession and the continuation of the ruling legacy of her father Peter the Great. Because she was unwed and childless, Elizabeth greatly feared that usurpers would sever the Romanov line after she was gone. Thus, she believed an awe-inspiring marriage ceremony would sanctify her adopted heir as the rightful claimant to the Imperial throne. Also, Elizabeth was sensitive to what the rest of aristocratic Europe thought about Russia. The wedding was an ideal opportunity to dispel the opinion that Russia was more uncouth Asian than enlightened European. The list of invitees included scores of continental bluebloods, who would see firsthand the grandness of her empire.

The empress was in haste to consummate the union of her Holstein heirs. But the formal arrangements were delayed. In the summer of 1744, Peter was wracked by sickness. The delicate teen was exhausted by the fast-moving events in his life and remained in pressure-free confinement in his living quarters. In late November, on a bitter cold carriage ride between Moscow and Saint Petersburg, the duke collapsed. By morning Peter showed blistering skin and a high fever, signs of the dreaded red plague—small pox. Johanna was panicked; she hurried Catherine to the capital away from her infectious fiancé. Elizabeth was frantic; she rushed back to the bedside of her stricken successor. The doctors gave the boy only a slim chance of survival. Haunted by memories of her own fiancé's agonizing death, the empress was steadfast throughout the ordeal, caring for and praying over her suffering nephew. Six weeks following the ominous diagnosis, Catherine received a message from Her Majesty: "Today I can joyously assure you that we may at last hope for a recovery. His Highness, the grand duke, has come back to us."

Elizabeth was stunned by how close her succession plan had come to ruin. She could wait no longer for a grandchild. In March, against the advice of the doctors treating the grand duke, the empress announced that the royal wedding would be held in July 1745. It was not much time to organize the social event of the decade.

The empress put aside all other affairs for six months to prepare. No detail was overlooked; no expense was spared. She studied the programs and menues of other high-profile royal marriages across Europe, especially the recent wedding of the dauphin of France, son of Louis XV, staged at Versailles. Elizabeth advanced a year's salary to the high nobility so that officers had at least four ceremonial uniforms and ladies at least five ball gowns. Shiploads of fine linen, lacey silk, and sumptuous velvet arrived from France, Italy, and Holland to outfit the court with new wedding wardrobes. She also decreed that members of the Imperial court must upgrade their coaches, which must be pulled by teams of at least six horses.

Elizabeth devised a wedding program that included ten days of banquet feasts, opera and theater, afternoon hunting parties, and evening masquerade balls. With so much to organize, the wedding date was pushed back to late August.

As the wedding drew nearer, the royal teens grew more apprehensive and despondent. "My heart did not foresee great happiness," Catherine said about her arranged future. "Ambition alone sustained me." Poor Peter was not fully recovered from his near-death experience. The scorching virus had left his impish face haggard and scarred. He wore a ridiculously oversized wig to conceal his disfigured countenance. Catherine and Peter did not see each other for nearly three months. When they were finally reunited on the grand staircase in the Winter Palace, Catherine gasped and recoiled at first sight of Peter's ravaged face. "Do you still recognize me?" he asked with a sad smirk. It was an unfortunate incident that the self-doubting adolescent never forgot or forgave.

On the day of the wedding, the empress was up before dawn, like an artist fiddling with her creation one last time before its unveiling. She met Catherine and helped dress the bride up and down, inside and out. Catherine sat patiently while different hairstyles were combed out for Elizabeth's consideration. Finally, Catherine was coaxed into a svelte eighteen-inch waist, intricately embroidered and lace-trimmed wedding gown, spun from glittering silver thread, lined with white feathered sleeves, and topped with a jewel-dappled cape. Johanna described the dress as "the most shimmering cloth that I have ever seen." A touch of makeup and then Elizabeth helped Catherine to don the heavy diamond-encrusted crown of the grand duchess. Mother-in-law and bride were ready.

Elizabeth's colorful gilded coach was pulled by a team of sixteen snow-white stallions the short distance down Nevsky Prospekt to the colonnaded facade of Our Lady of Kazan Cathedral. Inside, the Bishop of Novgorod presided over the three-hour ceremony, in which the couple exchanged vows amid swirling incense and flickering candles. Then the threesome rolled back up crowd-lined Nevsky Prospekt, leading a procession of more than a hundred fancy coaches to Admiralty Square for the reception. Elizabeth oversaw every sensual detail of the party that followed, from the the foie gras mushroom sauce at the wedding banquet, to the gurgling fountains of wine at the gala ball, to the fragrance of soap in the toilets, to the riverfront fireworks finale. At 10:00 P.M., Elizabeth even escorted the bride and groom by hand to the royal boudoir, and with a knowing wink bid them good night.

Love and Marriage

Atop the red velvet vastness of her wedding-night bed, the newly crowned grand duchess drifted, alone. At sixteen, Catherine may still have been naive about the intricacies of intimacy, but she at least knew that something physical involving her new husband was supposed to happen. So she waited. She adjusted the fit of her pink Parisian negligee. She sat upright, crossed her ankles and kicked her heels against the silver-gilded bed frame, reclined on her left arm, then on her right arm, then slowly lowered the back of her head onto a stout embroidered pillow, and studied the swirly detail in the canopy above. Hours passed. At last, the door to the plush apartment pushed open and the seventeen-year-old grand duke made a stumbling entrance, before collapsing in a muttering drunken heap.

Next morning Catherine's marital mentor, Madame Kruse, coyly inquired about how the duchess had "slept." Catherine smiled nervously, looked down and said nothing. She was reasonably sure that she had not done anything wrong, but was fearful of spoiling everyone else's good time, especially the empress's.

Each evening during the wedding carnival Catherine was escorted back to her bedchamber. But while fireworks illuminated the Saint Petersburg sky, she sat in candlelit silence. To counter the boredom, Catherine smuggled books into the honeymoon suite, hidden in her flowing gowns. The grand duke made occasional appearances, but said little, and stayed well clear of his new wife and the big mattress. Instead, he summoned his servants to keep him company until, stupefied by drink, he passed out. Catherine always knew that Peter was a bit peculiar, but in a childish and quirky way; ever since his illness, he showed a morose and malicious side. Catherine was confused, hurt, and embittered by the rejection, but outwardly resilient.

When the festivities ended, things did not improve between Catherine and Peter; indeed, they got worse. Peter was a bundle of resentments, and now he was heir to the throne of a country that he openly despised and married to a woman that he suddenly detested. The months following the wedding were the hardest for Catherine. Peter ridiculed his new wife in public, and boasted of a romantic liaison with a court maiden. The incorrigible Johanna was sent packing a month after the wedding. Catherine would never see her mother again. Despite her new status, the grand duchess felt more alone than ever.

The empress, meanwhile, was a control freak, determined to be the only source of influence on her new daughter-in-law. To Catherine's dismay, her young girlfriends at the court were forbidden from talking to her after the marriage, including her closest Russian friend, Mademoiselle Zhukova, who was banished from the capital. The empress assigned the severe Madame Schenk to act as Catherine's main attendant and chaperone. Catherine referred to her new chamber lady as Argus, the ever-watchful hundred-eyed monster guardian of Greek mythology. Young Catherine was alone and unhappy, though ever gracious and alert in the company of the court.

Catherine and Peter managed to coexist; they had no choice. The empress desperately wanted an heir. She posted guards outside the couple's living quarters to make certain that they spent nights together. But behind the red velveteen walls, Catherine read Montesquieu and Plato, while Peter played with toy soldiers and hunting dogs. Catherine could tolerate finding his army dolls under her pillow, she got used to the stench of his defecating hounds, she learned to lose to him at cards rather than endure his insufferable sulking, and she even sat through several performances of his one-man puppet shows; but she drew the line with the duke's violin playing, which she likened to a scraping saw. Catherine thought her husband was immature, indiscreet, and dimwitted; but she also feared him, knowing that one day he would be the all-powerful emperor, and his whims would become law.

Besides reading, Catherine's main diversion was horseback riding. She already was a skilled rider from childhood. She found escape from the dreary solitude in exhilarating open runs through the countryside. Of course, the empress disapproved of Catherine's rambling ways, as well as her riding style. Catherine preferred to straddle her steed, not to sit sidesaddle, as norms of aristocratic femininity dictated. The empress considered Catherine's equestrian frolics not only unladylike, but also the probable cause for why she still had no grandchildren. The artful grand duchess, however, designed a special English saddle with an adjustable pommel and stirrup, so that once she was beyond sight of her keepers, she could swing a supple leg over her favorite gray steed, and race and jump with the best of Her Majesty's chevaliers. If the stable grooms were later quizzed about Catherine's riding habit, they answered honestly that Her Highness used a "lady's saddle."

Years passed, and the royal progenitors remained childless. The empress eventually came to regret her choice of heir apparent. At first, she accused Catherine of not showing sufficient love and affection to her husband. But her court spies told a different story. Elizabeth finally accepted that Peter was a flake, and probably impotent. And while Catherine may have been ignored by her husband, other rising officers at the court took note of the young woman with long brunette curls and alluring blue eyes. The empress decided it was time for an alternative succession plan. She assigned Catherine a new chaperone, Madame Choglokova, who let it be known that patriotic duty sometimes transcended marital fidelity. Choglokova began to host intimate soirees in her private quarters with the grand duchess and socially suitable cadets, leaving the young ones alone for long spells with ample wine and subtle encouragement.

This was how Catherine became acquainted with Sergei Saltykov, a junior court officer of rakish repute. The handsome Saltykov won Choglakova's favor with his noble pedigree, good humor, and outrageous flattery. He managed to turn up everywhere that Catherine went, eager to show off his dash and wit. When the Duchess asked Sergei right out what he hoped to accomplish, she was struck silent by his direct reply: to make love to the woman that he secretly worshiped and longed for. It was foolish, treasonous, and intoxicating.

Catherine described Sergei as "remarkably handsome, with no equal in the grand court." For weeks she playfully parried his advances, while eagerly anticipating the next thrust. Now in her early twenties, Catherine craved the attention of the bold prince, who in looks and demeanor was a complete contrast to her diminutive and dull husband. During a summer hunting holiday, Sergei and Catherine broke away from the party and strayed into a sun-splashed field of tall wildflowers, where she at last consented to be his lover. Thus began Catherine's first clandestine affair.

Catherine's fling with the tall dark prince lasted for little more than a year, and it did not end well. During these exhilarating months, she miscarried twice, almost fatally the second time. In February 1754, she finally gave birth to a son. The exultant empress immediately gathered the baby in her arms, named it Paul after her older brother, and carried it to a nursery set up in her apartment. Cannons boomed and bells rang out across the empire in celebration of the newborn heir. Once more, Catherine was left alone and in tears.

She did not see her son again for six weeks; thereafter, by order of the empress, she was kept apart from her child. He was, after all, a state treasure, a new hope for the ruling dynasty. Meanwhile, Saltykov visited her less often. By now, his ardor had waned, and new courtly conquests inspired his passion. After the baby's safe delivery, the satisfied empress waved a hand and sent the prince charmer far away from the capital, on what became a perpetual foreign mission.

Catherine went on to have three more children, but did not raise one of them. She never received maternal affection from self-obsessed Johanna, and any innate nurturing instincts were quashed by dynasty-obsessed Elizabeth. Poor Peter, meanwhile, openly mocked the charade of his paternity, remarking to friends over cards that he had no idea how he kept producing heirs, since he hardly ever touched his wife.

Attention-starved and unloved as a girl, Catherine made up for it as a young woman. Her furtive affair with Saltykov awakened a desire to be indulged and aroused. She was soon swept up in another secret seduction with twenty-three-year-old Stanislaw Poniatowski. The gentle Polish prince loved the grand duchess, and readily took any risk to see her. He crept in and out of bedroom windows, scaled palace walls by moonlight, and donned wigs in the disguise of servants or chamber ladies, whatever it took for an intimate hour with Catherine. Even Peter complimented the stealthy suitor on his ingenuity in finding ways into the royal apartment. The affair resulted in Catherine's second child and ended only when Poniatowski was called back to Warsaw. In the not too distant future, however, Catherine would make him the king of Poland, though what Stanislaw really wanted was to marry her.

Elizabeth's entourage was hardly reserved about sex. Now as the aging empress became more reclusive, court dalliances became more conspicuous. Catherine's unabashed husband Peter essentially lived with his mistress, Mademoiselle Vorontsova. Catherine also had grown more confident in her physical prowess and more daring in her romantic liaisons. She liked having admirers. She liked having sex. She liked having power. After her devoted Polish lover departed, Catherine became involved with a young artillery officer, Grigory Orlov, whose reputation soared among the ladies at court for his exploits both on the battlefield and in the bedroom. Their lustful affair became a fatal attraction.

Dangerous Liaisons

Saint Petersburg in winter is stilled by eighteen hours of darkness each night. In December 1761, a disquieting gloom set over the Imperial court as the once radiant Empress Elizabeth lay dying. On Christmas day, Peter and Catherine were summoned to Her Majesty's chamber. The faintly lit room had a heavy aroma of sacramental incense, which burned her eyes. Next to the bed the empress's paramour softly sang a Ukrainian lullaby, while a priest in the corner chanted the Orthodox Song of the Dying. Still conscious, the empress spoke. Despite her doubts, Elizabeth stuck with the plan to bequeath the throne to her adopted nephew. She made Peter promise to safeguard her adopted grandson Paul, and pass the throne on to him when the time came. She also asked that he look after the well-being of Razumovsky, her longtime lover. She said nothing about Catherine.

A few hours later, the head of the Imperial senate emerged from the bedroom and announced to the crowd of disconsolate courtesans: "Her Imperial Majesty, Elizabeth Petrovna, has gone to sleep with our Lord. God save our beneficent sovereign, Emperor Peter III."

With the passing of the empress, Catherine was now vulnerable. Peter already once forced a confrontation between Catherine and Elizabeth, when he tried to have his wife banished from the court, claiming that she was excessively proud and quarrelsome. Catherine nimbly fended off the challenge. On another occasion, Elizabeth urged Peter to heed his wife's good sense when he took the throne. But as autocrat he was not bound to that request. Peter I had already established the precedent of consigning his first wife to a nunnery, and then marrying his mistress and placing her on the throne. Catherine feared her fate.

Not surprisingly, the tenure of Peter III got off to a shaky start. The new tsar antagonized the military by making peace with his idol Frederick II, just as the Prussian nemesis was on the verge of defeat. He offended the devout by taking property and privileges away from the Church and belittling Orthodox customs. He infuriated Russia's foreign allies by reneging on existing treaties, and then declaring war on Denmark over some disputed pasture land in Schleswig-Holstein. To his credit, Peter abolished the Secret Chancery, the tsarist special police force used to terrorize the elite; though without a spy service, he unwittingly made himself more susceptible to a coup. His margin for political error was thin.

During fifteen years as Elizabeth's understudy, Peter never outgrew his reputation as a whimsical buffoon. He was averse to serious conversation; and, if anyone questioned his frivolous remarks, he responded by squishing up his face and sticking out his tongue. By contrast, Catherine during this time appeared more regal. Unlike her husband, Catherine possessed keen political instincts. She cultivated alliances at the court in anticipation of this moment. So thorough was the grand duchess that two-thirds of the elite believed they were her closest confidante. Despite her careful preparations, Catherine was inadvertently constrained from acting when the empress died. She was six months pregnant.

In the spring of 1760, a wounded war hero arrived in the capital, and immediately had the courtesans panting for every scintillating detail of his latest escapades. Lieutenant Grigory Orlov was one of five soldier brothers, famed for their daring in the war against Prussia. The family achieved minor noble status under Peter the Great, who initially condemned their grandfather to the executioner's block. But the emperor was so impressed by the elder Orlov's cool disregard for death, after watching him boot a severed head out of the way and lower his own head in its place, that he was spared the axe and promoted to a new regiment that Peter was forming. The feral fraternity of Orlovs was popular with the troops, while brother Gregory was a favorite of the ladies. He was sweetly handsome, strong as a bull and—according to court gossip—endowed like one, too. He arrived in town brandishing a sash of newly won medals and escorting a celebrity prisoner of war, a captured count and aide-de-camp of Frederick II. Gregory was immediately embroiled in scandal after seducing Princess Kurakina, mistress of a powerful minister. If Gregory was not being challenged to a duel, then he was likely issuing a challenge. Catherine swooned.

Catherine and Grigory struck up a torrid romance. He fathered her third child. Grigory not only sated Catherine's sexual appetite, but could help satisfy her political ambition. In the sultry summer of 1762, they contrived the ultimate conspiracy. The Orlovs cultivated support for Catherine among the military regiments in the capital. They talked up her Russophile credentials, while doling out vodka and kopeks. As Empress Elizabeth had already shown, the path to the power in Russia went through the barracks of the elite guardsmen.

Next, Catherine allied herself with the erudite Count Nikita Panin, who helped persuade an influential contingent of court nobles to defect to her side. In addition, the elder prelates of the Orthodox Church were eager to rid themselves of the apostate Peter. Finally, Catherine maintained a close friendship with Madame Dashkova, the younger sister of Peter's mistress. Through Dashkova, Catherine kept tabs on her talkative husband, who was scheming to imprison his wife and place his mistress on the throne. Catherine felt cornered. She confided in a letter: "I will either perish or reign."

The Time Has Come

In summer, the night sky over Saint Petersburg has an eerie white glow. On the night of June 27, one of the Catherine's coconspirators, Captain Passek, was arrested and charged with treason. When word reached the Orlovs, they leapt to action. Catherine was out of the capital at the summer estate of Peterhof. At Peter's behest, she was supposed to organize a party to celebrate his name day, which occurred on June 28. The emperor was scheduled to arrive around midday in the company of a hundred-some revelers.

Alexei Orlov, the mastermind of the coup, galloped to Peterhof before daybreak. Entering Catherine's bedroom, he whispered: "Matushka, wake up. The time has come." The pair was soon hurtling by coach through whirling dust clouds on the road back to the capital. Peter, meanwhile, arrived at Peterhof, wearing his favorite blue Prussian officer's uniform. He found no one waiting. Undismayed, he quickly deduced that Catherine must have planned a surprise party for him, and he gleefully skipped through the palace, throwing open doors to empty rooms.

On the outskirts of the capital, Grigory Orlov met Catherine's coach. He escorted her before the assembled guard regiments, who gathered around closely to swear their allegiance. Donning the dark green uniform of the Preobrazhensky Regiment, just as Elizabeth had done twenty years before, Catherine mounted her tall stallion and with sword drawn led a parade of priests and soldiers down Nevsky Prospekt, amid the excited clamor of church bells. Back at Peterhof, Peter was in a rage; his wife had defied his orders and ruined his party. His bored guests sought shade in the summer gardens.

Catherine's triumphant procession stopped before the Kazan Cathedral, where the Archbishop of Novgorod was waiting to consecrate the coup and proclaim Catherine autocrat over all of Russia. She then walked to the palace to meet Panin, who had the head of the Imperial senate ready to recognize her sovereignty on behalf of the high nobility. With her son Paul at her side, Catherine strode onto a balcony to acknowledge the wild cheering of tens of thousands of soldiers and city residents. In late afternoon, a lone horseman arrived at Peterhof mansion and reported to the emperor: the regiments were in revolt and the throne had been seized. Peter collapsed into the lap of his mistress and wept.

In the capital, a force of more than ten thousand guardsmen assembled to ride out and arrest the deposed ruler. Catherine, in Russian military attire, led the march. At Peterhof, Peter's friends convinced him to flee by boat to Holstein, but when they reached the Kronstadt naval fortress, they were refused passage. His authority was no longer recognized. The anguished emperor retreated to his country estate. Aware of the mismatch, he dismissed his own troops rather than put up a fight. Instead, he wrote Catherine a letter, in French, in which he apologized for all his rude behavior, promised to change, and offered to share the throne. Receiving his messenger along the road, Catherine rejected the offer. Peter now composed a second letter in which he would agree to abdicate the throne as long as he and his beloved mistress could go live in exile on the other side of the Baltic in his ancestral Holstein homeland. Catherine accepted.

Catherine turned her force around and returned to the palace in Saint Petersburg. She turned her attention to consolidating her victory and taking over the affairs of an empire. Catherine would reign for thirty-four years, presiding over a golden age for Russia, and making her court among the most esteemed in all Europe.

Peter, meanwhile, was separated from his mistress and placed under house arrest under the guard of Alexei Orlov. What happened next remains uncertain, except the fact that Peter was dead. It is widely assumed that practical Alexei murdered the ex-emperor to avoid potential counterclaims to the throne and to open the way to royal marriage for his brother. A more convenient and documented version comes from a letter that Alexei wrote to Catherine, in which he assumed full responsibility for the "unfortunate accident," stating that a drunken Peter had become belligerent and the guards used excessive force to restrain him. Finally, the "official" version of Peter's death, issued by the Imperial court to the public, declared that the emperor succumbed to a nasty bout of hemorrhoids.

Catherine's complicity in this act has never been proven, and she displayed revulsion and tears when told of the death. But then again, she was, before all else, a master politician.

5

TEMPLE OF ARTS

The Wine Merchant

An exuberant squeal resounded through the maze of stacked wine casks, cramming the ground floor of the Achterburgwal row house. At a front desk adjacent to the entryway, two startled Dutch merchants turned quickly, pageboys swishing, to locate the source. But the gigglers escaped unseen. The Braamcamp boys were playing hide-and-seek again. Father Jan Braamcamp apologized for the interruption, and the pair went back to talking business. In the 18th century, the Achterburgwal district was a favorite location for Amsterdam's wealthy traders.

By the mid-1700s, the Dutch Golden Age had passed. A century of on-again-off-again war with England wore down the imperial ambitions of the merchant republic. But while Dutch fluyts no longer dominated the ocean waves, Holland's compact seaport cities were still among the richest in the world. Dutch entrepreneurs never stopped calculating how to increase profits and reduce risk. And, in doing so, created modern capitalism. Few global commodities in the 18th century could reach consumers without a helping hand from the Dutch.

Jan Braamcamp had done well to ensconce himself at the center of Dutch commerce. He was born in the eastern town of Rijssen, where the Braamcamps once occupied positions of power and wealth. But as the youngest child in a large Dutch family, there was not much left for Jan to inherit when his father died. So the littlest Braamcamp set out for the city.

By the mid-1600s, Dutch merchants had cornered the global wine market, and Amsterdam was its center. Dutch traders shipped Rhineland Rieslings east, sailed Spanish Muscatels north, and transported French brandies everywhere. Jan saw his opportunity. He quickly learned the wine trade and opened shop as a vintner. The city was awash in small-time wine merchants, trying to get in on the oenological boom. There was enough business to go around; but with so many traders, it was difficult to strike it big. To enhance his prospects, Jan joined the Amsterdam guild of wine merchants, the *Wijnkopersgildehuis*. It was here that Jan became acquainted with Gerrit Wentink, one of the guild's most prominent traders.

When the unfortunate Wentink tippled his last, Jan felt obliged to console the grieving widow, Hendrina van Beeck. The twenty-eight-year-old vintner must have been a comforting presence, for the pair was married in January 1699. Jan not only gained a wife, but a thriving wine business, too. The matrimonial merger enabled Jan to rise from the lower ranks of small vintners to the upper echelon of wine traders. He was elected as an officer in the guild. His business interests became transcontinental, establishing ties with wine brokers in Portugal. The European wine market was flourishing, and so was Jan Braamcamp.

Life with Hendrina was good. Following the wedding, Jan moved into her four-story townhouse in the Achterburgwal district. The neighborhood ran along the Singel Canal, in the Old Town center (today's red-light district). Hendrina's first marriage bore no offspring, but seven little Braamcamps arrived within ten years of her second. Their firstborn son was Gerrit, in 1699, followed by three younger brothers, Dirk, Rutgers, and Herman. Sadly, all three sisters died in infancy. Hendrina was a devout Catholic, and Jan converted without fuss. The mother insisted on a strict Catholic upbringing for the children. In November 1699, Gerrit was baptized in the Church of the Three Hooded Crows, one of Amsterdam's few Catholic churches.

As was common practice, the sons were introduced to the family business at an early age. Before he was a teenager, Gerrit was following his father around the shop, taking on the tasks of trade such as accounting, inventory, shipping, and receiving. The boy merchant was eager to learn, and mature beyond his years. Satisfied with Gerrit, Jan sent his second oldest, Dirk, to Portugal, to serve as an apprentice at Cremer and Co., a Dutch trading firm in Lisbon. The family-run Braamcamp business was in good form, when tragedy struck. In 1713, Jan took ill and died. The father was just forty-two years old. Second-time a widow, the savvy Hendrina took over the family's affairs. Gerrit was only thirteen years old, but his days as a trainee were over. For the next few years, mother and son worked to keep the business profitable in the hyper-competitive market. Then, in 1721, misfortune fell on the family again: Hendrina was dead. The Braamcamp wine business did not seem likely to survive.

Rise of the House of Braamcamp

Still grieving the loss of their dear mother, the Braampcamp boys gathered for the reading of Hendrina's last will and testament. A gray-haired lawyer in flowing black velvet drew papers from a leather pouch. He removed a pair of round gold-rimmed spectacles and brought the documents near his somber face. Gerrit, Dirk, Rutgers, and Herman were each bequeathed 4,000 florins. Not a fortune, but a generous inheritance for certain. The family enterprise, however, was worth much more. Here the Braamcamp matriarch revealed her favoritism and confidence in the eldest. Gerrit was named sole owner of the wine business, and primary caretaker of the two youngest brothers. Gerrit was twenty-one years old.

Brother Rutgers fumed, as he had expected to share ownership and management of the firm. The sixteen-year-old resented being placed under the guardianship of his older brother. Their sibling bond was irreparably strained. Gerrit was unsentimental in business affairs. Rutgers was forced to look outside the family firm for income, finding employment with other wine traders. Gerrit was more devoted to eleven-year-old Herman. He arranged an apprenticeship for his youngest brother in Portugal with Cremer and Co., where Dirk was already employed. Unfortunately, Hendrina's unexpected death came before Gerrit reached the minimum legal age for ownership of a trading house in Amsterdam. He was forced to wait therefore until age twenty-five, before assuming full control from the guardian of the estate. It was a rough start for the young merchant.

Lean years followed Hendrina's death, as Gerrit struggled to keep the trading house solvent and to ward off predators. While the firm remained active in the wine market, Gerrit diversified his portfolio through the family's Portuguese connection. But even when he recognized an attractive deal, the firm was perpetually short of capital. Gerrit, however, did not miss every opportunity that came his way. He began spending his time at Arnold Clumper's hardware store, and investing his affection in young Elisabeth Clumper. In 1727, the son of the wine merchant married the daughter of the ironmonger. Like the Braamcamps, the Clumpers were practicing Catholics, and the couple was married in the Church. The bride came with a dowry of 21,000 florins. Fortune was shifting in Gerrit's favor.

Braamcamp's big business break came in 1736. After years of painstaking preparation and lobbying, Gerrit orchestrated a joint venture with three other investors in a timber importing operation. His partners were well placed to facilitate the necessary transactions to make it work. They included a bookkeeper of the Dutch East India Company, a town clerk of Amsterdam, and a captain of the Dutch Admiralty. The contract called for Gerrit's partners to put up 10,000 florins each, while Gerrit provided his "vigilance" and "expertise." Although he did not invest any cash, Gerrit was entitled to an equal share of the profits. So as not to jinx things, the contract invoked "God's Blessing" on the company. Whether it was Divine Will or Braamcamp Brains, the partnership was a huge success. After the first five years, the profits generated by Gerrit's trading deals surpassed 240,000 florins. Gerrit's equal share came to 60,000 florins. The joint company continued until 1748, when Gerrit bought out his partners.

Gerrit was on his way. He renamed the trading house Geraldo Braamcamp and Co., in a gesture to his Portuguese connection. He expanded into industrial enterprises—a lumberyard, a sawmill, an iron foundry. He invested in real estate—commercial properties, warehouse space, historic residences. In the ritzy Kloveniersburgwal neighborhood, he renovated and converted two adjoining mansions into the city's most luxurious hotel, the Arms of Amsterdam.

The Braamcamp branch in Portugal also prospered. His brother Dirk rose from apprentice to full partner in the Lisbon trading firm, which was renamed Cremer and Braamcamp. Gerrit's younger brother Herman also thrived. His Catholic faith was a useful asset for social climbing in aristocratic Portugal. Herman married Maria Ignacia Almeida Castelo-Branco, first lady of Morgado da Luz. Her father, Manuel, was a military brigadier, wealthy landowner, and first governor of Rio de Janeiro. His Portuguese vineyards produced some of Iberia's best wine.

Herman and Gerrit remained close. Herman named his first son Geraldo, to honor his brother. When still a boy, Geraldo moved to Amsterdam to apprentice with his uncle. Gerrit adored the lad and treated him as a son. Back in Portugal, nephew Geraldo rose to prominence, and was named the first baron of Sobral and a Knight of the Order of Christ.

But for all Gerrit's success, life was not complete. Gerrit and Elisabeth, alas, shared an empty house. Their first child, Arnold, was born in July 1728, in the couple's first year of marriage. Arnold survived the perils of infancy, only to take ill and die before turning six. Two years later, Elisabeth gave birth to a second child, a daughter named Cornelia Elisabeth. But the baby girl did not make it through the first year. The Braamcamps did not have any more children. Then, in September 1742, Elisabeth suddenly died. His beloved wife was interred in the New Church. The devastated husband was alone again. He sought relief from the inner pain. Life and love were temporary. Gerrit yearned for the eternal, and found it in the enduring beauty of art.

Golden Age Connoisseur

"Any good Dutch collection," expounded Heinrich Wilhelm Tischbein, "must contain a self-portrait by Rembrandt, an elaborate sketch by Rubens, and a picture by Dou." Almost seventy years after his death, Gerrit Dou still ranked among the "Big Three" of Golden Age masters. Tischbein was an accomplished German portrait painter and a recognized European authority on Old Masters. His judgment as to what constituted a "good collection" included more than two dozen 17th-century artists and was the accepted standard for 18th-century collectors. As trader Braamcamp entered this unfamiliar new marketplace, Tischbein's list was a useful starting point.

After the "Big Three," the list included Gerrit's student Frans van Mieris, and Gabriel Metsu. They were followed by Adriaen van Ostade, David Teniers, Gerard ter Borch, Nicolaes Berchem, Gerard de Lairesse, and two pieces by Philips Wouwerman (one from his early and one from his late period). Some artists were noted for a specialty: a portrait by Anthony van Dyck, a landscape by Aelbert Cuyp, a calm sea by Willem van der Velde, a stormy sea by Ludolf Bakhuysen, a church interior by Pieter Neefs, some cattle by Adriaan van der Velde, and, of course, some oxen by Paulus Potter.

Braamcamp embraced his newfound object of devotion. For the widower merchant, art collecting was not a passing infatuation, but a long-term commitment. He wanted a collection to rival Amsterdam's most illustrious merchant family dynasties. To do this, Gerrit needed help. Braamcamp was a virtuoso at buying and selling in a dozen different commodity markets, but in gauging value in the art market he was a novice. Gerrit contacted Engel Sam in Rotterdam, his longtime friend and partner in the timber trade. Known as "Smart Sam," the bon vivant was an art sophisticate and good painter in his own right. Gerrit persuaded Sam to move to Amsterdam and serve as his mentor and advisor.

In the commodity exchanges, Gerrit recognized the benefit of keeping company with expert and well-connected associates; he applied the strategy to his new endeavor. The upper echelon of Amsterdam's art community comprised an exclusive club of Protestant collectors and dealers, who depended on one another for precious tidbits of information on the whereabouts and movements of Old Masters. Exclusive, but not restricted. With enough money, even a Catholic could gain entry. Braamcamp struck an acquaintance with two of Amsterdam's most prominent art dealers, Dirk van Diemen and Jan Matthias Cock. The two high-end dealers were crucial in helping to assemble a legendary collection. Gerrit's business credo was to never overpay, for anything. But if his art counselors agreed that a particular painting was an indisputable masterpiece, he was prepared to make a generous bid.

The collection began modestly. In 1743, Gerrit's name appeared for the first time in the margin of an auction catalogue. Two years later, in April 1745, van Diemen procured a small 8 x 6-inch picture of a country inn, an officer in yellow tunic and red sash enjoying a drink, painted by Willem van Mieris (son of Frans). The astute van Diemen paid just twenty-one florins for the piece, which resold thirty years later for 1,000 florins. The merrymaking tavern scene was a fitting early acquisition for the son of the wine merchant.

Gerrit was eager for more. When gossip circulated among his art acquaintances that some Old Masters would soon come onto market, he was determined not to miss out. Opportunity indeed arrived, not once, but twice: in The Hague, the sale of the impressive collection of Jacques de Roore; and, in Amsterdam, the estate sale of Johannes Coop.

Braamcamp authorized art dealer Wannaar, a regular player in The Hague art market, to act on his behalf at the de Roore sale in September 1747. His deputy did not disappoint. With Lot 108, Wannaar secured a superb Rembrandt portrait for 125 florins. The dealer paid considerably more, 470 florins, for a historical painting by Gerard de Lairesse. The large panel showed Abraham entertaining three angels, with wife Sarah looking on. Inspired by his strong Catholic faith, Gerrit showed a preference for bible-themed historical paintings in general and by Lairesse in particular. Gerrit eventually owned at least six paintings by the Liege-born artist.

The de Roore auction was a good learning experience for Gerrit, who chose not to pursue several of the pricier pieces. Wannaar was outbid on Frans van Mieris's finely painted portrait of *A Man in Red Velvet*. This prize went to Willem Lormier for 812 florins; however, nine years later Gerrit paid just 505 florins for the same Van Mieris at Lormier's estate sale. The painting eventually landed in the Louvre.

If the de Roore auction was a modest success, then the Coop sale surpassed Gerrit's own high expectations. The Coop auction brought Gerrit another Rembrandt, one of the artist's most famous paintings, *Storm on the Sea of Galilee*. In this scene, Christ is a calming figure for the distressed apostles, caught in a violent tempest in Peter's fishing boat. The monumental canvas, more than five feet high and four across, was painted in 1633. During the Golden Age, the painting resided with Amsterdam alderman Jan Hinlopen, in one of Holland's most celebrated private collections. Gerrit nabbed it with an intimidating bid of 600 florins. Much later, *Storm on the Sea of Galilee* earned notoriety as the plundered gem in the Gardner Museum art heist in Boston in 1990. Rembrandt's only seascape was never seen again.

The Coop sale brought more Golden Age masters into the fledgling collection. Gerrit picked up three paintings by Gabriel Metsu. These included the clever companion set—*Student Writing a Letter* and *Young Lady Reading a Letter*—purchased for 500 florins. Metsu was another of Gerrit's favorite painters, and he eventually owned more than a dozen works by the Leiden artist. In 1747, van Diemen scored for 1,000 florins Metsu's ultimate masterpiece, *Visit to the Nursery*, which today hangs in the Met in New York City. The Coop sale also reaped a first-rate Adriaen van Ostade, a farmhouse interior with twenty partying peasants. The Braamcamp collection eventually counted more than ten paintings by van Ostade, the Golden Age master of Dutch country life. Finally, Gerrit grabbed two works by David Teniers the Younger for 730 florins. Painted on copper, the pair depicted a military company and a drummer. The Coop auction put Amsterdam's sellers and buyers on notice. If Braamcamp collected pictures the same way he traded commodities, he would be a force to reckon with.

The fervent competition for Old Masters on the Dutch art market energized the plump and pious widower. An inventory of Gerrit's acquisitions, in 1752, added up to 172 paintings. Contemporary art historian Jan van Gool, who was on familiar terms with every major collector in Holland, complimented Gerrit as "the famous merchant, connoisseur, and lover of the noble arts." By this time, Gerrit was two-thirds of the way to the coveted Big Three. Two paintings by Gerrit Dou were listed in the 1752 inventory, including *The Wine Cellar*, featured in de Bye's one-man show. The risqué scene of a flirtatious couple sent on an errand to fill a wine pitcher in a dark basement was among the artist's most popular. Braamcamp also owned a second Dou, depicting a young surgeon examining a woman in an armchair by candlelight, viewed through an arched portico. Then, in 1757, the reliable van Diemen struck again, seizing a companion set of Dou window scenes—*Trumpeter at a Window* and *Woman Carrying a Fruit Basket*—for a startling 4,150 florins. Three years later, Gerrit acquired one of Dou's early Tobit pictures, created in Rembrandt's studio.

The final piece of the Big Three, "an elaborate sketch by Rubens," managed to elude Gerrit for years. At last, in October 1754, Gerrit got his chance with the estate sale of Jeronimus Tonneman. While the forty-one paintings put on the block were certainly of interest, it was the thousand drawings that aroused excitement among dealers and collectors. Gerrit directed Jan Cock to act as agent at the sale. The proceedings were only just underway when Cock captured Lots 7 and 8, with a high bid of 1,350 florins. The prize was a companion set of Rubens drawings—*The Last Supper* and *Jesus Raising Lazarus*—described as: "masterly sketches done *en grisaille* for a larger picture." Cock was not finished. He further bolstered Braamcamp's collection with a superb Hendrick Goltzius rendering of Danae, for 300 florins.

It took Gerrit a little more than ten years to complete Tischbein's list of a "good Dutch collection." A second inventory of his art acquisitions, in 1766, catalogued 378 paintings. The Tonneman sale marked not only the rounding out of his Dutch collection, but the beginning of his Italian collection, when the alert Cock for just 400 florins scored *Moses Meeting the Pharaoh's Daughter* by Veronese. In 1765, Gerrit seized the rare opportunity to bid on some Renaissance Old Masters, when the Elector of Saxony was forced to put his outstanding collection on the block. Gerrit devoured eighteen works at the sale, including canvases by da Vinci, Titian, and Tintoretto.

Gerrit's life was transformed by art collecting. It was no longer a hobby or investment, but an evangelical mission. He savored the attention his collection received and embraced the role of patron of the arts. He doted on young promising artists, commissioning works and inviting them to study his masterpieces. He spent less time at the bourse and commodity exchanges, and more time in the salons and theater houses. The once reserved wine merchant now felt sufficiently plucky to court the flamboyant Italian ballerina Madame Monti, during her extended stay in Amsterdam. The provocative prima donna, however, was not interested in anything more than champagne and flattery from the awkward socialite. It was all just as well for the good Catholic widower.

Temple of Arts

When Gerrit first started his collection, he lived along the IJ canal, near the city's old shipyards. From his parlor window, Gerrit looked out at the crown cupola of the Dutch East India Company and the teetering masts of fluyts being loaded and unloaded. It was a convenient location for business purposes, but more to the liking of gin-swilling dockworkers than cognac-sipping art lovers. Gerrit knew that as much as one's art collection was an indicator of social status, even more so was one's place of residence. He would have to move.

Gerrit found a temporary location to hang his precious paintings along the fashionable Kloveniersburgwal canal: the celebrated Trippenhuis. Once home to the fabulously rich Trip brothers, the palatial edifice was constructed for the obscene cost of 250,000 guilders. The Trip family fortune was made in the arms industry, which their new home reveled in. The monumental facade was inspired by the ancient Temple of Mars in Rome. It was extravagantly decorated with Corinthian pilasters, wild stags, gun barrels, mortar-shaped chimneys, olive branches, and the family crest. In 1750, Gerrit met with Elisabeth van Loon, the widow of Louys Trip's grandson, and signed a lease to rent the first-floor antechamber. In 1755, Gerrit bought the adjacent property, at 31 Kloveniersburgwal, for a steep 22,000 florins, which he used as a private residence.

Only three years later, he was on the move again. In a rippling curve along the Herengracht, the Patrician's Canal, the most affluent Golden Age merchants concentrated their assets. The Golden Bend, as the neighborhood came to be known, epitomized the swank and swagger of the 17th-century Dutch merchantocracy. Making special exceptions to the city housing code, town officials granted building permits for much larger lot sizes in the Golden Bend. Here the rich and powerful built tall townhouses, with lush interiors and boasting facades. And here, Gerrit Braamcamp would make his statement, flaunt his fortune, and consecrate the "Temple of the Arts."

It was a rare opportunity, in 1758, when one of these grand domiciles came on the market. Gerrit knew well the gray stone mansion at 462 Herengracht, named for its original owner, Guillaume Sweedenrijk, and designed by neo-classicist architect Adriaan Dortsman. Its straight-lined facade was austere and precise. High atop the rooftop balustrade, full-figured likenesses of Flora, the Roman goddess of abundance, and Mercury, god of commerce, stood in dutiful silence. Sculpted images of Faith and Love presided over the arched portico of the central entryway. The edifice effused Golden Age bourgeois values of orderliness and success. Its one quirky embellishment was a wrought-iron front handrail twisted into the shape of hissing serpent heads, inspiring the sobriquet, "The House of Snakes."

Upon hearing that the Sweedenrijk was for sale, Gerrit hastily arranged a walk-through. Upon entering, he made a slow circle, admiring the sculpted marble foyer, the gracefully gilded stucco reliefs over the doorways, and the grand bending staircase. The ceilings were decorated in swirling plaster designs and painted with mythology motifs. Most important, the generous-sized rooms featured ample wall space, flat panels, luxuriously clad in undulating green silk. But was it enough space to display the collection? At nearly fifteen meters wide and four stories high (including attic loft), the Sweedenrijk was grandiose by Amsterdam standards, though modest for the Golden Bend. Gerrit scrutinized the interior, envisioning various arrangements of his paintings. It was difficult to imagine how they would all fit. Fortunately, the Sweedenrijk occupied an oversized lot. Gerrit's solution was to build a salon addition over the back courtyard.

Exiting the front yellow oak doors, Gerrit gazed across to the canal's north side and recognized the stately homes of several of Amsterdam's most esteemed merchants: at 475 Herengracht, the palatial French-inspired duplex of Matthew de Neufville, whose family of merchant bankers made a fortune selling gunpowder to Prussia in the Seven Years' War; and at 465 Herengracht, the gleaming crown-topped townhouse of Thomas Slicher, former colonial governor of Dutch Malacca. Gerrit was inspired. Negotiations were brief. Shortly, Amsterdam residents made way for a caravan of crated masterpiece paintings departing from the Nieuwe Market and traveling the short journey down the Kloviensburgwal, crossing the Amstel and the Herengracht, before pulling up to Braamcamp's new showcase.

Gerrit put his business affairs aside to act as curator. The symmetrical Sweedenrijk gave him two floors and eight good-sized rooms to work with, plus the back salon. He managed to fit scores of paintings in each space. Gerrit organized the collection thematically, in museum fashion. But it was also a home, where Gerrit went about his domestic routine surrounded by his masterpiece paintings.

Only the large canal-front reception room, located immediately to the right upon entry, was dedicated solely to picture viewing. Here Gerrit displayed his most prized pieces, including Potter's large-paneled *Drove of Oxen*, Metsu's *Visit to The Nursery*, and a ter Borch interior scene, which today hangs in the Louvre. The other rooms were crammed with tables, chairs, bureaus, and beds. More than thirty paintings and three bulky sideboards hugged the walls of the dining room, just behind the reception area. Another thirty-plus paintings crowded the living room on the front left. The widower's bedroom, to the back left, was kept dimly lit, a solemn sanctuary for his religious-themed works.

On the second floor, the lavish yellow and silver-trimmed guest bed-room, on the front right, was given over to the Italian masters. A second red-silken bedroom, on the front left, featured portraits and tronies. Another sixty paintings were located in two upstairs back offices, one of which also contained gold, silver, and porcelain art objects, while the other contained Asian-themed art and furniture. Gerrit preferred to indulge his guests in the back salon, sitting in French armchairs, admiring several score masterpiece paintings and gazing at the garden outside. Gerrit purchased the abutting property, and then joined the two back courtyards to make one large garden, which was an ideal place to arrange his eighty-two curvaceous statues.

It was Gerrit's intent to make his new home a cultural landmark. The Sweedenrijk would no longer be known as the "House of Snakes," but would become a "Temple of Arts." Gerrit made certain to keep Amsterdam informed when celebrities came calling. The monthly gazette, *The Mercurius*, found royal sightings along the Herengracht especially newsworthy. The paper reported that young Dutch stadtholder William V was so enthralled by Gerrit's paintings that he excitedly returned with his consort for a second viewing. And King Christian VII of Denmark, traveling incognito (with sixty attendants), made a special stop to view the collection. For Europe's enlightened aristocrats, a pilgrimage to Braamcamp's Temple of Arts was compulsory. Gerrit hosted the likes of: Prince Louis Joseph de Bourbon of Condé; Grand Duke Charles Frederick of Baden; the progressive Prince Frederick II, Landgrave of Hesse; the wordly Jesuit Gabriel Francois, Abbé de Coyer; Count Michal Mniszech, royal chancellor of Poland; Swedish diplomat Count Ulrich zu Lynar; Corsican patriot Pasquale Paoli; and, Count von Schmettau, ambassador to The Hague, who swooned before Paulus Potter's *Oxen*, much to Gerrit's delight. The Vatican archivist, Cardinal Giuseppe Garrampi, praised the collection for its fine taste and excellent arrangement.

Gerrit's home was a hub not just for art lovers, but for artists as well. Painters from across Europe came to Amsterdam to admire and study the collection. Gerrit welcomed them warmly, and encouraged them to make copies of his Old Masters. He hosted several artists-in-residence. Gerrit for a while acted as patron and mentor to Jacob Xavery, the godson of Amsterdam artist Jacob de Wit. Xavery's artistic talents, however, were mediocre. When Gerrit finally gave up on him, the ungrateful Xavery sneaked out of Amsterdam with a trunk load of stolen goods and paintings, leaving behind a large stack of unpaid bills. It was a frightful embarrassment. Fortunately, the young painter Joseph Laquy turned out to be a more successful protégé. Born in Germany, Laquy made a modest reputation as an original artist, but became better known for his copies of Old Masters from the Braamcamp collection; most notably, Gerrit Dou's cherished triptych, *The Nursery*.

The Nursery Comes Home

Isaac Rooleeuw was a wealthy Golden Age wool trader in Amsterdam. Like many of his entrepreneur peers, he was also an avid art collector. In 1696, the Mennonite merchant journeyed to Delft for the estate sale of Jacob Dissius, whose collection contained twenty-one paintings by Johannes Vermeer. Rooleeuw won the most anticipated piece of the day, *The Milkmaid* (today in the Rijksmuseum); less than five minutes later Isaac scored again with *A Woman Holding a Balance* (today in the National Gallery in Washington), spending 330 guilders for the pair. When Isaac returned to his townhouse home at 35 Nieuwendijk, overlooking the River IJ and bustling central waterfront, he hung the companion Vermeers alongside the centerpiece of his collection, Gerrit Dou's triptych, *The Nursery*.

Isaac was the first documented owner of Dou's famed masterpiece. By the turn of the century, however, Rooleeuw's reign over the wool trade was at an end; the family business was bankrupt. To pay off debts, Isaac was forced to sell his cherished artworks, widely recognized as one of Holland's most important collections. Amsterdam's leading art broker, Jan Pietersz Zomer, organized the catalogue and sale. The auction was held in April 1701, at the Nieuwezijds Inn. Thirty-seven lots, with many rare and valuable pieces, were put on the block. Isaac's prized Vermeers brought in 433 guilders. But the day belonged to Gerrit Dou. Rooleeuw's friend, renowned art dealer Jan van Beuningen, bought *The Grocer's Shop*, which eventually ended up in the hands of King Louis XVI of France, and later in the Louvre. The biggest prize was *The Nursery*. Zomer described the piece as "a capital work, uncommonly skillful, and best known by the artist." The bidding was not for the fainthearted or tightfisted. The beloved triptych sold for an unprecedented 4,025 guilders. This painting alone nearly matched the 4,083 guilders which the remaining thirty-six auction items raised in total.

The bold bidder was merchant Jacob van Hoek, who also took home Vermeer's *Milkmaid*. The Rooleeuw auction gave Jacob the chance to finally best his brother Adriaan van Hoek, who already owned a well-known Dou, *Astronomer by Candlelight* (today in the Getty Museum in Los Angeles). Van Hoek hung his new Dou in the place of honor next to—not Vermeer—but Paulus Potter. For a pricey 2,000 guilders, Jacob acquired Potter's *The Farmyard* from fellow merchant Quirijn van Biesum. This painting was commissioned in the Golden Age by the Dowager Princess Amalia, widow of Stadtholder Frederick Henry and guardian of young William III. The art-loving Amalia wanted to display one of Potter's bucolic farmscapes over the mantel in the reception hall at her court. But the urinating bovine at the center of the scene was a bit too realistic for the princess's tastes, and she withdrew the offer after preview. Nonetheless, *The Farmyard*, or as the painting affectionately came to be known, *The Pissing Cow*, became one of Potter's best-known and most popular works (located today in the Hermitage, Saint Petersburg). In 1719, the extravagant van Hoek met his fiscal reckoning. Forced to declare bankruptcy, van Hoek's masterpiece collection was liquidated. Advertisements went out in February, and Europe's elite collectors immediately began refiguring their budgets.

On April 12, 1719, the hammer dropped at the Oudeszijds Inn, a favorite auction site in the city center. More than one hundred items were sold that day. The van Hoek estate generated the substantial sum of 16,858 guilders. More than one third of the take, however, came from one single item. Even though the sale included pieces by Vermeer, Rembrandt, Metsu, and Potter, the feature attraction was Gerrit Dou's *The Nursery*. The teeming assembly of dealers, aficionados, and curious surged forward when the famed triptych was carried up to the platform. Loud gasps, whistles, and applause drowned out the auctioneer as the winning bid was announced—6,000 guilders. Nearly 2,000 more than what van Hoek had paid, and one of the highest prices ever offered for a painting in Amsterdam. The amount was comparable only to the Italian Renaissance masters Raphael and Titian. The winning bid came from French banker Samuel Bernard.

In the early 1700s, Versailles may have been the richest court in Europe, but Louis XIV was not the richest man in Europe, nor was he even the richest man in France (at least, in liquid assets). That distinction went to Samuel Bernard. Bernard amassed his fortune through speculation on war and the slave trade. In 1708, when royal coffers were depleted by the War of Spanish Succession, the Sun King cast his charm on banker Bernard, who was so warmed in the glow that he agreed to lend His Majesty nineteen million francs. Louis never repaid the debt, but instead bestowed on Samuel the title of count of Coubert. Although his talent was in finances, Samuel craved a place in the world of art, so he became a collector. Bernard's private collection had few rivals in early 18th-century Paris.

To the dismay of Dutch patriots, *The Nursery* departed the Netherlands. It moved to Bernard's opulent residence, at 46 rue du Bac, until the banker's death in 1739. The count's title, provincial domain, Paris mansion, and art collection were passed down to his son, Samuel-Jacques Bernard. The Bernard estate was valued at the phenomenal sum of thirty-three million livres. Yet it took only ten years for the estate's self-indulgent heir to squander it. In 1753, Samuel-Jacques died, deep in debt. Among his estate's countless claimants was Voltaire, whose 8,000 livres pension was mismanaged and lost by the younger Bernard. Before things turned badly between the two, Voltaire had the chance to visit 46 rue du Bac, where he studied the acclaimed art collection and first encountered Dou's masterpiece triptych.

When Samuel-Jacques died, Parisian agent Eberts prepared the auction of the Bernard estate and the sale of *The Nursery*. Eberts set an audacious price of 24,000 livres for the triptych. There were no takers. Eberts decided to hold on to the picture until one of Europe's high-stakes collectors came calling. The wait was not long. Frederick the Great coveted Dou's masterpiece. In 1754, the Prussian king offered 16,000 livres for *The Nursery;* the family insisted on 20,000. Eberts started negotiations, but mounting war expenses forced Frederick to suspend them. Nine years passed before the family was persuaded to reconsider their asking price.

Princess Marie Victoire, the margravine of Baden, was a wealthy benefactor of Catholic causes and a kind patron of the arts. In February 1763, the margravine expressed interest in *The Nursery*, though she never had seen the painting. Eberts responded reassuringly: "Your Serene Highness, this picture is so beautiful that it overwhelms all others. It does not deserve its own room, but the construction of its own château. It is impossible to see it without feeling enthusiasm and inspiration from its most rare beauty." He proposed 18,000 livres.

In the meantime, word had reached Braamcamp in Amsterdam that *The Nursery* was on the market. Gerrit immediately offered Eberts 15,000 livres. The agent informed the margravine of her competitor, and gave her one last chance to buy the triptych for 16,000 livres. "It is true," Eberts said, "that 16,000 is a large amount for an unseen picture, but the price will not surprise after you see it." He then appealed to her aristocratic sensibility: "nothing will equal my chagrin, if the painting passes into the hands of this Dutch amateur." But Marie hesitated. And in August 1763, Braamcamp agreed to Ebert's counteroffer of 15,500 livres. *The Nursery* was sold.

A spontaneous gathering of Amsterdammers lined the snake iron railings at 462 Herengracht, watching two workmen carry a large crate into the marbled foyer. The workers pried open the lid and pulled out clumps of straw padding. The master of the house gawked, his round eyes burning with anticipation. A wide black chassis decorated with a painted fleur-de-lis was lifted from the crate. A conspicuously empty space was already made on the wall in the front parlor, next to Paulus Potter's *Oxen*. Gerrit fumbled to pull open the side panels, and froze. He gazed into the soft blue eyes of Dou's invitingly tender nursing mother. People nudged into Gerrit's stooping back and peered over his shoulder. A hush went through the crammed hallway, a sniff and a tear. The son of the wine merchant had done it. The pride of the Golden Age, Gerrit Dou's beloved triptych, was back home in Holland, where it belonged. Safe in the Temple of Arts.

6

THE TSARINA'S SALON

A Player is Born

When Catherine took the throne, Frederick II of Prussia was her ruler role model. Four years after becoming empress, she sent to Frederick for his approval a copy of a list of enlightened principles to guide her reign. "Like the crow in the fable, I have decked myself out in peacock's feathers," she scribbled in a self-deprecating note to the king, knowing that Frederick would recognize that her proclamation was plagiarized from Montesquieu. In the Age of Enlightenment, Frederick the Great was the prototype Philosopher King. He was a considerate autocrat, who devised a legal code that conferred equal rights to his subjects; and, a military mastermind, who expanded his borders while balancing enemies on three sides. Yet, at heart, Frederick was an artist. He composed classical scores, penned erotic poems, and was a virtuoso flautist.

Catherine owed much to Frederick. He was first her most influential patron, and later her most intelligent rival. Catherine embraced Frederick's notion of enlightened autocracy. When the king of Prussia was not tending to state affairs, he retreated to his summer palace in Potsdam, Sanssouci (French for "without a care"). Its fountains and pools, terraced gardens, and hilltop villa were designed at Frederick's insistence in perfect geometric proportion. In Sanssouci's dome-capped Marble Room, the king played sonatas with Mozart and debated statecraft with Voltaire. He also boasted an outstanding art collection. Frederick made his court one of the continent's leading cultural centers, a worthy competitor to Versailles. The king even liked to sign his letters with the self-anointed sobriquet, *le Philosophe de Sanssouci.*

Catherine wanted not just to emulate Frederick, but to surpass him. But while she was conversant in philosophy, literature, and music, Catherine knew next to nothing about painting. She could rattle off the names of the Old Masters, but standing before a canvas she did not know her Caravaggio from her Botticelli. The newly crowned tsarina understood, however, that great monarchs are surrounded by great masterpieces. So when the opportunity arose to acquire Johann Gotzkowsky's collection of Old Masters, Catherine pounced. It was especially sweet to know that the paintings were intended for Frederick.

Johann Gotzkowsky was born a Polish blueblood without an inheritance. As a small boy, he was apprenticed to a trader, and proved an apt learner. The ambitious lad moved to Berlin and made a substantial fortune selling jewelry, porcelain, and silk to the rich and powerful. Frederick was so impressed with Johan's entrepreneurial skills that he made him chief supplier to the Prussian army. It was a mutually beneficial relationship, for a while at least. Gotzkowsky became the biggest employer in Berlin, despite a chronic tendency to overextend his resources, especially when the interests of the king were involved.

In 1751, Frederick gave Johann an unusual commission: to assemble an art collection for Sanssouci that would equal those of the French and English imperial courts. As with all requests from the Prussian king, the Polish merchant acted with zeal. Frederick's collection already brimmed with modern French masters, especially his favorite, Antoine Watteau. But it was missing Italian and Flemish Old Masters. Johann spent more than three years working his international trade ties to locate such rare works.

To please his patron, he bid to win whenever an Old Master became available. Gotzkowsky gradually stockpiled more than three hundred paintings.

But while Gotzkowsky was tracking down artwork, Frederick was gearing up for war. In the Seven Years' War, Russia, Austria, and France allied to curb Prussian expansion in Central Europe. The conflict forced Frederick to shift priorities from cultural acquisition to territorial preservation. Military expenses drained the treasury. When Johann went to Sanssouci to present his bill for the paintings, Frederick was broke. He deferred payment. Gotzkowsky could not argue with the powerful patron who had made him rich. Johann instead hung the pictures on the walls of his Berlin mansion, and waited for Frederick to buy up the lot. But before that day arrived, he suffered his own financial setback.

Frederick's military campaigns battered Johann's business interests. Wartime inflation, devalued currency, and blocked trade routes drove Gotkowsky to the brink. To make the best of a bad situation, Johan agreed to import a large shipment of Russian rye, with the intent of reselling at a profit to Berlin's bakers. Unfortunately, the grain arrived spoiled, and he could not unload it. His Russian partners ignored his complaints and demanded payment. Gotzkowsky faced financial ruin and, perhaps, physical harm, unless he could satisfy his Russian creditors.

Gotzkowsky pleaded his case at the Russian Embassy in Berlin, where Catherine's ambassador suggested a solution: swapping debt for art. Johann was horrified. Gotzkowsky's paintings were for Frederick, who had made clear that he still wanted them. But Catherine loved the idea. It was absolutely devilish. She would consider nothing else to settle Johann's debt than Frederick's paintings. Johann was loyal to the king, but he was also a businessman. And so Gotzkowsky "sold" 225 paintings to the Russian empress. Catherine's plunder included such masterpieces as: Hals's *Portrait of a Young Man*, Steen's *The Idlers*, and Veronese's *The Resurrection*.

It was a dazzling debut. In one fell swoop, the Imperial Russian court at last owned an art collection to boast of: more than two hundred Old Masters, including at a least a dozen widely acclaimed masterpieces. Even better, the former Fräulein Princess dealt the Philosopher King a humiliating jab in the bargain. Frederick never forgave his former protégée, whom he thereafter disparaged as a poser and hussy. Aristocratic salons across the continent buzzed with the news of Catherine's conquest, partly astonished and partly contemptuous. It would take more than ten score paintings, they said, to tame a savage land and wash clean the bloodstained hands of a usurper.

In Catherine's time, war and wealth were not the only measures of great power status. European sovereigns also tried to outscore one another with cultural victories. Artistic treasures were greedily amassed and ceremoniously displayed. It was not enough simply to be enthroned; a monarch should also be "enlightened." Accordingly, showcase palaces were built, ancient worlds were plundered, classical symphonies were orchestrated, and masterpiece paintings were flaunted. Political power was entwined with social prestige, which if not conferred through birth, could still be acquired by great wealth and good taste. Nothing showed good taste more than an Old Master. For Catherine, the rumors about how she came to the throne (a murderous coup) compelled her to cast her reign in the most favorable light—as an enlightened monarch and a woman of refinement. Art collecting was a means to that end.

With the Gotzkowsky purchase, Catherine was now a major player. Aristocratic Europe's high stakes competition for Old Masters would never be the same. The scale of the purchase was unprecedented. Ecstatic with her triumph, Catherine wanted more. But the empress realized that to become a player in this game, she needed expert assistance. For this, she looked to her erudite ambassador in France, Dmitry Golitsyn, and his philosopher friend, Denis Diderot.

French Connection

Being Monday, Madame Geoffrin prepared her Parisian townhouse on rue Saint-Honoré for a weekly dinner party. At one o'clock, the reliably prim hostess ushered her guests through a thick-curtained threshold into the parlor, where a dozen men in breeches, buckles, and white stockings huddled in conversation.

Madame Geoffrin's dinner parties were legendary. Not for the food, but for the conversation. Her home served as a salon to learn about and debate the latest goings-on in art, science, and politics. In absolutist France, private salons were sanctuaries where unconventional and uncensored ideas could be aired without fear of punishment. Not to mention that they were the most satisfying centers of gossip-mongering. An invitation to rue Saint-Honoré was a coveted status marker. Madame Geoffrin kept her guest list short and exclusive: only the crème of the Parisian cognoscenti and occasional foreign dignitaries were included.

For a while, Voltaire led the discussions, until inevitably the tetchy philosopher and snooty hostess got their egos in a snit. "Voltaire is madder than ever," Madame told a friend. She was not the only one who thought so. When Voltaire finally departed Paris for Sanssouci, King Louis thanked Frederick for "one less lunatic" in his realm. Madame Geoffrin's reputation was secure, and she had no trouble attracting new talent to her dinners, including Rousseau, Montesquieu, and Madame Pompadour. These days, however, discussions were led by the fiery philosophe Denis Diderot.

In her familiar bonnet and drab velvet dress, Madame Geoffrin directed the enlightened ensemble to a room with cabriole chairs atop a sumptuous crimson carpet. Idyllic landscapes by Van Loo and Boucher cluttered the walls. House servants silently attended, as invited guests noisily conversed. Besides Diderot, art critic and founder of the *Encyclopédie,* the guests included esteemed art critic Baron von Grimm, art collector and dealer François Tronchin, neoclassical sculptor Étienne Falconet, and others.

Where is Dmitry Alekseevich? a guest asked, when it was noticed that one of Madame Geoffrin's regulars was absent.

Have you not heard? came the response. Our young friend is probably busy with his new job. Prince Golitsyn is now officially Russia's ambassador to France.

In 1763, Empress Catherine decided that Russia needed better representation at the court of Louis XV. So she reassigned to Saxony the presiding French ambassador (who also happened to be her first lover), Sergei Saltykov. While signing the order to transfer Saltykov to Dresden, Catherine could not conceal the lingering bitterness: "Hasn't he committed enough follies already?" It was true that Saltykov was not the most diligent of envoys, mostly spending his time running up gambling debts and bedding down French coquettes. But it was also true that he never desired to be in the foreign service, and was only sent abroad because of the schemings of Catherine's autocrat mother-in-law.

It was no coincidence that Catherine's new ambassador was already a favorite of Madame Geoffrin. Catherine aspired to turn her court into a cultural mecca, as Frederick had done at Sanssouci. But Saint Petersburg was far removed from the European intellectual scene, where rue Saint-Honoré was the epicenter. Through her new ambassador, the ever-flattering Russian empress struck up an amiable correspondence with "your most charming" French Madame. Indeed, no Russian was better connected to the Parisian salon scene than Dmitry Alekseevich Golitsyn.

Dmitry Alekseevich was bred for the diplomatic corps. He could trace his ancestry back to the founding house of the Grand Duchy of Lithuania. Golitsyns served at high levels of military command and state administration during Russia's long rise from fringe principality to expansive empire. The worldly Golitsyns were valued diplomats, heading Russian embassies in Persia, Berlin, and London. His cousin Alexander Mikhailovich was vice chancellor and trusted foreign counselor to Her Majesty; while another cousin Dmitry Mikhailovich was the ambassador to Austria. Working together, Dmitry Alekseevich in Paris and Alexander Mikhailovich in Saint Petersburg plotted to fulfill Catherine's ambition to make Imperial Russia a cultural powerhouse.

Dmitry was the Enlightenment personified. He had resided in Paris since the mid-1750s, living the life of an intellectual aristocrat. His dabblings in chemistry and economics gained him membership in the Royal Society of London for Improving Natural Knowledge. He was a confrère of Diderot and his circle of *Encyclopédistes*. His wife, Adelheid von Schmettau, was the beautiful daughter of a Prussian field marshal and active participant in the mostly male Parisian salon scene. Most importantly for Catherine's purposes, Dmitry Alekseevich possessed an expert's knowledge and ardent appreciation of fine art.

Catherine pressed the new ambassador to introduce her to his friends. The empress was a prolific letter writer, devoting two hours a day in her chambers to quill and ink. Through correspondence, Catherine cultivated personal relationships with Enlightenment luminaries. She flattered Voltaire, who was soon exchanging weekly letters with Her Majesty filled with advice on governance, the latest news, and sauciest gossip. She subscribed to Baron Melchior von Grimm's *correspondance littéraire,* a critical newsletter for Europe's cultural elites, and soon became the liberal baron's pen pal. She struck up an intimate postal friendship with François Tronchin, a Swiss banker, playwright, and connoisseur. Catherine further enticed French sculptor Étienne Falconet into her circle of highbrow confidantes with the largest commission of his career, a monumental tribute in bronze to Peter the Great, which brought the artist to Russia for eight years.

The more guarded Denis Diderot was a tougher sell. Shortly after taking the throne, Catherine surprised the French philosophe by offering to publish his encyclopedia and welcoming him to her court. Wary of an autocrat's intentions, he politely declined the invitation. Referencing the tsarina's recently departed husband, Diderot told friends: "I too am prone to hemorrhoids, which, as we all know, can be a fatal affliction in Russia." Diderot's cool reply disappointed Catherine. But Golitsyn devised a plan.

Diderot was devoted to his writings on literature, philosophy, and art, and to compiling his encyclopedia of useful knowledge. Unfortunately, these activities did not generate much income. Disdainful King Louis had no interest in finding a place in his vast bureaucracy for the devout atheist. In 1765, Diderot needed a dowry for his daughter. But with an empty purse, the forlorn philosopher announced the sale of his precious library of rare books and manuscripts. Golitsyn persuaded Catherine to intervene. The tsarina offered to buy the library for a thousand livres more than Diderot's already expensive asking price of 15,000 livres. However, since she had no immediate need for the library, the empress requested that Diderot look after it for her, for a fee of course, paid in advance. Catherine, in effect, offered Diderot a lifelong salary to act as custodian of his own library. The dedicated cynic conceded to the tsarina's generosity: "Great Princess! I bow at your feet."

Europe's most knowledgeable art critic had joined forces with its most ambitious art collector. It proved mutually rewarding. Diderot's allegiance to his new patron was earnest, and he proved indefatigable in helping Catherine build a superior art collection. Almost immediately, Diderot alerted Golitsyn to a significant Old Dutch Master that was being sold by the Duke d'Ancezume in Paris—Rembrandt's *Return of the Prodigal Son.* Created in the artist's abject later years, Rembrandt empathized with the painting's subject. Golitsyn sprang at the chance to bag the beloved masterpiece for Catherine. It was only the beginning. With Golitsyn, Grimm, Tronchin, Falconet, and now Diderot, Catherine had recruited a dream team of art advisors. Soon the Russian empress would redraw the cultural treasure map of Europe.

Urge to Splurge

"I am not a lover of art," Catherine confessed, "I am a glutton." It was an honest assessment. When aroused, Catherine's passion was unquenchable, no matter the source of the craving: eager young officers at court, territorial conquests against the Turkish Sultan, or the latest play by Beaumarchais.

Stirred by the Gotzkowsky purchase, the empress channeled her desires into art collecting. So much so, that in less than twenty years she amassed along the banks of the Neva an art collection equal to that of Versailles, which had taken French royals four centuries to accumulate. She infuriated Europe's snobbish aristocrats, who would rather sneer at Russia's cultural shortcomings.

The first potential big score for Catherine's "French Connection" came in April 1768 with the death of Louis Jean Gaignat, a secretary to King Louis. Diderot had viewed Gaignat's treasures firsthand and was astounded. He immediately wrote to Falconet in Saint Petersburg: "The Monsieur had collected wonderful works of literature without almost knowing how to read and wonderful works of art without being able to see anything more in them than a blind man." He told Falconet to inform the empress of the opportunity. Catherine empowered Diderot to act as her agent at the sale.

Parisian art dealers anticipated a fierce battle. Diderot's main competitor would be King Louis's influential foreign minister, the duke de Choiseul. For the duke, the competition was not just about art, but about geopolitics and social prestige. De Choiseul had made his way to the pinnacle of power and wealth through noble birth and a strategic marriage. He epitomized the vanity and extravagance of the Old Regime aristocracy. And he was a thorough Russophobe. He was the main force in the French court behind an anti-Russia foreign policy. De Choiseul feared Europe's ascending power in the east, and arranged an alliance of buffer states—Poland, Austria, and the Turks—to isolate Russia. He also desired to depose the tsarina. "My policy toward Russia," he said, "is to remove Catherine as far as possible from the affairs of Europe. Anything that will plunge her into chaos and have her return to obscurity is of advantage to my interests."

Diderot may have been an expert appraiser, but at auction he proved an inexperienced buyer. Even though Diderot had the tsarina's money to play with, he was consistently overmatched in the fast-paced bidding by the high-rolling blueblood. Parisian high society was smug over the comeuppance that the duke delivered to the discourteous critic and his uncouth patron. Catherine was dismayed to learn that her agent managed a mere five paintings from the highly touted sale. Diderot explained in a letter to the empress that he was following an intuitive sense of value, and refused to follow de Choiseul's reckless bidding.

Diderot's instincts, as it turned out, served Catherine well. He prevailed in the furious fight for Bartolomé Murillo's *Rest on the Flight into Egypt*, a Spanish Baroque masterpiece depicting Mary and Joseph with their sleeping infant. It cost 17,000 livres, the second most expensive piece at the sale. When Murillo's canvas was unveiled in Saint Petersburg, Falconet gushed, "we should fall on our knees before it." Diderot also captured a lush rendering of Aphrodite and the Triumph of Galatea, by the adored French artist Jean Baptiste van Loo. Finally, Diderot landed three small panels by Gerrit Dou—the companion set of nude *Bathers*, first displayed at de Bye's one-man show for Dou in 1665. When the tantalizingly rare pieces were uncrated, Falconet described them as "jewels."

Revenge for Catherine was sweet four years after the Gaignat auction, when ill fortune befell the arrogant de Choiseul. His incessant political scheming this time went too far when he tried to promote his sister as new royal mistress, following Madame Pompadour's death. The king's wrath could not be assuaged, and the duplicitous duke was sent into early retirement, *sans* income. To maintain a noble lifestyle of immoderate leisure, de Choiseul was forced to sell off his treasured art collection. Diderot and Catherine enjoyed the last laugh, buying several of the same paintings that the duke had won at the Gaignat auction, but for half the price. "It is too bad for the empress," Alexander Golitsyn wrote to cousin Dmitry, "that she could not buy the entire cabinet *en bloc*."

In 1768, Prince Golitsyn was reassigned to the court of William V, Prince of Orange, in The Hague. The move meant new prospects for old paintings. One of Catherine's greatest hauls soon followed, when Austria's liberal-minded ambassador to the Netherlands, Johann Karl von Cobenzl, died in Brussels. The count had served in this post for nearly twenty years, during which time he amassed multiple prized paintings, as well as northern Europe's greatest collection of master drawings. This time Golitsyn devised a different buying strategy. Her Majesty, he suggested, could be assured of obtaining the best pieces, if she preempted the auction of individual items and made an offer on the entire collection. Catherine consented. The plan worked. The Cobenzl sale included several unforgettable pieces, including: Rubens's boldly sensuous depiction of *Venus and Adonis* and Gerrit Dou's haunting portrait of an *Old Woman Unreeling Threads*. The tsarina was at a loss, however, for what to do with the more than four thousand drawings and sketches that came with the sale.

Catherine's next big raid on a fellow monarch's cultural treasure came against King Augustus III of Saxony. Augustus was one of Europe's high-stakes art players, whose relentless pursuit of Renaissance Old Masters earned Dresden the nickname of "the Florence of the North." Like Catherine and Frederick, he was in a hurry to build a collection that would evoke awe across the continent. And the king did just that, in 1754, when he acquired Raphael's *Sistine Madonna*, commissioned by Pope Julius II in 1510 as an altarpiece, and featuring history's most famous pair of cherubs. The winning bid at 120,000 francs was the highest price ever recorded for a work of art at the time (a record that held until the 19th century). Catherine's target was not the king's paintings, however, but those of his crafty chancellor Count Heinrich von Brühl, whose private collection of Old Masters was the envy of Central Europe.

King Augustus expected that von Brühl's artworks would eventually end up in the royal collection, especially since they were bought with unauthorized drafts from the royal treasury. But fate intervened. In October 1763, the monarch and the minister died within days of one another. The priceless paintings were seized by the royal court. But the von Brühls were a powerful family and contested the action: they argued that it was not their fault that the king was oblivious. After a lengthy inquiry, von Brühl's heirs were awarded custody of the paintings. Catherine's agent in Dresden, Ambassador Beloselsky, swooped in. He offered the family a staggering sum of 180,000 Dutch guilders for the count's 600 paintings and 1,000 drawings. It was agreed. The artwork was hastily packed in leather valises, carted off to the Hamburg waterfront, and stowed aboard a ship bound for Saint Petersburg.

Catherine loved when these large shipments arrived. She canceled all other affairs and presided over the unloading of her cultural cargo. When the empress was informed that morning that a vessel from Hamburg had just arrived, she hurried out to the river embankment next to the Winter Palace. More than a hundred Italian masters were on board, including Raphael, Titian, and her first Caravaggio.

As Count von Brühl's paintings were being uncrated and catalogued in Saint Petersburg, Diderot was sniffing out another prize for Her Majesty in Paris. It would prove to be Catherine's greatest score.

Twilight of Aristocracy

By this time, Europe's once mighty noble class was in irreversible decline. Just around the bend, revolution was stalking. Yet the heirs of aristocracy still enjoyed lives of privilege and leisure, while spending down their family fortunes. With a wistful shrug, beloved old artworks were removed from ancestral halls and sold to the highest bidder.

In Paris, Diderot understood the historical forces at play. He also knew, more specifically, which aristocratic households were cash poor and art rich. He kept a close eye on the most vulnerable collections, such as the Old Masters belonging to the once prosperous Crozats. Diderot "exploded like a volcano" when he heard that this famed collection might be for sale. He nabbed his savvy friend François Tronchin to help compile an annotated inventory for Her Majesty. The persistent philosopher then pursued his quarry for two years before finally capturing it all in a stunning triumph.

The humble-born Pierre Crozat was a tax collector from Toulouse and a gifted opportunist. He became financial agent to King Louis XIV's favorite nephew Philippe II, Duke d'Orléans, whose art collection was second only to Versailles. The impressionable Pierre saw how art facilitated access into French high society. He learned to be an astute collector and active patron, keeping Antoine Watteau busy painting the ceilings throughout his Montmartre mansion. At the time of his death, in 1740, Crozat possessed the most fêted private collection in Paris. His paintings were bequeathed in batches to various family heirs, including niece Louise Honorine and her philandering husband Duke de Choiseul; but eventually the magnificent collection was reassembled by Crozat's youngest nephew, Louis Antoine, baron of Thiers. It was the baron's death, in December 1770, which electrified Diderot.

The news that Catherine was in negotiation to buy the entire Crozat collection roused passionate indignation in the velveted parlors of Paris. *Quelle horreur!* It was bad enough for France's blue bloods to lose the collection, but to lose it to Russia's ill-breds was as emasculating as it was mortifying. For his part in the national tragedy, Diderot was scorned. Already accustomed to his role as noble nemesis, the philosopher reveled in the controversy. He took as much satisfaction in teasing the French aristocracy as he did in pleasing the Russian monarch. He wrote to Falconet: "I arouse the most genuine public hatred, and do you know why? Because I am sending you paintings. Art lovers cry out, artists cry out, the rich cry out. And the empress acquires them, even while she wages war. This is what humiliates and embarrasses them the most."

The Crozat heirs knew with whom they were dealing. They made Diderot an obviously inflated proposition. Diderot, however, was in no mood to haggle. He was anxious to conclude negotiations before other high-stakes players could mobilize, particularly the King. Louis XV's feelings toward Catherine and Russia were no less inimical than Duke de Choiseul's. This was the same Louis whose arranged marriage to the future Russian empress Elizabeth was quashed by the condescending courtesans at Versaille. Catherine, meanwhile, was tenaciously mocked by the French press as an insatiable slut or a power-mad murderess. The empress neither forgot nor forgave the intended slights of the French haughty class. Catherine would now have her revenge. She advanced Diderot the funds.

In early 1772, the Crozat collection arrived in Saint Petersburg. Catherine was ecstatic. She swooned when her servants hoisted side by side two panels of Greek mythology's most famous reclining nude, Danae, one by Titian and the other by Rembrandt. As each crate was unpacked the cultural stock of Saint Petersburg rose precipitously higher. Italian, Flemish, Dutch masterpieces of the highest quality: Veronese's reverent *Pietà*, Rubens's bigger-than-life *Bacchus*, Giorgione's serene avenger *Judith*, and Raphael's chivalric hero *Saint George and the Dragon*. The Crozat coup vaulted Russia to the forefront of Europe's Old Master collections.

Things were going well for the empress, who could not help but brag to Voltaire about her conquest: "You were not deceived when you were told that I increased by one-fifth the pay of all my military officers, from marshal to ensign. At the same time, I bought the collection of paintings by the late M. de Crozat, and I am now in the process of purchasing a diamond the size of an egg."

Catherine's art splurging became more restrained after the exorbitant Crozat purchase. That is, until 1779, when news came from London that the legendary Walpole collection was for sale. Sir Robert Walpole, first earl of Orford, was a political colossus of the early 18th century. As Britain's first prime minister, the Whig party leader guided the new constitutional monarchy by effectively balancing power between Commons and Crown for more than twenty years. Sir Robert was as passionate about art as he was about politics. He assembled a collection of Old Masters that was unsurpassed in Great Britain. To provide a showcase setting for his grand art collection, the Earl built Houghton Hall, a palatial estate in the Norfolk countryside. There, the august collection remained until the third Earl of Orford, grandson George, devised a scheme to get out of debt.

In fairness to George, much of the debt was inherited from the previous stewards of Houghton Hall. Still, the Walpole scion's penchant for gambling and drinking did not improve household finances. In October 1778, George quietly contacted James Christie, proprietor of a recently opened art auction house in Pall Mall. Like Empress Catherine, entrepreneur Christie was taking advantage of the great sell-off by the profligate aristocracy. George hired Christie to itemize the collection, assign market values, and seek prospective buyers. Fearing his countrymen's scorn, George urged Christie to keep things quiet. But when the auctioneer was observed meeting with Alexis Musin-Pushkin, the Russian ambassador to Great Britain, Walpole's intentions were no longer secret.

George's plan for personal refinancing provoked public recrimination. The Walpole collection was viewed as a national treasure and should not leave British shores. Walpole's own son lamented: "I should wish the paintings were sold to the Crown than to Russia, where they will be burned in a wooden palace in the next insurrection." In Parliament, the radical Whig John Wilkes, an alumnus of the University of Leiden, fought to prevent the sale. "The Walpole collection," Wilkes roared, "was superior to most collections in France, scarcely inferior even to that of the duke d'Orléans. I hope that it may not be dispersed, but purchased by Parliament for the British Museum."

As political controversy swirled, Baron von Grimm warned the empress that London was rife with rumors that a cabal in the Commons was ready to seize the collection outright. Indeed, a motion was put forward to acquire the artwork for a national gallery, but the Russian empress countered by driving up the cost even higher. Catherine would not be denied a cultural victory over the mighty British Empire. She reassured Grimm: "Your humble servant has her claws on the paintings, and will no more let them go than a cat a mouse."

Christie calculated the collection's worth at 40,550 pounds sterling. Only Catherine was willing to pay the exorbitant sum. The hammer dropped on the Walpole collection. It was a sullen day for the Empire, already struggling to hold onto to its North American colonies. A London gazette related the somber news: "We are informed that much to the dishonour of this country, the celebrated Houghton collection of pictures, collected at vast expense by the late Sir Robert Walpole, is actually purchased by the empress of Russia." In marked contrast, the grateful earl of Orford was in such high spirits that he decided to rename his favorite racing greyhound "Tsarina."

The Walpole package contained more than two hundred paintings, teeming with Italian, French, and especially Flemish Old Masters. Highlights included: Rubens's sprawling biblical *Feast in the House of Simon the Pharisee* along with a set of prized sketches; a van Dyck windfall of fourteen portraits; and, Frans Snyders's proto-surreal masterpiece *Bird's Concert*. More religious-themed gems included Bartolomé Murillo's *Crucifixion*, Rembrandt's *Abraham's Sacrifice of Isaac*, and Nicolas Poussin's *Holy Family*. In 1779, the paintings were loaded onto the frigate *Natalya*, for transport from King's Lynn to Saint Petersburg. Tragedy was barely averted, when the *Natalya* was damaged off the coast of Holland. Fortunately, the precious cargo was safely transferred to another ship for the remainder of the journey to the Russian capital.

Back in Paris, the debt-ridden Comte de Baudouin had been pestering Grimm for several years to persuade the continent's most extravagant collector to make him an offer he could not refuse. He had a discerning cache of Flemish and Dutch masters, including nine Rembrandt portraits. Finally, in 1784, Catherine relented. She wrote to Grimm: "The world is a strange place and the number of happy people very small. I can see that the Comte de Baudouin is not going to be happy until he sells his collection, and it seems I am the one destined to make him happy." Catherine sent Grimm 50,000 rubles for 119 paintings. When Baudouin's pictures arrived, Catherine told Grimm that she too was "tremendously happy."

The Baudouin sale was Catherine's last large-scale art acquisition. By this time, she had already accomplished her primary goal of making the Imperial Russian court in Saint Petersburg a "great cultural power" of Europe. The empress's passions were shifting to putting on new plays, putting down peasant revolts, and putting out for Prince Potemkin. Yet her two decades of art splurging had lasting effect.

The tsarina's lavish spending sprees transformed the European art market and provoked patriotic reaction. Her unrestrained pursuit of Old Masters hastened the spread of an opinion that Europe's great private collections belonged not to the individual owners, but to the cultural wealth of the nation. This idea inspired the founding of public art institutions, such as the National Gallery of the British Museum and the French Louvre. As such, Catherine's compulsion to collect and obsession to outbid inadvertently helped to redefine the relationship between art, power, and people in the modern world.

Minerva's Playhouse

In ancient Rome, Minerva was goddess of wisdom and culture. The daughter of Jupiter, she inspired and defended those dedicated to knowledge and creation. For Catherine, myth became muse. The empress viewed herself as the "Russian Minerva, Patroness and Protectress of the Arts." She encouraged the likeness. Images of Catherine wearing Minerva's high-crested winged helmet were cast into commemorative coins, carved in ivory cameos, and painted onto fine porcelain plates. She even commissioned Flemish sculptor Jean-Pierre Tassaert to carve a life-sized marble figure of herself and Italian painter Gregorio Guglielmi to paint a ceiling fresco of herself in the guise of her favorite goddess. But the empress lacked a proper venue in which to play Minerva.

When the ship arrived with Catherine's first major purchase, two-hundred-plus paintings from the Gotzkowsky collection, the empress fretted: she had no suitable space to display her spoils. Frederick had his Sanssouci; Catherine would have her Hermitage. The more she heard about Frederick's Potsdam retreat, the more she coveted her own stylish sanctuary: a place removed from state affairs and court intrigues; a place reserved for stimulating conversation, soothing music, and exquisite artwork; part salon, part stage, part trophy room.

Just twenty miles outside the capital were the gilded gardens of Tsarskoe Selo, where Empress Elizabeth had her favorite builder Bartolomo Rastrelli fashion a swanky rotunda for entertaining purposes. The inside was a modern marvel, with each dining table fitted with mechanical dumbwaiters. Following aristocratic fashion, Elizabeth gave her garden rotunda a French nickname, *l'Ermitage*. Catherine considered this site for her art collection, but it was both too far away and too flamboyant. Catherine wanted to keep her stash close by. So she decided to build her own "Little Hermitage" along the Neva Embankment next to the Winter Palace, where she lived and worked.

Like Elizabeth, Catherine loved to build. She confessed to Grimm: "We have a mania for building. It is a fiendish thing and consumes so much money, but the more I build, the more I want to build. It is as addictive as alcohol." Unlike Elizabeth, Catherine loathed ostentation in her buildings. For her new Hermitage, the tsarina passed over Rastrelli, whose rococo creations were like whipped cream, she said. Instead, she gave the commission to Yury Velten, Rastrelli's longtime assistant.

In a restrained Baroque style, Velten produced a two-story South Pavilion, bordering Palace Square. At this time, construction was also underway on a new gallery for the Academy of Arts on Vasilievsky Island. Catherine viewed its progress from her palace windows. She was so taken by this building's elegant simple lines that she commissioned its Classical Revivalist architect, Villain de la Mothe of France, to design the next phase of her Hermitage. Mothe crafted a three-story neoclassical North Pavilion, along the riverfront. He then connected the two facing pavilions with long open galleries, surrounding a hanging garden courtyard. This structural ensemble became Catherine's salon, the Little Hermitage.

The empress paced the halls of her new playhouse in solitude. She contemplated the plaster walls, an empty canvas to be filled. She envisaged various arrangements for her artworks. Catherine alone decided which of her favorites would be displayed, and how. The Flemish masters Rubens, Bruegel, and van Dyck adorned one gallery wall; the Italian masters Tintoretto and Veronese the opposite side; while Dutch masters Hals, Rembrandt, and Steen were placed where everyone who entered would see them. The smaller scale Dous were grouped together and hung low, so visitors could admire the lifelike detail of the Leiden fijnschilder. When new acquisitions arrived, the empress took care and pleasure to find their right place among her treasures.

The empress's days were full of formality—counsels, ceremony, correspondence; but the evenings were given to informality—conversation, games, entertainment. Intimate parties of a dozen or so select guests gathered at night in the Little Hermitage. To assure the proper atmosphere, Catherine composed a list of ten rules For the Behavior of All Those Entering These Doors:

1. All ranks, swords and hats shall be left at the door;
2. Haughtiness in all forms shall be left at the door;
3. Act merry, but do not upset or break anything;
4. Sit, stand or walk as you please, regardless of others;
5. Do not talk loud, or give others an earache or headache;
6. Do not argue too passionately or angrily;
7. Do not sigh, yawn or anything that fatigues and bores others;
8. Agree to participate in any innocent games suggested by others;
9. Eat and drink as you please, but always leave on your own legs;
10. All that is said and done here must stay here after you leave.

As punishment for those who violated the rules one through nine, the empress made them guzzle a glass of ice water and recite passages of poetry. Those who trespassed against the tenth rule, however, were forever banned from the premises.

"My pictures are beautiful," the empress told Falconet. "When can you come see them?" Catherine was most comfortable in this combined setting of high culture and casual socializing. Philosophers discussed, musicians played, poets recited, and actors performed. While Frederick composed his flute sonatas at Sanssouci, Catherine tried her hand as a playwright, using the Hermitage theatre to stage her comedies. Invited guests played whist and bridge and other gambling games. Catherine was always eager to make a wager, even though she most often lost. Silver serving trays of food were laid out, alongside brimming crystal decanters of wine and vodka. Inevitably, at some point in the evening, the empress escorted guests to the galleries to view her most recent Old Master triumph. Here in the Little Hermitage, Catherine was indeed the Russian Minerva.

In mid-March 1771, the empress sat down with her vice chancellor for the morning briefing. Through the tall palace windows, she could see the Neva was finally stirring, as late winter ice crackled and churned. Alexander Golitsyn read to Her Majesty a letter just arrived from cousin Dmitry in The Hague: An extraordinary opportunity, the Amsterdam merchant Braamcamp is dead. His famous Temple of Arts, filled with rare and precious Old Masters, soon will go to auction.

7

SALE OF THE CENTURY

The Controversy

T he luster of the Golden Bend dimmed as word passed along the row of canal-front mansions. On June 17, 1771, the master of Sweedenrijk, at 462 Herengracht, perished in his sleep. Gerrit Braamcamp, age seventy-one, was dead. Amsterdam lost an eminent citizen—virtuoso trader, visionary builder, celebrity patron.

News of Gerrit's death circulated throughout the seaport and surrounding Dutch towns, then spread to the kingdoms and realms beyond. Jacob Bicker Raye ran the Dam Square Fish Market, but gained fame for the diary he kept for forty years about life in 18th-century Amsterdam. On June 17, 1771, Raye eulogized: "Lord Gerardo Braamcamp, after prolonged declining illness, has died; he was known throughout the world for his renowned cabinet of precious paintings and other works of art, which no foreign ruler or guest who came to our city could avoid visiting." Indeed, the Temple of Arts was one of Holland's last great collections of Golden Age masters. For this reason, the fate of the Braamcamp collection stirred a national controversy.

By the late 18th century, it was increasingly rare for a Dutch merchant to launch an ambitious private collection. The contemporary art critic Jan van Gool of The Hague calculated that in 1700, it was possible for a Dutch art lover to compile a major collection for a cost of 10,000 florins; but by 1750, the same cabinet cost 50,000 florins or more. Van Gool lamented that "only princes and speculators could afford such prices." The inflation of the Dutch art market was driven by voracious demand for a select group of painters. The value of Leiden fijnschilders tripled and quadrupled in the first half of the 18th century. "A Dou that once cost five or six hundred guilders," van Gool observed, "now costs fifteen or sixteen hundred guilders." Dutch merchants were nothing if not practical, and investing in Golden Age artwork was simply too much "dead capital to hang on the wall."

The precedent for breaking up a Golden Age collection was set on high by the Dutch stadtholder Willem III. In 1713, desperate for cash, Willem cannibalized the royal collection at an auction at his country estate Het Loo. The House of Orange owned Europe's most complete assemblage of Flemish Old Masters. Lot number one at the Het Loo, Anthony van Dyck's vivid historical religious painting, *Rest on the Flight into Egypt*, fetched a record price of 12,050 florins. Later, both English and Dutch connoisseurs shuddered when van Dyck's masterpiece ended up in the hands of Catherine the Great, after the Walpole sale. The stadtholder also parted with three Dou paintings at the Het Loo auction. The cultural status of the House of Orange was never the same.

In less than a generation, Dutch merchants had become sellers, not buyers of Old Masters. In August 1733, the collection of Adriaen Bout, brimming with Baroque masterpieces, was dispersed across the continent. The sale of 175 paintings included Italian masters Veronese and Titian, as well as Flemish luminaries van Dyck and Rubens. But it was the fine painters from Leiden who captured the day: the four highest bids were for three paintings by Gerrit Dou and one by Frans van Mieris. Bout's fijnschilder gems left Holland for good. Another rich Golden Age collection was that of art dealer Willem Lormier, which went to auction in 1763 in The Hague. Lormier's five first-rate Steens ended up in England, Scotland, Ireland, Germany, and Russia.

The dispersal of Golden Age collections was driven by market economics, but it roused patriotic indignation. The Age of Nationalism was fast approaching in Europe, and the Dutch were in the vanguard. The once loose alliance of coastal trading cities had grown into a tight collective since the formation of the Dutch Republic. A defining feature of Dutch identity was an embrace and celebration of the Golden Age past—its enterprise, its science, and especially its art. Jan van Gool decried the dismemberment of such collections. "I consider the noblest lovers of art to be those who do not sell their artistic marvels at any price, so that the art of our most celebrated masters will not be sent out of the country, forcing us to go to others to see that which we once owned."

Patriotic sentiment was all well and good, but an art dealer had to make a living. High-end art broker Gerard Hoet explained his situation: "The profits I make in the domestic market are so meager that they would barely amount to 100 guilders were I to draw up the balance. I actually buy up more from the art lovers than they from me. If one should ask, where are the paintings? Then let it be known, I do most of my business abroad."

The clash between market and nation came to a head in the Braamcamp sale. The case against breaking up the collection was forcefully made by Cornelis Ploos van Amstel. The Amsterdam dealer-collector was a frequent visitor to the Temple of Arts. Given his familiarity with the collection, Ploos van Amstel was asked to assist with settling the estate. He accepted the task with a heavy heart. So fine a collection, he implored, has never had an equal in comprehensiveness or taste, and it deserves to be kept together as a memorial to its creator, who was famous throughout Europe. But Braamcamp was a businessman first, and a nationalist second.

In 1761, Gerrit composed a last will and testament, which made explicit his intentions for the Temple of Arts. He bequeathed to his brothers only the family portraits and sculptures. The rest of the collection should be sold, item by item, at public auction, within ten months of his death. The sale should be comprehensive, including paintings, drawings and etchings, sculptures, porcelains, silver and gold, furniture, and finally the temple itself, the Sweedenrijk mansion. Leaving nothing to chance, Gerrit concerned himself with the details of the advertisements and catalogue for his estate sale. The socialite merchant knew that a public auction for his estate would generate enormous publicity as well as profit. Gerrit wanted to astound money-obsessed Amsterdam one last time.

Even the commission-hungry brokers recognized the irreparable cultural loss. In a gesture of civic goodwill, they announced a grand show for the general public, a fitting farewell to the Temple of Arts. To the relief of Gerrit's Golden Bend neighbors, the event would not take place at 462 Herengracht. Instead, the collection would be displayed at the Arms of Amsterdam, the city's most spacious luxury hotel, where Gerrit had presided as innkeeper-in-chief. In anticipation of large crowds, the organizers printed 12,000 tickets, but more than 20,000 spectators showed up. The exhibit ran for three weeks, hosting on average a thousand people a day, seeking a final glimpse of the Temple of Arts.

On Her Majesty's Secret Service

In the summer of 1771, Catherine was at war. The Russian tsarina was contesting the Ottoman sultan for the rolling lands that lead down to the Black Sea. In June, Russian troops were marching against Ottoman fortifications along the northern coast. The empress boasted to Voltaire: "My army has taken Perekop and with three columns entered the Crimea. I will press relentlessly for a signed surrender from the Tartars." The French philosopher was delighted by Mustafa's misfortune: "Madame, is it true that you have taken all of Crimea? I will agree to be your trumpet, announcing all of your victories."

But Catherine's was a two-front war. The Southern campaign was geopolitical, taking territory from the Turks. The Western campaign was geo-cultural, jousting with fellow sovereigns and high nobility for artistic trophies. On the Western front, Catherine's chief commander was her envoy extraordinaire, Dmitry Alekseevich Golitsyn. Upon learning of Braamcamp's death, Dmitry rushed off a letter to cousin Alexander Mikhailovich Golitsyn, vice chancellor at the Imperial court in Saint Petersburg. "In regard to the sale of the Cabinet of Braamcamp," Alexander responded to Dmitry, "I leave it entirely up to you to decide how to make the best acquisitions at a reasonable price. I would like you to send the entire catalogue to the empress."

When the parcel arrived from The Hague, Catherine cut short a council with her military advisors over the latest reports from the Crimean front, and instead huddled up with her artistic advisors over the choicest items in the Braamcamp catalogue. Prince Alexander relayed Her Majesty's orders to Prince Dmitry: "It is preferred to have several good pieces at a bigger price, than to have many ordinary pieces at a smaller price." Catherine specified her main targets: Metsu, van Mieris, Teniers, ter Borch, and Lairesse. At the top of the empress's wish list was *The Nursery*. These are "desirable masterpieces that may never be available again," Alexander Mikhailovich wrote, "especially the work by Gerrit Dou."

The competition would be fierce. Golitsyn must outmaneuver the continent's most aggressive players. Certainly, Catherine's favorite adversary, the king of Prussia, would be preparing a big strike. Frederick was already acquainted with the Temple of Arts. He was a buyer at Braamcamp's downsizing sale, in 1766, where he picked up a piece by Watteau. It was hardly secret that Frederick desired *The Nursery*. The Prussian monarch had made several bids on Dou's triptych already. Dmitry worried that Frederick might now have an inside advantage at the sale, since employing Gerrit's younger brother Herman as his royal agent in Portugal. Golitsyn could only hope that Prussia's war debts would curb the king's appetite.

More powdered bigwigs were keen to wage battle. In France, King Louis XV would want to add to the continent's largest art collection and to deny victory to his sworn enemy, the empress of Russia. Perhaps even more a threat was the French king's ex-prime minister and avowed Catherine antagonist, Duke de Choiseul, who was well informed about the Temple of Arts, having acquired a Metsu at the 1766 mini-auction. Though retired from office, the vainglorious duke was still living the high life at his Chanteloup estate outside Paris. Farther south, the enlightened king of Spain, Carlos III, let his intentions be known that he too would be a player at the auction.

Meanwhile, across the Channel, the duke of Wellington, the earl of Derby, the marquess of Bute, and other titled connoisseurs were ready to reach into the deep pockets of the British Empire. Dmitry, likewise, expected to hear from the margravine of Baden. Like Frederick, she had previously tried to acquire the triptych, and would surely be looking forward to a second chance. And, finally, Dmitry could not discount a reckless proposition or two from the king of Poland. With Stanislaw August, it was personal. The Polish potentate was hoping to attract the attention of his political patron and ex-lover, Empress Catherine, on whom he still had a crush.

Besides the continent's usual high-stakes players, Golitsyn also feared that a domestic player might emerge to contest the biggest prizes, impelled by patriotic sentiment. Cornelis Ploos van Amstel, the art dealer and estate organizer, would do all he could to keep as many paintings in the country as possible. Other local contenders included Pieter van Winter, who boasted a valuable collection of 180 paintings in his Keizersgracht home; and, the banker cousins Henry and Jan Hope, whose laudable collection adorned the walls of Villa Welgelegen in Haarlem. Leading the Dutch charge would be the prince of Orange, Willem V, who was dedicated to restoring what was once Europe's premier collection of Flemish and Dutch Old Masters. Dmitry, like all of Amsterdam, knew that the stadtholder held a special affection for the Temple of Arts.

With so much competition, Dmitry needed to be cunning to secure the spoils. His strategy was to deploy several agents, a few familiar and a few unknown. The bids would be submitted on behalf of anonymous patrons (common practice still). The agents would be privy only to their own specific targets. With discretion and diversification, Dmitry would try to conceal the buying intentions of the empress. The auctioneers had an interest in selling high for the estate and rival agents had an interest in spending down the tsarina's bankroll. So Dmitry sought to create uncertainty during the bidding in hopes of keeping prices to more reasonable levels.

The prince chose Adriaan van den Bogaerde, a savvy dealer and experienced bidder, to serve as a clandestine agent for the second-tier prizes on his list. Dmitry then quietly contracted B. J. Tideman for his primary target, Dou's triptych. Golitsyn was obsessed with winning the triptych. Dmitry knew that Dou's masterpiece would come to the block early. He instructed Tideman to top any rival bid. If the price climbed too high, the ambassador would have to forgo the other items on Catherine's list. But it would be worth it. Capturing Dou's triptych would signal a balance-shifting victory for Russia in Europe's geo-cultural war.

Lot No. 53

On a sultry summer morning, columns of tricorne-topped Amsterdammers converged on the posh corner of Kloveniersburgwal and Rusland. They gathered around the lavish Arms of Amsterdam. The thirty-room inn had been opened for barely a month when its celebrity owner died. As part of the costly renovations, proprietor Braamcamp insisted on a commodious grand hall, which could also serve as the city's main auction venue. It was here, as specified in Gerrit's will, that more than three hundred pictures from the famed Temple of Arts were put up for sale, on July 31, 1771.

Auction season was the springtime, with April considered the prime selling month. In summer, the big-money merchants left town. But the Braamcamp auction was more than an estate sale, it was the social event of the year. And so, the covetous and curious swarmed around the hotel entrance, hoping to catch a glimpse of the arriving players. An utterance of recognition sounded—"Russische ambassadeur"—as Dmitry Golitsyn made his way inside, in a dashing waistcoat and linen ruffles, his graying hair pulled back in a tight bow.

Over his beaked nose, Dmitry scanned the room for hints of the opposition. Amid the throng, he spied Tethart P. C. Haag, court painter to the Dutch stadtholder. Dmitry knew that van Haag was Willem's chief art expert and charged with making acquisitions. A small commotion to the rear of the hall announced the arrival of the flamboyant French dealer Desrivaux, darling of the Parisian salon set and designated buyer for Duke de Choiseul. They are all here, Dmitry reckoned, with fat purses no doubt.

The familiar figures of Jakob van der Schley and Pierre Fouquet strode to the front podium. Prominent dealers and artists both, they would preside over the sale. The room was called to order, the first lot brought forward—a winter canal scene by Hendrick Avercamp—and the bidding was underway. Dmitry gained a better vantage point on the side of the crowd. With fifteen-score paintings on the block, the pace was brisk. Sold to Willem Meyer for 113 florins. If the bidding lagged, the dealer-organizers van der Schley and Fouquet swooped in and grabbed up pictures for good prices, speculating on future resales. But van der Schley's winning bids, the ambassador knew, could just as well be placed on behalf of one of Catherine's many rivals.

The first painting to break the thousand florins mark was lot no. 14, a mountain landscape and hunting party by Haarlem's Nicolaes Berchem, taken by Amsterdam's Pieter Locquet. Bold, thought Dmitry. He gave Locquet a squinting once-over, wondering if the dealer-collector might emerge as a more formidable contender than expected. Moments later another Berchem landscape sold for more than two thousand florins, this time to van der Schley. Dmitry again pondered who else was backing the sharp auctioneer. Soon Cornelis Ploos van Amstel made his first move. Short on cash, but long on smarts, he took a Bruegel and a Berchem in quick succession for less than a thousand florins. Dmitry could not help but admire the discerning dealer. He chose his marks carefully, ready to pounce on any Golden Age master that came within his limited price range.

Duke de Choiseul now made a move, as Desrivaux landed a piece by Bartholomeus Breenbergh, an admired master of bible themes. Then, in an instant, van der Schley grabbed three high quality interiors by Gerard ter Borch. The last fetched 1,800 florins. Who would pay so much? Dmitry sighed. With the room still buzzing, a fourth and final ter Borch, *The Card Players*, was snatched up by Ploos van Amstel, for a paltry 305 florins.

Golitsyn spotted his special agent Adriaan van den Bogaerde, moving through the hall, and turned his attention to the auctioneer. A pair of Isaak Koedijk paintings was brought forward. The multitalented Koedijk was a naval officer turned merchant turned artist, whose skill with the brush bought him an appointment as court painter to Shah Jahan, the Mughul emperor of India. Lot no. 44 was a popular interior scene, in which a man descends a spiral staircase holding a shushing finger to his lips, as he spies on his servant and maid in a lustful romp. Dmitry was sure the empress would love this piece, and he ranked it high on the list. But he was not the only one. The painting quickly surpassed the morning's top prices. One thousand, two thousand, three thousand florins. Van den Bogaerde's rapid replies signaled to the competition that he would not be denied: "4,300 florins." This was getting expensive for a Koedijk, especially with so many valuable pieces still to come. The room deferred. Catherine was on the board. Bogaerde was not done, and he took the second Koedijk for the empress at 1,700 florins.

Next up was an Amsterdam cityscape by Jan ten Compe, *A View of the Old Mint Tower*. Before the crowd had recovered from the Koedijk purchases, Fouquet grabbed this piece for an anonymous buyer. It was not Catherine, but a delighted Prince Dmitry, who went wobbly when the 1,200 florins sale price was announced. There was no time to enjoy the victory. The organizers were ready to bring forward the Dous.

Braamcamp owned six paintings by the Leiden fijnschilder. It was the second in the set, lot no. 53, that the crowd had come to see: the pride of the collection, *The Nursery*. Van der Schley recited the catalogue description: "A richly furnished interior in which a charming woman is seated at a covered table. She is dressed in a yellow satin petticoat embroidered with ermine. She is suckling an infant, which she has just taken from the cradle next to her . . ." Dmitry watched his secret operative B. J. Tideman ease in closer to the front. The game was on.

Offers came fast and furious, within moments the triptych was beyond reach of all but a few. Five thousand florins, six thousand, seven thousand. The room hissed with excitement. The bidding spiraled upward. Nine thousand, ten thousand florins. A roar sounded. Who was Tideman's backer? Frederick? Choiseul? Catherine? The bids climbed higher still. Eleven thousand, twelve thousand. The crowd was staggered. Ploos van Amstel watched in dismay as van Haag, the stadtholder's agent, dropped out of the bidding. Tideman never wavered. He pushed the price higher and higher: "14,100 florins." This time there was no reply. Crack! The hammer dropped.

Gerrit Dou's masterpiece, *The Nursery*, was sold. Golitsyn beamed. Tideman's work was done for the day. He exited the hall in haste. As another Dou was brought forward, *A Surgeon Examining a Woman*, the room was still pulsating from lot 53. Where was the triptych bound? Rusland? *Jammer!* In the commotion, van der Schley snatched up lot 54 for a just 700 florins, an improbable price for an exemplary Dou genre scene. Dmitry recovered his concentration. Her Majesty's list still needed attending.

As expected, the Braamcamp auction was an international battle royale. King Louis of France grabbed a coveted van Mieris, while Duke de Choiseul snared a Wouwerman. Poland's King Stanislav took home two Rembrandts and a Wouwerman. Prussia's King Frederick picked up two paintings by the Venetian-influenced German artist Hans Rottenhammer. The kings of Belgium, Denmark, and Spain all scored paintings from the Temple of Arts. British bluebloods were active as well, with Lord Mount Stuart, the 1st Marquess of Bute, ending up with five pictures, including works by Metsu and de Hooch.

Golitsyn admired the persistence of van den Bogaerde, his covert agent, who claimed a succession of top prizes for the empress, including a pair of Metsu interiors, a van Ostade interior, two Wouwerman landscapes, a van der Velde pastoral, a Storck river bank, and a van Goyen village scene. As the day progressed, suspicions were raised that van den Bogaerde was in service to the Russian ambassador. Dmitry expected this, and took care to deploy yet another secret buyer for what was the second most anticipated item in the catalogue: lot no.167, by Paulus Potter.

On the wall in Braamcamp's front room, next to *The Nursery*, hung Potter's *A Large Herd of Oxen*. It was the centerpiece of the collection until the triptych arrived. The bucolic immensity, nearly five feet by seven feet, depicted a herdsman and dog driving ten robust bovines along a country road. Dmitry spied his agent D. Boumeester in the crowd as the bidding got underway. Again, the competition was intense, and the price shot past five thousand florins. Potter's portraits of cows and bulls had become a "must-have" rarity for any serious collector. Boumeester pushed the price past six thousand, but the bids kept coming. It was now the second costliest item of the day. Seven thousand, eight thousand. The bidders dwindled. Boumeester's eyes flashed and he topped the nine thousand mark. He would go to five digits if necessary. No one followed. The hammer sent a loud clap through the hall. Sold for 9,050 florins. Catherine captured Potter's prized oxen.

Dmitry was elated. It was a sensational score. The loyal prince had won a dozen paintings for his liege, including four of the five highest-priced items at auction. Golitsyn's only top tier miss was Rembrandt's *Storm on the Sea of Galilee*, which sold for 4,360 florins to Dutch banker Jan Hope. But there were few regrets on the day.

Dmitry eagerly informed Saint Petersburg of the results. On August 16, 1771, cousin Alexander responded: "Monsieur, I have seen your letter regarding the Cabinet of Braamcamp. I cannot refrain from expressing gratitude for this new level of your skill. Your service is truthfully a great pleasure." The news of Catherine's latest coup shot through the art world. Dmitry's enlightened ally, François Tronchin, sent his regards: "I beg your Excellence to permit me to offer all of my congratulations; I knew some of these Braamcamp paintings, namely the Gerard Dou, one of the most significant and most precious in existence."

Sale of the Century

The prince of Orange, in 1718, sold sixty-eight paintings from the royal collection for the satisfying sum of 60,021 florins. Four years later, in 1722, Jacques Meyers of Rotterdam dealt 264 paintings for a handsome sum of 51,194 florins. It took more than a decade for the 50,000-florin mark to be breached again, when Adriaen Bout of The Hague went to market with 175 paintings. Twelve years after the Braamcamp sale, in September 1783, art dealer Pieter Locquet's outstanding collection of 501 paintings, featuring many Golden Age masters, topped the six-figure mark, garnering 116,790 florins. These sales represented the premier collections of the day, and most lucrative sell-offs in 18th-century Holland. Yet they all paled in comparison with the Braamcamp auction. The first day saw 313 paintings sold for the exorbitant sum of 252,109 florins. The follow-up sale of etchings, prints, and some additional paintings brought the total up to 261,669 florins. Just as Gerrit had hoped, it was the "Sale of the Century."

Piece by piece, the Temple of Arts was dismantled. First the paintings, next the prints and drawings, then the sculptures, followed by the curios, jewelry, and furniture, and finally the house itself. Although the art received the most attention, Gerrit's final testament also called for the liquidation of many of his real estate and commercial interests. The great sell-off started on the last day of July, six weeks after Braamcamp's death, and concluded just before Christmas. An inventory of Gerrit's assets drawn up nine days after his death totaled more than a million florins. If Gerrit's wealth was converted to 21st century values, he would have been a multi-billionaire. Fellow Amsterdammers liked to say that Braamcamp "could make gold from wood."

The fears of Dutch nationalists were realized. Gerrit's most cherished Golden Age masterpieces departed Holland and were shipped across the continent and across the Channel. The stadtholder had a miserable day of it, spending less than 1,200 florins and netting only three paintings. But at least a few valued pieces remained in the homeland. Several Dutch merchants salvaged what they could afford from the wreckage. Jan Hope was among the most active bidders, taking home a dozen paintings, including works by Metsu, Wouwerman, de Hooch, and Holbein, as well as Rembrandt's seascape.

Thankfully a couple of the cherished Dou paintings eluded foreign buyers, too. Van der Schley bought *The Surgeon's Shop* for just 700 florins before reselling it to Paulus van Spijk, who brought the piece home to Leiden. *The Wine Cellar*, meanwhile, ended up with Pieter van Winter, as part of an excellent Golden Age collection of nearly two hundred paintings. While all Dutch art lovers mourned the loss of *The Nursery*, van Winter at least grabbed Willem Joseph Laquy's full-sized copy of the triptych. And Ploos van Amstel picked up Laquy's sketchbook of colored drawings of the figures painted in *The Nursery*, which was all he could afford.

Yet it was not without a touch of irony that Europe's most pampered nobles grabbed up artworks celebrating the most prosaic motifs. Urinating livestock, neck-wrung cockerels, fornicating servants, and drunken gadabouts were destined for the gilt salons of Versailles, Sanssouci, Buckingham Palace, and the Hermitage. But the aristocracy was in decline. In the next century, the bourgeoisie—the Rothschilds, Rockefellers, and Morgans—would step forward and affirm their newfound elite status by procuring the same Old Masters. And, finally, in the 20th century, the masterpiece collections of the capitalist robber barons would be converted into national museums for the people. The Golden Age would come full circle.

In 1771, however, most Amsterdammers were less concerned with cultural posterity and more interested in the inheritance. They were eager to see how the great fortune would be divvied up, and how much acrimony it might arouse. But there were no drawn-out disputes or scandalous squabbles. Gerrit was as shrewd in the business of his death as he was in trading commodities in life. He routinely revised his will in response to ever-shifting commercial fortunes and family relations.

Just as when matriarch Hendrina died, the elder Braamcamp was not particularly generous toward his younger siblings. In his final testament, Gerrit favored his nephews over his brothers, especially the sons of his youngest brother Herman, who was now a brilliant success in Portugal. Gerrit's steadfast Catholic sentiments were also displayed in the inheritance. He left money to the Staats family, his fellow Catholic neighbors in the Golden Bend; and, he bequeathed a large sum to an Amsterdam orphanage for Catholic youth. Perhaps, these instructions revealed Gerrit's lingering sadness for his own children, who did not survive him.

Braamcamp was especially fond of his brother Herman's oldest son, Geraldo Wenceslao, who had come to live with him on the Herengracht. Young Geraldo was the closest relation that the elder Braamcamp had to a son, and an heir. Gerrit left 20,000 florins to his namesake nephew—quite a fortune for an eighteen-year-old. In the last version of his will, Gerrit even scratched out the name of his brother Rutgers as the recipient of his family pictures and personal mementos, and wrote in Geraldo's name instead. It was Gerrit's hope that Geraldo would succeed him in the family business in Amsterdam. This was an overwhelming task for the inexperienced Lisbon youth. Nephew Geraldo needed help, which he thankfully received from his uncle Rutgers, who finally got his chance to run the family business.

The trading house Geraldo Braamcamp & Co. continued to operate for four more decades. When Rutgers passed away, the Portuguese branch of the family took full control. Finally, in 1819, the business was dissolved, ending the run of one of 18th-century Amsterdam's great merchant houses, started more than a hundred years earlier by a poor wine merchant from Rijssen.

Throughout the autumn of 1771, a flurry of activity enveloped 462 Herengracht, as artwork, statues, furniture, silverware, tapestries, carpets, and a plush wardrobe were crated up and carted away. Finally, on December 23, 1771, Bicker Raye recorded in his diary that "a number of Gerrit Braamcamp's properties were sold in the Herengracht neighborhood, including a small house used as a distillery in his younger years." The Sweedenrijk mansion passed into the hands of another storied family of entrepreneurs, the van Eeghens. The closing of the Temple of Arts did not disrupt the business of Amsterdam. The city's industrious merchantocracy hummed along as before, though with a bit less flair. The legacy of the Temple of Arts, however, was enduring. The 1771 Braamcamp sale remains a celebrated and value-enhancing citation in a painting's provenance. The auction dispersed so many masterpieces that it is nearly impossible today to pass through the Dutch and Flemish rooms in any world-class art institution without glimpsing at least one painting that once hung on the walls at 462 Herengracht.

Dam Square

Prince Golitsyn crossed the cobblestones of Dam Square. Skirting a queue of patient workhorses and laden sledges at the old Weigh House, Dmitry strode past a tight corridor of redbrick storefronts on the Damrak. He moved with serpentine purpose through the dockside commotion of rolling barrels, treadwheeling lifts, and perspiring stevedores. Across the jetty, a hundred tall ships bobbed on the IJ, waiting to be unloaded and reloaded.

The auction was over, but the ambassador's business in Amsterdam was not complete. Her Majesty's masterpieces required transport. It was August, and the Baltic sailing season was winding down. The voyage from Holland to Russia took at least a month. By mid-autumn, yowling winds and crackling ice would make the northeast Baltic too dangerous for most vessels to risk. Dmitry fretted that he might not find a Saint Petersburg–bound ship still in port. He knew where to inquire—at the shop of merchant Lodewijk Hovy.

Hovy and Sons was one of the last Dutch trading houses heavily invested in Russia. After Peter the Great's visit to Holland in 1697, Dutch merchants gained advantage over their English rivals in the lucrative Baltic route that traded manufactured goods from factories in the West for raw materials from forests in the East. The most active Dutch firms sent representatives to establish overseas offices in Russia. Lodewijk was the offspring of such an arrangement. His father, Jan Hovy, was a ship's surgeon, who found the enticements of Russia to his liking. He married Moscow native Catherina Stark and started a successful trading house in Saint Petersburg, where son Lodewijk was born. But Dutch dominance in the Russian trade was short-lived, as the British regained the advantage after Peter's death. In 1749, Lodewijk relocated to Amsterdam, where he became director of the Muscovy Trade Company for the next thirty years. This was where Golitsyn found Hovy, surrounded by barrels and papers. Dmitry was in luck. Lodewijk knew of a ship scheduled to sail in a few weeks to Saint Petersburg.

Hovy sent Dmitry to see the shipbroker Tamme Beth, who was organizing a voyage. The shipbroker was responsible for the business details of the venture: selling cargo space, financing the journey, keeping expense accounts, and contracting a captain and crew. One of Amsterdam's most successful freight traffickers, Tamme Beth was employed by several trading firms and held ownership shares in a half-dozen vessels, including the *Vrouw Maria*. Tamme Beth acquired the vessel in 1766, at an auction on Kattenburg wharf. According to the bill of sale, Tamme Beth was a co-owner of the snow-styled two-masted brig, along with merchant Coenraad Vissering. The purchase record also named Danish-born Reynoud Lourens as shipmaster, with a small ownership stake. The team of Tamme Beth and Lourens was at the forefront of the Russian trade.

In June 1771, the *Vrouw Maria* was moored on the IJ along the Amsterdam waterfront, having just returned from Lisbon. When Captain Lourens reported to Tamme Beth, he learned that his next assignment would take him north again to Saint Petersburg. It promised to be a lucrative trip. Tamme Beth had already sold space to thirty-four merchants. Reynoud consented at once. But there was not much time. Lourens set a departure date of late August, which would give him only two months to unload his Portuguese cargo, sign up a new crew, stow the freight, and procure his own goods to resell in Russia. He must keep to schedule if the *Vrouw Maria* was to be safely back in Amsterdam before the Baltic winter arrived.

By early August, the cargo was accounted for and stacked in Tamme Beth's warehouse. Now the grueling labor began of carting the freight to the dock, transferring the heavy goods into yawls, and rowing out to the ship. While one squad cranked the windlass in unison to haul barrels and chests up to the main deck, another squad lowered the cargo into the sweltering hold. The 85,000 pounds of sugar and sacks of coffee were distributed evenly around the lower compartments. These goods from the colonial plantations of the Americas would provide needed ballast for the vessel during the journey. More goods came onboard. The cargo list noted dyes, fabrics, and metals: 18,000 pounds of red madder, 3,200 pounds of blue indigo, 4,700 pounds of crimson brazilwood, 1,200 pounds of cotton, 725 pieces of fine linen, 10,000 pounds of zinc, and 250 pounds of mercury.

Reynoud was pleased with the progress. While overseeing final preparations, Tamme Beth arrived dockside with an urgent message. He had just spoken with Lodewijk Hovy, who was most anxious to get additional cargo onto the *Vrouw Maria*. We would favor the Russian ambassador, Tamme Beth reminded Reynoud, by honoring the request. But this was no ordinary cargo. It was a consignment of crated masterpiece paintings for the empress herself, as well as ten casks of silver for Hovy. These highly valuable items should be stowed safely and discreetly deep in the hold. So Gerrit Dou's triptych along with eleven other masterpiece paintings were concealed in the belly of the *Vrouw Maria*. A few days later, Tamme Beth delivered to Reynoud a packet of official documents with the seal of the Russian empress to be presented to the toll collectors at Elsinore. A crate containing hundreds of clay tobacco pipes from nearby Gouda was thrown on top of the cargo, and the hatch was closed.

The voyage was now behind schedule. Rainy weather kept the *Vrouw Maria* in port for several more days. At last the skies cleared. On September 5, 1771, the *Vrouw Maria* raised anchor and headed out to sea, for the last time.

8

CATHERINE'S TREASURE SHIP LOST

Turku, 1771

t is with much regret that we learned yesterday that the Dutch ship carrying the paintings bought from the Cabinet of Braamcamp has been wrecked near Åbo (Turku) off the coast of Finland," wrote Alexander Mikhailovich to cousin Dmitry Golitsyn in The Hague. "The situation is less than favorable. The ship has taken on six feet of water, and I fear that our precious things will be damaged." Unbeknownst to the vice chancellor, as he wrote these words, the *Vrouw Maria* was already lost to the Archipelago Sea.

Two gray shadows appeared in the opaque fog. Reynoud Lorens ordered his men to dismantle their makeshift camp on the bare granite skerry. Sloshing into the shallows came two uniformed customs officials to gather what was left of the salvaged goods. Captain and crew boarded an open launch and pushed off into the breaking surf. As they left the desolate outer archipelago, the vaporous shroud lifted. The sea was strewn with rocky outcrops and pine-topped islets. To the east, the island of Noto came into view. Above its tawny cliffs, Lourens could make out a small wooden chapel, a windmill, and huddled red shanties of the fishermen who helped salvage the *Vrouw Maria*. The packed boats maneuvered through a narrow passage between the larger islands of Nagu and Storlandet. Entering the inner archipelago, the oarsmen pushed past Själö, and its lonely leper hospital. Finally, the crew sighted the mainland and a coastal town. Rising above the rooftops was a pious brick tower and cupola of the Turku Cathedral, Finland's tallest man-made structure.

Turku was the capital of Finland, the easternmost province of the Swedish empire. Situated where the Archipelago Sea meets the Aura River, it was long the homeland of the Finns, a pagan Baltic tribe, distinguished by language and custom from their Germanic and Slavic neighbors. Turku was a market center for agriculture, fishing, and commerce. The name derived from the Slavic word *torg*, meaning trade. In the Northern Crusades, in the 12th century, the Christian Swedes, led by legendary King Erik, patron saint of Stockholm, conquered the Finns. Across the Gulf of Bothnia came Swedish lords and settlers, whose politics and culture came to dominate the southwest coastal regions and archipelago islands. The Swedish kings made Turku their base, built a cathedral, a fortress, and an academy, and changed its name to Åbo.

The sailors lurched into the mouth of the Aura, and headed upriver to the Old Great Square. For the *Vrouw Maria*'s Dutch-speaking crew there was not much to learn from their Swedish-speaking guides. But the Danish captain had a grasp of the local dialect. On portside, Reynoud tilted his head back to take in the imposing keep of Turku Castle, seven stories high and twelve feet thick. Behind this granite guardian, in the castle courtyard, was the residence of the governor-general. It was October 11, 1771. For Governor Christoffer Rappe, the agreeable boredom of life as a provincial viceroy was about to be disturbed.

As the king's appointee in Turku, Baron Rappe was responsible for overseeing the salvaging of shipwrecks in Finnish coastal waters. He was by now informed of the most recent craft to fall victim to the archipelago's treachery, a Dutch snow-brig sailing to Saint Petersburg. Local salvors had already delivered a portion of the cargo to the Turku customs house. It was all routine, until the baron met the captain.

Messages were immediately sent off to his superiors in Stockholm, and almost as quickly letters began arriving back, festooned with Swedish and Russian imperial seals. Where are the crates destined for Empress Catherine? Who has the precious artwork? The governor ordered his customs agents to interrogate the captain and crew, open and inspect every box and barrel brought in, and tell him at once what was salvaged. With a mounting sense of dread, Baron Rappe, governor-general of Finland, knight of the Order of the Polar Star, dictated a reply to his superiors: "Unfortunately, Her Majesty's paintings are not included." The governor rightly surmised that this was only the beginning of the affair.

Art of Diplomacy

When the *Vrouw Maria* plunged into the Archipelago Sea, Catherine was preoccupied trying to contain an outbreak of plague in Moscow and an uprising of Poles in Krakow. But the exhausted empress dropped all business, and called for the Swedish ambassador.

Relations between Sweden and Russia were anything but amicable. Since Peter the Great's expansionist westward thrust, the Swedes were under assault from the Slavs. In the Great Northern War (1700–1721), Russia finally overtook Sweden as the reigning Great Power of the Upper Baltic. In the 1740s, the "Hats," a Swedish political faction known for their French sympathies and tri-cornered chapeaus, launched a war of revenge against Russia. Their plan was to capture the capital and impose a humiliating peace on Peter's daughter, Empress Elizabeth. It was a disaster. Instead of Swedish troops seizing Saint Petersburg, the Russian army occupied Turku. To get the Russians to leave, the Swedes conceded even more territory from their shrinking realm. The "Hats" were not deterred, however. Anti-Russian sentiment was still rife in Stockholm in Catherine's time.

In May 1771, Sweden crowned a new sovereign. At age twenty-five, King Gustav III was Catherine's junior by seventeen years, and, like her deceased husband Peter III, a scion of the House of Holstein-Gottorp. As such, the Swedish king was a second cousin to the Russian tsarina. In addition, they both owed their vaulted status to the same manipulative patron, Frederick the Great. In Gustav's case, Frederick was a first uncle. Just prior to taking the throne, Gustav had been enjoying the bonhomie of Parisian high society. He was a favorite at Versailles, and a protégé of Catherine's enduring antagonist, Duke de Choiseul. Gustav was on the throne for barely five months when the *Vrouw Maria* sank in his waters.

Catherine did not know what to make of young Gustav. "We are like a circle in a square," she told Grimm. She neither held him in high regard nor trusted his intentions. His Francophile leanings were a worry. Ever the smooth operator, Catherine was now motivated to become better acquainted with her cousin. Any hope of retrieving the precious cargo lying at the bottom of the Archipelago Sea would require the cooperation of Swedish authorities. It was time to resort to diplomacy to get what she wanted.

Catherine turned to her most able and experienced foreign advisor, Nikita Panin. Gentlemanly and Western cultured, Panin honed a survivalist instinct amid the cloak-and-dagger politics of the Russian court. Finding Peter III incompetent and insufferable, Nikita became a principal plotter in Catherine's regicidal coup. More importantly, Panin was well-known and respected in Europe, and especially in Stockholm, where he served as Empress Elizabeth's envoy for twelve years. Nikita's knowledge of Swedish politics was unmatched among Catherine's advisors. The adept foreign chancellor also had a personal incentive to take charge: his own expensive bundle of luxury goods was aboard the *Vrouw Maria*.

Panin at once summoned Sweden's ambassador to Russia, Baron Fredrik von Ribbing. Though the two diplomats shared similar backgrounds and positions, they could not have been more opposite. Panin was self-assured, widely admired, and the most accomplished womanizer at Catherine's court (no small feat there). Von Ribbing was overly cautious, easily offended, and the most conspicuous cuckold at the Swedish court. His wife Eva Helen Lowen was an ultrachic countess and indiscreet temptress. Eva was eager to please, just not Frederick. She kept Scandinavian high society humming to her latest erotic exploits, including foreign dignitaries, military officers, and noble sons. With so many intimate connections, it is no wonder that King Louis recruited Eva to be his French spy. Of course, Nikita had the good manners not to bring up any of this to Frederick. His interest was only to find the *Vrouw Maria*.

Panin relayed the grim details of the wreck. It was urgent, the foreign chancellor insisted, that the Swedes muster all available means to save its cultural treasures. Panin drew von Ribbing into his plan, which was a multifront diplomatic offensive. First, he would direct Empress Catherine to write to King Gustav, invoking the special bond between sovereigns and making the matter a personal favor to Her Highness. Second, he instructed the Russian ambassador to Sweden, Ivan Osterman, to press the case with government officials in Stockholm, most notably the prime minister, Count Ulrik Scheffer, the king's most trusted foreign adviser. The portly Prince Osterman played his part with enthusiasm and skill. Eager to display his quality to the empress, he sent a jolt through Swedish officialdom.

Finally, Panin targeted Governor Rappe in Turku. He dispatched a special envoy, Major Thiers, to badger the baron and supervise the salvage, armed with this message: "We have learned that there was stranded near Åbo the Dutch ship of Captain Reynoud Lourens, carrying chests of priceless paintings for Her Imperial Majesty. As they are most susceptible to damage and require much care, I am sending Major Thiers to recover and transport them. I have furnished him with this letter, Monsieur, so that you will give him all the assistance that he will need to complete his errand. I do not doubt that you will do your utmost in this matter which personally concerns Her Majesty, the empress, and which will be commended by His Majesty, the king of Sweden." Only days later, Major Thiers barged in on Governor Rappe, waving a fistful of papers and demanding to take control of the salvaging operation. The resolute Russian overwhelmed the distressed Swede.

In these early weeks after the wreck, there was much confusion on the Russian side. On November 18, Dmitry Golitsyn, in the Hague, wrote to Tronchin: "I have been all these days in the biggest despair. The ship carrying the Braamcamp paintings was stranded and wrecked on the coast of Finland. They already sent me the news from Amsterdam that everything was lost." But then Falconet wrote from Petersburg to Golitsyn reporting that "the empress had recovered everything, and they hope there will be no damage, as the water did not have time to destroy the paintings." Dmitry passed this happy news to Tronchin, only to retract the report two weeks later. "Alas! Monsieur, I led you in error, just as I had myself. I have just finally learned from a reliable source that the ship was submerged in the water several hours after it was wrecked. It was not possible to salvage even a single one of my paintings."

Science of Salvaging

Baron Rappe knew but one man in Turku who could rescue him. He sent word for Karl Gustav Fithie to come to the governor's palace. Fithie was owner and operator of the Northern Diving and Salvaging Company, a privileged position inherited in 1762 from his British-born father Robert.

At the time of the *Vrouw Maria's* sinking, wreck salvaging along the Swedish coast was a well-organized, government-supervised business. But this was only a recent development. Previously wreck salvaging was conducted in feeding frenzy fashion, with archipelago islanders as the top feeders. Shipwrecks were such a boon to these poor communities that desperate islanders were known to take the initiative on stormy nights to build signal fires in the wrong location, hoping to lure disoriented sea captains closer to the rocks. The Crown's salvage reform created an official network of coastal reeves, or shipwreck constables, recruited from local communities. By conferring status and compensation, the islanders stopped competing with and started cooperating with Sweden's customs officials. The Swedish Crown also licensed two professional salvage firms, a Southern Company in Helsinki and a Northern Company in Turku.

Rappe informed Fithie that he must organize a search and salvage expedition for Catherine's lost ship. Fithie protested, saying that it was already winter in the outer archipelago. Rappe countered that this was a matter of politics, not meteorology. Depart at once, or else. Fithie prepared his boat for the fifty-mile voyage from Turku to the outer archipelago. He gathered on board the coastal reeve and several islanders, who assisted in Captain Lourens's rescue effort. They would identify the place where the *Vrouw Maria* was last afloat. If he could locate the wreck quickly, there was still a chance to salvage it before the archipelago surface transformed into an icy turbulence. After all, Fithie's company was at the leading edge of preindustrial underwater salvaging.

Finding the wreck is the first challenge in underwater salvaging. Fithie was fortunate to have firsthand accounts of the *Vrouw Maria's* sinking. But even if eyewitnesses could identify a precise surface location, underwater currents and obstructions made it difficult to pinpoint the actual resting site. In the murky waters of the Baltic, salvors located sunken vessels not by seeing but by feeling. Fithie used sounding leads—heavy metal pins attached to thick ropes, sectioned off in fathoms to indicate depth. The technique involved dragging the lines and leads along the seafloor in a grid-like pattern, making note of the depth and obstacles. The systematic crisscrossing was repeated until a sounding lead struck the wreck. Think needle and haystack.

If finding a wreck was the most difficult task, then working underwater was the most intimidating. Fithie would try to tow the *Vrouw Maria* into the shallows, where divers could more easily reach the vessel and access the cargo. For large ships, this technique involved thick harness cables and anchor lines connected to two floating hulks, which served as pontoons over the wreck. The straps and hooks were worked under the hull and sideboards of the sunken craft in a makeshift cradle. The stringing of the cables was performed at low tide, and relied on the force of the rising high tide to lift the vessel off the floor. Once the wreck was clear of the bottom, wind and rowers lugged the floating hulks to a more suitable excavation site. As early as 1545, the English employed this technology to try to raise Henry VIII's vaunted flagship the *Mary Rose*.

Shallow or deep, underwater salvors still need to breathe. Advanced salvaging companies like Fithie's employed the latest in underwater breathing machines. This preindustrial diving bell was a large open-bottom barrel connected to a manual-operated pump at the surface. It was used in 1531, when Roman emperor Caligula's long-lost pleasure barge was salvaged from the bottom of Lake Nemi. In the 1680s, Bostonian William Phips employed a similar barrel-and-pump to recover thirty tons of silver from a sunken Spanish treasure galleon off the coast of Hispaniola. In the 1700s, the diving bell was improved by astronomer Edmund Halley, of comet fame, with a multi-barrel system for an increased supply of compressed air, and a window for underwater visibility. With these innovations, Halley was able to remain down at a depth of sixty feet for as long as an hour.

Finally, there was the chore of lifting sunken cargo off the ocean floor. Salvaging barges featured capstans, pulleys, and cranes attached to grappling irons, as well as baskets and nets to raise heavy objects to the surface. In the 1660s, a diving bell and heavy-duty tongs were used to salvage fifty valuable bronze cannons from the Swedish warship *Vasa* in Stockholm harbor. More than a century later, Karl Fithie's Northern Salvaging Company was well equipped to raise Catherine's cargo of masterpiece paintings to the surface. If only he could find it.

It was late October by the time Fithie set out from Turku. The islanders led him to a location in the outer archipelago, where the foundering brig was last seen. It was as he had feared; ice sheets were already forming over the area. Fithie ordered the crew to pack up the sounding leads and ropes. He took out his sextant and chronometer and recorded the coordinates. The outer rim of the archipelago was a sweeping seascape with few distinguishing landmarks. Fithie took a long look around, and carefully wrote down his position in a notebook. Captain Karl then turned his boat around and headed back. The search for the tsarina's treasure ship must wait until spring.

Business of Shipwrecks

"Regarding the ill-fated Braamcamp paintings bought by the empress, Major Thiers was sent as envoy to Åbo to see what was salvaged," Alexander Golitsyn informed cousin Dmitry in October. His letter confirmed the worst: "Major Thiers reported that the ship ran aground against a big boulder twenty versts from *terra firma*, and that the ferocity of the wind caused the ship to list so that only very little of the cargo could be saved. Unfortunately, Her Majesty's paintings were in the part of the boat that became entirely submerged. Meanwhile, the captain refused to turn over to Major Thiers the cargo that was recovered. It defies belief. Apparently, they pretend there is some sort of law about it in Sweden."

Despite the Russians' incredulity, the Swedes had devised a rule-governed process for handling salvaged goods from shipwrecks, which did not allow individual claimants to help themselves. Instead, Swedish salvaging rules required: making an official declaration of the wreck at the Swedish Admiralty and Customs Service; assessing value and selling off the salvaged goods at auction; and, finally, sorting out the competing claims on the proceeds of the auction among the freighters, buyers, and salvors. Anxious to be done with the whole affair, Governor Rappe commanded the process to move forward, with or without Catherine's paintings.

The Turku maritime court was called into session. Reynoud Lourens was led into a candlelit chamber to face a table of inquisitors. The captain retold the story of his voyage: how his ship was blown far off course by a hurricane and smashed on a rock; how his crew mercifully found refuge on a nearby skerry and rowed back to save the ship with assistance from the islanders; how the bilge pumps failed and seawater filled the hold; and, how the ship sank before it could be fully salvaged. A stooped-over scribe recorded the testimony. The panel of examiners asked some follow-up questions, while Reynoud referred to his logbook to answer. After brief deliberation it was resolved to accept the captain's declaration. Reynoud was absolved of any negligence. Relieved, Reynoud rose and gathered his possessions to take leave. The captain's log, he was reminded, must remain with the court as evidence.

Reynoud was next put to work by the Turku customs house to help compile an inventory of the salvaged goods, to identify the owners and buyers of the goods, and to assign values for the salvage auction. On October 26, about two weeks since the *Vrouw Maria* vanished into the sea, the Turku customs house sold off the recovered goods. The auction inventory listed more than eighty items. These included the props and equipment to outfit an eighty-five-foot double-mast sailing vessel. Especially valuable were the sails, including two studding sails made of durable lightweight fabric. Other items included raw materials for Saint Petersburg's artisans: bulky chests containing rolls of coarse wool and fine linen; casks of indigo, brazilwood, and other dye stuffs; and, merchant Lodewijk Hovy's ten barrels of silver ingots. The auction also sold off exotic consumer goods from Holland's far-off colonies, including coffee, tea, and tobacco. And, finally, the salvaged crates yielded a cache of fine-crafted personal accessories and extravagant knickknacks: six pair of long cotton stockings, a dozen ivory eggs, one mechanical music box, and a carton of gold-framed mirrors to better admire oneself with.

While Captain Lourens may have satisfied the Swedes of his honesty and competence, the Russians were not persuaded. They viewed the proceedings as a legalistic farce and the captain's exoneration as an inexcusable insult. The intimidating Count Panin insisted to the beleaguered Governor Rappe that he make a special exception in this case. The baron intervened and cut short the sale. A selection of items belonging to Catherine's courtiers was removed from the auctioneer's table: a box of cartouche-packed tobacco snuff, destined for the nostrils of the foreign chancellor himself; a chest of leather-bound books, claimed for the cabinet of Vice Chancellor Golitsyn. To placate the Russians, these exempted items were re-crated and sent to Saint Petersburg, without paying the salvaging costs. Karl Fithie objected, but Governor Rappe overruled. It was preferable to forego the fees than to endure the pestering Panin. Swedish customs officials were also wary of incurring the ire of Lodewijk Hovy, who was experienced in contesting salvage cases abroad, and so his ten barrels of silver were also allowed to proceed to Saint Petersburg without further delay. Following the auction, all that remained was to divvy up the proceeds between the Swedish salvors and the Dutch freighters.

On the last day of October, the *Amsterdam Courant* first broke the news about the *Vrouw Maria*: "Along the Finnish coast, the ship of Reynoud Lourens on its way from here to Saint Petersburg stranded on the rocks in a forceful storm. The ship's bottom level was filled with water and dissolved sugar. The shipmaster sought help in Åbo." The ship's broker Tamme Beth at once sent a notice around to all those who booked freightage. Next, he went to Amsterdam notary Salomon Dorper to verify the ship was officially lost at sea and to assume power of attorney on behalf of the freighters, "to retrieve all goods possible, reimburse all salvage costs, and settle all possible conflicts." The experienced broker managed to keep confusion and disputes to a minimum. Most of the traders who bought space on the *Vrouw Maria* were protected against maritime misfortunes. Throughout November, the Amsterdam Insurance Company reimbursed the policy-holding freighters, whose wares, Tamme Beth confirmed, were either damaged or lost aboard the vessel. The *Vrouw Maria*'s sinking did not bankrupt anyone.

Tamme Beth's agent in Turku, Reynoud Lourens, reached an amicable settlement with Karl Fithie and the Northern Salvage Company. By December, the business of the wreck was concluded. Reynoud was free to leave. Most of his crew had already departed. But captains returning home without their ships are not always warmly received by employers and investors. Lourens did not return directly to Amsterdam. He spent Christmas in snow-spired Stockholm. Early in the new year, Reynoud finally went home. It was good to be back along the bright and bustling IJ waterfront, after three months in subdued Nordic darkness. Amsterdam hosted a small Danish community, where Reynoud appreciated the familiar company, especially that of Dorethea Ipsen, his future wife.

There were no lasting recriminations for the loss of the *Vrouw Maria*. Lourens remained in good standing with the local merchants. In fact, in spring 1772, Reynoud was enlisted as shipmaster of the *Johanna en Pieter*, another Tamme Beth–managed trader. Less than six months later, Lourens sailed the *Johanna en Pieter* through the Danish Sound, across the Baltic, and down the Neva, carrying a new load of luxuries for Russia's aristocrats. Arriving in August, Reynoud made certain not to linger. He departed Saint Petersburg long before the gales of autumn were astir. As his vessel passed the outer archipelago, he stood at the starboard rail, staring out at the gray emptiness.

For Amsterdam's merchants, the wreck of the *Vrouw Maria* was an unfortunate accident, a temporary setback, particularly nettlesome for the shipbroker Tamme Beth, shipmaster Reynoud Lourens, and investor Lodewijk Hovy. But they were businessmen, accustomed to risk and prepared to deal with loss. For Amsterdam's art lovers, however, the news was wrenching. On November 10, the *Netherlands Mercury* reported: "the ship of R. Lourens, heading for Petersburg and loaded with precious paintings from the cabinet of Braamcamp, is lost in the sea, without any of the cargo salvaged." It was a cruel fate for the Temple of Arts and for Gerritt Dou's triptych.

Treasure Ship Lost

In late autumn, Empress Catherine invited the reluctant Ambassador von Ribbing to the Winter Palace to report on salvaging efforts. The ornamental splendor of the setting contrasted with the cheerless countenance of the envoy. The baron avowed that his government had acted with haste and done all that was possible. The best salvage company in the Baltic hurried out to the far reaches of the archipelago where the ship had wrecked. But the ice-coated sea prevented the salvors from sounding for the sunken vessel. There was no further information at this time.

After von Ribbing's visit to the palace, Alexander Golitsyn delivered the depressing news to cousin Dmitry. "Your grief over the lost Braamcamp paintings is most justified, Monsieur. The rarity of the pieces is even more hurtful than their considerable costs. I will have nothing more to say about it until their expedition sets out in springtime." Catherine, meanwhile, could not wait that long. The empress announced a generous reward, promising to make wealthy the person who could locate the *Vrouw Maria*. News of the bounty quickly spread through the scattered settlements of the archipelago.

Nikita Panin kept the pressure on Swedish officialdom and remained hopeful about the prospects for the recovery of the artwork. In a letter to Governor Rappe, Nikita spouted optimism: "The painters and connoisseurs, who study all things related to art, reassure us about the survival of the paintings as long as they are under the water at a depth where there is little rubbing and friction or shuffling and rolling. The freezing point matters, however. What they fear most is that when leaving the water the chests of paintings should not be encased in ice, otherwise they will be totally damaged." He even sent a team of restoration specialists to Turku, ready to go to work on the sopping canvases as soon as they were found. For now, however, they could only wait for the spring thaw.

Wintertime brings barely six hours of daylight to the archipelago. The low-lying sun makes glossy orange streaks upon the soft pink and gray sky, tinting the frozen sea and frosted islets below. There is not much for the islanders to do except stay inside, mend their nets, eat dried cod, and tell fish stories. This season, the conversation was about ermine sacks of riches that the Russian empress was dangling before their wild eyes. The fishermen knew that come springtime Karl Fithie would return with his boatload of mind-bending salvaging gear, and they could forget about the tsarina's reward. A spell of warmer weather in early February split the ice covering in the outer archipelago. A fated chance to beat Fithie to the prize.

Von Ribbing and Rappe were delirious. Inform the empress, inform Osterman, inform Panin. An island fisherman has located the wreck. In The Hague, the dedicatedly rational Dmitry Golitsyn could not restrain his glee-fulness. "It was discovered in thirty fathoms underwater, but they are going to lift it," he wrote to Tronchin. "God knows if we will save anything? Yet, it is so beautiful to take every measure to preserve the artwork and blame only ourselves if we can't. You have no idea, Monsieur, how happy I will be if I learn that the dozen paintings I know are inside the ship are saved."

Karl Fithie was given the fishermen's report on the location of the *Vrouw Maria*. Thirty fathoms, or 180 feet, was deep. He prepared the heavy equipment needed to raise the sunken vessel by the pontoon-and-cradle system, complete with floating hulls, extra-long hawser cables, grappling hooks, and kedges. In late May, when winds and waves were their most cooperative, Fithie led his salvage flotilla back to the location. He sounded the spot pinpointed by the fishermen, and found a large submerged rock. He continued sounding the area identified as the wreck site, gradually expanding the search outward. Back and forth, marking the depths, crisscrossing the surface, dragging the floor, making a rectangular grid. On June 5, Fithie was back in the governor's office. The fishermen were wrong; there was no ship. It is not possible to search the entire outer archipelago. The tsarina's treasure was lost.

The empress was not convinced. The dashed hope of the February report put Catherine in foul temper. Like the Red Queen, she insisted Governor Rappe dispose of Fithie and find a new salvor. To accommodate Her Highness, the baron ordered the Southern Salvaging Company to scour the archipelago for the sunken brig. But by summer's end, the Helsinki salvors came to the same conclusion: the *Vrouw Maria* was gone.

In the Russian court, reality set in. "The Braamcamp paintings are lost without recourse," Dmitry Golitsyn bitterly informed Tronchin. "The ship was never recovered; it was people who wanted to gain the reward by pretending to have discovered it at thirty fathoms under the water. As soon as we went to retrieve it, we discovered nothing other than their deception; and I was truly angry. I would have liked to know, at least, in what state are those paintings that passed eight months in the water."

By now, Dmitry was apprised of the whole story of the wreck. He explained to his friend how the magnificent cultural treasure was lost: "I do not know how to express to you my pain but you can imagine it. You would never guess what is the cause of all my sadness and what augments my pain. Shall I tell you? Devotion! Yes, Monsieur, devotion! And here, my story is verified in the captain's log; because you can imagine well that I did not neglect anything to know the *when* and *why*, etc. The ship was thrown by a gust of wind near the coast of Finland. The sea was agitated, and the captain, not knowing his latitudes, was proceeding with caution, probing the depth as they sailed ahead. But when the hour of evening prayers arrives, he leaves everything, abandoning the care of his ship to one sole sailor, to a deck boy perhaps, and goes to howl out litanies with the rest of the crew. And it's at the strongest of their wailing that the ship was wrecked on a shelf of stone. I am consoled in my misfortune for this reason, which is so beautiful that it is almost a pleasure to have suffered."

The disaster forced Dmitry to rethink the logistics of Catherine's next great art acquisition, the Crozat collection. In April 1772, he discussed his options: "As for me, I am all the more the declared enemy of the sea, as for some time I have had incredible bad luck with it. It is enough that I send just a few things on a boat that it sinks; not including that of the Braam-camp paintings, I had three last year that played the same trick." But after considering various land routes between Paris and Petersburg, Dmitry gave up the idea as too complicated and too costly. The Crozat collection was entrusted to the sea. The 158 paintings, purchased for 460 thousand ecus, were wrapped with infinite care then sealed by hand in seventeen solid cases, under the keen surveillance of Her Majesty's devotees Diderot and Tronchin.

By the end of summer, in 1773, the empress came to terms with the loss of her paintings and gave up harassing the Swedes. She wrote to King Gustav: "Monsieur, my brother and cousin, nothing is salvaged. The *Vrouw Maria* has been taken by the sea. It is lost and I will have to deal with it."

Catherine was distraught. She looked for sympathy from Voltaire: "The paintings that I bought in Holland, from the Braamcamp collec-tion, were all lost on the coast of Finland. I have had rotten luck this year in such matters, there is no way to console myself. Well, there goes sixty thousand ecus. What can I do?" The flattering philosopher tried to soothe the disconsolate sovereign: "Allow me to say to Your Majesty that you are incomprehensible. Just when the Baltic Sea swallows up sixty thousand ecus worth of paintings coming to you from Holland, you take another 450 thousand livres of paintings from France. Then you buy another thousand rarities in Italy. But, where do you get all this money? Have you plundered the Sultan's treasury without the press talking about it? We French have peace, but still we are penniless."

For Catherine, art collecting was an infatuation, turned obsession, turned power trip. For the Golitsyns, art collecting was a passion, inspired by the wonders of human creation and artistic beauty. Dmitry was inconsolable. A child of the Enlightenment, Dmitry held a deep affection for the Dutch Golden Age, whose accumulated achievements advanced so mightily the causes of art, science, and humanity. All these themes were embodied in Gerrit Dou's masterpiece triptych, *The Nursery*, delivered by a hand whose unsurpassed skill inspired nothing less than awe and reverence. The archipelago's abduction of the triptych could not be measured in ecus, it was a cultural tragedy of momentous proportion. In Saint Petersburg, cousin Alexander concurred: "The loss is irreparable; the rarity of the pieces cannot ever be reunited or replaced. For the world of art, the loss of these paintings is nothing less than mortifying."

PART TWO

9

AGE OF REVOLUTION

Eclipse of an Artist

An icy crust topped the Galgewater canal as winter settled over Leiden in December 1674. Gerrit Dou's studio, at no. 3 Galgewater, was quiet. Weary and ailing, the sixty-one-year-old artist had stopped painting. Fearing the worst, Gerrit decided to take stock of his assets. He contacted a lawyer and revised his will, for a third and last time.

Unlike Rembrandt, whose last years were wracked by insurmountable debts, Dou was blessed with prosperity. He owned three houses on Kort Rapenburg, and a glinting heap of Dutch guilders. The artist remained to the end single and childless. In his final testament, Gerrit bequeathed the bulk of his estate to loyal housekeeper and niece Anthonia van Tol. Despite the occasional rumors, the nature of their relationship was never revealed to be anything more than what proper appearance suggested. Anthonia inherited real estate and 15,000 guilders from her bachelor uncle. Gerrit allotted an additional 4,500 guilders to local causes and institutions. His strength never returned. Six weeks after sorting out his affairs, the artist was dead. The loyal Leiden son was interred in the city's monumental Pieterskirk, the same Gothic shrine where long ago as a teen apprentice he fitted stained glass panels. On February 9, 1675, a simple entry in the church registry noted: "Mr. Gerrit Douw, painter."

More than a hundred years after his death, Gerrit's paintings were still coveted high-culture commodities. In 1780, the duke of Rutland wrote: "I am at last in possession of a Gerard Dou. The price was 3,000 florins, a very great price considering the size of the picture, but a very small price considering the great demand for the works of this master." Dou's paintings continued to accrue value into the 19th century. *Penitent Magdalen* sold for 170 guilders in 1735, and for 1,400 guilders in 1833, eventually finding a home in Stockholm's National Museum; *A Hermit Making a Rosary*, with Dou's signature on the crucifix, sold for 655 guilders in 1762, for 1,310 guilders in 1810, and for 3,469 guilders in 1836, before arriving at the Rijksmuseum. Meanwhile, Dou's paintings remained valued currency in political diplomacy. In 1799, King Carlo Emanuele IV in Italy presented the French Counsel with one of Dou's best-known works, *The Dropsical Woman*, which eventually was displayed in the Salon Carré, the room of highest honor in the Louvre.

Through the first half of the 19th century, Dou's deft depictions of real life were regarded as the epitome of artistic virtue. The prolific Dutch writer Johannes Immerzeel, in his comprehensive three-volume study of Dutch and Flemish painting, published in 1842, said that Dou's "beautiful manner" was unsurpassed by any artist and bore "the stamp of rare genius." Similar sentiment prevailed across the North Sea, where, in 1829, John Smith, England's foremost expert and dealer in Dutch and Flemish art, described Dou as: "a perfect master of all the principles of art, united with consummate skill and labor, which enabled him to produce the most perfect specimens that ever came from a painter." So impressed was Smith that he chose a lithograph copy of a Dou self-portrait to feature on the title page of his definitive eight-volume anthology of northern Old Masters.

At the 1857 "Art Treasures of the United Kingdom" at the Manchester Art Gallery, four British-owned Dous were selected for display, including one from Queen Victoria's collection. The show catalogue drew special attention to *Girl at the Window*: "This picture is not only of the first class for the delicate execution of all the objects but the subject is more feeling and dramatic than usual." The five-month extravaganza was a celebration of the nation's cultural wealth and largest art exhibit ever staged in Great Britain. It attracted more than one and a quarter million visitors, including US consul to Liverpool, Nathaniel Hawthorne.

The American author, a literary savant of descriptive narrative and allegory, felt an immediate kinship to Dutch genre paintings. In his diary, Hawthorne wrote: "I spent an hour looking at the Old Dutch Masters, such lifelike representations, even the photograph cannot equal. These Dutchmen got at the soul of common things. Gerard Dow seems to be the master among these queer magicians. A straw mat in one of his pictures is the most miraculous thing that human art has ever accomplished, and there is a metal vase with a dent in it that is absolutely more real than reality. It is strange how spiritual and suggestive the commonest household article—an earthen pitcher, for example—becomes, when represented with entire accuracy."

Hawthorne's praise echoed what art critics had been saying about Dou for two hundred years. But the Manchester show turned out to be a last fling for aristocratic Europe's cultural sensibility. The art world's standards of merit and taste were about to be overturned.

◆

In 1839, British attorney Miles Berry filed a claim in the central patent office in London on behalf of French artist Louis Daguerre. Patent no. 8194 was for "a new or improved method of obtaining the spontaneous reproduction of all the images received in the focus of the *camera obscura*." The "daguerreotype" transformed the relationship between art and reality. Technology created an image of reality that could not be matched by hand and brush. The age of photography was underway, and the world of painting moved on. Realism made way for Romantics, Impressionists, and Expressionists. The Leiden fijnschilders were in for a letdown. Gerrit Dou's virtuoso talent ceased to enthrall.

In the second half of the 19th century, modern notions of art and the artist took hold. High art was no longer monopolized by high aristocracy.

Art was for the people, not the princes. Public institutions became the guardians of culture. The Louvre Palace opened as a museum in August 1793, displaying 537 newly liberated paintings, free of charge, for those Parisians who grew bored with the entertainment provided by the busy guillotine a few blocks away. The outstanding royal collections of Mauritshuis in The Hague and the National Gallery in London went public in 1822 and 1824 respectively. Meanwhile, the artist was recast in a more Romantic role. The modern caricature of the artist took shape; aloof and disaffected, penetrating and unfiltered. Art was not a craft, but a calling. Style surpassed precision, inner mood bested outward appearance, spontaneity trumped method. On canvas, gritty peasants and despairing prostitutes became icons of humanity, while Gerrit Dou's thrifty shopkeepers, dedicated scholars, and pious hermits fell out of step with social progress.

When it came to the Dutch Golden Age, no individual did more to promote the "modern" perspective than Théophile Thoré-Bürger. "Art changes only through strong convictions, convictions strong enough to change society," wrote Thoré-Bürger, a Parisian lawyer turned journalist, turned political partisan, turned art critic. And with each turn, "Citizen Thoré" grew more strident. In 1848, he cheered on Parisian rioters as they toppled King Louis Philippe from the French throne, and applauded the revolutionary fires that scorched Europe's surviving strongholds of aristocracy. The following year, the High Court at Versailles banished the agitating pundit from the realm. Relocating to the nearby Netherlands, Thoré-Bürger trained his critical eye on the Dutch Golden Age. Not one to gush over quaint notions of beauty and nature, Thoré-Bürger propounded that art and politics were inseparable. In applying this dictum, the wannabe revolutionary decided that Gerrit Dou was on the wrong side of the barricades.

Writing under a pseudonym to fool French censors, Willem Bürger (aka Théophile Thoré) published *Museums of Holland* in 1860. The study evaluated artists less on composition and color, and more on nationalist aesthetics and social vision. In Thoré-Bürger's influential tome, Rembrandt was extolled as undisputed genius of the Golden Age and prototype of the modern artist. Rembrandt, of course, did not need to be "discovered." Thoré-Bürger added little to the praises of Rembrandt penned two centuries earlier by art critics Sandrart and Houbraken. The French radical did, however, create a suitably modern, and mostly mythologized, biography of the artist as unappreciated prodigy, forthright witness, and willful loner. Besides helping to construct the modern cult of Rembrandt, Thoré-Bürger pumped up the reputations of two other Golden Age artists. Of Johannes Vermeer's *View of the Town of Delft*, he wrote: "Amazing! Here is someone of whom we know nothing in France and who deserves to be known!" And, he was thoroughly smitten with Frans Hals's *The Merry Drinker*: "a valiant companion, who lives and laughs, and is happy to be in this world." In terms of refashioning tastes, Thoré-Bürger's *Museums of Holland* christened the modern triumvirate of Dutch superstars—Rembrandt, Vermeer, and Hals.

Thoré-Bürger did not only enhance the status of undervalued artists, he willfully maligned the reputations of others. He derided Golden Age notables Nicolaes Berchem, Gerard de Lairesse, and Adriaen van der Werff for being too accommodating to their princely patrons and for trying too hard to imitate the flamboyant Italians. But the French influencer was especially unsparing toward the Leiden fijnschilders, whose small pictures, he insisted, lacked social significance and personal insight. He once panned a painting for being "the last degree of Willem van Mieris." Thoré-Bürger saved his most jeering critique for Gerrit Dou, whom he mocked for being "precisely contrary to Rembrandt."

Gerrit labored to create an illusion of reality, concealing his brushwork from the viewer. But it was precisely Dou's polished finish and exquisite detail that Thoré-Bürger disdained most. "True art," he sneered, "has nothing to do with such futile preoccupations." Dou's uncanny replication of reality, Thoré-Bürger scoffed, was nothing more than a "conjurer's trick." With the rise of Impressionism and Expressionism, brushwork was tantamount to a personal signature, an emphatic stylistic statement. Dou's long-revered technical skill was now artistic sacrilege. At least one thing Thoré-Bürger said about Dou was true—his paintings were small. The critic used size to discriminate, downgrading Dou from other Golden Age artists and assigning him to a separate category of "small precious masters."

The Modern Art breakthrough was no less of a cultural revolution than the Golden Age had been two centuries before. Even by Thoré-Bürger's modern standards of art, however, his attack on Gerrit Dou seemed unjustified. The idea that Dou was somehow out of touch with Thoré-Bürger's notions of art and society was inconsistent. Dou was offered and refused the honor to be a court painter for a king. Like Rembrandt, he painted self-portraits and hermits. Like Vermeer, he painted domestic scenes of middle-class households. Like Hals, he painted ordinary people. He did not run off to Amsterdam seeking fame and fortune, as Rembrandt did; nor did he indulge the rich and powerful with his portrait skills, as both Rembrandt and Hals did. In choosing subjects, it was Dou who influenced Vermeer, not the other way around. Gerrit painted what he wanted to paint: Dutch city dwellers caught in the act of doing what they typically do—a mother nursing, a scholar studying, a shopkeeper weighing, a cook chopping. That is, "the people." Dou was a leading cultural revolutionary of the Golden Age, but he was now out of favor with the social revolutionaries of the Modern Age.

◆

To mark its arrival as the mecca of capitalism, New York City staged a festive showcase of American industry and wealth in 1909. The date coincided with the 300th anniversary of Henry Hudson's sail-powered navigations and the 100th anniversary of Robert Fulton's steam-powered inventions. The city hosted street parades with marching bands and floats, river parades with tall ships and naval vessels, Wilbur Wright soaring in the daytime sky and fireworks exploding in the nighttime sky. New York's landmark buildings and monuments were transformed into an electric, illuminated wonderland. The Hudson-Fulton Celebration also paid tribute to the city's Dutch heritage with a splashy special exhibition of Golden Age masters at the Metropolitan Museum on Fifth Avenue. It was a chance for the New World's industrial barons to flaunt their Old World aristocratic artifacts. "Some little astonishment will no doubt be felt in European art circles that it was possible to assemble in New York one hundred and fifty paintings of the first importance," boasted organizer Wilhelm Valentiner in the exhibition catalogue.

By the late 19th century, the world art market was transformed. In Europe, sumptuous private collections became a rarity. As the ennobled became indebted, aristocratic heirs cashed in their cultural inheritance for a last few cases of sparkling cuvée. The decline of Europe's nobility coincided with the rise of America's bourgeoisie. The New World's nouveaux riches eagerly consumed the Old World's old masterpieces, as a validating adornment of their arrival. Of course, these new American players were no more welcomed by the "old guard" than Russian Empress Catherine had been a century before. The director of the National Gallery in Berlin, Ludwig Justi, in 1910, summed up prevailing continental opinion about these frontier connoisseurs: "the denuding of European art collections for the benefit of America and Americans is to cast pearls before swine."

In the process of building world-class collections in the United States, the influence of French critic Thoré-Bürger was paramount. Wilhelm von Bode was a German art historian and museum curator, who claimed that he always carried a copy of *Museums of Holland* under his arm. Bode visited the United States, in 1893, to see the Chicago World's Fair, and along the way, stopped to advise America's new elite collectors, including Andrew Mellon, Henry Frick, and Joseph Widener. Bode's student and protégé was the same Wilhelm Valentiner who organized the Hudson-Fulton exhibit and personally counseled the wealthy on value and taste.

The Met's grand presentation of Dutch paintings occurred eighty years after the esteemed British art critic John Smith praised Gerrit Dou as the Golden Age's "perfect master." Much had changed. The exhibition organizers saw fit to include works by thirty-two Dutch artists in the show, in perhaps the most remarkable assemblage of Golden Age masters ever presented in the United States. What was even more remarkable was that the show did not include one piece by Gerrit Dou. Not only Dou, but his once acclaimed student Frans van Mieris was also excluded. The show's big-city organizers made a point to include a belittling note about the "circumscribed surroundings in Leyden" in contrast to "cosmopolitan Amsterdam." Only one reviewer, American naturalist painter Kenyon Cox, even bothered to mention Dou's omission, which, he snorted, "was not regretted."

For two centuries, Gerrit Dou had been the art world's reigning Dutch superstar. But the Hudson-Fulton exhibition confirmed that the circle had come full around. The teacher was above the pupil once more. Rembrandt, rightfully, was recognized as the most modern of Dutch Old Masters. His roughly textured panels were visionary, his intensely earnest subjects timeless. "The most prominent place in the exhibition is naturally occupied by Rembrandt," who, the catalogue effused, mastered "the art of breathing the divine spirit of genius upon what is ordinary. For Rembrandt painted with a sympathetic understanding of the pathos and mystery of human life." While Rembrandt was always at the forefront of Golden Age artists, the exhibition elevated two other artists to celebrity status, Frans Hals, who "painted in a passion of eagerness with a wonderfully sure hand," had twenty-one pieces in the show; while Johannes Vermeer, who "had more of the modern spirit than most of his contemporaries," was represented with six paintings.

Dou suffered further indignity when he was not even included in the catalogue's list of Rembrandt's "three best pupils," an honor that instead went to Ferdinand Bol, Nicolaes Maes, and the uninspiring Philips Koninck. The Hudson-Fulton show was a watershed. Dou did not simply suffer a decline in rank, he was effectively expunged from the discussion of Golden Age masters. Nor did his absence raise eyebrows, as he was barely known to Gilded Age collectors. For the Americans, size mattered. Derided as the "Leyden miniaturist," Dou's finely detailed small pictures could hardly command attention on the wall of a Newport mansion.

Though it was meant to impress European *haute société*, the showcase of Old Dutch Masters in the Hudson-Fulton exhibition instead confirmed that "art collecting in America is the fad of millionaire ignoramuses." Perhaps American collectors could never truly appreciate the art of a bygone past, an aristocratic and European past. The 20th century would be a modern century, an American century. New York, not Paris, would become the hub of the Western art world, where Rothko and Warhol would create a kind of art that could not be more distant from Gerrit Dou and the Leiden fijnschilders.

Gerrit Dou's fall was precipitous and swift. One morning in Paris, in 1899, the curator of European Old Masters at the Louvre and a staff assistant entered the Grand Salon Carré, where the museum displayed its most prized paintings. Passing da Vinci's *Mona Lisa*, the curator paused and pointed at a picture on the wall. A grim-faced doctor studies a beaker of urine as a limp elderly patient surrenders to her fate. It was Dou's *Dropsical Woman,* a resident of Salon Carré for nearly a hundred years. The worker clutched the ebony frame and removed it from the hanger. Heels clacking on the parquet floor, the pair exited the hall to find a less prominent place for the panel.

Death of an Empress

"Men will never be free until the last king is strangled by the entrails of the last priest," wrote Catherine's *philosophe* pen pal Diderot. And while Yemelyan Pugachev never read Diderot, the illiterate army deserter turned peasant rebellion leader was moved by likeminded sentiment.

In September 1773, Pugachev declared that he was none other than Tsar Peter III, Catherine's dead husband, coming out of hiding to reclaim the throne from his treacherous wife, liberate the peasants from the shackles of serfdom, and restore traditional religious beliefs to Russia. These proved to be popular positions, especially since the empress had consolidated power by accommodating the self-indulgent nobility at the expense of the overburdened peasantry. Under the guise of an avenging Peter III, the charismatic Cossack attracted an enthusiastic following for his counter-kingdom. Pugachev's Rebellion was a year-long marauder's march, moving between the Volga River and Ural Mountains, terrorizing provincial towns, torching manor homes, and exhorting peasant serfs to take revenge on their noble lords. It finally ended in September 1774, when Catherine's loyal regiments cornered and slaughtered the 10,000-strong insurgent army at Tsaritsyn (later the site of far greater carnage under the name of Stalingrad). Pugachev was captured, caged, and carted to Moscow, where a public beheading and quartering was staged as a fitting finale to the audacious adventure. It was in the midst of this murderous mutiny that Diderot arrived in Russia to debate the empress on the benefits of empowering the people. His timing could not have been worse.

Catherine wooed her cultivated French confidantes to visit her rehabilitated Russian realm. Voltaire had earlier sojourned to Potsdam for a royal chinwag with Frederick the Great, which predictably concluded with a spat and acrimonious parting. Retiring to his cozy country estate at Ferney, Voltaire could not bear to contemplate another jarring journey eastward. He declined Her Majesty's invitation, citing advanced years and ill health.

"I am older, Madame, than the city where you reign," he explained, "but if I were younger I would make myself Russian." Diderot also sent his regrets to Catherine, at least at first. But a mixed sense of obligation and curiosity caused him to reconsider and pay a call on his generous benefactor. In May 1773, Diderot departed for Holland, where he was a house guest of confrère Prince Dmitry Golitsyn, who spent the next three months coaxing the apprehensive philosopher to carry onward with his errand. One day toward the end of summer, a handsome coach rode up to the Russian ambassador's front door, conveying Prince Naryshkin with orders to escort Catherine's big catch to Saint Petersburg.

Diderot arrived in early October, just in time for the first snowfall. Catherine was preoccupied with suppressing the uprising of her renegade subject, Tsar Pretender Pugachev, celebrating the wedding of her successor son, Grand Duke Paul, and craving the touch of her favorite lover, Prince Grigori Potemkin. Exhausted from the journey, Diderot excused himself from the festivities, claiming that he had lost his powdered wig en route. The French philosophe's real interest in Russia was to tutor the obliging empress on the principles of enlightened statecraft. Catherine arranged for the pair to confer for two hours each day in her private study. Diderot poured all his energy and intellect into these sessions. What would begin as a mutual give-and-take inevitably became a one-sided harangue. He lectured, interrogated, and criticized his star pupil. Catherine resorted to rearranging the furniture because of Diderot's constant habit of jabbing his forefinger into her sovereign thigh to make a point. "I am obliged to place a table between us," she wrote, "to protect myself and my limbs." As long-distance letter writers, Catherine and Diderot enjoyed a charmed rapport. But as face-to-face interlocutors, relations were strained. Diderot later told friends that the empress had "the soul of Brutus in the body of Cleopatra." Diderot stayed for five months, waiting for springtime before traveling home. Catherine was generous and polite throughout, and much relieved when her exhausting guest departed.

Catherine enjoyed being included by Europe's liberal literati. When she first took the throne, Russia's enlightened despot and France's intellectual dissidents were coconspirators in peppery discussions about advancing the cause of civilization. But the constraints of power kept these ideas separate from practice. "I have listened to all the inspirations of your brilliant mind," she said to Diderot, "but you forget that you work on paper, which is smooth and flexible, while I work on human skin, which is more sensitive and irritable." Toward the end of his life, Diderot penned a long treatise for Catherine, urging her to abdicate the throne, abolish the monarchy, and establish a new government of the people. He decided to keep it in his drawer. It was for the best. Catherine by this time was more a conservative cynic than idealistic reformer.

◆

Catherine was a role model of 18th-century enlightened governance—adopting Montesquieu's code of law, baring a taut limb for a small pox inoculation, taking counts of the people, property, and wealth of the realm, founding schools, libraries, and hospitals. And, of course, the Minerva of the North was a most generous patron of arts and science. But Pugachev's Rebellion gave the Russian empress advance warning of the coming aristocratic reckoning. Europe's long run of empire and autocracy was winding down, and a new political play featuring nations and democracy was revving up. Nowhere, of course, was this transition more evident than in revolutionary France, where the national razor decapitated 40,000 bluebloods in the name of fraternity and equality. Diderot died five years before the deluge.

The empress recoiled at the reports of violence unleashed by the Revolution. Her longtime nemeses the Bourbons were deposed, imprisoned, and put to the blade. From its Parisian epicenter, revolutionary shockwaves rippled across Europe. In Sweden, Catherine's estranged cousin King Gustav was shot in the back at his own gala costume ball in 1792. Among the masked assailants was the miscreant son of Sweden's ambassador to Russia, the baron-wittol Fredrik von Ribbing. While in Poland, Catherine's estranged lover King Stanislaw August was beset with an armed uprising in 1794. The rebellion seeking to rid the country of Russian influence was led by soldier of revolutionary fortune Tadeusz Kosciuszko. When Robespierre's radical utopia finally crashed in France, a new beast rose from the rubble. In her final years, Catherine was busy making alliances to contain Napoleon's empire-building crusade. Once disparaged and belittled by the continent's aristocratic elite, Catherine's Russia now stood as the bulwark of their Old Regime Europe.

By 1796, Catherine was sixty-seven years old, graying, fleshy, and fatigued. After thirty-four years on the throne, her health had declined. She endured splitting headaches and excruciating leg pains. The tsarina still maintained her formidable daily routine, overseeing the myriad details of running an empire. Of late, she was distressed by the failure to arrange a politically useful marriage for her oldest granddaughter and by a resurgent French assault on the Italian peninsula. She was pleased, however, by her army's latest victories along Russia's southern frontier. At home, meanwhile, Catherine fretted about the inevitable succession. It was no secret that the empress favored her bright-eyed grandson Alexander over the legitimate claimant, her maladjusted first son Paul.

On the evening of November 4, a few court intimates gathered in the Hermitage salon, where her old favorite Prince Naryshkin's parodies had the empress relaxed and laughing. Feeling spent, she begged her company's forgiveness and retired to an early bed. The next morning, Catherine as usual rose before dawn, took a cup of black coffee, and disappeared into her private apartment to sort through a pile of correspondence. She never reemerged. By late morning, a personal attendant went to check on the tsarina and found her sprawled behind the door of the bathroom. She had suffered a stroke.

Catherine's limp body was propped up on a mattress on the bedroom floor, hardly moving, faintly moaning. For the next thirty-six hours, doctors, priests, counts, and servants huddled over the stricken sovereign. They anxiously hung on each flutter of life, but she never regained consciousness. Her breathing became labored and halting. She was draped in a white silk fabric with gold braiding. The last rites were administered. At 10:00 P.M., on November 6, the procurator-general appeared before Her Majesty's sobbing court and read from a proclamation in his trembling hands: "The Empress Catherine is Dead."

She had come to Russia at the fresh age of fourteen, as little Sophie, the precocious princess from Stettin, modest but confident, agreeable but resolute, making the most of her audition before the empress. On the occasion of her fiftieth birthday, Catherine playfully composed her own epitaph. It read: "Having come to the Russian throne, she wished to do well, and to bring her citizens happiness, freedom, and property. She easily forgave and hated nobody. She was merciful, considerate, and cheerful by nature. With a republican soul and a kind heart. She had many friends, liked being with people, and took pleasure in her work. And, she loved the Arts."

◆

Autocrats make bad parents. At least Catherine did not murder her firstborn son in a fit of paranoiac rage as did predecessors Peter the Great and Ivan the Terrible. Instead, she just drove Grand Duke Paul batty with a combination of explicit slights and implicit threats.

Raised by his grandmother, Paul was never endeared to his mother. Paul did not wait long to undo Catherine's policies and assert his own preferences. During his short reign, he managed to antagonize most of the ruling elite. In a public gesture intended to right past wrongs and spite his mum, Paul had Peter III exhumed and interred in the sacred Romanov burial sanctuary, the Peter and Paul Cathedral, in a tomb right next to Catherine. And in case anyone should not be clear about the new regime, he compelled Catherine's coconspirator in Peter's murder, elderly Count Alexei Orlov, to walk behind the funeral carriage, cradling the weighty Imperial crown on a pillow. So insecure was Paul when he took the throne that he built a fortified castle in the middle of the city and locked himself in. Of course, just because you are paranoid does not mean that people are not out to get you: Paul's reign was cut short when his palace guards strangled him to death with the bedroom drapes. Catherine's legacy would be preserved after all.

In 1801, the throne passed to Catherine's darling grandson, Tsar Alexander I. He was everything his father was not—gallant, gracious, and good-looking. Alexander excelled at charming others, from fetching countesses in the bedroom to preening generals in the war room. After spending several days looking across the negotiating table into the cerulean eyes of the Russian monarch, Napoleon swooned: "If I could not be me, then I would want to be him." Alexander led Russia to the top of the Great Power hierarchy in Europe, with the unintentional help of the Little Corporal.

Indeed, Alexander was trying to avoid a fight with Napoleon, who thought the backward Russians would be a pushover. His 600,000-strong invasion force arrived just in time for winter, but other than vandalizing the Kremlin, Napoleon had little to show for the effort. Hungry, frostbitten, and dispirited, the overextended Grande Armée was forced to retreat. The War of 1812 was a defining event for Imperial Russia, stirring nationalist exaltation and orchestral inspiration. Alexander chased Napoleon all the way back to France. When the Russian army reached Paris, the fearful French groveled before its commander-in-chief, Tsar Alexander. The Russian occupation was belated comeuppance for all the smears and insults that had been heaped on the Romanovs since Peter's time. And it was a decisive victory for Old Regime Europe. Less than twenty years after Catherine's death, Russia was the continent's most feared military power and most influential political broker.

Alexander was also committed to continuing Catherine's cultural legacy. And postrevolutionary France was just the place to pick up a few more Old Masters for the Hermitage. In gratitude for not leveling Paris, as Napoleon had done to Moscow, French prince Talleyrand presented Alexander with keys to the city and introductions to the city's most available high-society consorts. Emperor Alexander became especially fond of ex-empress Joséphine, the "rose of Europe." With Napoleon sent packing, Alexander made himself comfortable at Château de Malmaison, Joséphine's palatial abode outside Paris. The premises were packed with four hundred paintings and assorted treasures, the looted spoils of her ex-husband's conquests. Alexander's fling with Joséphine was passionate, but brief. She died of pneumonia only two months after their first meeting. In 1815, the bereft tsar paid nearly a million francs to his paramour's children for the most prized pieces in her collection. It was the most expensive and impressive art acquisition since Catherine's time. The haul was especially rich with Dutch Old Masters, including Gerrit Dou's late career masterpiece, *The Herring Seller*.

Alexander acquired more than art for Russia; he also added territory. Another unintended consequence of Napoleon's wars was a rift between Sweden and Russia over Baltic sea lanes. Rather than negotiate a solution, both sides saw it as an opportunity. In February 1808, war was declared. The Swedes prepared for a naval assault come the spring thaw, but the Russians sent their army over the ice for a winter surprise. Hostilities dragged on for a year, before Sweden was forced to cede the eastern province of Finland.

In March 1809, representatives of Finland's four estates—landed nobility, town burghers, Lutheran clergy, and peasant farmers—gathered under the steeply tapered roof of Porvoo Cathedral, fifty miles east of Helsinki, to receive their new overlord. As a gesture of goodwill, Tsar Alexander journeyed two hundred miles from Saint Petersburg to the medieval fortress town to formalize the administrative details of Russian annexation. The Imperial throne was transported for the occasion and installed on a raised platform. Alexander posed majestically above the assembled, having donned a decorated black waistcoat and blue satin sash. He courteously accepted oaths of allegiance from his new subjects and proclaimed the Grand Duchy of Finland. Alexander's terms were lenient. He did not impose strict Imperial order, but granted local autonomy and preservation of existing institutions. It was an auspicious start to the new relationship.

The mutual good feelings of Porvoo did not last long. As the 19th century moved forward, subsequent Russian rulers were less mindful of local sensitivity and Finnish patriots more assertive about national identity. By the late 19th century, Russian tsars felt increasingly threatened by their non-Russian subjects. In response, the Imperial administration became more ambitious, seeking not just political control but cultural domination as well. In Finland, this led nationalist-minded intellectuals to form an organization—the Archeological Commission—dedicated to discovering and preserving the history and culture of the Finnish people. The work of the Archeological Commission was not overtly political, so it was tolerated. Compared to the riotous Poles, Finnish nationalists just wanted to dig around ancient burial mounds and medieval church foundations.

At the onset of the 20th century, most of Europe was transformed by the Age of Revolution. Russia, however, remained an outlier, where the divine rights of sovereigns and the prerogatives of aristocracy still reigned supreme. Nearly one hundred years after Catherine's death, in 1894, Tsar Nicholas II ascended the throne, when his father, Alexander III, a real autocrat's autocrat, died suddenly. Nicholas was of less steely stuff. Most contemporary accounts agreed: he was a good guy but a lousy leader; covetous of his power to decide, although he could never make up his mind.

Catherine's legacy now rested on the shoulders of an imperial inheritor, who was both half-hearted reformer and irresolute reactionary. The combination proved revolutionary.

The three-hundred-year-old Romanov Dynasty was finally toppled by the strains of the First World War. Old Regime Europe was no more. The Russian Revolution was even more ferocious than its French forerunner. The Tsarist Empire was torn asunder. And in 1917, Finland declared independence. Its claim of territorial sovereignty included the adjacent coastal waters and the hidden treasures contained therein.

10

GRAVEYARD OF WRECKS

Borstö Island, 1953

I n the predawn gloom, Sven and Nils Andersson dragged an open-topped *faering* into the cold surf, sloshing over the stony beach of their remote Borstö Island home. It was early fall in the Archipelago Sea. The brothers muscled the clinker-style rowboat over the swell and through the vapor toward deep water. They lowered a hemp-stitched driftnet, poised to intercept a silvery shoal of migrating herring. But their outing was spoiled, as the anchor line of the netting ensnared an unmovable object below. The Anderssons cursed their bad luck, cut the line free, and rowed back home against a blushing dawn.

Borstö lies in the outer reaches of the Archipelago Sea, sixty miles south of Turku, Finland. The island is near the fairway, the narrow sea lane where steady winds favor ships sailing to and from Russia, and dangerously close to the archipelago's unyielding boulders. Standing watch over this precarious stretch of sea is the Hag of Borstö, a carved wooden figurehead, mounted atop the island's highest cliff. Salvaged from a 17th-century galleon, the lonely widow offers silent testimony to the treachery that lurks below. In 1742, when the Russian military occupied Turku, the Swedish Crown converted the desolate island into a navy outpost. Borstö's first permanent settler was Abraham Thomasson, who also served as salvage constable. It was Abraham who recovered an old chest that washed ashore from an unknown wreck, which he duly delivered to the Turku customs house. As it turned out, it was the captain's trunk from the same shipwreck that the Andersson brothers had just snagged two hundred years later.

The seafloor in this area was known to be at least one hundred and twenty feet deep, while the herring nets reached only half that depth. Yet it was not the first time that Borstö fishermen had encountered this mysterious underwater hazard. Sven sat up on a smooth granite slab and oiled his leather boots, as Nils mended the net. It is a shipwreck, wheezed an old coot, who joined the brothers on the beach and recounted his own tale of nets getting caught and ripped. "My family has kept a record of all the wrecks here for 400 years," retorted Sven. There is no shipwreck in those waters. Nils, meanwhile, held up a section of netting and examined the rusted iron markings on the line. Maybe it is a shipwreck. If it is, Sven said, it must be "very old."

By chance, a team of Finnish navy divers pitched camp on Borstö the next summer. The islanders approached the visitors with a request: please find out what is mangling nets in one of the best fishing spots. Using only a few distant landmarks as a guide, Nils led the navy divers to the location where the brothers' driftnet was caught the previous fall. The Finnish frogmen secured their scuba tanks and dive belts and vanished into the dark sea. They soon resurfaced with an answer. The nets were catching on the upper spars of a well-preserved wooden vessel, probably a merchantman, at least two hundred years old. The mystery ship came to be known as the Borstö Wreck.

News of the shipwreck stirred seafaring imagination. Was it Catherine the Great's fabled art wreck? Alan Gustafsson, a Finnish journalist based in Turku, wanted to know. Gustafsson reported on the discovery with unconcealed delight. "If closer investigation proves that the Borstö Wreck meets expectations," he wrote, "we must not avoid any effort to salvage it. By all accounts a veritable treasure of maritime historical value is lying on the sea bottom off Borstö. There is nothing similar in all Scandinavia." Gustafsson assumed the role of chief advocate for the wreck. He used his press column to tantalize readers and galvanize officialdom: "The Borstö ship may be an international sensation." In 1958, Gustafsson's lobbying paid off.

The matter of the Borstö Wreck had by now reached the desk of Nils Cleve, director of the State Archeological Commission. Cleve was Finland's top archeologist, and a national hero. His fieldwork unearthed evidence of an early Finnish Iron Age culture along the embankment of Lake Köyliö, vindicating Finnish folklore. Köyliö was the site of the legend of Lalli, Finland's first freedom fighter, a bad-tempered peasant who supposedly chased the pillaging crusader Bishop Henry onto the ice-covered lake and killed him with an axe. Cleve was intrigued by the prospects of the Borstö Wreck, but knew little about marine archeology. The Archeological Commission was staffed with diggers, not divers. He contacted the navy to bring him out to the archipelago to investigate.

In September 1958, the *Kallanpaa* pushed off from the dock at Borstö. On board were director Cleve, three navy frogmen, and Sven Andersson, sputtering directions inside the wheelhouse. Securing an anchor line to the wreck, the divers descended into the murky depths. Diving equipment in the 1950s had come a long way from Karl Fithie's 18th-century diving bell. Jacques Cousteau's revolutionary self-contained underwater breathing apparatus (SCUBA) was more than a decade old. But diving techniques were still rudimentary. The Finnish frogmen had trouble with the depth and darkness. One diver injured his eardrum and was forced to return to the surface. The other two gathered as much information as possible during two short descents to the seafloor. Cleve devoted just one day to the underwater exploration. It was not enough time.

Aboard the returning *Kallanpaa*, Cleve jotted down the main details gained from the excursion: "The vessel has three masts and it lies sunk in the mud with its masts upright. There are no gun ports. It is obvious that the wreck is no man-o-war, but instead an ordinary merchant vessel, probably from the 18th century." The meager findings were a major disappointment. "The inspection did not produce any appreciable results," Cleve wrote in his journal. Lacking financial resources and underwater expertise, the director was at a loss about what to do next. Journalist Alan Gustafsson, however, was undeterred. He devised a plan to solicit outside funding to contract a private salvaging company to raise the mystery ship on behalf of the Archeological Commission. But bureaucrats are covetous of control. Gustafsson's proposal was rejected. And for the first (but not last) time, Finland's cultural guardians refused help from outsiders to recover a lost treasure from the Graveyard of Wrecks. "The secret of the wreck still remains to be solved," scowled Gustafsson, "but why must it remain a secret?"

Graveyard of Wrecks

"The vessel though her masts be firm, beneath her copper bears a worm." And so *teredo navalis* earned a literary callout from no less than American transcendentalist loner Henry David Thoreau. Better known as the shipworm, *teredo navalis* is, in fact, not a worm, but a tiny clam, which uses its knifelike shell to burrow into hunks of underwater wood. The resulting hole becomes home for the hungry mollusk, which continues to scrape at the wood and take in nourishment from cellulose-enriched water. Once a shipworm digs in, the tunnel extends ever deeper and wider. And when a community of shipworms digs in, the hull of even the sturdiest vessel is transformed into a subaquatic Swiss cheese. Even New England's vaunted clipper ships, as Thoreau laments in his ode to the bitty bivalve, were destined "to sink in the Indian seas." Hence, *teredo navalis* earned the nickname "termite of the sea."

The shipworm thrives in warm and salty waters, such as the Caribbean. Columbus, as it turned out, carried more than tobacco and chocolate back from his New World adventure. El Capitán also gifted Europe a few things the continent would rather have done without: its first dose of syphilis and a hull riddled with shipworm. The newly arrived *teredo navalis* quickly dug into a Mediterranean feast of two millennia's worth of shipwrecks. On the northern end of Europe, however, the wood-devouring clam did not fare as well.

With more than 250 rivers and streams draining into its basin, the Baltic Sea is more brackish than salty. Whereas the salinity level of ocean water is around 3.5 percent, it is closer to 1 percent in the Baltic. The temperature, meanwhile, runs from chilly to freezing, with 50 percent of the surface covered in ice during winter months. The Baltic's northernmost waters, including the Archipelago Sea, are the least salty and most frigid, which is why *teredo navalis* prefers to dine elsewhere. Besides being long on ice and short on worms, the Baltic exhibits minimal tidal movement, measured in inches instead of feet. Thus, once a sunken vessel settles down, there is not a lot of thrashing about on the seafloor. All together this means that Baltic shipwrecks, including very old wooden wrecks, tend to be well preserved.

With more than 20,000 officially documented wreck sites, from an estimated total of 100,000 plus, the Baltic Sea is known as "the Graveyard of Wrecks." Resting on the Baltic's dark silty floor are dragon-carved Viking longboats, fat Hanseatic sailing cogs, cannon-wielding Elizabethan galleons, and pummeled Prussian battleships. The oldest underwater discovery in the Baltic was a dugout tree trunk canoe, dated to 5000 B.C.E. In 2010, Nord Stream, a Russian-operated underwater pipeline project, surveyed twelve historic wrecks at a depth of 400 feet in just one thirty-mile corridor. Underwater cameras showed these vessels to be in good shape, with three old wooden hulls still fully intact.

While Scotland has her Nessie, the Baltic has its own sub-maritime mysteries. In 2003, the "Baltic Ghost" wreck was discovered off Gotland Island by a diving team searching for a lost spy plane. When echo sound indicated a large unnatural object, underwater cameras were turned on. Instead of a DC-3 fuselage, robotic eyes revealed an eerie vision of primitive wood carved figures, manning the deck of a fully intact 17th-century fluyt. But perhaps the most enigmatic item in this underwater museum is the "Baltic Anomaly," an unidentified sunken object, lying three hundred feet down in the middle of the Gulf of Bothnia. In 2011, Swedish wreck hunters stumbled on this immense oddity, which displayed an unnatural metallic composition and an uncanny resemblance to the *Millennium Falcon*.

Not just old wooden brigs, but their sunken cargos stay well preserved in the Baltic. In 2010, a trading vessel was discovered at a depth of 160 feet near the Åland Islands. The "Champagne Schooner" yielded more than one hundred bottles of Veuve Clicquot, from the venerable Reims champagne house. The Baltic's chilled temperature and muted light provided ideal storage conditions for the 170-year-old bottles, which luckily landed on their side. The first salvaged bottles put on the block, in 2011, set world auction records for champagne. After spending nearly two centuries at the bottom of the Baltic, the decanted beverage was described as spicy, smoky, and sugary.

As the playing pond of northern Europe's great powers, the Baltic preserves the sunken remains of multiple centuries of naval warfare. Among the many casualties of war resting on the Baltic seafloor is history's most lethal maritime disaster, the wreck of the *MV Wilhelm Gustloff*. In May 1937, Germany launched a sleek state-of-the-art cruise ship, for overworked Nazis to catch some rest and relaxation. Pressed into military service as a hospital ship and floating barracks, the Nazi *Titanic* was mobilized in 1945 for the Wehrmacht's mass evacuation of Poland, with the Soviet Red Army closing in from the east. The cruise liner, built to accommodate 2,000 passengers and crew, was crammed with 10,500 retreating troops and desperate civilians.

Leaving Gdynia on January 30th for an overnight passage to Kiel, the captain opted against a shoreline route, fearing underwater mines in the shallows, and headed further out to sea, where a deadlier menace lurked. The lumbering prey was stalked by Soviet submarine *S-13*, which slammed three torpedoes into the *Gustloff*'s hull. Fiery explosions and gushing seawater set off a panic. Only one lifeboat was lowered. The ship foundered on its side and sank in less than one hour. It was the greatest loss of life in a single shipwreck in maritime history—as many as 9,400 souls slipped into the freezing water and drowned, twenty miles from the white sands of Pomerania.

Of all Baltic shipwrecks, none is more renowned than the mighty Swedish war galleon *Vasa*. On August 10, 1628, a festive crowd gathered in the late afternoon on the Stockholm waterfront to witness the maiden voyage of His Imperial Majesty's new flagship. Resplendently adorned and prodigiously armed, the *Vasa* was built to be the fiercest warship ever to cruise the Baltic Sea. The rise of Sweden's northern empire dated to the early 1600s, during the reign of King Gustav II Adolf, one of early modern Europe's foremost military figures. The Lion of the North was feared as a bold commander and brilliant tactician. He built a naval fleet to extend his influence across the Baltic to the shores of continental Europe. The king pinned his hopes of victory on the floating juggernaut *Vasa*.

The ship was built in the image of Gustav Adolf, majestic and ferocious. At a cost of 40,000 *riksdalers*, it was the most expensive item the Swedish state had ever invested in. More than four hundred workers and two years in the making, the *Vasa* was a towering menace, with an elevated stern for tactical height advantage in ship-to-ship combat, and twice the firepower with double-decker gun platforms. It carried seventy bronze cannons and three hundred battle-ready sailors. Just as much attention went into the decorations. Nearly five hundred brightly painted wooden sculptures adorned the behemoth, including likenesses of the king, some Greek gods, and an assortment of scary sea monsters and seductive sea nymphs. But on its maiden voyage disaster struck. A strong wind broadsided the top-heavy vessel and seawater poured through the opened gun ports, which were preparing a thunderous salute. The lower decks were deluged. And with the Swedish lord admiral as witness, the *Vasa* began to sink. The captain hastily abandoned ship, while terrified sailors, most of whom could not swim, were dangling from the rigging and flailing in the waves.

Gustav Adolf's invincible warship journeyed less than one mile before settling into the mud at the bottom of Stockholm Harbor. Of course, there was an inquiry, though everyone knew the cause of the ship's ruin. Its hull was too narrow, its aftcastle too tall, its top weight too heavy, and its ballast too light. But since it was the king who insisted on a design that was more beast than boat, the investigators naturally attributed the sinking to "an act of God." Several attempts to raise the galleon failed. It was too heavy. More than fifty cannons were salvaged in a remarkable feat of preindustrial technology. After that, the *Vasa* lay undisturbed for three hundred years.

Concealed in a muddy tomb on the harbor floor, the *Vasa* long evaded her would-be rescuers. Until the summer of 1956, when a lead sounding keg smacked her hull, dropped from a rowboat above by Anders Franzén. The curious Franzén worked a corer into the mysterious hard mound and brought up several small samples of black oak. It was an old shipwreck. The bespectacled Franzén, in khaki military jacket and scarf, was a familiar figure around Stockholm Harbor. He spent all his free time either researching old wreck locations in the naval archives or plying the coastal waters with his sounding equipment. By 1950, Anders correctly identified six historic wrecks in the waters around Stockholm. Yet his quest was to find the *Vasa*.

In early September, the Swedish Navy's chief diving instructor, Per Edvin Falting, descended on the spot in a helmeted diving suit. Falting could barely see a foot in front of him through the stirred-up mud on the soft harbor floor. He was about to start his ascent when he bumped into "something solid, like a wooden wall." Climbing upward, Falting discovered a row of "rectangular openings . . . the cannon ports." Climbing a bit higher, he gawped at a second row of cannon ports. Falting resurfaced and congratulated Franzén—the *Vasa* was found. The discovery roused the nation's consciousness. Having grown accustomed to the role of peaceful and prosperous social democrats, Swedes delighted in being reminded of their glorious imperial past. King Gustav VI Adolf was positively giddy, and urged the navy to commit whatever resources necessary to salvage the historic prize of his royal ancestor and namesake.

Almost five years later, on April 24, 1961, the *Vasa* was finally lifted from the water. Not unlike the day she was launched, the *Vasa*'s raising was occasion for an impromptu holiday. A gallery box of royalty, admiralty, and celebrity was crouched up front, while scores of journalists were perched nearby. The shoreline was packed with spectators, schools were dismissed early, and the rest of Sweden watched on television. When the great warship was hoisted above the surface, seawater and mud roared over the decks and out of the portholes. It was a spectacular sight. Anders Franzén was the first to step aboard.

Little did anyone then realize that lifting the wreck would be the easy part. The *Vasa* was well preserved in the cold depths of the Baltic, but in the atmosphere above sea level her component materials began to deteriorate rapidly. Wooden planks dried out, warped, and split; iron bolts holding the ship together crumbled and disintegrated. Conservationists never faced such a task. A special moisturizing solution was concocted and sprayed over the oak timbers for the next seventeen years. All the iron fixtures were eventually replaced with stainless steel. The maintenance was never-ending. Still the raising of the *Vasa* was an astounding triumph of marine archeology. The venerable royal war galleon became the symbol of Stockholm and pride of Sweden, and an inspiration to other nations. And no country was more captivated by the *Vasa* than Finland.

Mystery Ship

Across the Gulf of Bothnia, Finland's chief archeologist Nils Cleve followed the *Vasa* story with interest and envy. The Finns, of course, had their own historic shipwreck from the age of sail, a perfectly preserved merchant vessel in the waters off Borstö Island. But what riches it held were yet unknown. Indeed, it was quite possible that the wreck was the *Vrouw Maria*, the legendary lost ship of Catherine the Great. Unlike the *Vasa*, Cleve's mystery ship had neither a royal patron nor a naval squadron to help reveal her secrets. The Archeological Commission over which Nils presided had never undertaken any major underwater projects. Finns descended from farmers, not sailors. It was welcome tidings, in early 1960, when the frustrated Finnish director received an unexpected Swedish visitor.

Anders Franzén was a shipwreck fanatic. The hero of the *Vasa* was now looking for more historic wrecks to locate and salvage, and he knew the Finns had one. Franzén proposed a collaboration between his amateur wreck hunting club and Cleve's Archeological Commission to explore the Borstö Wreck. Anders could provide a team of divers with their own vessel and equipment, and, more important, with expenses covered. They would document the physical details of the wreck, try to learn her identity, and salvage her cargo. Anders would get the glory, Nils would get the artifacts. Cleve readily agreed.

For three summers, between 1960 and 1962, the Swedes came to Borstö and investigated the anonymous wreck. Anders became busy with the *Vasa*, and turned the project over to Gösta Bojner, a trusted colleague and experienced wreck diver. Cruising into the archipelago on a converted trawler, the *Fram*, the Swedish coed crew was an immediate sensation. The divers brought their wives and girlfriends, who served as the on-deck support team. Their Finnish hosts could not help but ogle the summer celebrities in action. Gösta showed off state-of-the-art diving equipment, dry-suits with air supplied from the surface, boat-to-diver radio communications, and underwater flash cameras. More captivating than the gear was the vibe. Exuding adventure and fun, something akin to the California surfing culture had arrived in Scandinavia. It was the early '60s and the world belonged to the young, the limber, and the tanned. The bushy blond Swedes at Borstö inspired a first generation of Finns to take up amateur wreck diving.

Bojner's team laid the foundation in Finland for the field of marine archeology. Finnish independence at this time was less than half a century old. The young country was still working out the defining features of its national identity. The standard story of the Finns was that they hailed from the northern Eurasian forests. The archeologists who cultivated this national identity had built their credentials by digging and sifting through old settlement sites, searching for evidence of a distinctively Finnish religion, language, and way of life. The national narrative was about simple but spirited, hardworking farmers, who had the bad luck to be stuck between two ambitious empires. There was strong opinion among these cultural custodians that the story of the Finns ended at the shoreline.

Nils Cleve was one of the diggers, but now he too was caught up in the coastline craze. Nils was a fixture upon the *Fram*'s breezy, sun-splashed deck. His familiar beret and wool overcoat seemed out of place among the chiseled Swedes. But he worked closely with Bojner's diving crew, learning the means and methods of underwater archeology, and seeking to know more about his shipwreck. With each dive, a few more pieces of the puzzle were revealed. The ship was a three-masted galliot, most likely from the 18th century, and given her size and shape, probably Dutch. But was it the *Vrouw Maria*?

Having determined that the wreck was a trading vessel, the Swedes next planned to explore the hold to see what it was trading. Using a deck winch and pulley cable, the crew lowered an empty oil drum down to the wreck site. The salvaging began. Aboard the *Fram*, anticipation rose in sync with the cranking whine of the winch, hauling the barrel back to the surface. Cleve and crew eagerly huddled around as it was lowered onto the deck. The trove eventually yielded three anchors, a wooden figurehead, and an assortment of nautical relics. More impressive were the salvaged old luxury goods—gold watches, silver snuffboxes, silk petticoats, and bejeweled bric-a-brac. But the most sensational item was a fancy French-made cariole, a two-wheel horse-drawn carriage. It was obviously intended for a person of lofty status. In total, Nils catalogued close to 200 pieces, a dazzling collection of near pristine Old World artifacts. The Borstö Wreck was arguably the best-preserved and best-stocked merchant shipwreck yet known in the world of marine archeology.

The news of treasures found in the Borstö Wreck caused the Finnish government to revisit its position on cultural heritage. In June 1963, Finland's parliament, the Eduskunta, passed the Antiquities Act. Soon after, the Archeological Commission was reorganized and given a new moniker, National Board of Antiquities (NBA). Prompted by the excavation of the Borstö Wreck, Part III of the Act was devoted to Marine Archeology. "The wrecks of ships and other vessels discovered in the sea or in inland waters, which can be considered to be over one hundred years old are officially protected," the legislation decreed. "The finder of a wreck," the Act continued, "shall immediately report the discovery to the National Board of Antiquities," while "the objects discovered in wrecks shall go to the state without redemption." The national homeland was effectively extended to the adjacent coastal waters, officially claiming that what lies therein belonged to the cultural heritage of the Finns. The Finnish experience was no longer confined to the margins of the continent.

The Swedes had got the Finns off to a good start. Nils Cleve thanked Gösta Bojner: "I wish to express deep gratitude not only for the sensational finds and the actual fieldwork but also for your personal contribution, your great interest and the excellent organization of all the work." But now the newly minted National Board of Antiquities would need to develop its own expertise in underwater archeology. A new Maritime Museum set up operation in cramped quarters on one of Helsinki's small harbor islands. In the early 1970s, Maritime Museum director Christoffer Ericsson organized the first all-Finnish underwater investigations of the wreck site. More physical details of the ship were learned and more fine-crafted luxury goods were salvaged. Yet no masterpiece paintings were uncovered. Ten years after the Swedes had gone home, the identity of the Borstö Wreck was still a mystery.

The Scion and the Sea

In the summer of 1950, Finnish maintenance workers in Kotka harbor discovered a 130-foot wooden hull, with a line of mounted cannons still ready to fire. The broken warship was a casualty of the Battle of Svenskund, the largest naval battle ever waged in the Baltic Sea.

In 1790, Empress Catherine's peevish cousin King Gustav decided to avenge Swedish pride and launched a surprise attack on his detested eastern rival. Russian spies in Stockholm gave the tsarina warning, and the king's forces were routed. Catherine might have taken all Finland, if not for the Swedish navy's startling victory at Svenskund (Kotka). On July 9, 1790, a Swedish flotilla of 250 ships, 450 cannons, and 14,000 troops met a Russian fleet of 200 ships, 900 cannons, and 18,000 troops on the edge of the harbor. Russia's confident commodore advanced on his quarry with every intention to devastate. But strong prevailing winds disrupted the Russian lines, and the Swedes repeatedly pounded their assailants with cannon fire. When it was over, the Russian side counted 50 ships sunk, including 10 large frigates, 1,500 men killed, and another 10,000 wounded or taken prisoner.

The shipwreck discovered in Kotka harbor was the *Sankt Nikolai*, one of the Russian frigates destroyed that day. The find set off a flurry of activity over the slain vessel. Among the curious was a teenage sailor whose imagination was set loose by the hundreds of artifacts the wreck yielded. At the helm of his small ketch, the lad gazed over the tranquil waves, seeing Catherine's and Gustav's mighty ships-of-the-line facing off, inhaling the sulfurous cannon smoke, and hearing the crashing of timbers. Young Christian Ahlström was hooked.

But it was just maritime daydreams. Christian was, he knew, destined to a career in the family business. The Ahlström Corporation was a Nordic industrial giant. In 1851, Christian's great grandfather, Antti Ericsson Ahlström, founded a grain mill in Pori, along Finland's west coast, quickly expanding to paper and saw mills. By the 1870s, Ahlström was leading a Finnish industrial revolution, with a sprawling shipyard and roaring ironworks. When he died in 1896, Antti was the richest man in Finland. By 1931, the Ahlström Corporation was Finland's largest industrial enterprise, with thirty manufacturing groups and five thousand employees. In 1937, the Ahlströms marked their status in stone, with a new corporate headquarters, the Industrial Palace, along Helsinki's downtown esplanade.

As a descendant of this distinguished clan, Christian too was eager to show his quality. But it would not be in the boardroom. Teased by tales of adventures past and treasures lost, his mind forever drifted to the sea.

"I used to work in the family company, but I did not like that at all," the spritely scion explained, "so I decided to shift to the history business." With the discovery of the Borstö Wreck, Christian managed to turn a pastime into a profession.

"I heard of the Borstö Wreck from a relative of mine who had been sailing in the Archipelago Sea," Christian recalled. With rapt attention, he listened to the descriptions of the Swedish divers and the priceless artifacts. His mind raced with questions. Where did the vessel come from? Where was it bound? How was it lost? Christian determined to involve himself in the mystery. "I assumed that everything would be much simpler than it actually turned out to be," he recalled. "I had no idea of all the new things that I would have to learn."

Christian was not a diver, so he found a way to contribute above water. Ahlström began spending less time in the corporate offices of the Industrial Palace and more time in the cramped cubbyholes of the National Archives. He explored long-dormant historical sources, uncovering fragmentary bits of information and piecing together the clues. Based on the salvaged cargo, a few assumptions were plausible. Gold pocket watches and silver snuffboxes were the high-status accessories of the high aristocracy, and in the eastern Baltic, that could only mean the Russian Imperial court.

If the ship was sailing to Russia, Christian surmised, then it could have come from beyond the Baltic, which meant it had to pass through the Öresund and Castle Kronborg, where the Sound Dues were collected. He contacted the archive of the Danish customs house in Copenhagen for information on eastward bound merchant ships between 1745 and 1755. Please be more specific, came the curt reply, your request includes more than 15,000 records.

Christian revised his strategy. He knew that salvaged goods from shipwrecks went to auction, so he went to Turku in search of old auction reports. Unfortunately, most of the old records were lost in Turku's Great Fire of 1827; only two boxes of documents survived. Among the few surviving records were some papers from 1746–1748. Christian examined these and found a sale receipt for a sea chest, turned in by the Borstö salvaging constable Abraham Thomasson, dated February 1748. And another document showed that Robert Fithie's salvaging company searched for a lost merchant ship near Borstö at this time. Christian now had some bits of information to return to the Sound Dues.

Back in Copenhagen, the customs house ledger for 1747 showed ninety-one ships bound for Saint Petersburg. One Dutch ship, in particular, caught Christian's attention. Arriving from Amsterdam to Castle Kronborg on October 15, 1747, its cargo was listed as "miscellaneous goods" and its master was Carl Paulsen Amiel. But Danish customs officials registered ships by number, not by name. Even if Amiel's ship was the Borstö Wreck, Christian had no way to confirm it. He expressed this frustration to the antiquated archivist, who suggested he might find the answer among the applications for exemption. Christian now learned about the Danish king's policy of excusing fellow sovereigns from paying the Sound Dues. He was presented with a colossal stack of old parchment letters.

Christian labored through the applications. The pile did not appear to shrink. His eyelids grew heavy, his attention waned. He was about to go home, when an ornately decorated letter caught his eye. He pulled out the document, handwritten in French. It was from Nikita Panin, the Russian ambassador to Copenhagen, requesting a tax refund for a French cariole for Her Majesty Empress Elizabeth, transported by shipmaster Carl Paulsen Amiel. There was a note from the Danish king Frederick: "the Russian minister to our court, Panin, has notified that a customs duty of 7 *riksdalers* and 22 silver *skillings* was levied on a carriage with equipment and harness packed in three crates and sent from Amsterdam to Saint Petersburg. Since the goods are intended for the personal use of the empress of Russia, no customs duty should be levied owing to the courtesy generally shown by princes to each other." Christian had found the Borstö Wreck.

Ahlström still did not know the name of the vessel, so he expanded his search to Holland to dig up information on Captain Amiel. The Amsterdam City Archive revealed that in 1747 Carl P. Amiel was the registered owner of a three-masted galliot. The mystery ship was revealed. The Borstö Wreck was not the *Vrouw Maria*, it was the *Sankt Mikael*. The ghostly figurehead recovered by Swedish divers a decade earlier was finally identified as Michael the Archangel, leader of the armies of God and patron saint of sailors.

Final Journey of the *Sankt Mikael*

By spring of 1747, Saint Petersburg had at last acquired the demeanor of an Imperial capital. Thanks to brassy Empress Elizabeth, gleaming stone mansions reflected on the canals in place of the rough wooden structures from Peter's time. And just to be sure that the regal ambience was not spoiled, Elizabeth forbid residents from hanging laundry out to dry on the trees.

On the eastern tip of Vasilievsky Island, a three-masted galliot pushed off from the dock in front of the long, arcaded bourse, where the commodities of the Russian forest—honey, beeswax, and fur—were traded for the crafted goods of Germany, France, and Holland. The ship's master was a recognized figure in the merchants' quarter. Carl Paulsen Amiel was a Dutch captain who took up residence in Russia, lured by the riches of the wild east. His vessel was loaded with hemp for Holland's sailmakers. A figurehead of his ship's namesake presided over the stern, the archangel Sankt Mikael.

By July, Captain Amiel was back in Amsterdam. The placid summer breeze belied the political tempests, which had unsettled Holland during the spring, when popular revolts rocked Rotterdam and French soldiers occupied Flanders. In the summer of 1747, the need for unity was utmost, so the otherwise fiercely independent Dutch provinces put aside their differences. The House of Orange, under Willem IV, was restored. After all, too much politics was bad for business.

Captain Amiel's return trip to Russia promised big profits. In late summer, Dutch stevedores loaded the *Sankt Mikael*'s hold with barrels of exotic raw materials, bolts of fine fabrics, bottles of mineral water, and crates of rococo-crafted luxuries that only Europe's wealthiest consumers could afford. Hand-glazed porcelain figurines and chinaware from the Meissen factory in Germany, fancy gold pocket watches from the goldsmiths of London and Paris, enameled copper and delicate gold-leaf snuffboxes from Holland and France, and tortoiseshell hand fans encrusted with Burmese rubies and diamonds. And the grandest item heaved over the rail was the stylishly wrought two-wheeled French carriage for Empress Elizabeth. By early September, the ship was ready. First Mate Fredrik Scheel shouted the order to crewmen Yeager and Ivanov, sails were raised, and the voyage was underway.

The North Atlantic leg lapsed more slowly than Captain Amiel had hoped. The *Sankt Mikael* did not reach Castle Kronborg until mid-October. Beyond the Sound, details of her voyage through the Baltic are unknown, as the *Sankt Mikael* left no known survivors. Her story can only be conjectured from the few documents uncovered at the Turku customs house and the underwater discoveries at the wreck site. Under normal conditions, the *Sankt Mikael* would have reached the Upper Baltic in mid to late November, the height of hurricane season. With fair winds, a three-masted galliot gave Captain Amiel a speed advantage; but in foul weather, such a vessel could be difficult to maneuver and incapable of making headway against strong oncoming winds. Circumstantial evidence suggests the ship was struck by a late autumn squall.

The vessel sank close to Borstö Island, within view of land, yet there were no reports by the islanders of any sightings, suggesting that the tragedy occurred either in the blackness of night or under thick cloud cover. The fateful blow caught the captain and crew by surprise, as the ship was abruptly seized, dragged down, and devoured whole by the implacable sea. Aside from one stray sea chest recovered on Borstö, the islanders did not report any traces of cargo or flotsam. Gösta Bojner's dive team found the ship's anchors secured on deck, indicating that there was not enough time to try to right the vessel if it was listing. The Swedish divers confirmed that the hull was intact, so the ship did not smash on one of the archipelago's boulders. The underwater investigation also showed that the gear on the main deck and cargo in the hold shifted to portside, as if the ship was pushed over in a storm, which might occur if the upper rigging iced over and the top-heavy craft was battered by strong winds.

The *Sankt Mikael* was not just a sunken ship, it was an underwater tomb. The wreck site yielded skeletons of at least three people and a small dog from the captain's cabin and nearby seafloor. Forensic analysis indicated the remains belonged to a middle-aged male, a younger female, and adolescent male. The skeletons added a touch of macabre to the mystery, particularly for those islanders who swear by the existence of archipelago ghosts. Moreover, a skull found in the wreckage showed signs of having suffered a severe, perhaps lethal, blow to the head.

The grisly discovery captured the imagination of Christian Ahlström, who shuddered to learn a further chilling detail. There was no dinghy found with the wreck. All ships carried a rowboat in the event they needed a tow or worse to abandon ship. It was curious that they found human bones but no lifeboat. Christian grappled with the revelation: "Perhaps the crew had escaped with the boat, leaving the passengers to certain death. The boat presumably held five or six persons, and there were at least that many crew members. Could they really have rowed away in cold blood, leaving the others onboard to the mercy of the raging seas?"

For scholars who enjoy the quest, the excitement of discovery is fleeting. The mystery of the Borstö Wreck was solved. What next? Christian recalled another stash of documents he had uncovered in the old Imperial archives in Stockholm. He rummaged through the box of papers and pulled out a letter from Foreign Minister Nikita Panin concerning a shipwreck with a valuable cargo belonging to Her Majesty, Empress Catherine. He now recognized the same signature scrawled thirty years earlier by then-junior ambassador Panin, asking the Danish king for a tax exemption. "Panin made good progress in his career," Christian mused. He scanned some other documents in the box. The ship was traveling from Amsterdam to Saint Petersburg. It too was lost in a storm in the outer archipelago. The captain survived. His name was Reynoud Lourens. His ship was the *Vrouw Maria*. Christian gasped in disbelief. He had stumbled on Finland's most celebrated shipwreck. But to find it, he would need help. He would need a wreck hunter.

11

THE WRECK HUNTER

Leningrad, 1985

T he Karelian woods were startled by a snorting motor coach, rumbling
eastward along the deserted King's Highway. Emerging from a snow-
clad birch canopy, the vehicle hesitated. The sudden change in scenery
hushed the passengers inside. After an anxious delay, the coach moved
forward, barely, creeping through a gauntlet of rickety watchtowers, razor-
tipped barbed wire, and Kalashnikov-wielding border guards. Welcome to
Soviet Russia.

Though only a hundred miles from their Helsinki departure, the riders
may have well arrived on Mars. It was an alien world. Across the border, the
smooth roadway skirting the northern coast of the Gulf of Finland gave way
to battered asphalt strips and packed dirt mounds, better suited for T-34s
than Volvos. They soon passed the medieval fortress town of Vyborg. For
four hundred years, Vyborg Castle secured the eastern edge of the Swedish
Empire, that is, until Peter the Great wrested away the strategic prize for

Russia. Craning necks pressed against the right-side windows to catch a glimpse of the citadel's imposing Tower of St. Olav. The coach trundled down Soviet M10, the "Scandinavian" Highway, bisecting the squelchy isthmus that separates the Gulf of Finland and Lake Ladoga, Europe's largest lake. This was the ancient Karelian forest, sacred to Finns, and forcibly ceded to the Soviet Union in 1944. The foreign visitors gazed out at the austere landscape, their ancestral homeland.

The intrepid band of travelers were employees of Helsinki-based Polar Diving Company, whose owner, Antero Parma, had splurged for an end-of-year holiday party in Leningrad. By the 1980s, Catherine the Great's former Baltic capital had become an offbeat weekend destination for venturesome Finns, who wanted to experience firsthand the dystopia next door. Aboard the caravan getting his first peek behind the Iron Curtain was ex-employee Rauno Koivusaari.

Rauno worked as a technician for Polar Diving for almost a year, "until [he] got bored and quit." Without a job to go to, Rauno decided to go back to the gym and work on his boxing skills, having once trained with Olli Maki, Finland's former lightweight champion. His strapping frame was testament to the intensity of his efforts. But Rauno did not take things too seriously, including himself. Most often a smile cracked across his chiseled features. That's why Antero Parma took a liking to the brash young man, who incessantly fiddled with the company's machines, looking for new ways to use the equipment. Parma had a hunch that his rolling holiday party would get an extra charge if Koivusaari came along.

Against a somber gray sky, the tarnished golden dome of St. Isaac's Cathedral came into view. The merrymaking Finns crossed over the ice-choked Neva and passed under the faded turquoise facade of the Winter Palace, where two centuries earlier Empress Catherine reigned over the continent's most glittering court east of Versailles.

Communism was not kind to Russia's "Window on the West." At a peak of nationalist fervor during World War I, the city was renamed from the German-sounding Petersburg to the Slavic-sounding Petrograd. In early 1918, when the Kaiser's gunboats sailed into the Gulf of Finland, the self-crowned government of Lenin and the Bolsheviks fled four hundred miles east. Moscow reclaimed the title of capital of Communist Russia, while Petrograd consoled itself as the Soviet Second City.

In Russia, it has always been the case that wealth and status flow from political power. The Bolshevik relocation to Moscow caused the Petrograd population to plummet by two-thirds. Those who remained were reduced to bartering and begging. The new regime needed a new identity. The city's name was changed again, in 1924, to Leningrad, in honor of the recently deceased scourge of the tsars. Russia's aristocratic world of extravagance and privilege was shattered. "For centuries, our grandfathers and fathers have had to clean up their shit," railed radical socialist Leon Trotsky, "now it is time they clean up ours." Noble pedigree became a marker for discrimination and exploitation. Family mansions were expropriated, churches were closed, art treasures were seized.

On June 22, 1941, Leningraders were basking in the summer solstice, when Foreign Minister Molotov interrupted state radio to announce "the most egregious betrayal in the history of civilized nations." That day German forces launched Operation Barbarossa, a full-scale military offensive across the Soviet Union's western border. At the end of August, the Germans captured the eastbound railway and Leningrad was cut off. Instead of a bloody street fight, the Nazis tried to starve the city to death. For nine hundred days, the city endured the longest military siege in modern history. Hundreds of thousands succumbed to starvation, corpses were strewn atop snow-covered streets, mass graves were dug on the outskirts. City scientists were pressed to develop something edible out of yeast, glue, and soap. A strict ration system was imposed, violators were shot. At last, in January 1944, the Red Army arrived in force. They pulverized the German front with more rockets and shells than were used at Stalingrad. Battered but not beaten, Leningrad was liberated.

The 1980s brought a thawing in the Cold War, and Russia's communist keepers were a bit less paranoid about capitalist visitors. Some dedicated tourists arrived in Leningrad to take in its classical high culture—masterpieces at the Hermitage and pirouettes at the Kirov. The attraction for many Finnish weekenders, however, was cheap vodka and caviar. "We rode our bus all over Leningrad," Rauno recalled, "and we partied as much as humanly possible."

These were the days when slick black marketeers stalked drab hotel lobbies, befriending foreigners and proffering favors. "At every stop," Rauno said, "we ran into locals who insisted on changing our Finnish marks into rubles." It was a tempting offer, given the stingy official exchange rate. "Pretty soon my pockets were filled with rubles and the Russians became interested in my stonewashed jeans and down jacket. But these were the only clothes I had to wear." Rauno spent much of the night fending off unsolicited propositions for his pants.

Rauno soon realized there was not much to buy in Russia, and he began to fret about going home with hundreds of worthless rubles. When a beefy black marketeer sporting a leather vest and walrus moustache approached him at the hotel bar, Rauno turned out his pocket and explained that he wanted to exchange his rubles back to Finnish marks. Leering at the wad, the moustachioed tout gestured to follow him out to the street. A red Lada, the ubiquitous Soviet driving machine, modeled on a 1965 Fiat, pulled up to the curb. The rear door swung open, and a hand beckoned the Finn inside. "I jumped into the back seat before thinking," Rauno said, "the door slammed shut, and the car screeched forward. That was when I realized that I made a huge mistake."

Rauno shouted to stop, but was restrained by the bushy-lipped thug. The car sped away from the center. He worked on the back door handles, but they were both locked. Rauno presumed that he was on his way to some remote site on the outskirts to be rolled by Russian gangsters. After twenty minutes, the car finally stopped at a red light. The driver turned back to check on the now quiet hostage. Anticipating the moment, Rauno leveraged a foot against the back door and unloaded "the hardest hook that I have ever thrown. The driver's head plopped limply onto the steering wheel." Rauno now kicked the back door with all his might, once, twice. The door flung open knocking back his captor. "He reached over to grab me and I hit him with a five-to-six combo." The dazed Russian goon fell to his knees. The adrenalized Finn fled on foot.

Rauno ran for what seemed like half an hour, avoiding the streetlights, trying to make his way back to the center. He finally stopped, out of breath and out of sorts. He had no idea where he was. He waited in the shadows until he spotted a taxi, then handed the driver a card with the name of his hotel. On the slow ride back to Leningrad center, Rauno rubbed his bruised knuckles and found a broken incisor embedded in the skin. Olli Maki had been a good teacher. "Seeing our hotel, I felt relieved and when the cab stopped, I gave the driver all the rubles I had. By the look he gave me, I knew it was too much."

An agitation of Finns crowded the sidewalk in front of the hotel, flanked by two flashing police cars and four dour-faced policemen. Rauno's old boss Antero was excitedly engaged with the impassive chief, when the cause of the commotion nonchalantly approached from behind: "Sorry I am late."

"God damn it, Koivusaari," said a ruffled but relieved Antero. Then noticing the blood splotch on Rauno's shirt, the old boss chuckled, "that will teach them." Chock one up for the Finns.

An Exceptional Finn

How do you spot the extrovert in a group of Finns? They are the one looking down at the shoes of the person next to them. "Reserved" is the word that Finns often use to describe their national persona. Neither overly cheerful, nor overly grim. Steady, reliable, practical; delivered with matter-of-fact modesty. It has been suggested that the Finnish demeanor is an evolved social strategy, shaped by the long, dark Scandinavian winter. Perhaps. Still, there are 5.5 million Finns, and plenty of exceptions. And most of his compatriots would agree that Rauno Koivusaari was one of the "exceptional" Finns.

For starters, he was not reserved. Since his youth, Rauno had a tendency to act first and think about consequences later. He was not averse to taking risks if he thought he would come away with a good story. He often got into trouble. But just as often, he got out of it, thanks to his lighthearted demeanor and the ever-playful glint in his clear blue eyes.

Rauno was born in 1964, on the fortress island of Korpo, in the Archipelago Sea, and he grew up an army brat. Rauno's father served in the Finnish military's coastal artillery. These units operated long-range gun batteries dug into island cliffs and mainland promontories along the coast. Sharing the Gulf of Finland with the Soviet Baltic Fleet kept Finnish defense forces busy, observing the red-bannered warships patrolling nearby sea lanes and watching for stealthy submarines sneaking into territorial waters. Rauno's mother was also busy, caring for her boys and supplying local shops with homemade *pulla*, the swirly sweet cardamom rolls that are a Finnish culinary staple.

The archipelago was Rauno's childhood playground. He swam in its chilled waters, scampered across its wave-splashed rocks, and explored its pine-rimmed coves. Impatient with the orderliness of the classroom, Rauno thrived in the outdoors. The pristine setting offered endless up-close nature lessons. When his family was stationed on Mäkiluoto, a popular birder haven, the youngster was an eager tagalong to visiting tripod-toting naturalists. He helped them set up field nets to snag flittering passerines and set out pigeon cages to lure hungry raptors. Rauno even had a favorite feathered friend, the Great Gray Owl. He would quietly lie in wait for a chance to observe the Phantom of the North dive bombing through two feet of snow to snare a tasty vole. "I disliked sitting inside studying, and I wasn't very good at any subject," Rauno conceded, "but every time there was a question about birds, I was the first to raise my hand."

Rauno learned things by doing, though his first venture into the sub-aquatic realm did not go especially well. A devotee of *The Undersea World of Jacques Cousteau*, Rauno badgered a local boat captain to teach him how to dive. Finally, on the agreed upon morning, the eager fourteen-year-old bicycled to the home of his indisposed instructor, who crawled out of bed bleary eyed and hungover. To get rid of the pesky kid, the captain handed over his dive gear and a few basic instructions, then closed the door in his face. Rauno somehow managed to pedal to a nearby lake. Going for his best Cousteau imitation, the teen pulled out a harpoon gun, borrowed from a friend, and strapped on a weight belt. Though in a breach of *Calypso* fashion etiquette, he was forced to keep his shoes and socks on, so that the oversized fins did not slip off his feet.

Rauno awkwardly waded out to a half-submerged rock and fumbled his way up. Looking down into six feet of water, he practiced breathing through the regulator one last time and rolled off: "I landed at the bottom on all fours. I was stuck in the mud. A small perch swam right against my mask, as if trying to see who was behind it. I aimed the harpoon but did not dare shoot at a target only a few inches from my head. I tried to swim but could not move. My efforts made me out of breath. I started to shake uncontrollably from the cold. The equipment felt incredibly heavy. I could only think of getting to the surface and fast. I managed to grab hold of a rock and pulled myself out of the water. I ripped off the mask and lay on my back, panting for a long while. I noticed that I was bleeding from the knees and elbows. Something did not go right."

At age fifteen, Rauno commanded his first vessel, a compact fiberglass Vator motorboat with a 20 hp Mercury outboard. On his first launch, the proud teen was showing off for a friend by jumping the wake of a lumbering tugboat. At full throttle, the speeding skiff pounded into the dense water wall, hurtled upward, upended the boys, and careened out of control over the rocks. With a mangled propeller, the craft limped home. "I was aching all over and had broken the motor on my maiden voyage." Undaunted, Rauno repaired his boat, invested in a map and compass, and with a bit more caution began cruising the archipelago. Whenever he had a few hours to spare, he would set out to prowl the hundreds of islets and inlets in his backyard sea. He became adept at tracking the deviously twisting channels. It was a talent that later served him well.

As soon as Rauno was old enough, he quit school. He fought with his parents about it, but stuck to his decision. "School just wasn't for me." He worked at odd jobs and took up amateur boxing. When he reached conscript age, Rauno joined the navy, "so I could spend my time on the sea, where I belonged." He spent his uniformed years playing Cold War cat and mouse games, chasing Soviet submarines around and laying sea mines. His commanders came to rely on him as helmsman of choice whenever their vessel went on alert amid the tricky passageways of the archipelago. As someone whose hobbies included driving boats and shooting things, Rauno enjoyed navy life. But when his stint ended, he decided not to reenlist. Instead, Rauno looked for something new to try.

An Obsession Is Born

No list of famous shipwrecks would be complete without the pride of the White Star Line, the *RMS Titanic*. At her launch, the Belfast-built luxury liner was the largest vessel ever to grace the ocean blue. The pomp and hubris of the modern industrial age were on full display, when the 50,000-ton behemoth cast off from Berth 44 of the Southampton docks at noon on Wednesday, April 10, 1912, for her maiden transatlantic voyage.

Just before midnight on the fourth day at sea, triumph turned to tragedy. Three bells sounded in the crow's nest, warning the bridge: "Iceberg right ahead." Cruising near maximum speed, at 22.5 knots, the *Titanic's* presumed watertight hull scraped the massive ice floe starboard side, its steel panels buckled from the force of the collision, and the North Atlantic gushed into its cavernous hold. The seawater entered at a rate of seven tons per second, overwhelming the ship's bilge pumps. The lower compartments, boiler rooms, and squash courts were quickly submerged. The wounded leviathan stayed afloat for three hours, before it keeled upward, snapped in two from the tremendous weight and plummeted 12,000 feet to the ocean floor. Fifteen hundred lives went with it, including a distant relative of Rauno.

When he was ten years old, Rauno watched a television show about the *Titanic*. The saga "mesmerized and devastated" the lad, who could not stop imagining what the frantic final moments must have been like aboard the ship. Still replaying the desperate scenes in his mind the next day, Rauno asked his grandmother if she had seen the show. She paused before answering: "I don't think that you were ever told that my mother's brother went down with the *Titanic*." Rauno was stunned by the revelation that his great uncle, whom he never knew, was an itinerant laborer aboard the star-crossed luxury liner, and as far as anyone knew, had perished in the disaster. An obsession was born.

Rauno's captivation with the *Titanic* was now personal. He learned as many details as he could about the tragedy. His imagination eventually wandered to "the slew of unfound wrecks lying on the bottom of the Archipelago Sea, some of them hundreds of years old." For the first time, he began to frequent the library. He scoured copies of the old shipping news and filled up notebooks with curious facts about the wrecks off the Finnish coast. Rauno wanted to know the details of each ship's tragic sinking, yet most wrecks remained a mystery, taking their stories with them to underwater graves. But these were not just fantasy ghost ships conjured from an old storybook. The archipelago contained real sunken ships, timeless relics, waiting to be discovered. Sometimes it is possible not just to imagine the past, but to see and touch it as well. Rauno learned to scuba dive.

Rauno's interest in shipwrecks eventually brought him into the social circle of sport divers. He began spending long hours with the Calypso diving club, founded by former navy divers in the early 1970s. The club took its name from the iconic research vessel of Jacques Cousteau. Rauno was welcomed in the club for his "archive of knowledge" about the numerous wrecks in the nearby waters. In exchange, he was treated to the collective experience of the club's underwater veterans, an invaluable resource for a novice diver. "At sea, unforeseeable things are bound to happen," he said, "so diving follows the same primary rule as warfare—always be prepared to react quickly to unexpected and changing circumstances."

Through his Calypso connections, Rauno found a new line of work—professional diver. He accepted a full-time position as submersible construction worker for a large company that built ocean piers. He enrolled in the Maritime Academy, where he earned certification as an underwater mechanic. Rauno had a knack for finding things underwater. Soon, friends and friends of friends were asking him to look for odd valuables dropped overboard—car keys, boat anchors, bottles of booze. Rauno enjoyed the challenge. To earn extra money, he started scavenging things that collectors would pay for, such as coins, cannon balls, anchors, and especially brass trinkets. Unlike gold and silver, brass retains its shine in the salty sea. The value of such artifacts, he learned, increased significantly if he could identity the wreck they came from.

He learned of an underwater stockpile of anti-aircraft artillery shells off the Hanko peninsula, jettisoned by retreating Soviet warships in World War II. Figuring that the brass casings would return a handsome profit, he set out with his brother in a small motorboat to salvage the discarded shells. The risky undertaking required digging up live ammo from the sea floor, transporting it over bumpy waves back to shore, and then dismantling the detonators to remove the gunpowder inside. While Rauno succeeded in not blowing up himself or his brother, he miscalculated the demand for brass. The venture barely broke even. To make a big score as a dive salvager, Rauno realized he needed more serious, and more expensive, equipment. He convinced Calypso club member and former navy diver Ari Ilola to invest in a partnership. Their new salvaging business was outfitted with a Cousteau-like Zodiac dive boat and, more significantly, a side-scan sonar.

During his time in the navy, Rauno became familiar with the military's classified means of seeing underwater. Side-scan sonar was first developed by ex-Nazi scientist Julius Hagemann to help the US navy look for lost hydrogen bombs in the ocean deep. The echo-locating device was encased in a torpedo-like shell, which transmitted fan-shaped images of the seafloor while it was towed behind the stern. The Finnish navy employed side-scan sonar to hunt for leftover World War II mines. The navy's chief side-scan technician was an acquaintance of Rauno's father, and he tutored the young seaman on how to operate the sophisticated apparatus. By the early 1980s, the US military's exclusive patent claim over Hagemann's invention had expired.

Rauno and Ari owned and operated Finland's first commercial military-grade side-scan sonar. With this high-tech advantage, their investment paid off. The team became regular contractors to insurance companies investigating boating accidents. Rauno developed a surgeon's touch with the sensitive device. His subaquatic detective skills eventually caught the attention of the Finnish police, and he began getting calls to search lakes and rivers for drowning victims. From the experience, Rauno developed a morbid expertise, understanding how panicked people behave in water and where dead bodies are most likely to be found.

Although Rauno was busy locating sunken crafts and retrieving lost cargo for insurance claims, it was just a job. A preferred job, which kept him outdoors and supervisor-free, but still just a job. "If I could do the same work above water, I would," he said. Rauno's real passion had not changed in twenty years. Shipwrecks excited him—treasure-bearing, history-laden shipwrecks.

Shipwreck Fever

The Calypso diving club is based twenty miles west of Helsinki, on the wooded peninsula of Kirkkonummi. The club organized weekend dive camps in the nearby sea. On one such outing, divers uncovered a stash of old tinted bottles. The divers bandied guesses back and forth as to the age and content of the bottles. One undamaged flagon still contained the original liquid contents. As the night went on, curiosity and vodka took its toll, and the full bottle was unsealed and sampled: "It tastes like alcohol," came the inconclusive conclusion. The colored glass antiques made good souvenirs, so plans were made for a return to the site. "Bottle Slope" thereafter became a regular destination for club divers, though the source of the bounty remained unknown.

Rauno was intrigued. He sifted through his research files looking for a shipwreck that might have spilled the old bottles. Eventually he stumbled on a captain's declaration for the 1840 wreck of a Prussian merchantman, accompanied by a detailed description of the course of events. The *Carolina Fredrika* was blown off course in a late September storm and smashed on the rocks near the Porkkala lighthouse. The crew scrambled into a leaky lifeboat and barely made it to the safety of a nearby islet. Rauno was in luck. The wreck declaration referenced the lost cargo, including 220 crates of rum destined for the Imperial Russian admiralty. He looked at a map and calculated the direction and speed of the wind. He identified a spot where the accident likely occurred, the islet where the crew was stranded, and the resulting debris line of the emancipated cargo. It matched up with the bottles recovered by the Calypso divers. At the first opportunity, Rauno pointed his inflatable motorboat out to the site, where he discovered the broken remains of the brig *Carolina Fredrika* on the seabed. The mystery of Bottle Slope was solved.

Rauno had a bad case of "shipwreck fever." Like any sports club, Calypso thrived on competition. The ultimate goal was to be the first to discover the resting site of a famous wreck. Of course, it was an ego boost to claim the laurels for making an important discovery. But to the winner also went the spoils. According to the "Law of Finds," if a ship is abandoned at sea, then the diver who later comes upon the wreck is entitled to what they can salvage. As Rauno described: "Whenever you discover a new wreck, you have to get to it quickly before anyone else beats you. This is because there might be something down there that would be just perfect for gathering dust on your bookshelf."

Those stricken with "shipwreck fever" are prone to dodgy behavior. "Wreck fever compels you to lie," Rauno stated bluntly. You lie to your friends, to your spouse, and most of all to your fellow divers. You tell your companions that you can't go out because you have to work late or tell them that you are going out to an already familiar wreck site. Never say anything to suggest that you may have found something new to explore. Because shipwreck fever makes one disinclined to share information, you need to become adept at eavesdropping on others and asking indirect questions. Always listening, always probing, always jonesing for one extra detail. "All this mysterious behavior causes paranoia and leads to legends being born," Rauno observed, "since everybody is constantly thinking that somebody else has found something historic." And just when you have regained your senses, a random comment from a fisherman unloading the daily catch on the pier reaches your ear, and the fever grips you all over again.

Finding lost wrecks in the wide ocean is not an easy task, but Rauno rose to the challenge. Besides his notebooks and side-scanner, Rauno had another advantage. He did not think about wrecks the same way as other divers. Instead, he tried to see the wreck through the eyes of the crew during the fateful moments when their vessel was foundering. He thought about his own close calls and instinctive reactions. Though each wreck was a particular tragedy, he began to notice recurring patterns with seafaring conditions and captains' mistakes. "In every case of maritime emergency," Rauno realized, "people have behaved and acted in the same way. When I'm tracking down a shipwreck, I always picture myself standing on the deck of the ship in peril, and try to ask myself what I would do if I were the captain."

By his mid-thirties, Rauno's reputation as wreck hunter was ascendant. He was admitted into the ranks of the Teredo Navalis Society. The Helsinki-based diving club was dedicated to marine archeology and closely affiliated with the Maritime Museum. Always short on resources, the museum recruited Teredo Navalis divers to help document and preserve Finland's underwater cultural heritage. Rauno became a regular on museum dive junkets to find old wrecks, explore the sites, and salvage artifacts. Rauno relished the opportunity to be involved with historic wreck projects. But he wanted more: he wanted a big score of his own: Ahab had his white whale, Cousteau had the British steamship *Thistlegorm*, Tommy Thompson had the ship of gold *Central America*, and Robert Ballard had the queen of shipwrecks, the *Titanic*. Helsinki was a long way from Hollywood. Did the

Gulf of Finland possess a legend in her depths? Rauno knew of only one such wreck: the lost treasure ship of Catherine the Great.

The *Vrouw Maria* was long a fixture of archipelago folklore. After the discovery of the Borstö Wreck, a revived interest in Empress Catherine's shipwreck took hold of a new generation of maritime romantics. Both marine archeologists and sport divers sought to solve the mystery and recover the masterpiece paintings. The *Vrouw Maria* was a favorite ghost ship story in the summer dive camps. Each season, a changing cast of divers would take a shot at the prize, acting on new information, a tipoff from a fisherman, or just a hunch. Teredo Navalis club official Petri Rouhiainen said: "From the early 1950s, they have been looking for the *Vrouw Maria*. The story was well known. Every diver knows the name. It is like the *Flying Dutchman*." The legend of the *Vrouw Maria* grew with every failed attempt. She came to be known as the "Holy Grail" of Baltic wrecks. In the summer of 1998, Rauno finally had a chance to win the chalice.

With an air of confidence, the Archipelago Maritime Society dive club, a rival of Teredo Navalis, announced plans for a search for the *Vrouw Maria*. The bold excursion was the inspiration of Erkki Talvela, a Helsinki business executive and avid wreck diver. The logistics of getting a dive boat and crew on the water for two weeks in the outer archipelago was an expensive and complicated undertaking. Erkki massaged his business relations to secure funding from several corporate donors. He also recruited a key player, maritime historian Christian Ahlström, whose relentless archival digging had unraveled the mystery of the Borstö Wreck. Since then, Christian had turned his attention to the *Vrouw Maria*. His enthusiasm for Empress Catherine's sunken ship was so great that he chipped in a few thousand euros from his family inheritance to the expedition. As the ambitious project came together in the winter of 1997, Erkki realized that one crucial component was lacking—an ability to see the ocean floor.

Talvela's team was equipped with underwater scooters and echo-sounders, but these gadgets were not powerful enough to discern the depths of the outer archipelago. He needed a side-scan sonar, and he knew who had one. Erkki had met Rauno earlier at a Maritime Museum dive outing. Erkki telephoned Rauno, and asked if he and his side-scanner would like to join the expedition. Rauno was taken aback. He was wary of getting involved with the rival dive team, but the thrill of making history was too tempting. He accepted the invitation. On the surface, it seemed an unlikely partnership. Erkki was well-heeled and well connected; Rauno was casual and clannish. On the inside, however, they shared one critical attribute. They both had a bad case of shipwreck fever. It was the irresistible force that brought them together, and the inevitable cause of their falling-out.

Erkki's plan was for Rauno to bring his own boat and crew to work the side-scan sonar, while accompanying his vessel and divers. The supporting role gnawed at Rauno; the tension was palpable. Erkki's first mate and good friend took an immediate disliking to Rauno, and vice versa. "It took two minutes," Erkki recalled, "and then they started. They had the same kind of personalities—not easy." They bickered over housing and over expenses even before they got on the water. It was an inauspicious start. Yet on the second day of the search, the ill-tempered mood was suspended when the outline of a shipwreck appeared on the side-scan sonar. The *Vrouw Maria* was found.

Or, so it seemed. The side-scan read-out showed a large and intact wreck, an old wooden vessel, about thirty meters down. Cheers went up. "The media was very interested," Erkki said. Rauno, however, was skeptical. It is too shallow, he said. If this was Catherine's treasure ship, it would have been spotted by the salvagers or islanders two hundred years ago. But the crew wanted to believe they had found the Grail, and spent the next two days exploring the wreck. When the divers finally reported that the ship's rudder was still in place, the disappointment set in. It was not the *Vrouw Maria*.

The search continued. But as Rauno followed Erkki's team around the outer archipelago, it became increasingly clear that they had no idea where next to look. "We spent too much time in too shallow water," Erkki realized later. The expedition was a bust. Annoyance turned to acrimony.

The experience left Rauno embittered. He felt misled and taken advantage of. But his close friend and diving buddy Petri Rouhiainen understood the real source of Rauno's rancor. "It is very difficult to put Rauno in somebody else's project," Petri explained. "He is a leader and wants to be the director." The 1998 misadventure left Rauno more determined. Having observed firsthand how *not* to conduct a major search project, he vowed to put together his own expedition to find the *Vrouw Maria*. And at least one positive development came out of the episode: Rauno became better acquainted with shipwreck historian Christian Ahlström. Here was someone whose knowledge of archival evidence surpassed his own. Rauno had a secondhand copy of Ahlström's book at home, still unread. When the summer dive season ended, he would crack it open.

12

GOLDEN AGE
SECRETS REVEALED

Decoding Dou

S
tanding amid the Old World charm of Dom Square, a bespectacled art
student, Jan Emmens, gazed up at the chiseled inscription on the brick
facade of University Hall: SUN OF JUSTICE ENLIGHTEN Us. This was
the Old Testament–inspired motto of Utrecht University. At this moment,
in the autumn of 1947, Utrecht was desperate to feel the sun's embrace
again. Holland was only two years removed from a sadistic Nazi occupation
and bitter "Hunger Winter," when nearly 20,000 Dutch starved to death.
Utrecht at least did not lay in ruin, as did Jan's hometown of Rotterdam. In
May 1940, the Luftwaffe hurled a spiteful torrent of bombs on the industrial
port in response to the Dutch army's unexpectedly spirited defense. In one
afternoon, the Rotterdam Blitz leveled the historic town center, destroyed
25,000 homes, and extinguished a thousand lives. If resistance continued,

the Nazi commandant warned, Utrecht was next. The Dutch surrendered, Utrecht was spared. Having survived the historic assault on Rotterdam, Jan was about to rewrite history in Utrecht.

From the 17th century's Baroque Realism to the 20th century's Abstract Expressionism, Utrecht remained an art town. In the Golden Age, it was home to the Dutch Caravaggists, led by Gerrit van Honthorst. These young artists sojourned to Italy to absorb the lessons of the Renaissance master straight from the canvas. Upon return, they added Carravaggio's empathetic humanism to the distinctively Dutch style of painting. Rubens was so impressed that he sat for a portrait by Honthorst. In the modern era, Utrecht was the birthplace of Piet Mondrian, whose primary-colored blocks upon white achieved pure artistic abstraction. Given Utrecht's cultural lineage, it is not surprising that its University was home to a prominent research center for the study of Golden Age art.

Jan Emmens was precocious and peculiar. Though accepted to one of Europe's finest art history faculties, he was not yet sure if academia was his path. He had a keen appreciation for art, especially Dutch art. But he was also a talented amateur artist, whose drawings drew comparison with the lasciviously twisting torsos of Egon Schiele. Jan was moved by writing as well as painting, devouring all forms of prose, verse, and wordplay. He was perhaps foremost a poet. And then there was history. Jan did not just have an interest in the past, but wanted to get inside it, to see things as contemporaries had seen them. Inherently creative and curious, Jan chose art history to satisfy his prodigious intellectual appetites.

The twenty-three-year-old settled comfortably into the grind of graduate school. Brushing a wave of chestnut hair from his forehead and pinching his horn-rimmed glasses as a prop, he entertained his classmates with spot-on impressions of their ever-so-serious professors. Jan's raw talent and self-initiative caught the attention of his teachers. He became a favorite of Professor Jan van Gelder, the doyen of Dutch art history in the Netherlands. Van Gelder was director of Mauritshuis Museum in The Hague and founding editor of *Simiolus*, the premier Golden Age art journal. Jan also worked closely with Professor William Heckscher, a disciple of the great innovator Erwin Panofsky. Heckscher described Panofsky as a "young, witty, acerbic, conceited genius," drawing new students to his classes like a magnet. Panofsky developed the "iconography" approach to art history, which looked for hidden social meaning in a painting's main subject and incidental objects. The idea excited young Emmens, who later described Panofsky as "the most brilliant and influential art historian of our time." Jan used the iconography approach as an intellectual key to unlock the hidden secrets of the Golden Age.

Jan thrived in the role of young apprentice. He combined his love for words and images in a master's thesis on Golden Age poems inspired by Golden Age paintings. He collaborated with van Gelder to produce a revealing reassessment of the mystique-shrouded Vermeer. At the academic raw age of thirty-four, he was distinguished with an appointment as director of the Dutch Institute of Art History in Florence, Italy. By day, he toiled to reconstruct the social context that shaped Golden Age painting, and by evening he crafted more lines for his poetry portfolio. "I lose myself in historical research," he said, "and find myself again in a poem." In 1961, Jan returned to Utrecht, at van Gelder's insistence, to complete his doctoral dissertation. This was Jan's most ambitious project yet—an iconographic reinterpretation of Golden Age hero Rembrandt van Rijn.

Rembrandt and the Rules of Art was possibly the most unwelcomed book on Dutch art history. Jan started out by eviscerating Frederick Schmidt-Degener, the field's premier Rembrandt-*ophile*. Schmidt-Degener studied at the Sorbonne before his appointment as director at the Rijksmuseum in Amsterdam. From this high perch, he promoted the Rembrandt legend of solitary nonconforming genius, while acquiring ever more Rembrandts for the collection and staging countless Rembrandt shows. The legend, Jan chirped, was Romantic rubbish. Rembrandt was a painter of the highest quality and original style, no doubt, but he was also a product of the same social setting and cultural constraints as his peers. Moreover, Jan provoked, there was nothing consciously transcendental in Rembrandt's brushwork. Instead, Rembrandt was simply a very good representative of the prevailing notions of art and beauty shared by his Golden Age peers. It is modern art historians, Jan said, who have wrongly removed Rembrandt from his historical context and assigned to him a faux biography and overblown persona. Jan concluded that the beloved Rembrandt myth revealed more about modern art critics than it did about Golden Age artists.

An art world demigod was shoved off his pedestal. It was an affront to national pride. Reaction was swift and shrill. "A disastrous book!" Who is this minion who deigns to "explain Rembrandt from A to Z" to his superiors? The dam was breached. Sides were drawn. Discussion of the Golden Age would never be the same. Jan was neither personally perturbed nor professionally harmed by the controversy. On the contrary, the venerable Society for Dutch Literature awarded *Rembrandt and the Rules of Art* its biannual prize. In 1965, patron van Gelder proposed protégé Emmens to the post of Lecturer in Dutch Art History at Utrecht University. Jan accepted; though he was never quite sure where he fit in. Was he a student of art or an artist who studied? In person Emmens was halting and self-effacing, but in written word he was eloquent and unflinching: "From today I will set my cowardice aside. From today I will be myself again." For Jan's next big project, he turned his attention to Rembrandt's long-forgotten student. It was time to reconsider Gerrit Dou.

◆

Who is "the artist"? This question was at the crux of the late 19th-century debate on art and society. The artist, came the response, was a Bohemian hero and free spirit, whose critical commentary offered a wiser, more attuned perspective on humanity. While Rembrandt epitomized the modern stereotype of the artist, his former student Dou was derided as the antithesis. A craftsman, not an artist; all exterior, lacking depth and soul. Done in by a modern generation of art critics, Gerrit's detailed small panels were mocked for being more industrious than inspiring, more persnickety than penetrating. The damage inflicted on Dou's reputation seemed complete and permanent. That is until Jan Emmens challenged the conventional wisdom.

When Jan Emmens was appointed to the faculty, the Art History curriculum gave scant mention to Gerrit Dou. Once lauded as the most dazzling Dutch master, he had become a Golden Age footnote. But Jan took to heart the words of 17th century critic Cornelis de Bie, who said that Dou's paintings "scatter all the darkness from our understanding, and bear our spirits higher than the stars." Jan wanted to see Dou's paintings through the same cultural prism as his original viewers had seen them. He applied Panofsky's iconography approach to Dou's best-known works. Disregarding style, he focused on the message. Through the positioning of primary subjects and arrangement of secondary objects, he asserted, the artist was testing a social norm, taking a moral stand, or tickling a collective funny bone. "Dou's canvases must not be considered solely as realistic genre paintings, as we have been accustomed to think," Jan wrote. When viewed through a properly reconstructed 17th-century filter, his panels were both substantively rich and provocatively engaging.

Behold Dou's legendary lost triptych and consider why this painting was so greatly admired during the Golden Age. *The Nursery*, Jan argued, celebrates the classical understanding of the elements of great art. Using Laquy's copy, he saw Aristotle's triad on creating art in the three panels—nature, learning, and practice. Jan directed attention to the center panel: "In the Netherlands at the time, mothers were recommended to breastfeed their babies, thus the woman in the foreground is not a wet nurse but the child's mother, dressed in all her finery." He continued, "the baby is of comparatively advanced age, the emphasis is therefore not on the birth but on the suckling of the child, or rather on the way in which the child is supposed to be fed." The adjoining panels, featuring familiar Dou subjects, a night school and a scholar sharpening quills, represented respectively learning and practice, completing the classical triad. Aristotle's ancient credo, Jan showed, was both well-known and widely embraced by Dou and his contemporaries.

Jan followed with a reassessment of *The Quack*, housed in his native Rotterdam. Painted in 1652, *The Quack* was Gerrit's most ambitious work at the time, a departure from his intimate genre scenes. The large panel depicted no less than fifteen characters, one dog, and a monkey. *The Quack* is a morality tale about willful deceit. In the scene, Leiden townsfolk take pause from their chores to indulge the sales pitch of a medicine-peddling huckster on the street outside the Galgewater studio, where we spy the artist eavesdropping at an open window. We are thus presented with a contrast: the quack deceives with a false promise of potent health and the artist deceives with a playful illusion of real life. One kind of deception is reproachful, or as Gerrit comments more vividly—via the mother positioned in the forefront wiping her infant's bare bottom—is shit. The deception of the artist, however, is admirable, natural, beautiful.

Next Jan set his sights on another Dou masterpiece, *Trumpeter at a Window*, held by the Louvre in Paris. The painting is quintessential Dou, an archway scene in which a festively garbed horn player locks eyes with the viewer while delivering a tune. In the background, the artist placed a mini–genre scene of men and women banqueters, emptying their tankards. The trumpeter is framed with a familiar accoutrement object from Dou's Galge-water studio, a bas-relief depicting a gang of unruly cherubs antagonizing a billy goat. The mournful musician, the carefree revelers, and the randy ram, according to Emmens, are fatefully interconnected. The trumpeter's song is a kind of last call, or last judgement, for the mirth-makers within, who are compelled by unquenchable thirst and unbridled lust. Through these waggish images, the artist delivers a portentous message: the pleasures of earthly indulgence are short-lived, while the hereafter is eternal.

With the iconography approach, Jan Emmens challenged reigning opinions about Dutch genre painting in general and Gerrit Dou in particular. His conclusions captivated. Instead of the usual one-dimensional descriptive analysis of genre scenes, Jan elaborated a multi-dimensional social-cultural analysis of these slice-of-life panels. In so doing, Emmens single-handedly escorted Dou back into the discussion of Golden Age art.

◆

In late 1971, the mood at the Institute turned grim. Jan Emmens was ill. At forty-seven years, Jan was just reaching his prime. He was professor of Art History and Iconography at the university and was collaborating on a monumental historiography of Dutch art. Although emotionally embattled, he still amazed his colleagues with a lecture on "new surprising discoveries" and continued to explore his "*enfant chéri*," Gerrit Dou.

In December, Jan Emmens died. "It is impossible to forget him," said Jan's former schoolmate. "His good-hearted and human" take on life and art was "a tonic we must now miss." Another fellow classmate recalled, "What most set him apart was an intensity of experience and expression, barely disguised by humor and irony, that had us all under his spell. He was, and remained, an absolutely exceptional figure." For the field of Art History, Jan's "merciless illness and premature death are a disaster."

Jan Emmens redefined the art world's understanding of Golden Age art. Long-standing narratives, including the sacred Rembrandt myth, were cast into doubt. "Modern views of artists," he wrote, "are in the first instance determined by modern needs and prejudices." Even scholars who rejected Jan's most audacious claims accepted his central conviction that "genre scenes in paintings like Dou's were not intended to be taken at face value." After Emmens, art historians would no longer see Dutch genre paintings as just descriptive glimpses of daily life, but would look deeper for insight into the mindset of Golden Age society.

Jan's legacy was assured not just by his written oeuvre, but by the circle of devoted students he trained. Among this cohort, Eddy de Jongh was perhaps the most zealous disciple. Where Jan may have teased and speculated, Eddy dug in and insisted. For de Jongh, Dutch genre painting was a virtual visual tour through a 17th-century red-light district. Eddy found erotic insinuation in almost every bulge and crevice that a painted panel had to offer. He generated controversy with his exposés on the promiscuity of a dead duck and chastity of a bunch of grapes. And similar to his teacher, de Jongh saw Gerrit Dou as the undisputed Golden Age champion of cramming smart and sassy messages into his small-paneled paintings.

In September 1976, a major exhibition on Golden Age art, entitled *From Teaching to Entertaining*, premiered at the Rijksmuseum in Amsterdam. Reflecting the influence of Jan Emmens, the show was dedicated to revealing the hidden meaning of Golden Age genre paintings. The selection of pieces was entrusted to Eddy de Jongh. The exhibit made obligatory inclusion of the reigning celebrity Dutch masters, Rembrandt, Vermeer, and Hals. But Eddy also included three works by Gerrit Dou—*The Nursery* (via Laquy's copy), *The Quack*, and the *The Young Astronomer* (on loan from Germany). De Jongh composed the catalogue notes on Dou, which could have been lifted from a Jan Emmens lecture. By giving the Leiden fijnschilder the spotlight treatment on the big stage of the Rijksmuseum, the 1976 show publicly returned Gerrit Dou to the front ranks of Golden Age masters.

Making a Map

"Turn out the light and go to sleep," growled Nina Koivusaari, "Don't you have any other books to read? Or are you trying to memorize that one word for word?" Husband Rauno murmured assent, without actually processing the request. It was 3:00 A.M. Rauno had been poring over the same few pages in the same slim volume every night for a week. Nina sighed, pulled a pillow over her head, and turned away from the lamp light.

Rauno read and reread *Sunken Ship*, Christian Ahlström's summary of his archival research, looking for clues to the final resting spot of Finland's most famous shipwreck. He scrutinized each minuscule detail of the eyewitnesses to the tragedy—Captain Lourens, the ship's crew, the island fishermen, and the Crown salvagers. A main obstacle to locating Catherine's lost ship was that information in the historical record was not only scanty, but contradictory. Contemporary accounts did not agree. Some said the ship had sunk at thirty meters, others were certain it was at fifty meters. Some said it went down three miles from Trunsö Island, others insisted it was two miles away. A discrepancy of one mile on the open sea was discouragingly vast. Still, another conjecture was that the wreck was not near Trunsö at all, but further south near Utö, the outermost inhabited island of the archipelago. For Rauno, however, the most dismaying assessment—an opinion that formed after several summers of fruitless searches by the salvagers and fishermen—was that the *Vrouw Maria* did not sink where it was anchored, but rather that its rope lines were severed and the ship drifted westward, eventually sinking closer to Sweden than Finland.

The Archipelago Sea had been Rauno's playground for most of his life. He was intimately familiar with its islands and skerries, deep channels and shallow shoals, seasonal wind and water patterns. Now, as he tried to divine the location of the *Vrouw Maria*, some of what he read made sense with what he already knew, but some did not. The evidence was insufficient to launch an expedition.

Rauno lingered over each bit of testimony, trying to imagine himself in the place of the actor who gave it. Who said what? Under what circumstances? Details about nearby islands, wind direction, and water level from the night of the wreck were the most crucial bits of information. But the crew would have been terrified, thrashing about in a violent storm, and in blackness. How could they know how deep the water was, where the submerged rocks were, or how close the land was? What instruments did they use to make calculations? How precise was an 18th-century compass anyway? Rauno struggled to process it all.

Propped against a pillow, Rauno caressed an open hand over his bristled dome, pondering the opposing statements. He recalled a comment that Christian Ahlström had once made: conflicting evidence does not necessarily mean that one is right and one is wrong; it may be that both are right in a way that we do not understand. Maybe the contradictions were not disagreements of observable fact, but differences of cultural reference. After all, these testimonies were gathered from people with distinctive languages and customs, and they were taken over two hundred years ago, when the names of places and units of measure were not standardized. As this realization set in, Rauno thought of how to reconcile the inconsistencies in the historical record. He needed an old map.

It was late November in Helsinki. A teasing sun made a low arc over the continent's northernmost capital. Rauno strode across Senate Square, pulling tight on his woolen collar as a cold blast from the Gulf urged him ahead. He sidestepped a fur-bundled couple chattering in Russian as he passed Helsinki Cathedral, built when Finland was still a Grand Duchy. Just behind the green-domed neo-classical colossus, he entered the National Archives and headed toward the Senate map room. He requested all existing nautical maps of the outer archipelago, from newest to oldest.

The archivist retrieved three cartographic renderings of the outer archipelago. First, he unrolled an up-to-date nautical map published by Finland's maritime administration, based on extensive hydrological surveys. This map was highly detailed with small islets and obstacles, safe channels, and depth readings. Rauno recognized the second map as the standard navigation map used in his navy days. This map, issued in the 1950s, contained large swaths of blank white space, where water levels were unknown. The third map was old and rare. It was a copy of an early 19th-century navigation map drawn by Sweden's Imperial Navy. Rauno had never seen this map before. On a large table, Rauno scanned the three drawings side by side. On the 1950s map, he noticed a tiny rectangular area that had been thoroughly sounded amid a large blank swath of unknown depth. He asked the archivist about this oddity. The 1950s map was based on a much older map, predating the 19th century, but which was lost. This compacted rectangle of depth soundings, the archivist surmised, was probably made for military purposes by naval pilots. Or salvaging purposes, Rauno thought. The archivist made large photocopies of the three navigational maps at Rauno's request. Later that evening, Nina Koivusaari found her dinner table had vanished under overlapping diagrams of the Archipelago Sea. She opened her mouth to protest, but Rauno without looking up put a finger to his lips: "Shh, I am thinking."

◆

Rauno needed to eliminate the numerous false leads contained in the eyewitness accounts of the wreck. Perhaps comparing nautical details on the three maps would help. He began with the easiest clue to unravel: water depth. Back in 1772, Anders Thomasson, a Borstö island farmer eager to reap Empress Catherine's reward, claimed to have hit the wreck with a sounding line at thirty fathoms. At that time, a fathom measured the approximate reach of a grown man's outstretched arms. So thirty 18th-century fathoms, Rauno calculated, was closer to fifty 20th-century meters. This depth seemed plausible, especially considering that the *Vrouw Maria*'s mainmast stood at more than fifteen meters above the deck. If the vessel had come to rest in more shallow waters, and the main mast had not broken, then the archipelago's herring fishermen would surely have snagged their nets on it by now. Rauno circled the places on the most recent map where the water level measured fifty meters.

Although the sea floor was more than twice as deep in spots, a typical anchor line could not reach the sea's lowest depths. Rauno knew that the crew had managed to anchor the ship after crashing on the rocks. From the boatswain's testimony, he also knew that before the wounded vessel was secured, several sounding leads failed to touch bottom. This meant that the ship had passed through one of the outer archipelago's deep channels. The captain's log recorded that strong east-southeast winds were blowing on the night of the wreck, so a rudderless craft would have been pushed along a west-northwest trajectory. Rauno now circled several spots on the new map, where the water level plunged to one hundred meters. The number of possible wreck locations was reduced.

The next clue to decipher was surface distance, the main point of contention among the eyewitnesses. Rauno carefully spread out the 19th-century map. He adjusted an overhead light, and noted that the old map, drawn without benefit of modern measuring tools, gave a remarkably accurate depiction of the physical details of the archipelago. In the lower right corner was a key. Rauno squinted at the minute scrawl denoting two units of measure—the old English league and the *tyska mil,* which was the old German *meile.* A league was the distance that a man could walk in one hour, or approximately three standard miles. The *meile* was a long outdated postal measurement, used in Prussia and Denmark, which approximated 25,000 feet, or about 4.5 standard miles.

Rauno rifled through his stash of notes and documents. In May 1772, Karl Fithie, the Crown salvager in Turku, reported that the *Vrouw Maria* sank three miles from the island of Trunsö. In July 1772, Hansson Sunn, the Crown salvager in Helsinki, wrote that the ship went down two miles from Trunsö. Could it be that the British-descended Fithie measured the distance to the *Vrouw Maria* with an English league, while the Swedish Sunn measured the distance with a German *meile*? It seemed too easy. Rauno pressed a straight edge to the paper, and marked off two German *meiles* in pencil, underneath it marking off three English leagues: the lines were nearly equidistant.

Sunn's report also noted that flotsam from the wreck washed ashore two miles away on the island of Jurmo. This was consistent with the captain's testimony that winds were prevailing from the southeast. But only deck items were recovered at Jurmo—neither barrels from a spilled-out hold nor planks from a shattered hull. From this, Rauno knew that the wreck did not drift toward Sweden, or else there would have been debris recovered further west. The *Vrouw Maria* was still in the outer archipelago, and likely still in one piece on the seabed.

Using the old 19th-century map, Rauno traced a line starting at Jurmo in a direction between three and four o'clock and the distance of two German *meiles.* Then starting at Trunsö, he traced a second line of similar length in a direction of six o'clock. The endpoints intersected. He pressed a knuckle against his chin and stared at the map for several minutes before marking the spot. He repeated the exercise with different trajectories, but nothing was as promising as this first location. He double-checked the depth with the newest map, and found that this site was one of those he had circled at fifty meters deep. Even more promising, the spot was just northwest of a deep, hundred-plus meter channel, so it was consistent with the boatswain's statement. Rauno also recalled from the captain's log that the salvage attempts were hindered by strong wave surges, and this particular spot was not near any rocky barriers, thus making it more vulnerable to swells.

There was one last clue still to examine. Rauno laid out the 1950s navigation map. His hand shook as he retraced two German *meiles* southward from Trunsö and then southeastward from Jurmo on the 1950s map. They converged right in the middle of the tiny rectangle that, according to the archivist, had been sounded by the Swedes two hundred years ago. The pencil dropped. Rauno knew where the *Vrouw Maria* was.

◆

Rauno needed to tell someone about his discovery, someone who could keep a secret. He chose Petri Rouhiainen, his closest friend from the Teredo Navalis club. As Petri put it, "we spoke the same language." Petri was twice Rauno's best man, and once his honeymoon companion (when Nina was waylaid by a work emergency). With his ursus-like frame and booming baritone, Petri had no trouble attracting attention. A business manager during the week, he was an avid sport diver on weekends. Gregarious, sharp-witted, and skilled at underwater photography, Petri was good company in the summer dive camps. It was Petri's idea, in 1988, to turn a casual junket to the popular Mulan Wreck into a serious underwater project. Let's do something different, Petri urged his companions. Let's do an archeological survey of the site, just for fun.

The Mulan Wreck was named for an islet off the Hanko Peninsula, a twenty-mile dagger of pine-scrubbed dunes and the southernmost point of the Finnish mainland. The peninsula was the site of a decisive naval battle in the Great Northern War. In July 1714, a Russian galley fleet, one hundred strong, overwhelmed an unsuspecting Swedish force, thus tipping the balance of power in the Upper Baltic. The Battle of Hanko marked the first victory of Peter the Great's fledgling navy and launched Russia as a great power. The old wreck, discovered by sport divers in the 1970s, was thought to be a relic of this pivotal contest.

The chronically underfunded and understaffed Maritime Museum never got around to investigating the Mulan Wreck. But if Teredo Navalis club divers wanted to conduct an underwater investigation, then the museum would provide laboratory analysis of whatever they brought up. Petri's plan was to compose a photographic montage of the wreck, while documenting its dimensions and collecting artifacts. No visual images of the Mulan Wreck existed. The water depth was only twelve meters, but visibility was poor. The plan required a level of ambition and ingenuity unprecedented among Finnish sport divers. It was autumn in the archipelago, which meant working on a rough windblown surface, while building supports for cameras and lights on a throbbing cold bottom. The final results surprised all. The Mulan Wreck was not from the Great Northern War in the 1700s, but in fact from the 1600s. It was a thirty-two-foot, single-mast clinker boat, transporting war booty, likely from the sacking of a Russian trading post on Lake Ladoga. The historic artifacts included flintlock pistols and moose antler powder-horns, silver coins and kopeks from the reign of Ivan the Terrible, two large bronze church bells cast in the 1590s at an Orthodox monastery near Novgorod, and hundreds of human bones, including those of a small child. Petri's amateur archeology project proved a huge success.

Petri was the only person that Rauno trusted to know that he had solved the mystery of the *Vrouw Maria's* location. He waited for an opportunity when they were alone to tell him. It came in the sauna.

Petri ladled some cold water from a pail and splashed it across a tray of hot rocks, fired by a squat wood-burning stove. A hissing rush of steam gathered against the low spruce wood ceiling and the temperature climbed above 150 degrees Fahrenheit. Petri sat back down on a white terry cloth towel draped over a pine bench, closed his eyes and inhaled the dry heat.

"I know where she is," Rauno said from the corner on the top bench.

"Where who is?" Petri asked.

"The *Vrouw Maria.*"

Petri waited for a punch line, but none followed. His eyes fluttered open and his head swiveled sideways. Rauno was serious. "And so," Petri demanded, "What exactly do you know?"

Rauno eagerly began to recount his experiment with the maps, itemizing the list of clues, each one leading to the same spot. Petri interrupted: "Don't talk anymore. I don't want to know anything." He told Rauno to stash his notes and maps in a safe and keep quiet about the discovery.

"I don't have a safe," Rauno dismissed.

But Petri's reaction injected a sense of urgency. Rauno knew that their rivals, the Archipelago Maritime Society, were organizing another expedition to find the *Vrouw Maria* in the summer. The pair ruminated in the sauna for a long time, exchanging ideas, forgetting to soak the rocks or feed the stove. The temperature dropped to a chilly 105 degrees Fahrenheit.

Rauno knew that the discovery of Catherine the Great's lost masterpiece treasures would count as a major wreck-hunting feat. If he was indeed right about the location, then Rauno wanted to plan something appropriately big. He talked about raising the wreck and building a museum. Rauno and Petri quickly agreed that this vision would never be realized if they simply handed the wreck over to the Maritime Museum. They had sufficient firsthand experience to know that the museum bureaucracy lacked not only the aptitude, but the ambition to lead a project of such scale. Nor was the Teredo Navalis Society equipped to conduct an underwater expedition of this sort. But what could they do? They were just two guys.

"I am good at finding things, but you are good at organizing things," Rauno said. They thought through the essential elements of a search for the *Vrouw Maria*. They needed a boat, a crew, equipment, and supplies. They needed financing, a lot of it. They needed discretion, and they needed publicity. They needed to do something like what Petri had done at the Mulan Wreck, but on a grander scale. "We wanted to do it in a professional way," Rauno explained. Petri proposed that they follow a business model. They would form a private chartered association, a legal entity with an executive board, organizational structure, and stated mission. It would be a serious enterprise, an incorporated team of underwater experts. It was necessary, Petri argued, to attract sponsors. By the time they vacated the sauna, the idea of the Pro Vrouw Maria Association was formed.

Petri and Rauno singled out several Teredo Navalis members, reliable individuals, both above and below water. Did they want to become partners in a private venture to find the *Vrouw Maria*? This startling invitation prompted both incredulity and interest. The *Vrouw Maria* was the Baltic diver's dream. The appeal of being part of a historic expedition was strong. The enterprise first acquired a chief executive officer and underwater lighting technician in Timo Puomio. Fluent in the fine print of founding a not-for-profit association, Timo sped through the incorporation process in a week's time. On January 25, 1999, Pro Vrouw Maria Association was a legal entity, with a chartered mandate and bank account. It was a transparent body, Petri insisted, its books open for scrutiny. The association was not created for personal enrichment, but to organize and finance the search for the *Vrouw Maria* as well as post-discovery research and recovery operations.

Pro Vrouw Maria Association next recruited Kalle Salonen, who had worked closely with Petri on the Mulan Wreck project. An expert diver, he was also Finland's premier underwater graphic artist. After that Petri Pulkkinen signed up, an experienced diver and underwater videographer, who by profession was an advertising executive. Pulkkinen designed the Pro Vrouw Maria logo. The association enlisted the services of a media expert, Mikael Martikainen, who was not a diver, but a documentary filmmaker. In 1997, Mikael was on a television assignment on the water near Helsinki when he first met Rauno, who was conducting sonar imaging of another 18th-century wreck, the *Kronsprins Gustav Adolf*. An avid maritime history buff, Mikael spent the day with Rauno, who regaled him with tales of Baltic shipwrecks and later recruited him to film the search for the *Vrouw Maria*. Finally, the association conferred honorary status on Christian Ahlström, who served as expert historian for the expedition.

Rauno remained confident about the *Vrouw Maria's* location, but was increasingly troubled by a potential dilemma. The archipelago had swallowed up thousands of vessels. Suppose they go out to the site and find an old merchant ship, how will they know it is the *Vrouw Maria*? The expedition would have at most two weeks on the water. Even a tight search area might hold two or more wrecks. In the gloomy green depths, it was nearly impossible to take in the full perspective of a ship the size of the *Vrouw Maria*. Instead, wrecks were investigated and photographed in sections. It could take weeks or longer just to date a vessel to the correct century. In outward appearance, the *Vrouw Maria* was a nondescript Dutch trading ship. Her distinguishing feature was her cargo, but Gerrit Dou's triptych would not be sitting on the deck when they arrived, it would be hidden in the hold. He knew that the *Vrouw Maria* had lost its rudder, but a broken rudder was not unusual for a wooden wreck in the rock-laden archipelago. Much expense and effort would be squandered if they ended up exploring the wrong wreck. They needed to know more details about the *Vrouw Maria's* physical appearance.

The team dispatched Mikael Martikainen to Amsterdam to consult the municipal archive. At the main research desk, Mika inquired about the *Vrouw Maria* but was rebuffed: they hadn't the resources to track down one small trader in their vast inventory. Not easily discouraged, he continued to probe and eventually engaged a kindly, silver-haired senior archivist, Peter van Iterson, who agreed to have a look around. When Mikael returned to Amsterdam two weeks later, van Iterson smiled and said he had found a few things, then brought out a small trove of documents, including a bill of sale for the *Vrouw Maria*, dated 1766, listing Tamme Beth as owner and Reynoud Lourens as shipmaster. The receipt included the overall dimensions of the ship, major repairs to the frame, and an inventory of equipment and rigging. Mika had struck gold.

One item in particular caught Rauno's attention. The kedge anchor was missing a fluke. The kedge is a lightweight anchor, which in the age of sail was mostly used to maneuver vessels in and out of narrow harbors. Rauno remembered that there was no mention in either the captain's log or crewmen's testimony of deploying the kedge during the *Vrouw Maria's* travails in the storm. If this was true, then the kedge must still be onboard. The missing fluke would serve as the team's critical indicator to recognize Catherine the Great's lost treasure ship.

13

RESTORING A MASTER

Bourgeois Baron

The first international loan exhibition devoted to the illusionistic and refined paintings of Gerrit Dou, one of the most esteemed Dutch artists of his time, will be on view in the Dutch Cabinet Galleries in the West Building." So read the press release issued by the National Gallery of Art in Washington, DC. The special exhibition, which opened in April 2000, kicked off a yearlong international tour, which restored the forgotten fijnschilder to the upper echelon of Golden Age masters.

The rotunda-crowned National Gallery of Art is one of the art world's grand venues. Founded in 1937, the neoclassical shrine adorning America's monumented midway was the bequest of banker Andrew Mellon. The savvy Pittsburgh financier invested in steel, oil, and railroads during the late 19th century industrial boom. By World War I, only John D. Rockefeller and Henry Ford boasted bigger fortunes among the American nouveaux riches.

Attuned to appearances, Mellon looked to Europe's clinging nobility for tips on how persons of wealth and status should comport themselves. He duly acquired the accessories of peerage: a manor house with tennis courts, a stable of thoroughbred racehorses, and a collection of masterpiece paintings. It was Andrew's friend Henry Clay Frick who got him hooked on art. Frick's fortune came in from the coke ovens and steel furnaces of Western Pennsylvania and went out on artworks for his East Side New York mansion. Andrew began more cautiously, the idea of spending five thousand dollars on a picture seemed a sinful fetish. Working with Frick's connections at the Knoedler Gallery in New York, Mellon procured the occasional Barbizon landscape or Baroque portrait from Britain's waning aristocracy, whose family inheritances followed their empire into the sunset.

During the get-rich-quick 1920s, Midas Mellon served three successive presidents as treasury secretary. He displayed his paintings at his luxury penthouse on Embassy Row, along with a set of priggish rules. Modesty prevented Andrew from bidding on nude paintings, even by the great masters, and piety prevented him from hanging religious paintings in the common areas, where his guests swigged whiskey and smoked cigars. The taciturn treasurer enjoyed the attention his pictures received from his new power-broking friends. He dug deeper into his pinstriped pockets and scored bigger gilt-edged trophies. He instructed the Knoedler Gallery to keep alert for rare Old Masters. Andrew traipsed along the same social climbing path as Empress Catherine before him, and he learned that there were few finer collections of Old Masters in the world than in the tsarina's salon.

In 1930, the Knoedler Gallery telegrammed Treasurer Mellon with extraordinary news: Empress Catherine's Old Masters were for sale. After the revolution, the communists had converted the Hermitage into a state-run museum. Now, the new regime was desperate for cash and fine art was one of the few liquid assets available. Comrade Stalin thus formed a group, Antikvariat (Antiquarian), to gauge prospects on the international art market. Antikvariat was staffed with loyal party apparatchiks, rather than knowledgeable art experts. They compiled an inventory of Hermitage masterpieces, wildly guessing at market values. They then discreetly contacted the few renegade capitalists who were still doing business with the pariah communists.

The first buyer in this clandestine art auction was the suave Calouste Gulbenkian, a British citizen of Armenian origin, born in Turkey, who made millions in Russia. For a pittance, Gulbenkian procured two Rembrandts, a Reubens, a ter Borch, and a Watteau, which he quickly resold for a handsome profit. The Russians wised up. They next approached American businessman Armand Hammer, whose Russian-born grandfather was a prosperous merchant under the tsars. Armand faithfully, and profitably, served Soviet Russia's governments from Lenin to Gorbachev as a business intermediary between communism and capitalism. Antikvariat submitted a list of forty Hermitage paintings to Hammer, who offered five million dollars for the bundle. The lowball bid was rebuffed: "What do you think we are—children?" The problem for Antikvariat was that they were trying to unload artwork worth millions, at a time when the world's millionaires were short on cash. Save one.

When Andrew heard that Catherine's Old Masters were for sale, the sedate septuagenarian lunged like a starving wolf. He mobilized the Knoedler Gallery to act as dealer-agent in the year-long secret negotiations. Desperate for foreign currency, the Soviet government dangled ever more enticing pieces before the leering eyes of America's banker-in-chief: $559,000 for two Rembrandts and a Hals in April 1930; $838,000 for a Botticelli in February 1931; and, $1,166,000 for a Raphael in April 1931. When rumors arose of these extravagant purchases in the midst of a wretched depression, the publicity sensitive plutocrat used the *New York Times* to deny knowing anything about it. "If this is not the time when an American citizen would be likely to buy the most expensive painting in the world, neither is it the time when the Soviet government would be likely to sell the rarest of its national treasures," the willfully ignorant broadsheet concluded.

The treasurer plundered the tsarina. He picked up twenty-one masterpieces, at a total cost of six and a half million dollars. For 150 years, Old Masters had flowed steadily from west to east. Now the direction was reversed. Soviet Russia was cashing in the cultural treasures of its Imperial past. Mellon's haul included an assortment of Italian Renaissance and

Dutch Golden Age masters. They were choice pieces from Catherine's most infamous grabs that had upset the geo-cultural balance of early modern Europe: two Rembrandts from the king of Prussia's art dealer Gotzkowsky; a Hals and Velázquez from the British Walpole collection; Rembrandt's *Polish Nobleman* from Habsburg Count Cobenzl; and van Dyck's tender portrait of a mother and daughter from Catherine's sworn nemesis the French Duke de Choiseul. Mellon also secured five pieces from Catherine's greatest score, the Crozat sale, including Raphael's *Saint George and the Dragon*.

Nothing conveys high status more than high culture. The aging Mellon applied this personal motif to the global ambitions of the United States. To be a respected force in a Europe-dominated world required not only military muscle and economic clout, but cultural capital as well. And Old Masters remained the preferred currency of good taste for great powers. In 1936, Mellon finally went public with his private collection, when he proposed to President Franklin Roosevelt the idea of a National Gallery of Art. The bourgeois baron bequeathed 120 paintings and financed the new gallery building. The Soviet government, meanwhile, kept the great art sell-off a state secret, denouncing America's Old Masters as capitalist forgeries.

Mellon inspired his connoisseur pals to contribute to his national art project. Most notably, the gallery acquired the collection of the late Peter Widener, trolley car king of Philadelphia, which included two thousand paintings, drawings, sculptures, and fine crafts. Like Mellon, Peter Widener's collection showed off several outstanding Dutch masters: Rembrandt's landscape *The Mill*, considered by some critics as his greatest work, and, Vermeer's beautiful *Woman Holding a Balance*, which once hung next to Dou's triptych on the walls of Isaac Rooleeuw's townhouse in Amsterdam. The newly arrived American bourgeoisie admired and identified with the mystique of the merchant-led Dutch Republic—industrious, pious, and rich.

The National Gallery reflected this preference for the Golden Age when it opened in 1941. But it was not until thirty years later that the museum hired a dedicated Golden Age specialist. It would be this same curator for Northern Baroque Art, who envisioned a special exhibition to reintroduce the art-going public to Gerrit Dou.

Yankee Curator

In 1973, deep-rooted New Englander Arthur Wheelock Jr. arrived in Washington, DC. The young art scholar was the recipient of a Finley Fellowship at the National Gallery. Arthur's one-year internship turned into a lifelong appointment. He made the Northern Baroque galleries a refuge of reflection and calm amid the spouting political hot pot that was the city outside. Arthur's benevolent reign over the Golden Age in the American capital lasted for forty-five years.

Descended from original Puritan stock, Arthur traces his ancestry to the Reverend Ralph Wheelock, who moved with his family from England to Massachusetts Bay Colony during the Great Migration of the 1630s. The resolute Cambridge-educated minister opened new settlements along the River Charles, raised funds to build Harvard College, and became known as "America's first public school teacher." The preaching patriarch's interest in the learned arts endowed a distinguished progeny, which included the founder of Dartmouth College, the founder of Wheelock College, a president of UC Berkeley, scholars, poets, soldier heroes, a Mormon missionary, two professional baseball players, and one eminent art historian.

Arthur Jr. was raised in Massachusetts, twenty miles west of the settlement started by his pioneer ancestors three hundred years before. He matriculated through the hallowed halls of New England Yankeedom—Phillips Exeter Academy, Williams College, and Harvard University. Arthur was nourished by the quietness and beauty found in the fine arts. He followed this passion, but only after recognizing that he was not destined to become the third professional baseball player in the Wheelock dynasty.

Barely a year removed from his doctoral defense on Delft painting in the Golden Age, Arthur was appointed to the staff at the National Gallery and to the faculty of art history at nearby University of Maryland. While Dutch and Flemish masterpieces were among the crown jewels in the National Gallery collection, they had lost some sparkle by this time. "When I came here in 1973," Arthur said, "there were no lights above or scrim lighting. And when the sun was out, it shined on the upper reaches and the paintings were in the shadow, with gold frames, on dark walls. And they were all dirty. So it was a nice brown experience." Nor was the gallery space well suited for the intimate renderings of the Golden Age. "The Dutch galleries are quite large and the panels where paintings hang are quite large," the curator explained. "It was more appropriate for large scale paintings, but Dutch art is not really large scale." Arthur spent his early years studying and cleaning the inventory.

By the 1990s, the Golden Age collection was in good form. The gallery rooms were brightened by a new lighting system and the paintings refitted into authentic Dutch frames. Arthur developed conservation treatments to remove the obscuring varnish from the surface of the three-hundred-year-old panels. His restoration program helped revive the original color and light of the delicate images and helped resolve several attribution controversies. Arthur also figured out a way to use the gallery space more effectively. It was impossible to subdivide the big rooms because "the architecture did not allow for it." Instead, he persuaded the stewards to bust through a wall, confiscate an adjoining storage closet, and create three cabinet-style gallery rooms. "I argued that we had no place to hang our small paintings," he recalled with a waggish grin, "though I never explained to anybody that we actually had no small paintings. Except the Vermeers and the Dou, of course."

Arthur's first love was Vermeer. His main contribution to Golden Age scholarship was an extensive study of the social setting of Delft in Vermeer's time and an intensive analysis of the artistic technique employed in Vermeer's panels. In the mid-1990s, Arthur pulled off a feat that was thought impossible—a solo Vermeer show. There were only thirty-five known Vermeers in existence, some of which in galleries that either couldn't or wouldn't lend them out. "If we can just get eighteen pictures," Arthur said, "we would have enough." Patience and goodwill won out. In November 1995, the show featuring twenty-one paintings premiered at the National Gallery for a three-month engagement. Neither winter blizzard nor labor stoppage deterred the Vermeer-adoring public. The exhibition was a smashing success, setting attendance records and winning rave reviews.

Arthur wanted to follow this success with another show. He knew there was more to the Golden Age than the Big Three. Instead of another Rembrandt show, what about a tribute to Rembrandt's greatest pupil, Gerrit Dou? Now that the gallery was refashioned with cozy cabinet rooms, it was possible to stage an exhibition of smaller panels. "Dou was a major artist," Arthur said. "He was somebody that I loved and really wanted. I thought his story was fascinating, and we had a Dou that was very interesting."

The Hermit was completed toward the end of Gerrit's career. In it, the mature artist revisits the theme of a contemplative life, with his signature technical precision and fluid movement. The painting belonged to the Prince Elector Karl Albrecht of Bavaria in the 18th century. It journeyed across the Atlantic, in the early 20th century, with American industrialist William Timken, who had been abroad on an Old Masters shopping spree. *The Hermit* became the National Gallery's first Dou, in 1960, a gift from the widow Timken. "You have all this symbolism that we now see as part of Dou's world," Arthur said admiringly. "Here is the hermit, the skull, and that little basket is open at the top, it's like pushing the stone off the tomb for the Resurrection. You have a dead tree, but there is some green growing at the top growing. All this symbolism adds a dimension to the thought process that goes into these works."

Still, it was only one picture. Was a solo show even possible? There were few Dou paintings in America. Gerrit's greatest masterpieces were mostly scattered throughout proud public institutions and reclusive private collections in Europe. Three hundred and thirty-five years had passed since Gerrit Dou had starred in the art world's first one-man show in Johan de Bye's front parlor in Leiden. Now Arthur would need to summon his inner diplomat once again to rekindle the old passion for Dou in the new cabinet rooms of the National Gallery.

A Gathering of Dous

There are one hundred and thirty or so verified paintings by Gerrit Dou. Less than half the number of known Rembrandts, but four times the number of Vermeers. If Arthur could do a show for Vermeer, then certainly he could do one for Dou. But no one had organized a Dou retrospective before, or at least not in three centuries. "You know where to find some of the paintings," Arthur said, "but others you don't. You have to figure out where are these paintings? They might be in private hands in Switzerland or Spain, and you have to start making contacts." Tracking down the fijnschilder's compact creations from Los Angeles to Lichtenstein posed a serious challenge. Wheelock would need help.

Arthur enlisted the services of his former student Ronni Baer, who was now established as curator of European painting at the Museum of Fine Arts in Boston. Inspired by an internship at the National Gallery, Ronni had made Gerrit Dou the subject of her doctoral thesis. In the course of research, she managed to view almost every available Dou panel. Her knowledge of Gerrit's oeuvre was unsurpassed and indispensable for staging the show. And, like any artist, Arthur needed a generous patron. He found one in the Shell Oil Company Foundation, the charitable arm of the multinational firm, headquartered in the Netherlands. Shell Oil was persuaded that a series of Golden Age exhibitions in the Dutch cabinet rooms was good for both corporate image and national pride. Besides the Dou show, the series eventually highlighted the works of some of Gerrit's closest acquaintances: Leiden friend Jan Steen, studio colleague Jan Lievens, and former student Frans van Mieris.

The key to a successful exhibit is not only the quantity of paintings, but also their quality. "To put on a show, there are some key paintings," Arthur said, "but are their owners willing to part with them?" Several of Dou's most acclaimed works belonged to institutions that were notoriously stubborn about lending their collections. "There are always some that are easy and some that aren't," Arthur acknowledged. Incrementally, through a combination of professional courtesy and hard bargaining, the show began to take shape.

"One of the paintings that was tricky to get was *The Quack* in Rotterdam," Arthur said, "It's a great painting. But it's huge. It's a huge painting on a panel. And they also had *Lady at Her Toilet*, again on a large panel. Now here are two major paintings by one artist, coming from the same institution. So, would they agree to that?" In the end, Arthur wooed both Dous from the Boijmans Museum. "It is partly a balancing act," he described, "They may need something from us in the future, especially something that is not Dutch. But this was an instance, fortunately, where I had a very good relationship with the curator there. These personal friendships are very important." Arthur also scored three works from the Rijksmuseum, including the early masterpiece *Old Woman Reading*, painted in Rembrandt's studio, and the deceptively three-dimensional *Painter with a Pipe and Book*, a brilliant trompe l'oeil window and curtain scene. "I had a nice relationship with the Rijksmuseum and we had already done an exhibition together," he said. Once it becomes clear that a show will have an impact, then a big institution is more inclined to participate. But not every big institution.

The Dropsical Woman was a featured highlight of de Bye's one-man show in 1665, and long hailed as one of the artist's foremost works. It spent the past two hundred years in the care of the Louvre, which, as Arthur knew, was not keen on sharing. "The French have a very French view of the world," Arthur commented, "You know, if it's not in Paris it's not worth worrying about." Arthur very much wanted this piece for his show. "It was a big, big panel." But this time personal charm had no effect. "The Louvre curator was one of the most impossible people in the world. He didn't do exhibitions and he didn't lend to exhibitions. So it was not here." Likewise, the Hermitage in Russia did not want to send its Dou paintings to America. The Hermitage had an important late work by the artist, *The Herring Seller*. The piece was doubly attractive for theme and provenance: a quintessential shop-keeper's window scene that had once been lovingly admired by the French empress Josephine. But Arthur understood that the political climate influences cultural cooperation. He did find a suitable replacement. *The Grocery Shop* was not only a vintage late Dou, but came straight from the collection of British Queen Elizabeth II.

Gerrit had a reputation for painting himself, a practice he picked up from his teacher Rembrandt. Arthur would need a selection of self-portraits to give viewers a visual record of Dou's physical and social development. He was aware that his institutional rival, the Metropolitan Museum in New York, had a good self-portrait from Gerrit's later years. But Arthur was able to avoid making the awkward request, when he found a rarely seen self-portrait from the same period in private hands in Boston. Even better, this 1665 self-portrait included a plaster mask under Gerrit's right elbow—the same accessory in the same position as another self-portrait in the show, painted thirty years earlier. The 1635 Dou self-portriat came from the Cheltenham Art Gallery in England, whose curator served as personal escort to the picture on its trip across the Atlantic. Gerrit was strapped into his own £1,700 club-class seat next to his chaperone, though the eight-inch half portrait had little use for the forty inches of leg room.

Arthur entangled his curator counterparts at the Dulwich Picture Gallery in London and Mauritshuis Royal Cabinet in The Hague in his scheme to reintroduce Gerrit Dou to the general public. The exhibit would spend time in both locales after its Washington premiere. Crucially, each museum had an outstanding item to offer: *Woman Playing the Clavichord*, another gem from the de Bye show in 1665, and *The Young Mother*, the Dutch Republic's gift to England's King Charles II in 1660. As Arthur regarded the Dulwich's *Woman Playing the Clavichord*, he could not help but notice how much the painting resembled Vermeer's *Lady Seated at a Virginal*. He surmised that "the remarkable similarity may well indicate that Vermeer derived his composition from the Leiden artist."

In all, Arthur succeeded in gathering thirty-four Dous for the tribute to the Leiden fijnschilder. By April 2000, Arthur was ready. But was the public? Staging a Golden Age art show that did not feature the Big Three was a risky venture. Once more Gerrit was challenged to escape the shadow of his towering mentor.

Master Painter in the Age of Rembrandt

Rembrandt was anything but absent from Gerrit's one-man show. His attention-commanding moniker was even included in the show's title. "It's because of his personal association with Rembrandt," Arthur explained, "that people always start by making comparisons." Gerrit's apprenticeship in Rembrandt's workshop and the two painters' career trajectories were explicitly written into the show's narrative. It was almost as if Rembrandt was reaching over Gerrit's shoulder and embellishing the panel on his easel, as he had freely done in the Leiden studio. And, just as in the past, Gerrit's unique qualities would stand out on their own.

Reviews of the show embraced Dou's time-tested Cinderella story arc, from humble origin to spectacular rise to dizzying fall to resilient comeback. "In the Golden Age of magisterial Rembrandt, exuberant Hals, and uncanny Vermeer, Dou was an international art star. He was wealthier than Rembrandt and more famous than Vermeer. The smallest of his paintings cost as much as a good house," wrote the *Washington Post*. "Despite his brilliance and his influence, Dou fell from favor in the second half of the 19th century," penned the *New York Times*, "only to be restored to prominence in the second half of the 20th century." "His unhappy fate gives us a rare almost blow-by-blow account of the vagaries of artistic renown, serving as a reminder that all glory is fleeting," noted the *Wall Street Journal*. "The present show," the review continued, "represents the latest and most exalted stage in Dou's rehabilitation." Indeed, fortune had changed once again for Gerrit, as National Gallery director Rusty Powell proclaimed: "Dou has been rightfully restored."

"It was an intimate experience," Arthur described the exhibit. At the entrance, visitors were introduced to *The Quack*. The busy street scene embodied the artist's talent for ultrarealistic brushwork and moralistic story-telling: it was a perfect starting point to engage Dou's métier with portraiture and genre painting. Entering the first room, *The Painter with a Pipe* was there to greet you, reaching over the stone ledge window frame, attracting your gaze, unmatched realism on display. The paintings were arranged to highlight the combination of "the provocative and the intimate" in Gerrit's work. The exhibit concluded with the *The Young Mother*, as the "bravura demonstration of Dou's technical skill."

Inside the cloistered Dutch cabinet, visitors became immersed in Gerrit's finely rendered snapshots of daily life of Leideners in their time. The critics raved about the artist's "brilliant and meticulous style." "Most of all," mused one reviewer, "he was preternaturally gifted at reproducing the textures of things. So great is his illusionism that there is almost no trace of brushwork in his paintings." "Dou did close-up magic," marveled another, "the details in miniature—an hourglass in candlelight, a vial of elixir, a Persian rug—were so utterly convincing one could scarcely believe one's eyes." So engaging were Dou's interactive models that spectators were taken into the confidence of the painted figures. "Dou invited viewers into a privileged, intimate world through these painterly tricks-of-hand," observed one spellbound reviewer, "He also used them for erotic scenes. In *Lady at Her Toilet* a woman before a mirror is associated with pride and lust. But who is she seducing? She looks directly at the viewer, and perhaps a male admirer, through the reflection in her mirror."

It is one thing for a lost artist to be revived in the public imagination, but another to generate the broad appeal of the Big Three of Dutch Art. "The show did enormously well," said Arthur. "Not like the biggest shows. But given the subject, it was still really popular." In its three-month run at the National Gallery, Dou attracted 128,753 visitors; by comparison, Arthur's Vermeer show five years earlier brought in 327,551 patrons over the same period. As one reviewer observed: "Dou used to be a giant. He's a little master now."

In September 2000, the show moved to the Dulwich Picture Gallery in London for a three-month run, before its final leg at Mauritshuis in The Hague. Gerrit's work was not as obscure to art-goers in Europe as in the United States. Dou could be found in most every major collection in northern Europe, since his fine panels had been so coveted for so long by royals and aristocrats. And, as a result of the renewed interest in the artist, Dou and the fijnschilders had already been featured in several special shows in the Netherlands and United Kingdom.

The feel-good energy of the Washington show carried over the ocean. The European art public was eager to include Dou as one of the premier Dutch masters. "Reputation is a fickle thing," wrote the *Financial Times Europe* when the exhibit opened in London. "This beautiful and fascinating show is a perfect exercise in critical rehabilitation. In the late 1920s, the Alte Pinakothek at Munich felt it perfectly reasonable to sell off a number of its works by Dou. How dearly, one wonders, their successors at Munich would like to have those pictures back." The show's December launch in The Hague, meanwhile, inspired equally enthusiastic praise: "There is a new recognition of Gerrit Dou, the painter, who was once world famous but later fell into oblivion, and is now acclaimed as a great artist again."

Reviews of the show provided art critics a convenient opportunity to revisit the Modernist reinterpretations of the Golden Age. Not all reviewers were ready to abandon Thoré-Bürger's alpha-soul takedown of Gerrit's small panels. Writing in *The Guardian*, Laura Cumming, who is admittedly partial to Spanish court painter Velázquez, described Dou as "the incredible shrinking master." Cumming seemed put out that Gerrit was even being considered for reassessment. "Dou is no sort of Vermeer. And he doesn't have a particle of Rembrandt's genius for psychology or emotion," she jabbed. "At their best, his details can be really startling. Small pleasures, maybe, but one wouldn't wish to understate them with absurd claims that Dou could have painted a single one of the Rembrandts in the National Gallery." But this regurgitated Romantic Rembrandt trope, commonly used to disparage Dou at the turn of the 20th century, was a distinctly minority view among critics a hundred years later, in the postmodern 21st century.

It was Jan Emmens who first deconstructed the Modernist critique of Gerrit Dou. Jan's influence was clearly apparent in the wider art world's reaction to Gerrit's one-man show. As one art journal succinctly put it: "In Modernism's aftermath high finish is cool." In the British weekly *The Spectator*, John Spurling elaborated: "[Dou's] best works can be read like plays by Chekhov: plain and undramatic at first glance, but richer, stranger and more stirring the more you look." Spurling continued, "Because of the beauty of the objects, the delicious play of light and air over faces, furs, feathers, wood, stone, metals, glass, vegetables and textiles, these paintings seem less laments than celebrations of humanity, amongst its own wealth of artefacts. The finest artefact of all, of course, is the painting itself, which still, three and a half centuries later, makes that whole world seem alive to us, but was and is the artist's illusion." And Ivan Gaskell, professor of Dutch Art at Harvard University, concluded that: "The exhibition will be a revelation to all who see it, whether casual visitors or specialists, and stimulate new lines of enquiry. Dou's achievements far exceed the sum of its parts. His is an art of astonishing complexity and intellectual profundity."

If Jan Emmens was responsible for returning Gerrit Dou to discussions of Golden Age masters among art historians, then Arthur Wheelock was the person most responsible for restoring Gerrit Dou to the attention of the art-going public. But while Gerrit's reputation was back on top in the art world, his most famous work, the oak panel triptych *The Nursery* was still at the bottom of the Baltic Sea.

14

CATHERINE'S
TREASURE SHIP FOUND

Meeting at the Museum

At the entrance to Helsinki's South Harbor stands the old Pilot House. Perched atop a natural granite platform on Hylkysaari ("Wreck Island"), the tall tawny facade was long a reassuring sight for seafarers entering the deceptively tranquil, rock-laden haven. But underwater scanners eventually replaced the human navigators. The harbor pilots moved out and the Maritime Museum of Finland moved in.

The Maritime Museum was the marine archeology appendage of the National Board of Antiquities (NBA), the government's main agency for overseeing Finnish cultural heritage. The museum was specifically charged with registering, identifying, and protecting the hundreds of old shipwrecks found in Finland's coastal waters. In spring 1999, with preparations for a summer search well underway, Rauno thought the time was right for the

Pro Vrouw Maria Association to seek favor for its quest to find the legendary shipwreck. He recruited project cofounder Petri Rouhiainen and filmmaker Mikael Martikainen for a meeting at the museum.

Rauno, Petri, and Mikael boarded a ferry at Helsinki's Market Square for the short ride to the South Harbor islands and the Maritime Museum offices. The team did not need official permission to search for the *Vrouw Maria*. Only two wreck sites in Finnish waters were off limits to diving: the *Sankt Mikael*, the Dutch galliot near Borstö, and the *Sankt Nikolai*, the Russian war frigate near Kotka. Rauno requested a meeting to inform the museum of the team's intentions and to discuss areas of joint interest should they find the fabled wreck. In the cultural bureaucratic hierarchy, the museum was a low status player and after-thought recipient of budgetary funds. To supplement its meager resources, the museum relied on the volunteer services and equipment of the Teredo Navalis divers. Most members of the Pro Vrouw Maria team were regular participants in museum-sponsored excursions and had amicable relations with museum staff. So Rauno's proposal for private-public cooperation in a dive project was not in itself unusual. That Rauno would be running the operation, however, was most unusual.

Debarking the ferry, the trio crossed a narrow footbridge to Hylkysaari and entered the old Pilot House. The building was crammed with the administrative offices and research facilities of the NBA's marine archeology staff, as well as a public museum holding more than 15,000 objects, and the national maritime archive. The visitors brushed past displays of model ships, nautical instruments, and navigation charts. Inside they were met by Sallamaria Tikkanen, chief marine archeologist, and Ulla Klemelä, chief conservator. The sides were already familiar with one another.

Sallamaria was a member of the Teredo Navalis Society—the first female recruit in the male-dominated club. Unlike her self-taught guests, Sallamaria was a graduate of the University of Helsinki's inaugural program in marine archaeology. Despite its wreck-rich coastal waters, Finland lacks a major research center dedicated to maritime archaeology and underwater conservation. So, from 1994 to 1995, Sallamaria traveled to St. Andrews in Scotland, to receive postgraduate training at the well-regarded Institute for Maritime Studies. She returned home as one of Finland's few certified divers with bona fide academic credentials. Finding employment with the NBA, Sallamaria quickly rose to become its leading maritime researcher.

Though they shared a common interest, Sallamaria and Rauno were a study in contrasts. While Sallamaria was reserved and cautious by temperament, Rauno was irrepressible and adventurous. Sallamaria earned her position through formal studies in ethnology and archeology, while Rauno's status derived from military training and practical experience. And, where Sallamaria embraced the virtues of cultural and environmental protection, Rauno relished the thrill of discovery and the spoils of salvaging. Despite the museum's need for cooperation, Sallamaria was not endeared to the "boys-on-holiday" culture of the community of sport divers. Likewise, Rauno did not have much regard for the boring bureaucratic routines of the museum staff. The meeting got underway amid forced smiles and ill ease.

Rauno started, and soon was gushing about the prospects of finding the *Vrouw Maria*. He was certain that he had figured out the location of the wreck. Furthermore, the Pro Vrouw Maria Association had assembled a highly skilled team of divers and underwater technicians, the best talent of the Teredo Navalis club, to perform the preliminary work of identifying, photographing, and documenting the wreck site. The discovery of the wreck was only the beginning, Rauno asserted. This was a long-term, game-changing project, which would lead to excavating the cargo, discovering the fate of the lost masterpiece paintings, raising the wreck, and making it the showpiece of a new museum, with a film documenting the project. Pro Vrouw Maria Association expected to cooperate with the Maritime Museum to do all this.

Rauno's grandiose vision stunned Sallamaria and Ulla. They protested. Do you have any idea how much it costs to raise a wreck? Who is going to pay for all this? The museum does not have these kinds of resources.

The excitement caused by the discovery of the wreck would create new sources of revenue, Rauno countered. The Ministry of Culture, corporate donors, the European Union. In the meantime, research and recovery efforts will be subsidized by revenue generated from merchandizing. Pro Vrouw Maria Association planned to register a *Vrouw Maria* trademark and they already had designs for T-shirts, model ships, and the like, to be sold through the museum, which would share a percentage of the profits.

Rauno's scheme for the *Vrouw Maria* was both fantastic and frightening. Sallamaria and Ulla were incapable of engaging their effusive interlocutor in a serious manner. "Okay then, the boys are off to have an adventure. To find Catherine the Great's lost treasure," Sallamaria smirked.

Rauno was provoked. "Don't you understand what will happen if we find the *Vrouw Maria*? It will be the greatest thing that has ever happened to you." He went on a rousing roll: "You will get media attention. You will get the people excited. You will get international fame. You will get serious funding for a change. You will get the new museum you want. Don't you see what the *Vrouw Maria* can do? She will lift you out of your swamp."

The Maritime Museum may have been a bureaucratic weakling, but it was still a bureaucracy, covetous of its authority. The very notion of a Pro Vrouw Maria Association aroused suspicion. This was not the usual gaggle of divers waiting to be told where to jump. It was an organized corporate entity, a potential rival. Rauno touched a nerve. "I hope you do not find it," Ulla blurted out.

Rauno froze mid-rant. He and Mikael exchanged wide-eyed glances. Ulla's unexpected salvo brought the meeting to a quick conclusion. Crossing back on the ferry, the team mulled over the portents of this strange reception at the museum—so incredible, so predictable. Did the Maritime Museum's chief conservator really not want them to find the Holy Grail of Finnish shipwrecks?

Getting Organized

Finland is for boaters. Finland's 5.5 million people own over 800,000 boats, one of the highest boat-to-people ratios in the world. The Helsinki International Boat Fair, held every February, is the largest boat show in northern Europe, drawing 300 corporate vendors, 10,000 patrons, and mega media coverage. It was the ideal venue to launch the Pro Vrouw Maria Association.

Mikael produced a smart promotional film, telling the tale of the *Vrouw Maria* and her priceless Golden Age cargo, touting the underwater talents of the team, and teasing about the celebrated wreck's impending discovery. The legend of the *Vrouw Maria* was the buzz of the boat show. Finland's largest newspaper, the *Helsingin Sanomat*, picked up the story and ran a front-page feature, embracing the expedition's adventurous spirit. The debut was a success. Momentum gathered as they moved to the critical task of fundraising.

The Pro Vrouw Maria team made a list of potential deep-pocket donors—philanthropic foundations and corporate sponsors—but their proposals were met with rejections. Enthusiasm waned. Without financial backing, there would be no expedition. Even more vexing, Rauno confirmed that the Archipelago Maritime Society were preparing another go at the *Vrouw Maria*. He was now aware that during the previous summer Erkki Talvela's search had come within a mile of the location. It was plausible that this time they would find the wreck. "Who is funding those bastards?" Rauno asked. As it turned out, it was Pro Vrouw Maria insider Christian Ahlström. Despite the previous year's misadventure, the *Vrouw Maria*'s most devoted patron tapped into the Ahlström family fortune a second time to help underwrite another search. Except this time, Christian hedged his bet by splitting the investment between the two diving teams.

Rauno fumed to learn that his partner was bankrolling his rivals. Not only was Christian a member of the Pro Vrouw Maria Association, he was privy to the new information about the ship's physical appearance. Still, Rauno understood the historian's motivation and recognized his importance to their team. Rauno was careful, however, not to divulge any details about the location to his collaborator. At least the venture finally had a sponsor.

Soon after Christian's contribution was counted, a letter arrived bearing the embossed logo of Honda Marine. Rauno sighed as he knifed open the envelope, having grown accustomed to rejection. Instead, he read an unfamiliar starter: "We are pleased to inform you . . ." Pro Vrouw Maria Association had hooked a corporate backer. Honda Marine was Finland's largest retailer in outboard motors. The company liked to be associated with outdoor adventure. Rauno was a perfect match with the corporate image. Fortunes were reversed. More donations followed. The bank account grew, surpassing 100,000 Finnish markka and nudging toward 150,000. It was not as much as they had hoped for, but it was enough to get them out on the water come summer.

Pro Vrouw Maria Association was still missing one essential component of a dynamic diving team—a boat. Rauno and Petri scoured the dockyards for a suitable vessel, but were frustrated by what was available within their tight budget. Petri suggested a practical alternative. They could hire the *Teredo*, which belonged to the Teredo Navalis Society. It was an easy negotiation, since Petri sat on the club's executive board. Instead of buying a boat, they would upgrade the one they already used.

The *Teredo* was a retired fishing boat, a fifty-foot side trawler, with the wheelhouse positioned aft, the trawl winch forward, and the net gallows along the side. The diving club purchased the *Teredo* on the cheap for their summer dive junkets. For this new mission, the boat would need to be refitted. The *Teredo*'s large fish hold, where hauls of herring and cod once chilled on ice, was converted into sleeping quarters to accommodate ten crewmen. The galley and mess area were expanded and updated. In the stern, the gunwale was cut down and a platform and ladders were installed for the divers. The main deck was remodeled to accommodate the expedition's equipment: diving gear and underwater instruments, a new air compressor, and a side-scan sonar system. And in a final Finnish touch, a sauna was installed. Besides the structural renovations, the *Teredo*'s rasping engines and creaking mechanical parts required an extensive overhaul. It was a substantial work order to fill, with the dive season only a few months off. While scrounging through boatyards, Rauno found a good support vessel, the *Baltic Eye*, a thirty-five-foot ex-naval patrol boat.

The last task was to assemble a crew. Rauno and Petri drew up a list of veteran divers, who possessed the combined skill and temperament necessary for the endeavor. The wreck was in deep frigid water, so participants must be experienced dry suit divers. Ideally, each crewman should possess an additional skill; especially useful were mechanical fix-it types, savvy high-tech types, and capable navigator types. Just as important, the crew must be able to cooperate on deck and get along with one another. The expedition would operate in a professional manner, in contrast to the imbibing recreational culture of the sport diving camps. To assure that participants were serious, Petri suggested that those selected put up a modest enlistment fee of 200 Finnish markka per week. When word got out that Rauno was leading a search for the *Vrouw Maria*, the team was besieged by a raft of enthusiastic recruits.

Rauno and Petri sat at the kitchen table and systematically went through the list of wannabe crewmen, matching skills and personalities. After several hours, they winnowed the names down to sixteen volunteers, including twelve divers. The roster contained former navy captains and firefighters, people who were accustomed to command chains and working in teams.

When they were done, Petri looked distressed: "Hey, what about me? I am not missing this, what is my role?"

"You're the cook," Rauno answered.

Petri thought about it for a moment, then picked up a chef's knife from the countertop and stabbed the air menacingly. "I like it," he said. "Nobody argues with the cook."

Midsummer

Midsummer is the time of year when Finns get in touch with their inner pagan. Before the encroachment of Christianity, summer solstice was the high holiday of the northern Baltic. White night revels involved spring potato picnics, fermented beverage consumption, and naked dance parties (at least two of these rituals are still widely practiced). The solstice signaled the transition from spring sowing to summer growing, and the critical interlude for appeasing nature's fickle spirits, whose mystic powers and mischievous penchants were enhanced during the midnight sun. Large bonfires were lit on midsummer's eve to frighten off phantoms, who might otherwise spoil the harvest or burn down a barn. Young maidens, meanwhile, delicately tucked seven wild flowers, picked from seven meadows, under their pillow, in hopes of seeing their future mate revealed in a dream. Along Finland's west coast and throughout the islands, revelers erected long-limbed maypoles, decorated with spruce garlands and jangly trinkets. Looking like a boa-clad ship's mast, archipelago maypoles protected fishermen and sailors against the Baltic's spiteful water demons.

Rauno chose midsummer as the launch date for Pro Vrouw Maria's expedition. From his many years in the archipelago, he observed that the sea was uncharacteristically placid during the fortnight which followed summer solstice. Under the best circumstances, the team would have only two weeks to find and survey the wreck. He hoped to avoid the diver's banes of bad weather and rough water.

In early June, the *Teredo* returned to her familiar dock slip in Helsinki's South Harbor. The twenty-two-year-old vessel sparkled with a fresh coat of white paint on the upper deck and wheelhouse, contrasted with a coat of serene blue on the lower sides and keel. A flurry of activity enveloped the boat as boisterous crewmembers loaded supplies, tested equipment, revved up air compressors, and rolled aboard Petri's freezer full of *makkara*, the sausage staple of Finnish holiday camps. The *Teredo*'s captain would have preferred less conspicuous preparations.

Rauno was suspicious that the *Teredo* was being watched by his rivals, and feared that they might try to follow him out to the wreck site. Unless a boat had divers in the water or was towing a cable line, etiquette allowed for one craft to trail another at a safe distance on the open sea. He was wary of the possibility of an awkward confrontation in the search zone. His apprehensions were affirmed just two days before the *Teredo*'s departure. That evening a couple of the Archipelago Maritime Society crew chanced upon several of Rauno's crew at a dockside bar. After splurging for successive rounds of beers and shots, they turned the conversation to the *Teredo*'s destination. At this point, Rauno intervened. "Thanks for the drinks guys, now fuck off," he said, escorting his tipsy crew from the tavern.

On Saturday, June 26, five days following midsummer, the *Teredo* set off from Helsinki for Jurmo Island, at the southern edge of the Archipelago Sea. A throng of friends, reporters, and well-wishers lined the waterfront. Representing the Maritime Museum was chief archeologist Sallamaria Tikkanen. The Pro Vrouw Maria Association crew impressed, donning crisp uniforms of collared short-sleeve khaki shirts and pressed navy-blue shorts, with the Honda Marine logo emblazoned on their caps. The media-savvy team organized a press conference, which drew Finland's largest newspapers and state-run television network.

The press rallied behind the expedition. "Another search is underway for the ship that sank carrying precious artworks. For the past few summers, different dive groups have been searching for the wreck. But this year's team possesses newly uncovered information about the location," effused the major daily *Helsingen Sanomat*. The media showed particular interest in the *Teredo*'s high-tech system. "The crew is equipped with state-of-the-art side-scan sonar, which takes 'aerial photos' of the seabed," the newspaper said, "Similar equipment is used by the special forces of the US Navy." Rauno explained to the reporters how the search process would work: "All sightings resembling a wreck will be checked by divers. It's not like there are huge letters on the hull saying '*Vrouw Maria*.' Identifying the wreck requires expertise." The press was eager to play along. Pro Vrouw Maria's search to find Catherine the Great's lost treasure ship was the perfect feel-good story to kick off the summer holiday season.

It was a brilliant send-off, but for one inevitable moment. While posing for photos, Rauno overheard Sallamaria offhandedly remark to a reporter: "There go the boys, off to play and have an adventure." An undercurrent of mutual acrimony briefly surfaced. The normally reactive Rauno bit his lower lip, and let the comment drift away on a Baltic breeze. Sallamaria was not heard from again. The fanfare concluded by mid-afternoon, and the *Teredo* was ready to shove off. Looking through the windscreen of the raised bridge, Rauno piloted the vessel out of the harbor. Picking up speed, the Finnish flag slapped at the wind high above the main deck. The quest was underway.

From the outset, a purposeful mood prevailed. The expedition was conducted with the semblance of a military mission. Acting the part of squad leader came easily for ex-navy man Rauno. And the *Teredo*'s crew followed its skipper willingly.

Rauno set a west-southwest course, for the 130-mile voyage. The *Teredo* journeyed partly at night, but never in darkness. As the hour grew late, the midsummer sky turned an eerie smoky blue and faintish yellow overhead. The first half of the trip ran along the southern Finnish coast, punctuated by two jagged peninsulas. Twenty miles west of Helsinki is Porkkala, whose southern tip is just twenty-two miles north of Estonia. Given its strategic value, the Soviet Red Army refused to evacuate Porkkala for more than a decade following World War II. The *Teredo* next came to the Hanko peninsula, where the crew stopped to refuel and sleep for a few hours. To the south they could see the great beacon of Bengtskär, tallest lighthouse in Scandinavia. Standing at the entrance to the Gulf of Finland, Bengtskär's gasoline-fueled spotlight and twenty-two-foot foghorn warned vessels as far away as twenty miles of the deadly danger in the waters nearby. This was the *Teredo*'s destination, the Archipelago Sea.

On Monday, June 28, at 4:00 A.M., the *Teredo* arrived at the island of Jurmo. Astern, the sun was rising, after lurking just below the horizon during the night. The island was a level and sparse heathland, except for one lonely tree, bent by the wind. Local lore has it that Jurmo was once covered in pine woods, like most of the archipelago, until its inhabitants incurred the wrath of the Swedish king with their false signal fires and wreck looting. In retribution, King Gustav Vasa, in the 16th century, sent his troops to incinerate the island's dwellings, farmland, and forest. Only a couple of islanders and a single tree, it is said, survived the royal reckoning. Jurmo was eventually resettled, as an incestuously self-contained fishing village. When the *Vrouw Maria* foundered on the rocks nearby, in 1771, the island's population was at an all-time peak of sixty residents.

On Monday morning, Rauno strode upon the same eroded granite slope that Captain Reynoud Lourens had alighted on more than two centuries before. Just beyond, the island moor was a knee-high palette of heather, juniper, and crowberry. On a bluff overlooking the leeside jetty, a freshly decorated forty-foot midsummer maypole jingled in the breeze. The island seemed frozen in time. In reality, Jurmo was much changed from the time of the *Vrouw Maria*. The onset of large-scale commercial trawling in the 1970s hastened the demise of the archipelago's quaint fishing villages. The signature red cabins were either abandoned or turned over to tourists. Jurmo survived, but barely, with a dozen full-time residents, eking out a living from subsistence fishing and farming.

The crew had a leisurely late start on the first morning, with coffee, black bread, and sausage, the same thing they would eat for every meal for the rest of the week. Mid-afternoon, Rauno called a team meeting on the main deck. In dress uniform, the crew made a semicircle in front of the wheelhouse. Rauno read off a list of rules for the expedition: no smoking anywhere onboard, as the boat carried 500 gallons of gas; no drinking beer during the day, and no getting crocked at night; uniforms must be worn at all times while on duty or whenever the press is aboard; no mobile phones around the side-scan equipment, when in use; and, whatever else you do, no stepping on the side-scan sonar cable, as it is very sensitive and costs 5,000 euros. Rauno then spoke of the rare opportunity the team had to make history. Based on his calculations, they had a 90 percent chance to find the

Vrouw Maria in the first two days. Otherwise, he cautioned, they had a 10 percent chance at best thereafter.

With clipboard in hand, Rauno barked out the roster and assigned tasks. The captain went up to the bridge, as the crew assumed their roles. Belching a dusky trail of exhaust fumes on the breeze, the *Teredo* chugged out past the harbor's manmade breakers. Even now, only Rauno and Petri knew their destination. Rauno pushed on the throttle and the converted trawler thrashed forward at fifteen knots toward the open water of the outer archipelago. Jurmo's midsummer maypole dwindled in the west above the frothy wake. A half hour later, the *Teredo* was idling over a shipwreck.

Treasure Ship Found

Rauno scanned the horizon for approaching vessels. Waves lapped against the hull. The *Teredo* was alone. A black inflatable was unhooked from a side davit and lowered to the water. John Liljelund and Kenka Lindström loaded scuba gear. To keep the team occupied, Rauno dropped the divers over the same sunken ship that the Archipelago Maritime Society had found the year before, now referred to as the *Donald Duck* wreck. At thirty meters down, it was a good spot to test the equipment and acclimate to the chilling depths. The water temperature was in the upper-50s Fahrenheit on the surface, but dropped to the mid-30s on the seafloor. Mikael opted to join the divers in the black inflatable with his video camera. It was only a practice dive, but the *Donald Duck* exploration was likely to be more interesting than trawling the open sea in a grid pattern.

Rauno steered the *Teredo* a mile southward into the search zone. Still wary of being followed, he swept the horizon again with binoculars for other ships. In the gulf to the south, he spied a twelve-story passenger ferry bound for Stockholm. Rauno checked his coordinates and eased into an idling position. He ordered the crew to ready the side-scan sonar.

The side-scanner was contained in a sleek yellow torpedo case, called the towfish, and ran freely in the water behind the boat, connected to a long cable line. It was crucial that the boat driver, sonar reader, and towfish operator coordinate their movements. The boat had to maintain a steady pace, not too slow, not too fast. The sonar technician had to identify vaguely shaped subaquatic objects, while anticipating potential hazards, especially rocks, which might appear suddenly on the screen. The side-scanner was sophisticated, expensive, and unlikely to survive an underwater wallop. It was the responsibility of the cable operator to maintain the proper depth for the desired scan range. Rauno preferred that the crew work the towfish by hand, instead of with a reel and crank, but it took practice to develop a feel for it.

It was now late afternoon, though the team still had six hours of daylight. On board, first mate Antero Kuhalampi took over the ship's wheel. Stationed at the sonar screen, Rauno fiddled with the calibrations on the instrument panel. Meanwhile, crewmen Arto Parkkanen and Tommi Lipponen rehearsed with the cable line. The primary search zone was a compact area of deep water, sheltered behind a barricade of submerged rocks. Rauno signaled to Antero to begin the first test run, and Arto lowered the towfish into the sea at a depth of twenty-five meters.

Rauno adjusted the emission frequency and an image of the seafloor fanned out on the screen. Suddenly, a massive object appeared, Rauno gauged its depth: "Pull up!" Tommi and Arto lifted the towfish in a rapid hand-over-hand motion, the cable line tangling at their feet. Rauno watched the screen and braced, as the side-scanner passed a few feet above a huge underwater boulder. Rauno exhaled a slow whistling breath. The search was almost over before it began.

Arto rearranged the cable line and lowered the towfish back down, this time to twenty meters. Rauno waved to the wheelhouse, and the *Teredo* moved forward. In a few minutes they were all in sync. Rauno studied a furrowed image of the seafloor slowly moving across the screen. Again, the sonar detected a dense mass, Rauno checked the depth reading: it was safely on the bottom, forty meters down. "Steady ahead," he called to Antero, and then, *thwack!* The towfish struck something solid. The screen became a scrambled mess. Another rock. "From where?" Rauno objected.

He manipulated the controls, and an image of the seafloor returned on the screen. The side-scanner was still working. Rauno stared at the readout. "I am not sure what that was, guys," he said, "but it was not a rock." Resetting the towfish at fifteen meters, the boat cautiously tracked over the unidentified object again, and then again. A sonar image began to take shape. It was a shipwreck. The side-scanner had struck her protruding mast.

Rauno tried to gauge the dimensions and shape. It was big enough to be the *Vrouw Maria*. And the muted lines on the screen indicated that it was wooden, not metal. Rauno studied the abstract sketch, and could readily envision an old sailing ship. He then double-checked the coordinates of the *Teredo*'s location. They were right in the middle of the primary search zone. Rauno bit down on a knuckle, consciously suppressing emotion. They needed to do another pass, he said, and lower the depth of the side-scanner. The crew could sense what Rauno was not saying.

The *Teredo* conducted several more tracking runs, producing a more resolute image of the mysterious sunken object. There was no doubt. It was a twin-mast wooden ship, in one piece, sitting upright on the seafloor at forty-one meters deep, with physical dimensions similar to the *Vrouw Maria*'s. That evening, Rauno displayed the side-scan images for all to see on the mess table. A collective whoop went up. Petri abandoned a skillet of sizzling sausages in the galley and walked back to where the crew was huddled over the readouts. He leaned into the scrum and scrutinized the unmistakable contours of a sunken ship, then turning to Rauno said: "Well, it took you all afternoon to find it."

The crew was in high spirits, but Rauno did not allow any celebrating that night. There was much work to perform the next day. And, until the divers went down to investigate, they still did not know if it was the right ship. Rauno instructed John Liljelund and Kenka Lindström that they would be the first dive tandem to explore the wreck.

Next morning the *Teredo* was back on the water over the wreck site. The sea was dead calm, shimmering bronze in the morning light. The dive conditions were ideal. John and Kenka purposefully put on their dry suits, body weights, and air tanks. The first task was to attach a buoy line to the vessel, marking the site on the surface for the *Teredo*'s crew and implanting a direct artery to the wreck for the other divers. It was a simple task, provided that they could see. John and Kenka plunged into the cold.

John Liljelund was a few feet ahead on the descent. After just two minutes his depth gauge read forty meters. He promptly halted his descent and kicked his feet out behind him, so he was parallel to the sea floor. The divers had to take care not to overshoot and touch bottom, kicking up clouds of silt and spoiling the mission. John swung his flashlight around in a half circle, but saw only blackness before him. He pivoted backward. There against the dimly greenish glow from the sunlight above was the looming silhouette of a large ship. He felt a chill from the silent specter. A hand reached out of the darkness, and touched his shoulder. It was Kenka. The divers fixed a cable line to the hull on the starboard side near the stern. After ten minutes, they began the deliberately halting ascent back to the surface.

The next pair of divers, Petri Pulkkinen and Timo Puomio, waited nervously for their turn. With Petri working the camera and Timo on lights, their task was to take the first video of the slumbering hulk. Petri led the way down, following the buoy line until the ship appeared before him. He froze in place. It was fantastic. He later told reporters: "As I went down for the first time, the view was simply amazing. The visibility was ten meters and the sunlight was filtering through the calm surface of the sea. The ship lay there intact and beautiful like a treasure ship straight from the fairy tales."

Timo moved past Petri toward the stern. He signaled to Petri to follow, and aimed his powerful flashlight—there was no rudder. They moved together around the aft end, recording the taffrail and damaged sternpost. Petri was exhilarated; he started to swim forward to circle the entire wreck, but Timo pointed at his watch and gestured upward, their ten minutes had expired.

The divers worked in groups of two and four, methodically moving around the hull. They measured the ship, examined the wooden frame, and noted bottles, dishware, and debris strewn around the main deck. The hatch to the cargo bay was open and crammed with crates. The evidence accumulated: it was the size of the *Vrouw Maria*, a merchant vessel, at least one hundred and fifty years old, and with a lost rudder.

The divers finally made their way to the bow, a wide blunt prow, typical of an 18th century trader. A forty-foot bowsprit projected from the frame into the deep sea's gloom. Swimming under the bowsprit to portside, John Liljelund pointed his light above and noticed the kedge anchor still dangling from the bow. With a dolphin kick, he propelled upward for closer inspection: the kedge was broken, it was missing a fluke.

Rauno gathered Petri and Mikael for an impromptu meeting below deck. They systematically compared the divers' observations and video footage with their research notes. The dismembered kedge was the *Vrouw Maria*'s unique identifying mark. Rauno tried to remain composed and focused on the survey work. He was reluctant to make the final call that this was the lost treasure ship of Catherine the Great.

That evening, Rauno went up to the *Teredo*'s bridge and telephoned Christian Ahlström, who was relaxing at his summer cottage on the Kirkkonummi moor, overlooking the gulf. In a calm voice, Rauno spoke: "I think we found it."

Ahlström's reliable veneer of upper-class reserve shattered on the spot. The diminutive doyen dropped the phone and danced wildly around the room. "I will join you as soon as possible," he gushed. The next day, Christian, in floppy sun hat, pranced down the main dock at Jurmo, where he joined the *Teredo*'s crew. "I still have no idea how he got there so quickly," Rauno said. Christian squinted at the sonar image of the wreck, and listened to Rauno's recitation of the evidence. Rauno concluded his presentation: "It might be the *Vrouw Maria*."

"Might be?" retorted Ahlström. "It might be that you have all lost your minds! Of course, it is the *Vrouw Maria*."

Rauno laughed, "Okay guys, if Christian says it is so, then it is so. We have found the *Vrouw Maria*."

Three Parties

"On the small island of Jurmo, people are still recovering from the celebration on Tuesday. After discovering the treasure ship the *Vrouw Maria*, the twelve divers were in high spirits," an obliging press reported to a Finnish nation eager for more details of the breaking story.

The *Teredo*'s divers were the first persons to look upon and touch the sturdy oak frame of the *Vrouw Maria* in more than two and a quarter centuries. After Ahlström's confirmation, Rauno finally relaxed, trying to absorb the immensity of the discovery. Somewhere inside the wreck were Catherine's masterpiece paintings, including Gerrit Dou's triptych. Could they possibly have survived?

That night the *Teredo* crew celebrated with champagne, vodka, beer, and sausages. Christian Ahlström had been consumed with finding the *Vrouw Maria* for more than twenty-five years. He described the moment as "the happiest day of my life," and he assured the crew that "the whole world is going to be crazy over this ship."

Rauno recalled only that "after Christian said it was the *Vrouw Maria*, we got drunk." The merrymaking on the *Teredo*'s deck continued for two more nights, serenading the island's staid residents until the wee hours. On Friday, Petri was working on the dock when a solemn-faced fisherman approached: "I understand that if you find a wreck, then you have a party. But you have found only one wreck, and you have had *three* parties."

Rauno, Petri, and Mikael discussed how to deal with the press. On Wednesday, the team revealed its secret. Within hours, the headline blared in the *Helsingen Sanomat*: "Wreck of Treasure Ship *Vrouw Maria* Discovered." By chance, the Finnish Broadcasting Corporation had a television crew nearby, filming a nature documentary. That evening, the story broke on Finland's most watched television news broadcast. A media storm hit Jurmo. For the next several days, the sedate island was abuzz with the chopping whir of helicopters, ferrying journalists to interrogate the crew and photograph the *Teredo*. On Thursday, the *Vrouw Maria* was the lead story in *Ilta Sanomat*, the popular evening tabloid and Finland's second largest newspaper. On June 30, the Associated Press picked up the story, which quickly spread to hundreds of media outlets around the world. The *Vrouw Maria* was an international sensation.

The incessant messages of congratulations and interview requests forced Rauno to make a new rule—shut off all mobile phones during work hours. The skipper, however, was not very good about following his own rule. "I've had to recharge my new phone up to three times a day," Rauno joked. He even received a call from Russia, though he did not understand the name. In a foreshadowing of events to come, the caller inquired when the raising of the ship would take place. Rauno replied that his team would only photograph the wreck, which now belonged to the Finnish government. "Says who?" came the mysterious reply.

It was not just the media that was interested in the *Vrouw Maria*. The Finnish Coast Guard began tracking the *Teredo*'s movements with a Super

Puma helicopter. Rauno was on friendly terms with the Coast Guard pilots, so when pressed, he reluctantly divulged the coordinates of the wreck site. Meanwhile, random boaters and sport divers converged on Jurmo. The crew stopped taking the *Teredo* out to sea, because she was too easy to spot on the water. Instead, the divers commuted to and from the wreck in the speedy, low-lying black inflatable. They used a green plastic bottle as a discreet buoy marker, to maintain the secrecy of the site.

News of the discovery gutted the plans of the Archipelago Maritime Society, which at that moment was making final preparations for their own search expedition. Refusing to accept total defeat, team leader Erkki Talvela tried to go around Rauno to finagle access to the wreck site. Two days after the discovery went public, Erkki phoned Rauno with chummy congratulations, then dropped a hammer on him. He said that the Maritime Museum had given permission to the Archipelago Maritime Society to dive on the *Vrouw Maria*, and that his boat would soon join the *Teredo* on the water. "No, we are too busy. You can't come," Rauno blustered. "I'll revoke your permission. If it is up to me, no one dives here except our crew." Erkki persisted, "I have done so much work, why can't I see it too?" Rauno ferociously guarded his prize. He contacted museum officials and reasserted his team's proprietary claim over the project. The museum conceded; Rauno was appeased. Erkki eventually satisfied his desire, when he participated in a later museum-sponsored dive trip on the legendary wreck. Still the wound from his confrontation with Rauno never healed. "He knew about all the work we had done," Erkki said. "In some ways Rauno can be a very small person."

It was true, however, that Rauno's team was busy. He was forced to create a buffer against the barrage of attention, so that the divers could continue to work. They had little more than a week to complete a preliminary archeological survey of the ship and wreck site. Meanwhile, in the second week, intemperate winds blew up from the southwest, threatening to cancel the scheduled dives. Also, during the second week, the *Teredo* lost its cook, as Petri had to give up his post over the frying pan and return to his office desk. Within hours of Petri's departure, Rauno approached one of the island fishermen and proposed a trade—a freezer full of sausage for a small portion of the catch of the day. The *Teredo*'s crew was most grateful when the swap was accepted.

Discovering the wreck turned out to be easy, while the work at hand was considerable. The depth of the *Vrouw Maria* meant that the divers had limited time underwater. A standard dive was thirty minutes in total, including a five-minute descent to the seafloor and a much slower fifteen-minute ascent back to the surface. The divers had to take care, rising from the seafloor in sequenced stop-and-start stages, acclimating to the changing pressure levels. The amount of time left was only about ten minutes. Working at this depth was physically demanding and required long rest periods in between dives. Water pressure is considerably stronger than air pressure; already at ten meters deep the level of ambient water pressure on the body is twice greater than at the surface. At forty meters, the *Vrouw Maria* lay at the outer limit for amateur divers, where the ambient pressure on the body was five times greater than at the surface. Individuals performed two or, at most, three dives per day, with required days off in between, to reduce the risk of nitrogen narcosis.

The divers were assigned only one manageable task per dive. Whenever a team resurfaced, the designated interviewer, Tommi Lipponenn, debriefed them for details of the wreck, while memories were still fresh. Later, in the evening, Mikael set up a monitor and the crew crowded around to gawk at the newest video images of the phantom wreck. "It was spectacular," Mikael said. The divers provided running commentary about what they had seen. Because of the darkness, it was impossible to capture a sweeping overview of the ship, rather the wreck scene had to be reconstructed like a jigsaw puzzle. Following each dive, the expedition's illustrator, Kalle Salonen, was able to fill in more of the details of the wreck's physical appearance. Section by section, a full portrait of the *Vrouw Maria* emerged on the pages of Kalle's sketchbook.

The vessel was eighty-five feet long and twenty-three feet at its widest point across the deck. The sturdy oak hull was well preserved in the chilled water. On the main deck, a strong-looking oak barrel windlass sat in the bow. Still upright, two broken pine masts stood in the fore and mid-ship areas, fifty feet and forty-five feet high. But the upper sections, the topmasts and gallant masts, were toppled over and lay across the deck. In the rear, a raised deck and captain's cabin were destroyed by a fallen topmast, probably from the jolt the ship took when it crashed on the bottom. It was a handsome ship, with decorative carvings along the rail. The wreck sat upright on the seabed, with a slight starboard tilt. With a few repairs, it was probably still seaworthy.

The *Vrouw Maria*'s great prize remained elusive. There was no sign of Empress Catherine's priceless masterpiece paintings. Two cargo hatches on the main deck were found open, just as Lourens's crew had left them the last night the ship was afloat. The cargo hatch at mid-ship was crammed with crates and barrels. On top of the heap was a broken box containing dozens of disc-like objects, which turned out to be eyeglass lenses, an 18th-century Dutch specialty. A second upturned crate spilled across the pile hundreds of long-stemmed clay pipes, a relic of the tobacco craze then igniting the Russian court. But the divers could not get in deeper without disturbing the precariously stacked cargo and risking entrapment inside.

In the second week, Maija Fast-Mattika of the Maritime Museum arrived on Jurmo. She was the only NBA employee to visit the expedition, but she was not an official representative. Rather, Maija just happened to be in the neighborhood, leading a tour of Australian marine archeologists. The Aussies heard the news of the discovery, and wanted to see the *Vrouw Maria* first hand. The Coast Guard transported Maija and company via helicopter to the island.

As it turned out, the Aussie archeologists were neither experienced with the depth nor familiar with dry suit diving. Wishing to accommodate the museum, Rauno ordered John Liljelund and Petri Pulkkinen to take the visitors to a nearby islet, and practice with the team's diving equipment at ten meters down. The Australians could not get the knack of it, and Rauno was forced to reject their request. Maija protested, but Rauno explained that "playing around in ten meters is totally different than diving to forty meters. Someone could get killed." There was goodwill, nonetheless, during Maija's brief visit. She expressed excitement and support for Pro Vrouw Maria Association's historic discovery. Significantly, she also gave approval to bring up a small sample of artifacts from the wreck.

The divers lifted six items. First was a ceramic bottle, lying on the main deck near the main mast. The bottle was still unopened, with a seal indicating that it was mineral water from Triers. Second was a corroded metal ingot. Rauno hoped it might be part of Dutch merchant Hovy's cache of silver. The divers next recovered an engraved medallion, later determined to be a packing seal from a crate of fine linen produced in Gerrit Dou's hometown of Leiden. Finally, the divers brought up three long-stemmed clay pipes, manufactured in Gouda, Holland. At the time, raising the artifacts seemed the obvious thing to do. However, this ad-libbed authorization of a wee excavation would become a major controversy in the legal battle still to come.

The *Vrouw Maria* was a Baltic legend. For 228 years her broken body lay at rest, cloistered in the cold dark depths of the Archipelago Sea. No longer. The fabled wreck had come back to the living, ready at last to give up her secret cargo. For those who would soon take possession of her, it was a terrifying responsibility.

By the third day, there were no longer any doubts that this was the *Vrouw Maria*. The Maritime Museum needed to be informed. Despite the cool reception Rauno received on Hylkysaari, there was never a question that the underwater work of Pro Vrouw Maria Association was being conducted for the benefit of the museum. That evening, Petri called the museum staff and left them a message: "Your Nightmare on Elm Street, we have found it."

PART THREE

15

FINDERS KEEPERS

On Holiday

A ghostly shipwreck, a lost masterpiece painting, a lustful tsarina, the news of the *Vrouw Maria's* discovery stirred imaginations in the summer of 1999. In all quarters, that is, except one: the National Board of Antiquities (NBA), bureaucratic overlord of the Maritime Museum. Despite Finland's long coastline and wreck-filled waters, the NBA had never been enthusiastic about marine archeology. And now Finland's cultural guardians were forced to deal with the Baltic Sea's most sensational underwater archeological find since the *Vasa*.

The *Vrouw Maria* made global headlines for one reason, Empress Catherine's stash of Dutch Old Masters, including the most valuable work of art produced during the Golden Age, Gerrit Dou's triptych, *The Nursery*. The Pro Vrouw Maria Association was committed not only to locating the shipwreck, but also to salvaging her high culture artifacts. The divers explored around the main deck and captain's cabin, aimed powerful spotlights inside through the hatches, and photographed the cargo hold. "We have seen the cargo through the bay doors, it seems intact, it hasn't moved about," Rauno told the Associated Press. "We saw barrels and boxes, but nowhere did we see the great art treasure of Catherine the Great. We hope that it is salvaged soon and we hope to participate when it happens."

The media bombardment that accompanied the discovery sent convulsive shocks through Finland's cultural bureaucracy. The NBA was quick to assert ownership of the wreck, but made scant mention of its incomparable contents. "The wreck legally belongs to the National Board of Antiquities," the press was informed. However, NBA director Professor Henrik Lilius made clear: "This thing is of such magnitude that it is not even worth discussing yet. We need to research the matter slowly and see what is going to happen." The director's initial appeal for restraint stood in contrast to Rauno's unbridled enthusiasm, offering a glimpse of the coming conflict between those who claimed the wreck and those who found the wreck.

On Friday, July 9, Pro Vrouw Maria Association concluded its operations in the outer archipelago and began a triumphant return voyage to Helsinki. "We were quite happy with our accomplishment," the skipper said. "We achieved what many had dreamed about for so long." Hopes were high that the media attention would lead to more sponsorships. As the *Teredo* plodded eastward with Finland's rocky coastline to port, the crew buzzed about what was next and Rauno shared his vision of "the greatest shipwreck museum the world has ever seen."

Two days later the *Teredo* was back in South Harbor. The first order of business was with the Maritime Museum. In two weeks on the water, the team conducted 120 dives on the wreck. They observed, poked, prodded, measured, photographed, and filmed the sleeping giant. Because of the darkened depths, the ship could only be studied and photographed in tight illuminated sections. These individual snapshots were pieced together to create a comprehensive picture of the whole wreck. The team compiled its findings in a thick binder, with Petri Pulkkinen's video footage and Kalle Salonen's spot-on illustrations. On July 11, Rauno delivered the research file and salvaged artifacts to the museum's conservation laboratory.

The *Teredo* captain was greeted by the museum's chief conservator. The last time the two had met, Ulla Klemelä stunned Rauno by saying she hoped the expedition would fail. Her mood had not changed. Ulla groused about having to work on Sunday. Rauno replied with a sheepish grin. She offered him a coffee. And then she filled out an NBA shipwreck report form—Reporter: Rauno Koivusaari; Report no: 15/306/1999. Rauno held up the team's research folder and began expounding on its contents, but Ulla was not listening. She was rifling through desk drawers, looking for an NBA shipwreck notification form. The *Vrouw Maria* was entered into the registry—Shipwreck: no. SMM 25/22. Next, Rauno handed over the container of artifacts. "This is not the way we do it," Ulla barked, objecting to the packing of the clay pipes. The startled wreck-hunter countered that this was the method of storing artifacts that he, and others, had always used, always with the approval of the museum. The conservator's officious pose was unwavering. Ulla rummaged through the box of artifacts, as she completed an NBA artifacts registration form—Underwater Relics: no. 1658. She pushed the paper at Koivusaari to sign, and the museum took possession of the salvaged items. The meeting was over. Rauno had not finished his coffee.

Rauno had expected a more welcoming reception. Pro Vrouw Maria Association had just pulled off the most spectacular feat of underwater discovery in Finnish maritime history. But instead of congratulations, the museum managed only a perfunctory handoff and a scolding. "It was the first slap in the face," he later observed.

Until now, Rauno assumed that the snide comments made by certain museum staffers came from jealous teasing. Once the wreck was found, he believed, a shared interest in Finnish maritime history would prevail and the museum would embrace his endeavors. He now revised this opinion. The disdain he felt directed toward him and his project was not personal, but bureaucratic. The museum did not view Pro Vrouw Maria Association as a partner, but as a rival. An unwelcome and unworthy rival.

As Ulla organized the forms in a neat stack, Rauno did a slow burn. He suppressed an impulse to seize back the research folder. He was aware, however, that in the pile of materials, there was no mention of the geo-coordinates of the *Vrouw Maria's* location. That information was contained in a separate notebook inside the field bag dangling from his shoulder. On the spot, Rauno decided to withhold the notebook. Anyway, it was not a secret anymore. The Coast Guard knew, so the museum also would find out soon enough.

On Tuesday, July 13, Mikael drove into Helsinki to the National Board of Patents to register the trademark name "Vrouw Maria" for the Pro Vrouw Maria Association. To Mika's astonishment, the clerk refused the application. The name was already taken, only yesterday in fact, said the registrar.

The "Vrouw Maria" trademark name was claimed by Matti Haajasalmi, director of the Society for Support of the Maritime Museum. Matti had heard of Rauno's plan to generate revenue through merchandizing, and apparently agreed that the wreck had commercial potential. When the discovery hit the press, Haajasalmi rushed back to Helsinki ahead of the *Teredo*, and early Monday morning went into the patent office. The Society was a quasi-independent organization, created to raise money through institutional grants and individual donations. It worked on behalf of the museum, but beyond its direct control. The Society operated on private incentive. A percentage of the funds raised for the museum were skimmed off as profit. Having seized the legal rights to the commercial use of the "Vrouw Maria" name, Haajasalmi left town for summer holiday.

The revelation hit hard. The team was incredulous that their idea, shared with the museum in good faith, had been nicked. "I never dreamed anyone could do such a rotten thing," said John Liljelund, the diver who first set eyes on the *Vrouw Maria*. On July 15, 1999, the team sent a formal letter to the Society: "The Pro Vrouw Maria Association is a nonprofit organization founded in order to search for the wreck of the *Vrouw Maria* in the Archipelago Sea, and after its discovery to assist the proper conservation and display of both the wreck and its cargo." The letter ended with a polite request to withdraw their claim on the trademark. The correspondence went unanswered.

"They are wrong if they think they will get away with this," Rauno spat. In the interest of diplomacy, it was decided that the good-humored Petri should call the principals to discuss the matter. But Petri's telephone messages were also ignored. Without anyone to talk to, Pro Vrouw Maria's burly cofounder became increasingly undiplomatic: "Please remove your trademark application before things start to go in the wrong direction. The behavior of the Society is wrong. Before this situation gets really bad, please remove your application. If you do not do it, then a storm will follow."

When Petri finally got hold of a museum staff assistant, she politely said there was nothing to be done since all responsible personnel were "on holiday."

Only a day after this latest snub, Petri at last received a response. The museum was calling to complain that in all the research materials submitted by Pro Vrouw Maria Association, it neglected to give the geo-coordinates of the shipwreck. Please tell us, where is the *Vrouw Maria*?

Petri rang back with a curt message: "Sorry, on holiday."

No Diving Allowed

"If it is, in fact, the *Vrouw Maria*, it is extremely valuable," said museum senior curator Marja Pelanne, "a sensational find on an international scale. We are not aware of any other wrecks that can measure up to this one. However, we had no chance to prepare for the discovery."

It was true that the Maritime Museum was caught unprepared for the *Vrouw Maria*, but it was not true that the discovery should have come as a surprise. Back in May, the museum was forewarned that the wreck would likely be found. Rather than heed the message, museum staffers scoffed at the messengers. Now they scrambled for cover from the media storm. Moved by involuntary bureaucratic reflex, the museum sent urgent appeals for help up the command chain to NBA bosses.

To get the NBA to pay attention to Finland's underwater cultural heritage, however, required the rare concurrence of a media-ringing event and a sympathetic director. One without the other was not enough to disrupt the status quo. The discovery of the *Sankt Mikael* during the tenure of Nils Cleve was one such coincidence, eventually leading to the creation of a dedicated Section for Marine Archeology and Maritime Museum. But while Catherine the Great's lost treasure ship was a more sensational news bonanza than the *Sankt Mikael*, Professor Henrik Lilius proved less supportive than Nils Cleve.

In summer 1999, three issues demanded immediate attention. The first was to safeguard the wreck site. "There are insanely valuable things down there," said Magnus Fabian Wenzel Hagelstam, art expert and owner of Finland's oldest auction house. "The tsar's court would acquire only the best of the best. The value of the cargo is almost impossible to estimate, we're talking tens of millions." The Maritime Museum was entrusted with protecting the hundreds of registered shipwrecks in Finnish coastal waters. The power existed more on paper than in practice. The gap between official mandate and operational capability was as wide as the Gulf of Finland. The Maritime Museum was chronically understaffed and underfunded. The maritime archeology staff was no more than a dozen employees, without a boat to call their own. By the museum's own reckoning, the looting of shipwrecks was rampant.

The museum implored the coast guard and navy to protect the wreck site. The coast guard was noncommittal: "Our mission is to guard the Finnish border. We can keep an eye on the wreck but we are not able to protect it." Rauno warned that while sport divers want "to sneak a peek and sometimes pick up a souvenir," the more serious threat was "international gangs of wreck looters." The navy's chief of staff, Heikki Salmela, agreed, adding that criminal syndicates were already known to deploy mini-submarines to pilfer artifacts from Baltic shipwrecks. Without naming the Russian mafia in particular, Salmela fretted about high-tech thieves slipping past the military's subaquatic listening posts. "We should knock on wood," said curator Marja Pelanne, "the wreck will be at the mercy of looters for an entire year."

Cooperative agreements were eventually reached with the coast guard, to check traffic on the surface, and with the navy, to install monitors below the surface. As it happened, the *Vrouw Maria* slumbered within the Archipelago National Park, in the bailiwick of the powerful Environment Ministry, causing further intragovernmental wrangling. Finally, in May 2000, the celebrity wreck was formally designated a "First Class Archeological Site." The protected zone comprised a circular area, 1,500 meters in diameter, where anchoring and diving were strictly forbidden. Only preapproved research vessels were allowed to linger in the zone, and specially-licensed divers were allowed to descend on the wreck. The authority to grant these licenses was entrusted to the Maritime Museum.

A second issue was resources. Culture Minister Suvi Lindén promised to hire at least one additional marine archeologist and to boost the museum's measly research budget. Lindén appealed to the Finance Ministry for an extra 1.5 million Finnish marks, but the request was rejected. "We tried to get the *Vrouw Maria* into the budget," said Lindén, "but we were unsuccessful." Instead, NBA director Lilius scraped together 50,000 Finnish marks for the *Vrouw Maria*. Lindén then proposed a special wreck fund, in which the Culture Ministry would allocate money directly to the project, bypassing NBA bureaucrats, and to which private corporations could make donations by becoming official sponsors. But Professor Lilius opposed this idea. "Let's first look at what kind of money is needed," said the ever-cautious director. "It is difficult for the Agency to negotiate seriously before it knows what it can offer to companies in return." The NBA prevailed, and no special fund was created.

The final and most contentious issue was making a wreck plan. In the summer of 1999, the Finnish press teased the public with giddy reports about raising the *Vrouw Maria*. The director of the Vasa Museum in Stockholm, wealthy benefactors in Finland, and experts in archeology and art were all consulted about the possibilities. Speculation focused on the masterpiece paintings. "Such a treasure ship is a fantastic thought, imagine what you could find in there," marveled a potential corporate sponsor. "We know for sure that this exact ship was loaded with case after case of art treasures," a historian testified. "If a work of Rembrandt is found on the ship, it will cause a worldwide sensation," salivated an art authority. "The condition of the cargo remains unknown. While porcelain and precious metals can withstand the effects of salt water quite well, the state of the paintings depends on several factors, such as the materials and paints used," came another opinion. Could Dou's Golden Age masterpiece be saved?

Culture Minister Lindén suggested the formation of a Wreck Study Group, composed of representatives of the Maritime Museum and Pro Vrouw Maria Association. For Rauno, the next step was obvious: reveal to the world the fate of the *Vrouw Maria*'s tantalizing cargo. He suggested lifting the ship off the seafloor with a harness and towing it to a customized underwater cradle in the shallows of South Harbor, where salvaging could commence. This was similar to what had been done with Sweden's *Vasa* and England's *Mary Rose*. But the notion of a cooperative public-private initiative was beyond the museum's comfort zone. The Wreck Study Group never convened. Rauno's team was never invited to join the museum's planning discussions.

Filmmaker Mikael Martikainen explained that the museum "stepped into big shoes all at once. And with all that international attention and significance, they were afraid to make mistakes. Maybe that is why they didn't consult us. They would do it by themselves, by the book."

On the government side, disagreement arose over what to do next. Suvi Lindén brought in NBA archeologist and museum administrator Pekka Honkanen as special consultant. Honkanen was keen on a *Vasa*-style rescue operation, but the NBA director was not. The expense of raising and moving the ship was extravagant, while the task of on-site salvaging was treacherous. "The National Board of Antiquities considers the research of the wreck and its cargo important," Director Lilius opined, "however, this is a very difficult, expensive, and time-consuming project." The NBA was looking for something less dramatic. They found a useful ally at the museum in Sallamaria Tikkanen. The museum's chief marine archeologist was also not eager to rummage for Catherine's lost treasure. "It is not now sensible," said Sallamaria. "First it is necessary to collect all available information about the ship, its materials, and its cargo."

Sallamaria was the top candidate to take charge of the *Vrouw Maria*. She was adept at both the academics of marine archeology and the management of the shipwreck registry. Her recent fieldwork focused on the Swedish warship *Kronsprins Gustaf Adolf*. Located near Helsinki in shallow depths, she oversaw the conversion of the wreck site into a public archeological dive park. But Sallamaria had never put together a project on the scale of the *Vrouw Maria*. Catherine the Great's treasure ship required a bold plan. And a bold plan required imagination, entrepreneurship, and confidence. Sallamaria wrote a grant proposal.

Working her academic contacts in the UK and the Netherlands, Sallamaria pitched the EU's "Culture 2000 Program" with a multinational shipwreck project. Her bid scored a million-euro award "to safeguard, monitor, and visualize" the *Vrouw Maria* and three other northern shipwrecks. The so-called MoSS project marked one giant leap for the Maritime Museum, and one small step for the *Vrouw Maria*.

In August 1999, a temporary thaw in relations occurred between the Pro Vrouw Maria Association and Finland's cultural bureaucrats. Culture Minister Suvi Lindén organized a public ceremony where NBA director Lilius bestowed a medal of honor on the discoverers. Rauno finally received the public acknowledgment that he craved, though he chafed to share the platform with the same museum personnel who had done nothing to help.

Rauno's springtime prediction to Sallamaria had come true. The public was engaged. The *Vrouw Maria* inspired a new generation of maritime enthusiasts, who took up wreck diving, marine archeology, and museum conservation. The low-standing Maritime Museum was uplifted by new resources from the Culture Ministry and the European Union. But as the museum consolidated its hold on the wreck, Rauno's worst fears came true as well. The MoSS project kept the museum busy for the next three years poking around the outside of the ship, without thinking about the precious cargo inside.

Pro Vrouw Maria Association, meanwhile, did not abandon its plans. The team intended to dive on the wreck and delve for the masterpiece treasure for Mika's unfinished documentary film. They invested in expensive floodlights and video cameras to capture high-quality underwater footage, and contracted with a production and distribution firm. But to go down on the wreck now required museum approval. An application was filed, permission was denied. Even when Rauno rewrote the application to include the museum's own archeologist Matias Laitinen as project supervisor, the request was refused. "They did not trust us," said Mika. "Perhaps they thought we were going to rob the wreck. Do you mind if we see if you have a Rembrandt hanging in your house?"

This did not mean that there would be no diving or filming next summer, however. The *Teredo* would sail back to the site, only Rauno would not be the captain. A documentary would be filmed, only Mika would not be the director. The museum had no interest in cooperating with Pro Vrouw Maria Association. Rather it wanted to thwart its rival once and for all. Rauno's team was embittered by the museum's stance. Their grand project had been usurped. The museum took their research, their trademark, their film, and their shipwreck. Rauno was not ready to give up his dream. He sued.

War of Laws

The underwater world of shipwrecks is populated with marine archaeologists, carefully uncovering and cataloguing objects of antiquity, and cultural looters, covertly ransacking and smuggling objects of avarice. Somewhere in between are wreck hunters. In the spirit of private enterprise and service of public enlightenment, wreck hunters tread a murky gray zone. Unloved by research-minded scientists and scorned by profit-seeking plunderers, wreck hunters have done more than either to locate the hidden remains, salvage the lost treasures, and share the haunting images of the most celebrated shipwrecks of popular lore.

Ever since Mel Fisher hauled up the first gold bar from the half-billion-dollar *Atocha* shipwreck off Key West, Florida, deep-sea treasure hunting has become a fast-moving, technologically sophisticated business. And in response, political authorities, in whose waters shipwrecks are located, have become tenacious in wresting away ownership for themselves. Fisher fought the state of Florida for ten years before the United States Supreme Court awarded the *Atocha's* glittering heap of New World plunder to the wreck hunter in 1992. In doing so, the Court upheld the centuries-old "Finders Keepers" principle of maritime law, which states that if something of value is lost and abandoned at sea, then the person who rescues it first becomes rightful claimant. The principle, as one might expect, is fraught with ambiguity. Always invoked, always contested, especially if the prize is a treasure-toting shipwreck.

Rauno's decision to sue the Finnish government did not come at one impetuous moment, but through an accumulation of slights. The Pro Vrouw Maria Association team was united behind its captain, and filed a petition of protest. But when a more contentious legal strategy was broached, the crew's solidarity shattered. Finns are not litigious. Whereas in the United States there is one lawyer for every 300 citizens and in the United Kingdom one lawyer for every 350 citizens, in Finland there is one lawyer for every 2,600 citizens. Finns, it seems, prefer evenhanded compromises to winner-take-all decisions. Behind this cultural norm is a legal diktat. Plaintiffs bear the cost of bringing their conflicts to court. The financial risk of losing is a strong disincentive to initiate a lawsuit. And for Pro Vrouw Maria's divers there was yet another reason to refrain. To join the lawsuit meant taking sides against the museum. Any individual who stood with Rauno would forego invitation to future museum-sponsored outings.

Man Smoking a Pipe (Self-Portrait), Gerrit Dou, c. 1650, Rijksmuseum, Amsterdam, the Netherlands.

Anna and the Blind Tobit, Rembrandt van Rijn, c. 1630, National Gallery, London, UK, *Art Resource*. Painted in Rembrandt's studio in Leiden, this painting has long been a subject of controversy. Was it painted by Rembrandt, Dou, or both?

ABOVE: Dou's childhood home on Kort Rapenburg in Leiden, the Netherlands. BELOW: Sign affixed to the facade of the Dou family house on the tercentenary of Gerrit Dou's birth. "Here lived Gerrit Dou, Born in Leiden 1613, Deceased in Leiden 1673." *Photos by Mara Vorhees.*

ABOVE: *Equestrian portrait of Catherine the Great*, Vigilius Eriksen, c. 1764, State Hermitage Museum, Saint Petersburg, Russia. BELOW: The Small Hermitage, built by Empress Catherine to display her art collection, now part of the State Hermitage Museum, © *October64, Dreamstime.com.*

ABOVE: *Portrait of Empress Catherine the Great, née Princess Sophie of Anhalt-Zerbst,* Fyodor Rokotov (?), 1780s, State Hermitage Museum, Saint Petersburg, Russia. BELOW: The Tent-Roofed Hall in the New Hermitage, now part of the State Hermitage Museum, displays 17th century Dutch paintings, including Catherine's rich collection of paintings by Dou and the Leiden *fijnschilders*. © *Rostislav Ageev, Dreamstime.com*

ABOVE: *Portrait of Gerrit Braamcamp*, Reinier Vinkeles after Jacob Xavery, c. 1766, Rijksmuseum, Amsterdam, the Netherlands. Xavery was an artist-in-residence at Sweedenrijk. BELOW: "The Temple of Arts": Gerrit Braamcamp's home, Sweedenrijk, on the Golden Bend of the Herengracht canal. © *Ahavelaar, Dreamstime.com.*

ABOVE: *Mint Tower viewed from Singel*, Jan ten Compe, c. 1751, Amsterdam Museum, Amsterdam, the Netherlands. Part of Braamcamp's collection, this painting was purchased by Russian Ambassador Dmitry Golitsyn for his own private collection and shipped to Saint Petersburg on board the *Vrouw Maria*. Unlike the Empress's paintings, *Mint Tower* was salvaged before the ship sank. BELOW: *Four Cows in a Meadow*, Paulus Potter, c. 1651, Rijksmuseum, Amsterdam, the Netherlands. An exemplary Potter landscape featuring farmyard animals. A comparable painting was part of Gerrit Braamcamp's collection, purchased by Empress Catherine (the second-highest priced item sold at the Braamcamp auction), and lost on the *Vrouw Maria*.

Triptych: Allegory of Art Training (The Nursery), Willem Joseph Laquy after Gerrit Dou, 1770, Rijksmuseum, Amsterdam, the Netherlands. Laquy painted this copy of Dou's beloved triptych when he was an artist-in-residence at Sweedenrijk. The original was lost on the *Vrouw Maria*.

ABOVE: The island of Jurmo, northwest of the *Vrouw Maria* wreck site. *Photo by Mara Vorhees.*
BELOW: The island of Jurmo in winter. © *Juka Palm, Dreamstime.com*

ABOVE: Finnish wreck hunter Rauno Koivusaari, discovered the *Vrouw Maria* in 1999. BELOW: Members of the Pro Vrouw Maria Association. Back-row from left: Ossi Lindberg, Arto Pakkanen, Tommi Lipponen, Petri Rouhiainen, Petri Pulkkinen, Kalle Salonen, Timo Puomio, Antero Kuhalampi, Rauno Koivusaari, Kenneth Lindström, and John Liljelund. Seated: Christian Ahlström and Laura Tuominen. *Photos by Kalle Salonen.*

ABOVE: *M/S Teredo* docked at Jurmo during the 1999 expedition. *Photo by Kalle Salonen.* BELOW: Clay pipes manufactured in Holland and destined for the Russian Imperial court. The pipes were excavated from the *Vrouw Maria* and are now on display at Vellamo Maritime Center in Kotka. *Photo by Mara Vorhees.*

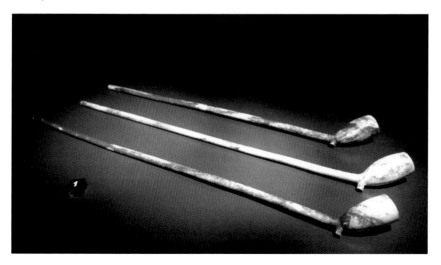

ABOVE: Bow of the *Vrouw Maria*, © *Petri Puromies*.
BELOW: Overview sketch of the *Vrouw Maria*, © *Tiina Miettinen, Maritime Museum of Finland.*

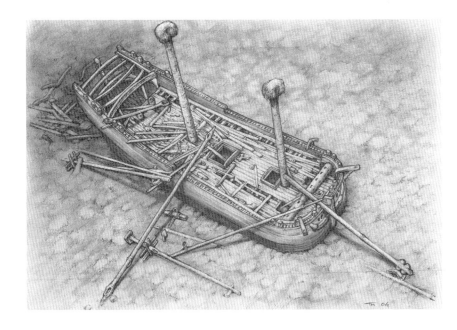

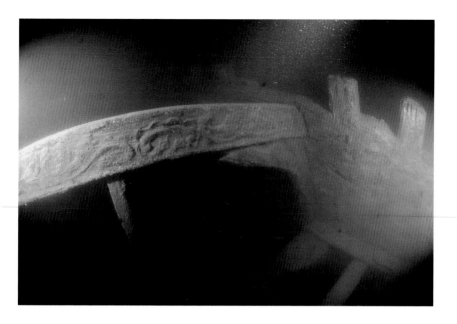

ABOVE: Decorative trim with laurel carving, detail on the *Vrouw Maria*, © *Erik Rådström, Finnish Heritage Agency (AKMA201221:89).* BELOW: Sketch of the stern of the *Vrouw Maria*, showing the location of the laurel carving, © *Tiina Miettinen, Maritime Museum of Finland.*

ABOVE: Divers investigate the bow of the *Vrouw Maria*, © *Petri Puromies*. BELOW: Sketch of the bow of the *Vrouw Maria*, showing location of the identifying kedge anchor portside, © *Tiina Miettinen, Maritime Museum of Finland*.

ABOVE: Maritime Museum researchers and volunteers (from left) Aki Leinonen, Kalle Salonen, Rami Kokko, Riikka Alvik, Immi Wallin, and Fredde Toivari watch divers descend to investigate the *Vrouw Maria* in 2012. © *Eric Tirkkonen, Maritime Museum of Finland.* BELOW: *M/S Muikku* anchored above the *Vrouw Maria* during the Underwater Project in 2012, © *Eric Tirkkonen, Maritime Museum of Finland.*

The beguiling Finnish archipelago at sunset, ©*Janusorlov, Dreamstime.com.*

"Once there was personal risk," Petri explained, "people no longer wanted to be involved. They did not want to give up their connections to Teredo Navalis Society or to the Maritime Museum." Petri did not join the lawsuit, but neither did he go back to diving with the museum. Underwater illustrator Kalle Salonen also wanted no part of the legal action. "Somebody might think that I am a traitor," said Kalle, "but I have always dived with the museum and I am good friends with them, too. Wrecks are wrecks, divers are divers, and I just wanted to dive." In the end, only Mikael joined the suit. Mika was not a diver, but a filmmaker. The museum's decision to deny Pro Vrouw Maria access to the site adversely affected Mika more than the others. "Fear of the costs and fear of the museum led most members to pull out of the lawsuit," he said, "but I was so bitter that I told Rauno I would stick with him to the end."

In December 1999, Rauno and Mika filed suit against the NBA in the Turku Maritime Court. They were represented by Jussi Kähäri, an attorney from Hill Dickinson. The venerable Liverpool-based firm specializes in maritime law, with past clients including White Star Line for the *Titanic* and Cunard Line for the *Lusitania*. Attorney Kähäri told the press that the NBA had shown his clients "a lack of respect and appreciation of their work." Rauno's lawsuit was a first of its kind. No one in Finland had ever before challenged the state for ownership of an object of cultural heritage.

The Finnish government was dismissive of the action. NBA director Lilius said that it was "embarrassing and unfortunate that this wonderful thing has turned into a property dispute." "The legislation is very clear," said Sallamaria, "and everyone knows it." A toxic mix of hotheads and sour grapes, surmised Marja Pelanne: "It is unfortunate that there is an argument about this, but we have done nothing against the law. This cannot go on forever. The mood will soon calm down."

Culture Minister Suvi Lindén commissioned NBA troubleshooter Pekka Honkanen to do a second report on the legal challenge. Honkanen concluded that the state's claim would stand up, and that the divers were not owed a salvage reward. But he also suggested seeking a compromise. The government consented to discuss Rauno's grievances. Lindén said she hoped to end the dispute "through negotiation, instead of litigation." The culture minister invited the wreck hunter to a meeting, urging him to drop the suit and offering to cancel the trademark registration. But Rauno said it was too late. "How can you possibly win?" said a museum lawyer, "Use common sense. The wreck belongs to the museum. The law is the law." It may be true that "the law is the law," but in the case of the *Vrouw Maria* there was more than one law.

Rauno's legal challenge was based on maritime law. Used to resolve private disputes on the high seas, maritime law is one of the oldest institutions of interstate cooperation, arising from ancient Mediterranean seafaring. Maritime law defines how the principle of "Finders Keepers" works in regard to shipwrecks. Accumulated precedent helps determine when a first salvor may become the owner of a wreck and its cargo; when the first salvor may take possession of all or part of the rescued cargo, but not the vessel; and, when the first salvor may be entitled to a reward for rescued cargo. In March 1990, Finland signed the International Convention on Salvage, endorsing these time-tested norms of salvage and reward. Rauno's lawsuit asked for all of the above: ownership of the wreck, ownership of the cargo, and a salvage reward.

The government's legal defense invoked the Antiquities Act of 1963, Finland's basic law for protection of archeological sites and cultural heritage. Accordingly, shipwrecks lying in territorial waters for at least one hundred years automatically become state property. The Act complies with the United Nations Convention on the Law of the Sea, which extends national sovereignty to adjacent waters. The potential contradiction of maritime law's notion of salvage rights with the Convention's notion of territorial waters provides the grist for the legal battles between wreck hunters and state authorities. In general, national sovereignty trumps maritime law, as long as national laws are codified and clear at the time of the find. But if national laws are not explicit, then a wreck hunter's claim may prevail. This was how Mel Fisher succeeded to fend off Florida's bureaucratic poachers from the *Atocha*.

As the lawsuit proceeded, Rauno was shunned by Finland's close-knit diving community. Once a fixture at the museum, he was now banned from the premises. The staff was forbidden to fraternize with the enemy. "It was very hard," said marine archeologist Riikka Alvik, "because he was my friend and we often dived together. But you had to take a side." And Maija Fast-Matikka remembered that "before, he was very close and we shared coffee every week. But the lawyers told us no more after the court case started." His boat and gear were removed from the museum's small pier on Hylkasaari. Nor was Rauno welcome any longer at the Teredo Navalis Society. Club members were mortified by the lawsuit, and felt betrayed, after lending him their vessel. It finally struck Rauno just how far things had gone, when he ran into a pair of Teredo Navalis divers on the Hanko dock and they would not even allow him to step onto their boat. "They really hated me." So that club members would not have to be reminded of the unpleasantness, Koivusaari was expelled from the Society.

Perhaps the biggest regret for Rauno was the breakup of the Pro Vrouw Maria Association. A few days past midsummer, in June 2000, the *Teredo* chugged back to the outer archipelago with new leading actors, but at least some of the same supporting cast. On board were five former recruits from the Pro Vrouw Maria dive team.

The divers found the wreck in good condition, as they had left it. There was no evidence of looters. There was a reason the *Vrouw Maria* held up so well for so long. She rested on a narrow patch of soft silt surrounded by a treacherous underwater moraine. Like a pearl in a craggy hard shell, the ship stayed snug inside this rocky barrier, protected from shunting currents below and snooping robbers above.

The museum party made camp at the old Coast Guard station on Bodö Island. They conducted eighty-two dives on the wreck over eight days. They clocked four hours of underwater film footage, took measurements of the external structure, studied the broken masts and rigging, and otherwise duplicated what Rauno's team had done the year before. The museum made no attempt to explore the cargo hold or to locate Empress Catherine's treasure.

While the museum was sizing up its new gift, the jilted gift bearer did not sit idly by. Rauno mustered what was left of Pro Vrouw Maria and headed back out to sea. The wreck hunter had found a new quarry.

The Silver Brig

"We sent numerous applications to dive on the wreck," Rauno said, "but they all boomeranged back at us." The loyal remnants of Pro Vrouw Maria, meanwhile, had organized their summer holidays around another diving expedition. Prospects were increasingly doubtful, and the mood turned glum. Until one winter's day, while keeping warm in the National Archives, Rauno uncovered a lost nugget among the old municipal court records. It was the captain's declaration for a 1782 shipwreck, the *De Catherina*, better known as the Silver Brig.

Eleven years after the *Vrouw Maria's* final voyage, Empress Catherine was still ruling in Saint Petersburg and Dutch merchant Lodewijk Hovy was still trading in Amsterdam. In summer 1782, Hovy contracted with Thomas Sabeck to provide a ship for the Russian Run. Hovy's cargo would include kiln-cooked clay tiles to adorn the townhouse rooftops of Catherine's courtiers and casks packed with silver ingots to supply Catherine's craftsmen. Sabeck chose the *De Catherina*, a reliable double-mast brig. Registered in Saint Petersburg, the ship had already made the Russian Run several times, though her young captain, Dutchman Joachem Anders, was making his debut at the helm.

The *De Catherina's* story is not unlike the *Vrouw Maria's*. The ship got a late start, compounded by bad weather. A week was lost when a North Sea gale ripped the mizzen sail, and the vessel returned to port for repairs. Still another week was lost at Castle Kronborg in Elsinore, when foul winds from the south kept her at anchor. It was mid-September when Captain Anders reached the Upper Baltic, and steered his ship toward the fairway. Here they met a defiant volley of wind and water from the southeast. First mate Knut Jensen ordered the drenched crew to take in the mainsail and raise the storm sail. Sometime past midnight, on September 16, the jib sail was torn off and the vessel was pushed off course. The *De Catherina* entered the menacing shoals of the Archipelago Sea. The helpless crew braced as the ship careened head-on into a large boulder. The hull split open and seawater roared in. The thrashing swell made it unsafe to abandon ship. The terrified sailors endured the tempest, clinging to top deck fixtures. When morning arrived and the sea relaxed, crewman Jorgen Winter was gone, stolen by the archipelago in the night.

First mate Jensen anchored the wounded vessel, and captain and crew rowed to a nearby islet. Later that day the Swedish salvage constable arrived, and together they returned to the foundering ship. The cargo hold was submerged. There was no saving the *De Catherina*. Salvaging what they could from the captain's cabin and main deck, they relocated to the waterfront town of Tammisaari (Ekenäs in Swedish), where formal statements were taken and salvaged goods were auctioned. The salvors were able to rescue only a small portion of the silver from the wreck. Back in Amsterdam, Lodewijk Hovy was enraged when the pittance from his share arrived. The salvors took 25 percent of the auction's proceeds as salvage reward, while Tammisaari town officials heaped additional taxes and fees on the settlement. Hovy filed a protest, suspicious of the salvage report's conclusion that the rest of his silver was lost.

For the next two centuries treasure hunters searched for the Silver Brig. In the 1880s, a Tallinn-based salvage company resolved to find Hovy's missing treasure. Two steamboats combed the area and discovered a double-mast Dutch wreck. But all they hauled up were jars of pickles and mustard. In 1967, another old wooden ship was found in the area, setting off a treasure feeding frenzy. This wreck yielded Madeira wine and British porcelain, but no silver. Not until Rauno thought to research the old municipal court archive had anyone seen the captain's declaration. He now possessed an eyewitness account of the *De Catherina*'s crash, but written in an extinct Old Swedish dialect. Rauno called historian Christian Ahlström to help decipher the document.

Just past midsummer, in June 2000, the Pro Vrouw Maria team was aboard the *Baltic Eye*, making for Jussarö Island, ten miles south of Tammisaari, where Captain Anders gave his sworn testimony two hundred years earlier. The declaration noted that the islet where the survivors camped had trees and vegetation. This meant that the *De Catherina* was not in the outer archipelago, where wreck hunters previously searched. It also said that the ship was conveying a load of roofing tiles, a distinct identifying feature. Rauno had narrowed the search zone to a swath of water northwest of the island. The team lowered the side-scan sonar and the boat began drawing a grid pattern on the gently rippling surface. On the first day, the sonar revealed a wooden wreck. Divers descended on the site and discovered a medieval cog, a favorite craft of Hanseatic traders and an unusual find in Finnish waters. The search recommenced.

After observing the methodical movements of the *Baltic Eye*, curiosity got the best of a local islander and he approached the vessel. Rauno told him they were looking for the Silver Brig, and the old-timer laughed. "Even if you found her," he asked, "how would you know with so many wrecks on the bottom?" Rauno answered that there were telltale signs, mentioning the clay tiles. The islander went from chuckling to choking. Not only was he aware of the roofing slates, but he was using them at his own house. He told the transfixed team a tale about navy divers who hauled up the tiles from the seafloor ten years earlier. An hour later the *Baltic Eye* was idling above another old wreck.

The ship lay in shallow water, twenty meters down. The divers reported it was a koff, about thirty meters long with two masts. The koff was a common Dutch trader in the 18th century, shorter than a fluyt, but wider across to pack more cargo. The ship's body was broken in two, its gut sliced open, and its contents—old brick tiles—strewn across the seabed. The long elusive Silver Brig was found. Unlike the *Vrouw Maria*, this wreck did not stay hidden for two centuries. The wreck site was visited before Rauno's team arrived. But until then its identity was unkown.

"Silver Brig shipwreck *De Catherina* found near Jussarö," exclaimed the *Helsingin Sanomat*. Though he was banned from the *Vrouw Maria*, Rauno was still stealing attention from the museum. "Marine archeology history is made once again by the Pro Vrouw Maria divers, who excelled last summer by finding the much prized *Vrouw Maria* shipwreck," gushed Finland's largest newspaper. "So far the divers have yet to locate the legendary silver." It was one thing for Rauno to outshine his rivals, but it was quite another for them to learn about the new find from the news. Collective indignation seethed through the Maritime Museum. According to the Antiquities Act, the finder of a shipwreck older than a hundred years must report the discovery without delay to proper authorities, and it is strictly forbidden to remove anything from the site. "If the search group raises a single artifact from the wreck," the museum threatened, "it will commit deliberate damage to an ancient object and will be subject to a police investigation. The penalty is two years imprisonment."

Rauno was not intimidated. He was in no hurry to accommodate the same bureaucrats who spoiled his *Vrouw Maria* project. Through his attorney's office, Rauno sent a terse notification to the museum, confirming that he had discovered an old shipwreck and promising more information "in due course." He was now technically in compliance with the law. NBA officialdom was not assuaged. They demanded that the district police shut down Pro Vrouw Maria's activities on the water. The police refused to cause a confrontation at sea, but agreed to start an investigation on land. "The National Board of Antiquities cannot demand a discovery notice," an incredulous Rauno told reporters. "We just came off the sea today. What was I supposed to do? Travel 100 kilometers by boat and car to the museum to file a report, when they would not even agree to cover the costs?"

Rauno was smug about his latest scandal. He had opened a second front in his personal war with the Maritime Museum. His nemesis was clearly provoked. The NBA refused to back down from the public challenge. But the coercive powers of the cultural bureaucracy were few. They slapped Rauno with an administrative fine of forty euros, but that would not make a proper example of the brazen wreck hunter. So the NBA pestered the district prosecutor to pursue a criminal case. Rauno was charged with committing an "antiquarian crime" against the state; it was another way of calling him a looter. But by the time the case was heard in court, two years later, the NBA still lacked evidence to support the charge. The Court found Rauno not guilty.

As for the silver, it was not found. It is possible, Rauno suggested, that it is still there, covered over by two hundred years of silt. Or, perhaps Lodewijk Hovy's presumptions about corrupt proceedings in the old salvage court were correct, and the Silver Brig's unaccounted for treasure was nicked from the wreckage long ago.

At the Maritime Court

In May 2002, oral arguments began in the case of *Rauno Koivusaari et al. vs. Finland* at the Maritime Court in Turku. The Maritime Court is composed of three professional judges and two sea captains. But this was a preliminary hearing to determine the merits of the plaintiffs' case. Only the Honorable Judge Nystrom presided.

Rauno's argument appealed to Chapter 16 of the Maritime Code, the "Finders Keepers" clause, asserting that he was rightful claimant to the wreck and cargo as finder and first salvor. On July 9, 1999, Rauno's crew raised six artifacts form the shipwreck, with the approval of Maija Fast-Matikka of the

Maritime Museum. This seemingly small act became the legal basis for Rauno's claim to first salvage rights. Moreover, his suit requested a salvage reward, arguing that Maija Fast-Mattika's consent constituted a *de facto* salvage contract.

The Finnish government's defense appealed to the superseding authority of national sovereignty. According to the Antiquities Act, the NBA is the exclusive claimant to the shipwreck and cargo. "The *Vrouw Maria* is a national property, a cultural heritage that cannot be assessed in money. The wreck has historic value, which makes it impossible to fix a salvage fee," argued Marianne Jalkanen for the Maritime Museum. The state had not partnered with the salvors. Nothing in the way of a salvage contract existed, as Maija was not empowered to negotiate such an agreement. The six artifacts were raised, with explicit understanding, for the purpose of scientific research by the museum.

In September 2002, Judge Nystrom rendered his decision: "Provisions of the Maritime Code were applicable to the operations aimed at salvaging the wreck and the property originating from it." The Antiquities Act and maritime law, the judge said, "were not mutually exclusive." This meant that the plaintiffs' grievance was legitimate, and the case would go to trial. The government was stunned. "The case should never have been allowed in the Maritime Court," said one perturbed museum official. Rauno and Mikael had won round one.

Who owns the treasure under the sea? The dispute in the Maritime Court was a bilateral conflict between a finder and proprietor. But with old shipwrecks conflicts are often multilateral. Who owned the ship? Under whose flag did the ship sail? Who owned the cargo? And when is a wreck abandoned? There were more than two legitimate claimants to the *Vrouw Maria*. It was a Dutch-owned ship, in service to Dutch merchants. Would present-day corporate legatees in the Netherlands step forward to press a claim? What is more, at the time of the *Vrouw Maria's* sinking there was no sovereign state of Finland. Sweden was then lord of the Archipelago Sea. What claim might Sweden make on the historic shipwreck? Finally, there was Russia. It was beyond dispute that the *Vrouw Maria's* treasure belonged to Empress Catherine the Great, who had paid dearly for the bounty within. The tsarina made every possible effort to retrieve her property after the tragedy. What would Catherine's heirs do now that it was found? Could the Finns fend off these challenges? And, if so, what would be their plan for the *Vrouw Maria*?

16

THE DUTCH RETREAT

"We've Found Your Wreck"

When the ship was found, it was quite a horrible situation," said marine archeologist Riikka Alvik. The *Vrouw Maria* sent the Maritime Museum staff into a dither. The long-neglected, low-profile section of the Finnish cultural bureaucracy was suddenly thrust into a glaring spotlight with a project more immense and confounding than anything seen before. Riikka described the situation inside the museum in the summer of 1999: "We had just opened a big exhibition, we had the Swedish warship *Gustav Adolf* to research, another medieval wreck, and a new wreck with loads of 16th-century pottery that needed urgent attention. We had an overload of everything, and zero resources to do it." Leaves were canceled, workdays extended, and nerves frayed. The Maritime Museum needed help.

According to the United Nations Law of the Sea, "objects of an archeological or historical nature found on the high seas should be preserved for all mankind, with preferential rights to the state or country of origin." In all respects, the *Vrouw Maria*'s country of origin was the 18th century Dutch Republic. There the ship was built, owned, and registered. By the Law of the Sea, it was reasonable to conclude that the Dutch were the rightful owner of the *Vrouw Maria*, while the Finns were just her responsible caretaker.

"The Netherlands was very important," said museum researcher Maija Fast-Matikka, "because the ship was Dutch." Maybe, the Finns reasoned, the Dutch will want it back. The museum reported the discovery to the Dutch Embassy in Finland, who responded with cheery congratulations and a promise to pass the information to proper authorities. Maija remembered a sharp-witted young maritime researcher from Holland, whom she had met earlier at an international conference on underwater heritage. "The first thing I did was to call my colleague in the Netherlands," Maija said, "and I told him that we've found your wreck. It is here in our waters."

The news of the Baltic legend roused the curiosity of Maija's acquaintance, Martijn Manders. At this time, Martijn was still an archeologist in training at the Netherlands Institute for Ship and Underwater Archeology. He was assigned to work with cultural attachés in the diplomatic corps, alerting them to the rich Dutch cultural treasures dispersed beneath the seas of the world. His subaquatic interests had begun in his student days at Leiden University, in Gerrit Dou's hometown, where a decade later he returned as lecturer, rising to the top post of University Head Teacher for Marine Archeology. Eventually, he also became head of Marine Archeology for the Cultural Heritage Agency. Apple-cheeked and blue-eyed, the charismatic Manders had a flair for getting others excited about the stories and science of underwater discovery.

At the Maritime Museum, there was hope that the confident Manders would get involved with the *Vrouw Maria*. "We invited him to come and see the wreck," Sallamaria Tikkanen said, "but he was too busy." It was not that Martijn was not keen to see the *Vrouw Maria* for himself, rather that he was preoccupied with his own 17th-century shipwreck. Above all, he was dedicated to the pursuit and protection of the sunken legacy of the far-flung Dutch maritime empire. Within a decade, Manders would be widely recognized as one of northern Europe's foremost guardians of underwater cultural heritage. And, as events unfolded in Finland, he would become linked to the fate of the *Vrouw Maria*.

Protecting the Treasures of the Deep

"The deep ocean is the largest museum on earth, it contains more history than all the museums on land combined," said wreck hunter Robert Ballard, famed for locating the *Titanic*, in 1985, at more than two miles down in the North Atlantic.

Beginning with Ballard's big find, attitudes toward this vast cultural underworld were transformed. Martijn Manders personified this shift in maritime archeology from adventure-seeking amateurs to academically trained professionals. "Much of what has been produced by humanity has been lost, thrown away, or left behind underwater," he wrote. "However, over the past few decades, our insights into this rich resource and the opportunities to protect it have improved considerably." Martijn was part of an international reaction to the rise of high-tech underwater profiteers, whose marine robots were capable of ransacking artifacts from piteous wrecks in the deepest abyss. While salvaging pieces of eight from a Spanish galleon may conjure the romantic, auctioning jewelry and pocket watches lifted from the *Titanic*'s drowned victims evokes the morbid. Tantamount to grave robbing, it offends public sensibility. "The tension between commercial salvors and maritime archeologists," he noted, "is a driving force in the global movement to safeguard shipwrecks."

Manders was fascinated by the ways in which the past gives meaning to the present, through the interplay of cultural artifacts and social identity. He especially understood how shipwrecks affect popular imagination. Hence came his inherent distrust of wreck hunters. "The commercial companies have a completely different starting point. They want to earn money from the heritage of shipwrecks. You never know for sure if their story is true or not. What is the difference between finding an ordinary necklace or finding George Washington's necklace? A big difference in price." At stake in this underwater competition, he warned, was control over cultural heritage: "What's most important is authenticity." And just as there are laws against looting artifacts from ancient pyramids, so there should be safeguards for cultural sites on the seafloor.

While still an apprentice archeologist, Martijn was selected for the Dutch delegation sent to negotiate the UNESCO Convention on Underwater

Cultural Heritage. In November 2001, the Convention agreed on a set of measures concerning the cultural treasures lying under the sea. These guidelines established principles of 'best practice' in the protection and preservation of maritime artifacts and archeological sites. The Convention proved popular with national cultural bureaucracies, such as the Finnish Maritime Museum, because it conferred to them responsibility for managing underwater heritage sites. Indeed, the Maritime Museum also sent a team of delegates to the UNESCO negotiations, although the Finnish government never ratified the final document. It was during these underwater rule-setting parlays that Martijn impressed the Finns with his fervent commitment to protecting shipwrecks.

In 2000, Sallamaria recruited the Dutchman as a joint collaborator in the EU-funded MoSS project, the research endeavor that included the *Vrouw Maria* and three other northern wrecks. The three-year program embraced the new scientific approach to shipwrecks, "from focused archeological excavation to managing the resource." The project promoted legal and physical protection, technical surveillance and on-site monitoring, and noninvasive means of access. At Martijn's behest, the MoSS project adopted a broken 100-foot Dutch merchantman in the Wadden Sea, a body of water between the barrier islands and coastal mudflats of the northern Netherlands. In the Age of Sail, the westernmost island of Texel served as an intertidal way station for larger vessels servicing Amsterdam merchants, without risking the bottom-dragging shallows. The historic Texel Roads area contained scores of old shipwrecks, which Manders concluded were best managed through in situ preservation.

The in situ protection strategy means leaving a shipwreck in place and undisturbed. It is a minimalist management tool for overwhelmed and underfunded scientists. Inspired by practices in land-based archeology, it seeks to curb looting and protect artifacts by keeping them hidden. The UNESCO Convention endorsed in situ preservation as the "first option" for underwater cultural heritage. But it was not the only option. Differences of opinion existed over when the in situ policy was the appropriate choice.

At the Finnish Maritime Museum, Sallamaria Tikkanen was a proponent of a strict interpretation of in situ preservation. Responsible for protecting Finland's underwater cultural heritage, the museum's chief marine archeologist found the in situ option a useful solution, given that there were so many wrecks and so few resources. Sallamaria's vision was "to develop virtual underwater museums," which could be accommodated with in situ preservation.

By contrast, at the Dutch Cultural Heritage Agency, Martijn Manders embraced a more flexible approach. Although he recommended in situ preservation for the Wadden Sea wrecks, he stressed that "there is a difference between *first* option and *preferred* option, and nothing in the UNESCO Convention says that in situ preservation must be the preferred option. If there is a good reason articulated and a good plan worked out, then excavating or even raising a shipwreck can be the preferred option, and still remain faithful to the UNESCO best practice standard." This was the case with the wonder wreck, the Dutch East India ship *Rooswijk*.

In 2004, the splintered hull of the *Rooswijk* was discovered on the Goodwin Sands, the notorious "ship swallower" off the coast of Kent in the English Channel. The state-of-the-line transoceanic trader went down in a wicked storm in January 1740, carrying a load of silver to the Batavia colony (Indonesia) to exchange for sugar and spice. As many as 300 lives met a final frigid reckoning in the disaster. More than a decade after discovery, Manders led a pod of divers on an international excavation of the site. The costly expedition was conducted under difficult conditions, but it was deemed an opportunity that should not be missed. The *Rooswijk* was "a treasure trove for archeologists," Martijn said. The wreck yielded chests of silver bars, thousands of Mexican silver coins, and a horde of historic artifacts, which were divvied up evenly among the contributors—public and private, professional and amateur, Dutch and English.

As demonstrated by the *Rooswijk*, salvaging shipwrecks and protecting the cultural treasures of the deep sea are not incompatible goals, as long as the excavation is conducted for the right reasons and with proper practices. "Each object on the seafloor tells a story," Martijn said. "Marine archeology techniques tell a story that could never be told in history books." The Dutch, as it turned out, could be very enthusiastic about excavating shipwrecks, just not the *Vrouw Maria*.

The Dutch Claim

"If the *Vrouw Maria* had been a Dutch East India ship, then we would have claimed ownership of her," Martijn said, "And we would also have expected to be involved in any decisions about what happens to her." But the *Vrouw Maria* was a private ship, not a government-owned ship.

In 1999, when the Finns first notified the Dutch Embassy of the freshly-preserved snow-brig lying in repose in the outer archipelago, they had expected the Dutch to get involved. After all, the Netherlands had a strong historic connection to the wreck. At the Finnish Culture Ministry, Päivi Salonen said, "the Dutch have always been interested in the *Vrouw Maria* and her story, so we have had a lot of contact with them about the ship." But not as much as hoped for. The Dutch deferred.

"It is a great find," explained Manders, "but we have to set our own priorities." It is not that the Dutch were neglecting their legacy of shipwrecks, on the contrary. "We are a big maritime nation, and a big part of our identity is related to the sea and seafaring, but we have already identified the positions of over 1,500 shipwrecks of high archeological value." The Dutch maritime empire spread to the far corners of the world, where the misfortunes of nature and misdeeds of man sometimes brought journeys to a sudden tragic end. At the Dutch Cultural Heritage Agency, Martijn leads a diving research team charged with looking after more than four hundred shipwrecks, from Brazil to Cuba, from Indonesia to South Africa. "So, yes, the *Vrouw Maria* is interesting," he said, "but so are these other shipwrecks."

While some empires are sustained by soldiers, the Dutch Republic was led by salesmen. Dutch merchant companies plied the seas in search of something, anything, that could be traded for profit. And no mercantile firm was more adept at making a deal, and backing it up with a forty-cannon gun deck, than the Dutch East India Company (known by the initials VOC). Part private multinational corporation, part state-within-a-state, the VOC was at one time the richest and best-armed oceangoing merchant company in the world.

It was the VOC that inspired Peter the Great, when he said: "If God gives me a lifetime, I will make Saint Petersburg into a Second Amsterdam." The first Russian tsar to venture abroad, Peter headed to the Netherlands, where he stayed in the living quarters of the rope master of the Dutch East India Company. Peter played the part of an apprentice shipwright. Everyone knew who the six-foot seven-inch "junior prince" really was, but they went along with the act. The tsar observed and assisted in every facet of the six-week shipbuilding process, from laying down the keel to hoisting the main mast. At its launching, the VOC presented the one hundred-foot, twenty-two-gun frigate to the delighted Slavic sovereign. It was the first acquisition in what would become Peter's Imperial Navy. Northern Europe's balance of power would never be the same.

In 2002, the Dutch East India Company celebrated the 400th anniversary of its founding. After two generations of collective penance for the cruelties of colonialism, Dutch society was again ready to embrace the swagger of its maritime past. Martijn was inspired. In 2007, he penned a proposal to conduct more underwater research, which the government eventually acted on. "At the time, we were doing nothing to preserve our maritime heritage, so I wrote up a vision of what we should do. The timing was right. It was accepted, and suddenly marine archeology is a booming business."

Given the popular upswell of maritime nostalgia, why did the Dutch forego their claim to the *Vrouw Maria*? Manders explained: "Our priority is with the India companies and Admiralty ships. The VOC was a private company, but it went bankrupt and the assets were taken over by the government. So all VOC shipwrecks belong to the Dutch government. At least that is what we claim. Of course, old colonies do not easily accept the claims of their former oppressors." By contrast, the *Vrouw Maria* never fell under state jurisdiction. The distinction is crucial for a society proud of having invented modern capitalism. "It is a Dutch ship in form and design, that's simple to see," Martijn said, "but it was private." The *Vrouw Maria*'s owners were insured for the loss, as were the merchants who booked cargo space from Lodewijk Hovy for the Russian Run. There are no known outstanding commercial claims from the Netherlands. The business of the wreck was long ago concluded.

It was not that the Dutch did not care about Catherine's treasure ship, quite the contrary. "I wanted very much to be involved," said Manders. "The *Vrouw Maria* is a great ship with a great story." But the Dutch were constrained from making a legal claim on the wreck. "Because the *Vrouw*

Maria was a private ship," Manders affirmed, "we cannot claim it. We have an interest in it, but my former governmental role didn't reach that far. We cannot take the lead." Citing UNESCO principles on underwater heritage, he said that "Finland is the coastal state where the *Vrouw Maria* lies, so we expect Finland to play a responsible role and show good stewardship." As for a plan of action, Martijn put the onus back on his colleagues at the Maritime Museum: "It is in Finnish waters, so Finland must lead the discussion and make the decision."

A Treasure Goes Home

Back in the summer of 1771, Empress Catherine's diplomat connoisseur, Dmitry Golitsyn was relieved. The envoy had a few more items to ship, and managed to get word to merchant Loedwijk Hovy on Dam Square just before the *Vrouw Maria* cast off for Saint Petersburg. The paintings that he and cousin Vice Chancellor Alexander Golitsyn acquired at the Braamcamp estate sale had been held up. While the word of the empress was enough to take possession of her auction acquistions, the ambassador needed to put down a deposit before he could collect his winnings. With a purse of clinking florins, Dmitry visited Amsterdam dealer Pierre Fouquet and gathered his prize. Now to gain the release of cousin Alexander's pictures.

Conveniently, two of Alexander's paintings were being held by Hovy, who had procured them on his behalf from auction dealers. Unfortunately, the chancellor found himself in an awkward position. The Russian ambassador presented the Dutch merchant with a promissory note from his cousin: "Messieurs, I am very obliged to you for the acquisition of the Italian and French paintings from the cabinet of M. Braamcamp, but the prices are enormous." Alexander asked Hovy to discharge the paintings to cousin Dmitry for a small fee and a pledge to settle the debt later. Hovy consented. It was good business to stay on good terms with his high-end Russian clients. Still, Prince Dmitry was in a snit. For some unknown reason, dealer Jan Yver had neglected to deliver to Hovy one of Her Majesty's paintings won at auction. And the ship was about to sail without it.

The *Vrouw Maria*'s skipper Reynoud Lourens was summoned by Hovy to pick up the additional parcels. The captain grumbled, the tsarina's cache of masterpiece paintings was already safely concealed in the lower hold. It would cause further delay to unload and reload just to unite the paintings. But Lourens too was wary not to offend Hovy's haughty client. Reynoud rubbed a leathery palm against his stubbly chin, and then offered to find space in his sleeping quarters. The captain's cabin was located in the rear of the *Vrouw Maria*'s main deck, under the aftcastle. With two hundred square feet, Reynoud normally had space to spare. But on this occasion, the room was already crammed with his personal stores that he hoped to sell for big profits in Saint Petersburg. He found a secure spot among the crates and barrels inside. By now, the captain was behind schedule. Lourens told Hovy that he could wait no longer. Golitsyn would have to send the missing painting on a different boat. And the *Vrouw Maria* weighed anchor.

When the painting finally arrived, Hovy packed up Pierre Mignard's *Jephthah and His Daughter* for the next Russian Run. Mignard's Old Testament scene depicted the triumphant Jephthah, who had promised God that he would sacrifice the first living thing he saw if he was victorious in battle, at the moment when his eyes, aghast, fell on his daughter. Catherine paid 399 florins for the piece, which arrived in Saint Petersburg on a different ship and entered the tsarina's salon in 1772. But the lone painting's arrival brought the empress grief instead of joy. A reminder of the dreadful loss of Dou's triptych and other Golden Age gems. Today, *Jephthah and His Daughter* is the only painting in the Hermitage confirmed to have come from the Braamcamp auction, though it was subsequently reattributed to Bon Boullogne, another 17th century French Baroque master and contemporary of Pierre Mignard.

Meanwhile, the pictures belonging to the Golitsyn cousins were salvaged from the captain's cabin before the *Vrouw Maria* was swallowed by the archipelago. Because they were among the last items loaded, these panels survived the star-crossed voyage. In Turku, the auction inventory list of salvaged goods referenced "one large painting in a gilt frame and five smaller paintings." But before the hammer dropped, these works were rescued from the block through the intervention of Russian Foreign Minister

Panin. Today the identity and whereabouts of the chancellor's paintings can only be speculated. It is possible that they were absorbed into the copious Golitsyn family collection, which was acquired en masse by the Hermitage in 1866. The fate of Prince Dmitry's impulsive splurge at the Braamcamp sale, however, is partially known.

Prince Dmitry was preoccupied with playing Her Majesty's hand at the auction; yet he still had a chit of his own in the game. Shortly before Gerrit Dou's prized triptych came to the block, he made a move on Lot no. 46, *A View of the Mint Tower in Amsterdam* by Jan ten Compe. The large piece profiled the Renaissance-styled bell and clock tower on Muntplein (Mint Plaza) from across the Singel Canal. Artist ten Compe was not a Golden Age master. He was a popular 18th-century painter, whose handsome depictions of Dutch towns were all the rage with contemporary collectors. The wine merchant Braamcamp acquired the *Mint Tower* for 400 florins directly from the artist sometime before 1752. It was the only ten Compe painting in the sale. Ever so fond of the urban Dutch lifestyle, the cosmopolitan Russian prince wanted it. Acting through the hand of dealer Pierre Fouquet, Dmitry scored the serene cityscape for a pricey 1,225 florins.

The painting adorned Dmitry's residence in The Hague, where he remained in Her Majesty's diplomatic corps for another decade before retiring to the life of a gentleman scientist. It was reported to be in Golitsyn's household in 1776. What happened to the painting after Dmitry's death, in 1803, is not clear. Curiously, in the late 18th century, Dutch artist H. P. Schouten painted a watercolor that depicts the *Mint Tower* on the trading block at another auction.

Active at the time of the Braamcamp auction, Schouten was acquainted with auction organizer Cornelis Ploos van Amstel. The scene, however, is not the Braamcamp sale. It takes place in the courtyard of the Old Side Gentlemen's Inn in Amsterdam, where an auctioneer is holding up the *Mint Tower* in a gold gilt frame to entice bidders. It is possible that the scene depicts a real auction that came later, perhaps when the retired Prince Dmitry was cashing in his assets. It has also been speculated that the drawing is simply Schouten's imagination at play. Still another report included the *Mint Tower* in the Golitsyn family estate in Russia in the mid-19th century. If this was the case, it did not end up in the Hermitage with the rest of the collection.

Maybe it was smuggled out of Russia by one of Dmitry's aristocratic descendants escaping the Bolsheviks' proletarian wrath.

In any event, *A View of the Mint Tower in Amsterdam* resurfaced in 1935, in London. But ten Compe's masterpiece did not stay in England for long. In October 1936, Mr. J. van Eck purchased Prince Dmitry's auction prize. The Dutchman then gifted the painting to the recently opened Amsterdam Museum. One hundred and sixty-five years after the *Vrouw Maria* perished in the Baltic Sea, the only traceable piece of her cultural treasure returned to Amsterdam, less than a mile from its former home in the Temple of Arts. Here the painting remains on display.

17

THE SWEDISH PATRON

At the District Court

I f we want to find something good about this conflict, then marine archeology has at least received a lot of attention," observed one volunteer diver for the Maritime Museum. Rauno's legal battle with the NBA kept the *Vrouw Maria* in the headlines, reminding the Finnish public of the extraordinary treasure awaiting rescue on the archipelago seafloor. After the Maritime Court ruled in the Pro Vrouw Maria Association's favor, in September 2002, a year and a half passed before the Turku District Court took up the case. Time did not diminish the hard feelings on either side.

Rauno and Mikael felt confident heading into the trial. The Maritime Court's preliminary decision validated the "Finders Keepers" principle in their case. Their legal team, meanwhile, was reinforced by the arrival of Jan Aminoff, who brought thirty years of maritime law courtroom experience. Their position was further bolstered by an independent assessment from Peter Wetterstein, Finland's leading academic expert on maritime law. The

Åbo Academy law professor was critical of the government's "rigid behavior" in the case. "The issue of ownership is not at all clear," asserted Wetterstein. "The purpose of the Antiquities Act is to protect valuable national cultural objects, while its application to foreign shipwrecks is quite flimsy. And how can we consider 17th-century Dutch paintings to be part of Finland's national cultural heritage?" The NBA scoffed at Wetterstein's opinion. "Lawyers can argue forever," sniped administrative director Heikki Halttunen, "but the wreck still belongs to the state."

After the startling setback at the Maritime Court, the NBA's defense team opted for a proactive strategy. First, they changed magistrates. Disappointed in Judge Nystrom's ruling, the defendants requested the appointment of a different, and presumably friendlier, senior justice to preside. They also demanded the case be tried before a collective panel of three judges. Second, they changed the law. To eliminate existing ambiguity, the NBA lobbied the parliament to amend the Antiquities Act. In December 2002, the Finnish legislature complied by revising the statute on cultural heritage to include explicit language on state ownership of old wrecks and cargo in territorial waters. Enforcement was made retroactive. Parliament did not disguise that this legislative quick-fix was meant to help the NBA with its lawsuit, despite the fact that the application of law ex post facto was generally prohibited in Finland.

In May 2004, the trial began in Turku. The judges sat stone-faced through the often heated exchanges between attorneys and eleven witnesses. Rauno's team cried foul on the revision to the Antiquities Act, and asked the judges to disregard the NBA's legal trickery. Otherwise, Aminoff stuck to the argument that Rauno was entitled to first salvage rights according to the established norms of maritime law. By contrast, NBA lawyers unfurled a patriotic homage to the sovereignty of national law, and then launched into a scathing personal attack on the plaintiffs. The mercenary Koivusaari, they said, was an ego-driven fortune seeker, robbing the nation of its maritime culture and abusing the court with frivolous claims.

Rauno was caught off guard by the assault on his character and motives. Forced on the defensive, he tried to explain that his interest in the wreck was not private gain but public good; he wanted to build a wreck museum. The proceedings became nerve-wracking over the lifting of the six artifacts, the basis of Rauno's claim to first salvage rights. The Maritime Museum's normally cheery Maija Fast-Matikka was caught in the middle and broke down in tears under cross-examination. Maija's carefully worded recounting of the circumstances surrounding the salvage "might have been the decisive point in the hearings," recalled Jan Aminoff. "Still when the case was closed, we were fairly optimistic that we had a good chance of winning at least part of our requests."

On June 16, 2004, the District Court issued a verdict on all counts in favor of the National Board of Antiquities. The Court ruled that *lex specialis*, a specific statute of national law, takes precedence over *lex generalis*, the general principles of maritime law. Thus, based on the tweaked Antiquities Act, ownership of the wreck and cargo is conferred to the state. Further, the plaintiffs were not entitled to a salvage reward. According to maritime law, a salvage reward is mandated only if a ship is foundering or its cargo in danger. Having rested peacefully in the outer archipelago for more than two hundred years, the *Vrouw Maria* did not fit this description. The Court further rejected the plaintiffs' argument that Maija's consent to raise the artifacts was a *de facto* salvage contract. Adding injury to insult, the judgement ordered the plaintiffs to cover all the costs of the trial, including the NBA's legal expenses, as punishment for wasting the court's time.

The NBA's pretrial preparations worked brilliantly. "The state should be ashamed for doing what they did," Jan Aminoff decried. "They played every trick they could to secure their position. They changed the Antiquities Act to include a provision which was entered into force retroactively." In addition, the NBA's insistence on a three-judge panel was crucial to the outcome, as the decision was not unanimous. A dissenting view sided with the plaintiffs on both first salvage rights and salvage reward. But this was only one judge's opinion against two. Finally, the NBA's tactic to villainize the wreck hunter as plunderer of the people influenced the mood of the Court. Aminoff acknowledged that the judges "took a negative attitude toward Rauno."

It was a devastating defeat. After the verdict, Jan Aminoff warned his dejected clients of the vagaries of the appeal process, which "could take ten years." The pair were worried less about time and more about cost. A quixotic gamble to overturn the District Court decision could lead the plaintiffs to financial ruin. Just when it seemed that Rauno's fight for the *Vrouw Maria* was over, there came an unexpected offer of support. Rauno's wreck-hunting skills had attracted an admirer, a rich admirer.

Adventures in Treasure Land

While the Finns invoked national sovereignty to legitimize their claim to the *Vrouw Maria*, there was a potential hitch. There was no Finnish state at the time of the wreck. In 1771, Finland and her coastal waters were an appendage of the Swedish Empire. It was a Swedish governor and Swedish diplomat who consented to help the Russian empress, and a Swedish salvage company that scoured the archipelago in search of the lost artwork. Just because the political map of Scandinavia had been redrawn since the night Captain Lourens was blown off course did not mean that the original host had no claim. The issue was not simply historical anecdote, but an unfolding present-day controversy regarding shipwrecks. Centuries after Imperial Spain had given up its New World colonies, for example, the contemporary Spanish state was still making ownership claims, sometimes successfully, on wrecks and treasures in the territorial waters of the sovereign nation-states of the Americas. If the Swedish state wanted to press a claim on the *Vrouw Maria*, there was precedent.

By the time the *Vrouw Maria* was found, however, the Swedes were already content with their resurrected relic of glories past, the *Vasa* warship. No official inquiries came from Stockholm to Helsinki about the *Vrouw Maria*. Still there was popular interest in Sweden about the discovery. "Finland has its answer for the Vasa Museum," the Swedish press reported. "Salvaging the wreck *Vrouw Maria*, near Åland, would be a benefit to marine archeology throughout the world." One Swede, in particular, was enchanted by the tale of the masterpiece-laden snow-brig, impressed by the ingenuity of the wreck hunter who found her, and enraged by the Finnish government's unceremonious seizure of the cultural treasure. "The *Vrouw Maria* could be the most valuable shipwreck in the world," said Kjell Edwall, virtuoso investor, dauntless adventurer, and Rauno's Swedish patron.

Kjell Edwall was many things, most of all an optimist. Quick-thinking and open-minded, he was adept at imagining market possibilities and creating business opportunities. Kjell was the consummate global capitalist, trading commodities, inventing technologies, taking risks, and independently wealthy by the age of forty. However, the riches that excited him most were not found on the stock exchange, but in history and legend. Since youth, he tingled at romantic narratives of treasure-seeking explorers in faraway untamed lands. With his personal fortune secure, Kjell sought to make his boyhood dreams a midlife reality. In 1986, the novice swashbuckler set out for the Ecuadoran highlands in search of the lost treasure of the Incas.

The bounty of gleaming gold and sparkling jewels was collected to ransom Incan Emperor Atahualpa, held hostage by Spanish Conquistador Francisco Pizarro. The outnumbered captors got antsy and killed Atahualpa before all the ransom arrived. According to myth, the undelivered portion of the gold, measured in hundreds of tons, was hidden in deep mountain caves, inaccessible to Iberian invaders. The blood-stained booty would tempt treasure hunters thereafter. Kjell made an exhaustive study of all firsthand accounts, and then took his own chance with history. Armed with a tattered hand-drawn map and ultra-sensitive metal detector, Edwall eventually led five expeditions into a remote mist-shrouded sector of the upper Andes, scaling over steep crags and slashing under dense canopies, looking for some trace of the treasure. In the end, the Emperor's ransom eluded his pursuits. Kjell took a liking to the adventurer lifestyle, nonetheless. By the mid-1990s, his fortune-seeking interest shifted from the mountains to the seashore, and from Incan gold to Spanish silver.

Thanks to the brazen and brutal Pizarro, Imperial Spain took control of the New World's most lucrative source of wealth—the bountiful mountain silver lodes of Peru and Bolivia. By 1600, the precious metal was routinely mined, minted, and hauled by ship from Lima to Panama, then borne on the backs of mules across the isthmus to the waiting Treasure Fleet on the Caribbean side. But not all the pillaged riches made it to Seville's counting house. Intemperate weather and incautious pilots caused some ships to founder along Ecuador's rocky Pacific coast. Kjell's quest now was to locate the wrecked remains of these unlucky carriers. And one great prize more than any other sparked his interest.

In 1654, the pride of the Spanish South Seas and flagship of the Pacific fleet, *La Capitana* (aka Nuestra Señora Jesus Maria de la Limpia Concepción), caused a royal fiscal crisis. The heavily armed and plunder-packed galleon had its underbelly ripped open by a jagged reef, dumping an estimated ten million silver pesos and ingots onto the seafloor. Salvors worked the wreck for almost a decade, recovering a third of the spilled loot. The rest of the shiny cargo went unaccounted for. If still on the ocean bed, as many believed, the treasure would be worth hundreds of millions of dollars. The contemporary Ecuadoran government sold exclusive search rights for marked-off coastal zones to top-bidding treasure hunters, who promised a fifty-fifty split on the salvage. Kjell purchased a 700-meter by 450-meter claim in a choice location near some submerged outer-barrier rocks, a sinister spot for any ship caught in a storm. Not surprisingly, he had competition. Several contending outfits were also on the water looking for *La Capitana*, including the notoriously skillful American wreck hunter Robert McClung. Almost immediately Edwall came into conflict with McClung over search claims. To play in this high-stakes game, the venturing Swede would need his own hired gun.

In late 2000, Rauno first heard about the Swedish tycoon recruiting a wreck hunter to look for Spanish gold. The timing could not have been better. Rauno was still brooding over the *Vrouw Maria*. His legal conflict with the NBA strained friendships, business relations, even his marriage to Nina. Ready for a change of scenery, he contacted the mysterious Swedish suitor. Rauno was soon meeting with Kjell and his partners; learning about Spanish conquistadors, Caribbean pirates, and the Treasure Fleet; and buckling into an airplane seat headed for Salinas, Ecuador, with side-scan sonar carefully stowed underneath. "The climate was warm, the sea was shimmering, adventures were bound to happen, and everything would be paid for. Why not?" he reasoned.

Rauno was in for some tropical culture shock. It started when his host Kjell set him up in a large 14th floor penthouse suite overlooking the Pacific, with a personal cook and maid. The living arrangements were not matched by the working conditions. Without access to a dive boat, Rauno had to hitch rides with local fishermen. It was difficult enough to work in the pitching surf on their rickety cruisers, but when conditions were right for fishing, the flummoxed Finn was often stranded on the beach, dive gear in hand, watching his hired skipper following the gulls out to sea. When he was diving in the inviting turquoise waters, Rauno was distracted by lurking bull sharks, venomous sea snakes, and breaching humpback whales. Meanwhile, his side-scan sonar remained a hostage of Ecuadoran customs officials, waiting for a financial incentive to grant its release. When the hydro-projectile was finally liberated, a new problem arose. *La Capitana* and her cargo were buried under 350 years worth of churning sands and debris, which the side-scanner's sound waves could not penetrate.

Rauno's treasure hunt was not off to a good start. He wanted to quiz the locals about the old Lima-minted coins that turned up occasionally on the street market, but his boss forbade it. Kjell was adamant about keeping their activities secret. The gag order frustrated the gregarious Finn, especially since everyone in town knew what they were doing anyway. Rauno eventually came to value caution as well. Cons, guns, and graft pervaded the local scene, and it was not always easy to distinguish the gangsters from the policemen. The experience gave him a newfound appreciation for the rule-obsessed Maritime Museum. "Thank god we have so many regulations back home," he later said.

In Salinas, Rauno became a regular at Choklo's bar, a beachside diver hangout. This was where he first encountered his rival for *La Capitana*, Robert McClung. The former Colorado police chief's resumé of historic finds was as impressive as Rauno's, including a booty-laden pirate wreck off Cape Cod, a thirty-gun British war frigate in New York Harbor, and a treasure-toting Spanish galleon in the Caribbean. A bit intimidated, but more intrigued, Rauno "was obliged to greet him." A table was cleared and the wary wreck hunters sat down together. Choklo's might never have hosted a more bravado-packed evening. McClung had been working Ecuador for five years, and had many stories to relate. "I found myself feeling awkward," Rauno said, "realizing that I did not have much to tell, despite the fact that we were diving in the best wreck area." The conversation came around to one spot in particular, which locals called *las monetas rokas* (the money rocks), where 17th-century silver coins washed up during low tide. McClung tried to investigate the adjacent area of sea, but it fell within Kjell's search zone. The American aquanaut then let loose an unfiltered and unflattering assessment of the Swedish mogul. Rauno was embarrassed by the barrage, and gallantly defended his boss. But inside, he was beginning to feel kinship with the fellow wreck hunter.

McClung boasted that he had already found *La Capitana*, although he had yet to locate her treasure trove. In 1997, he uncovered the timbered skeleton of a wreck that fit the description of the broken behemoth. And he salvaged about five thousand silver pieces and assorted artifacts of the period. But McClung had trouble getting others to believe him. Spanish colonial records were precise about *La Capitana's* salvage site, and McClung's wreck was in a different location. His rivals insisted that he must be on top of one of the many unknown wrecks, and so they continued with their own searches. Rauno was not convinced either, the evidence was contradictory. Later, while poking around historical sites in Lima, Rauno learned something that explained the mystery. A century after *La Capitana* went down, the Tsunami of 1748 devastated the shoreline village fronting the wreck site. The fierce storm, Rauno surmised, unleashed a powerful tidal wave that scraped the heavy hull across the seafloor. "Without a shadow of doubt," Rauno declared, "the wreck McClung found is *La Capitana*."

If Rauno was right, then the tsunami also explained why the missing silver was not recovered. The treasure was likely still interred not far from the original salvage spot. This area of sea, however, was outside the boundaries of Kjell's claim. Rauno never got the chance to test his theory. "After four years of chasing a ghost ship," Rauno was ready to return to Finland, though he was not going alone. Rauno had made more than one memorable acquaintance at Choklo's bar. Giselle Mansilla grew up in a family of professional divers. But after her brother died in a diving accident, she had no interest in the sport. Nor did she have any interest in Finland, which she associated with Vikings and snow. Yet Rauno convinced her that he was the "Indiana Jones of the Baltic Sea," and Giselle was smitten. And so Rauno resigned his commission as Kjell's chief wreck hunter, though the Swede and Finn remained united by their mutual interest in another treasure ship.

"One day I was driving with Rauno into Guayaquil," recalled Kjell, "and he looked very sad." Kjell pressed his friend about what was bothering him. Rauno had just received bad news from his attorney in Finland about the lawsuit against the NBA. Not only had he lost the case at the District Court, the judges slapped a punishing fine on him as well. "He had to pay a lot of money to the Finnish court," Kjell said, "so I decided to help him."

Kjell wanted to be involved with the *Vrouw Maria*. By now he was familiar with the saga of Catherine's lost treasure ship and Rauno's defiant legal battle. The risk-taking, self-made adventurer was a staunch advocate of the "Finders Keepers" principle, and had a vested interest in seeing a wreck hunter prevail over state bureaucrats in a court of law. But Kjell's fascination with the Baltic legend ran deeper. It touched his love of history, and his desire to make history. More than anything else, Kjell's adventuring was about the thrill of discovering renowned relics of the past for the cultural enrichment of the present—Atahualpa's ransom of Incan gold, *La Capitana's* plunder of Spanish silver, and now the *Vrouw Maria's* clutch of Golden Age masterpiece paintings. He concocted an amazing plan for raising the wreck and displaying her art treasure to the world. From this point, Kjell would underwrite the case of *Koivusaari et al. vs. Finland*.

At the Appeals Court

"The dispute over the *Vrouw Maria* shipwreck for ownership and salvage reward is headed to the Appeals Court," reported the *Helsingin Sanomat* in late August 2004. Just ten weeks following the District Court's emphatic knockdown, Rauno and Mika agreed to go another round. Their fortitude was stoked, and subsidized, by their Swedish patron. Still, even with Kjell's largesse, it was not an inevitable decision. The pair anticipated that more invective would be heaped on them. "It was quite hostile," recalled Mika, who with Rauno was condemned for trying to expropriate the national culture. "It was a Dutch ship, with a Dutch captain and crew, and a Russian-owned cargo. What did Finnish cultural heritage have to do with it?" the exasperated filmmaker asked. "And it was so shameless that they changed the law during the court case," he continued, "when it was really just typical Finnish jealousy all along." This time the friends entered the fray without expectations, but with pride and principle intact.

In early March 2005, the third skirmish in the *Vrouw Maria* custody battle commenced in Turku. In the Finnish legal system, the Appellate Court hears the same claims and evidence as the District Court, in a kind of expedited retrial. The Appellate Court's three-judge panel called twelve witnesses to provide testimony. Attorney Jan Aminoff again took the lead in presenting Rauno's side. To the appellants' relief, the bench struck a more balanced pose than in the previous trial. Once again, attention focused on the salvaging of the six artifacts. The judges lingered over the statements of Maija Fast-Matikka and Marja Pelanne, pushing them to recall exactly what was said aboard the *Teredo* in the summer of 1999. On March 23, the court issued its judgement. The plaintiffs were simultaneously vindicated and vexed.

The Appellate Court rejected the legal foundation of the District Court ruling. "The Antiquities Act is not superior to the Maritime Code," the Court concluded. "Furthermore, the Antiquities Act contains no provisions that prohibit the application of the Maritime Code's provisions on salvaging shipwrecks. Both laws are applicable to the matter under examination here." But the Appellate Court's opinion only overturned the District Court's legal reasoning, it did not overturn the practical implications. While the decision recognized Rauno's claim as first salvor, the Court launched into a legalistic catch-22, saying that he could only exercise first salvage rights with the owner's consent. And, based on the amended Antiquities Act, the NBA was still owner of the wreck. At least Rauno and Mika scored one redeemable victory, when they were given relief from the onerous fine imposed by the District Court.

Though the ruling disappointed the plaintiffs, the Appellate Court's decision offered a sliver of hope. It acknowledged Rauno's status as first salvor, though it was short on the legal details. Jan Aminoff pointed out that the judges "did not discuss the question of whether the mere fact that the divers had raised a number of objects from the wreck constitutes salvage." Kjell urged the boys to try their luck again. The fight for the *Vrouw Maria* would now go to the highest court in the land, the Supreme Court of Finland. Kjell firmly believed that the wreck legally belonged to the first salvor, and that the courts would eventually get it right. Confident of this, the Swedish patron moved forward with an ambitious plan for the *Vrouw Maria*.

The Swedish Plan

The *Vrouw Maria* was not your average treasure wreck. She did not flaunt a roguish pirate pedigree with glittering booty-brimming coffers, nor did she brandish fighting credentials with tarnished battle-tested cannons. The ship itself was an exceptionally well-preserved but ordinary 18th century merchantman. Yet the *Vrouw Maria* contained a cargo like no other. "You know the triptych by Gerrit Dou is on board," Kjell enthused. "That's the most precious piece of art in the world." Indeed, *The Nursery* was once the most revered painting of the Dutch Golden Age. This was what made the *Vrouw Maria* such an extraordinary shipwreck. And this was why Kjell planned such an extraordinary museum.

Kjell did not simply hand Rauno a blank check to cover his legal expenses. Instead, he saw the cost of the lawsuit as an investment in a vision. Kjell approached the *Vrouw Maria* with the same big risk/big reward style that he brandished in all business affairs. On his initiative and capital, Kjell founded a corporation in partnership with Rauno called Vrouw Maria Explorations. The company would subsidize the legal battle, with an understanding that if a court were to recognize Rauno's claim, then first salvage rights would be transferred to the company. In this way, Kjell would become part owner of the legendary wreck and cargo. But the lawsuit was not the company's only concern. Kjell also devised a scheme to bring the *Vrouw Maria* to the world. He contracted a host of deep-water salvors, shipwreck conservators, art restorers, and museum consultants to devise a Swedish plan.

Museum design has come a long way from its 19th century neoclassical heyday. Since Frank Lloyd Wright sketched an ascending spiral of ramps to display Solomon R. Guggenheim's modern art collection along New York's Fifth Avenue, museum outer walls have become as attention-grabbing as their inner wares. Museums are more entertainment complexes than temples of contemplation. Following these trends, Kjell believed that the *Vrouw Maria* should have a fitting showcase. Not only would the Vrouw Maria Maritime Museum be a space dedicated to art and seafaring, it would be seaworthy as well. The shipwreck museum would be an actual ship.

The Swedish plan would custom-fit a museum into the frame of a converted Baltic cruise liner, a refurbished and reinforced midsized car ferry. It would bring the 18th century snow-brig and her 17th century masterpiece cargo to the people. The two lower decks would feature museum exhibits and the two upper decks would provide a restaurant and hotel. The centerpiece of the museum would be an immense salt water aquarium, in which the *Vrouw Maria* would reside. The museum ferry would remain in port for a year in each of the three locales where the *Vrouw Maria*'s story unfolded—Amsterdam, Saint Petersburg, and Helsinki. The *Vrouw Maria* was an international story, and so it would be an international museum.

For the interior, Kjell turned to the imaginative Fredrik Arvas, a Swedish business consultant and investor in the Ecuador project. The tech-savvy Arvas fashioned an online experience of the futuristic museum ferry to promote the plan. "I wanted to do something different from what was out there," Fredrik said. "I wanted the museum to be an active experience, an environment for people and dialogues to come together. There is too much passive consuming, I want co-creation." In Fredrik's design, the lower museum floor would use multimedia displays to tell the stories of the ship, and the wreck; while the upper museum floor would feature the salvaged art treasures, telling the story of Dou's triptych, the Golden Age masterpieces, and Catherine the Great's art collecting. Fredrik also wanted visitors to observe the work of art restoration and wreck salvaging in process behind the glass aquarium walls. "It would be really fun if that was possible," he said. "People like to be part of something that is going on."

The idea of placing a raised wreck in an aquarium tank was not new. The Bremen Cog in Germany and the Nanhai One in China offered variations on this wreck conservation technique. But there was no museum on the scale and ambition envisioned in the Swedish Plan. By keeping the *Vrouw Maria* in a salt water tank, with water conditions and pressure similar to the archipelago seafloor, the designers hoped to avoid the serious and expensive conservation problems that occurred with the *Vasa* when she was lifted out of the water.

Reactions to the Swedish plan ranged from astounded to skeptical, but Kjell was not deterred. His plan was to create a multinational, multifunctional conservation complex: enlightening visitors on history and art, advancing the science of marine archeology, and entertaining the general public at leisure. The museum as spectacle, a floating Guggenheim. But

Kjell's vision would never come to be if a court did not recognize Rauno as the *Vrouw Maria*'s rightful claimant. In autumn 2005, another chance for the wreck hunter to make his case had arrived.

At the Supreme Court

In the early 2000s, while Rauno was looking for *La Capitana* in Ecuador, the Maritime Museum was looking at the *Vrouw Maria* in the Baltic. As part of the EU-sponsored MoSS project, museum divers measured the ship extensively, gauged the temperature and oxygen level of the water, confirmed that the metal ingot raised by Rauno was made of zinc, and determined that the clay pipes were made in Gouda. The signature accomplishment of the MoSS project was a three-dimensional rendering of the wreck by marine archeologist Stefan Wessman. The computer-generated sketch was then fashioned into a still-life model, arranged in a table-top aquarium tank. It depicted the *Vrouw Maria* on the seafloor, the *Teredo* on the surface, and miniature toy divers descending in between. Sallamaria's final MoSS report bragged that "this model may seem old fashioned in other parts of Europe, but in Finland this is the first one of its type." It was a stark contrast to Kjell's outlandish plan for a life-size aquarium with the real *Vrouw Maria* inside.

What made the *Vrouw Maria* a legendary shipwreck was Gerrit Dou's triptych and the Dutch masterpiece paintings. But during the three-year MoSS project, the Maritime Museum chose not to explore the contents of the wreck. Regarding the cargo, Wessman admitted that "there is still a lot to learn about this ship, the inside still remains mostly a question mark." At the end of the EU-sponsored project, the fate of the *Vrouw Maria*'s art treasure was still no closer to being known than on the day that her wraith-like image first appeared on Rauno's side-scan sonar screen. It was now more than six years since that jubilant midsummer afternoon, and Rauno was once again headed to court to reclaim his find.

The venue for this fourth round was the Supreme Court in Helsinki. This time the NBA was as anxious as Rauno to revisit the previous ruling. Although the NBA's ownership claim was upheld by the Appellate Court, their lawyers objected to the opinion that the Antiquities Act does not automatically overrule maritime law. The NBA wanted the Supreme Court to reject this position so as to preempt future challenges to the Antiquities Act. By this time, Rauno was reconciled that he could not get around the retroactively revised Antiquities Act. The Supreme Court, by constitutional mandate, is not allowed to contest the validity of legislative acts. As Jan Aminoff explained, the ownership issue "was dead beforehand, and we did not want to harm the rest of our appeal." So Rauno dropped his claim to the wreck, and instead petitioned the Court to recognize his status as first salvor and right to a salvage reward.

On November 23, 2005, the Supreme Court issued a terse statement. The Court "refused leave to appeal." This meant that the Supreme Court would not reopen the case and that the judgement of the Appellate Court stands. Neither Rauno nor the NBA were satisfied with this anticlimactic nondecision.

While the Supreme Court was the last legal stop in the Finnish justice system, it was not the end of the line for a justice-seeking Finn. Rauno had at least one more option. The battle for the coveted snow-brig was heading west, to Strasbourg, and the European Court of Human Rights. Before that case was heard, however, another challenger for the *Vrouw Maria* appeared on the eastern horizon. It was the Finnish government's worst nightmare. Empress Catherine's heirs were finally putting in a claim on Her Majesty's lost treasure.

18

THE RUSSIAN ADVANCE

Moscow, 2007

At the corner of the Old Arbat and the Garden Ring stands one of Moscow's "Seven Sisters," the iconic Russian-Gothic skyscrapers commissioned by Stalin to signal the communist capital's arrival as a modern metropolis. Since 1953, the crenulated landmark has housed the Ministry of Foreign Affairs. In early July 2007, the diplomatic chiefs of Finland and Russia convened here for a day of negotiations. Talk was about border controls, timber tariffs, and the usual list of bilateral concerns. Toward the end of the meeting, the Russian minister introduced to his Finnish counterpart a fresh item for discussion—the *Vrouw Maria*.

Later at the closing press conference, Sergey Lavrov announced "a new area of cooperation" between Russia and Finland: "a joint project to recover valuable art objects from the ship *Vrouw Maria*, which sank long ago in Finnish waters while carrying precious paintings from Holland to their buyer, Catherine the Great." The details, the Russian foreign minister promised, would be worked out by a collaborative expert group. "I am sure that the realization of this project will not only be important for Russian-Finnish relations, but for all of Europe as well."

The Finnish foreign minister, Ilkka Kanerva, had been on the job for less than three months, and did not yet appreciate just how stubborn was the government's culture bureaucracy, the National Board of Antiquities (NBA), regarding its underwater trophy. Kanerva mumbled a half-hearted commitment to the Russian foreign minister. "While the wreck belongs to Finland by law," he said, "Finland would be happy to cooperate in a project. Russian enthusiasm could make the *Vrouw Maria* a hugely spectacular event." The NBA disagreed. Less than two weeks after the meeting in Moscow, the head of the NBA's Archeology Department issued a clarification: "We have already said that the wreck will remain in place at this time. We will examine it for as long as it takes to determine its condition. And we will go inside it as little as possible." But the Russian foreign minister was undeterred. While the wreck lay in Finnish waters, the cargo inside was the property of Her Majesty, the Empress Catherine II.

There were legitimate grounds for Lavrov's assertion. The Russian claim hinged on a legal interpretation of "abandonment." In maritime law, abandonment is the act of deserting a shipwreck and sunken cargo, with neither hope of recovering it, nor intention of returning to it. If a vessel is determined by law to be abandoned, then the "Finders Keepers" principle applies. But just because a property is lost at sea does not automatically mean that it is abandoned. Maritime law generally recognizes the validity of original owners, as long as they have not formally relinquished their claim or accepted compensation for their losses. Despite the two-plus centuries between the *Vrouw Maria*'s sinking and discovery, a Maritime Court might possibly recognize Catherine's heirs as rightful owners of the masterpiece cargo.

The *Vrouw Maria*'s rival claimants all knew this. Dutch marine archeologist Martijn Manders spoke frankly. "The Russians are correct. The art was owned by Catherine. As long as she did not take out insurance on it, then they still own it." Swedish patron, Kjell Edwall, meanwhile, tracked down a descendant of the Romanovs living in Denmark and convinced them to renounce the royal family's claim on the artwork. This signed document,

Kjell said, meant the cargo is formally abandoned, and should go to the first salvor. The Finns also were aware of the merits of the Russian claim, and repeatedly insisted that the *Vrouw Maria* had been abandoned, making the Finnish government the rightful owner.

The Russians knew better. Catherine's extensive efforts over several summers to locate the wreck and salvage the cargo signaled that the property was not willfully abandoned. Nor did the empress accept any insurance claim on the paintings, at least there is no record of such. The passage of time was merely incidental. The tsarina amassed her fabulous art collection with monies drawn from the Russian state treasury, in her capacity as Russian head of state. That the Russian state was led by the Romanov family at the time was coincidence. The throne was permanent, the occupant temporary. The cultural wealth accumulated under the Old Regime monarchy belonged to its institutional successor, not to a divested count from Copenhagen. Historical legal precedent was on Russia's side—the rightful heir to Catherine's masterpiece paintings was the present-day Russian state.

The *Vrouw Maria* was now on the agenda of Finnish-Russian relations. By this time, Russia was increasingly vested in its pre-Revolutionary past as legitimating symbols for its postcommunist present. And Catherine the Great's treasure ship was the perfect story to enhance the old Imperial mystique. The Russians formed an ad hoc committee of private sponsors, scientific experts, and public officials who conspired to raise the wreck, salvage the cargo, and restore the artwork. They fanned public interest in the legend of Catherine's lost treasure ship and the Golden Age masterpieces aboard. Leading this cultural campaign to rescue the *Vrouw Maria* was a former Red Soviet engineer turned New Russian entrepreneur, Artyom Tarasov, the country's self-proclaimed first millionaire.

Russia's First Millionaire

A man in a hurry pushed ten kopeks through the window of a sidewalk kiosk. "*Pravda*, please." He snatched a copy of the *Communist Party Daily* and read: "Socialist cooperatives are a progressive and useful form of activity. They open up extensive opportunities for citizens to do productive work and to earn income based on the amount and quality of that work." There was no mistaking the gist of the new Law on Cooperatives, concluded Artyom Tarasov. After sixty years of criminalization, private business was legal again.

Russia's communist experiment was coming to an end. Lenin's Revolution did not bring a proletarian paradise. Instead, the social order that replaced the tsars and aristocrats was a bloated dictatorship and perpetual austerity. Soviet Russia was ready for change. In March 1985, the young lawyer Mikhail Gorbachev was promoted as Communist Party head and charged with the task of rejuvenating Soviet socialism. Operating on the assumption that a more vibrant society would stimulate a more productive economy, Gorbachev introduced a series of radical reforms. Censors were reined in, party bosses were voted on, and private entrepreneurs were welcomed back. But three generations of overbearing communism had dulled people's sense of how to operate in an open society, except for a restless few.

Perhaps it was ancestry that prepared Artyom Tarasov for the rough-and-tumble world of postcommunist capitalism. He was descended from a family of prosperous Armenian traders, sable-flaunting and theater-loving grandees of old Moscow. Although the family's oil business and Moscow mansion were confiscated by the Revolution, at least a few Tarasovs remained in Russia and adapted to the proletarian project. Artyom's intellectual parents found work in photography and academia. They proudly schooled their son on family history. The brainy boy gained admission to Soviet Russia's elite schools for engineering and economics. A careerist Communist, Tarasov was methodically making his way into the privileged club of Soviet manager-scientists, when Gorbachev came to power and offered an alternative path to status and wealth.

Blazing a trail into the unknown, Artyom registered Moscow's tenth newest cooperative, and named it "Progress" before he even knew what it would sell. Tarasov understood that the basics of business was supply and demand. And one thing in big demand was official residency permits to live in Moscow, which, he knew, were automatically issued to anyone marrying a local. Artyom became a marriage broker. "We received 4,000 potential customers in the first five days of operation," he said, "raising 100,000 rubles ($172,000), when the average wage was still 130 rubles per month ($224)." On the sixth day, city authorities revoked the co-op's license for being "an immoral business." Undaunted, Artyom and partners began a new start-up, "Tekhnika," which peddled foreign-brand electronics and computers. Importing these goods required foreign currency, which the co-op procured from high-end prostitutes for three times the official exchange rate. "A computer would cost us 1,500 rubles ($2,500)," he recounted, "and we would then sell it to a state-owned enterprise for 50,000 rubles ($85,000)." The venture thrived: "We were walking around with suitcases full of cash."

Artyom's success was fueled by irrepressible self-promotion, luring backers for his ever-grander schemes. But immodesty proved his undoing. In 1989, Tarasov told a *Moscow News* reporter that "he was Russia's first legal millionaire." The claim astounded. He was invited on the popular late-night television program *Vzglyad* (*The View*), where he repeated the claim and told the audience how they could get rich, too. His guest spot prompted thousands of letters to the show's producers, half suggesting Artyom be appointed the next prime minister and half suggesting he be lined up against a wall and shot. The authorities launched an investigation. Accusations flew—business fraud, tax evasion, embezzled funds. Artyom worked his Communist Party connections, but to no avail. Gorbachev himself, they whispered, was behind the indictment. Tekhnika was closed, its property and bank accounts seized. When the KGB finally came for Artyom, he was already on the tarmac at Heathrow.

From self-imposed London exile, Artyom watched the self-destruction of Soviet communism. In December 1991, the worn-out Gorbachev resigned his post, and with the stroke of a pen, the Soviet menace was no more. Russia was in transition. Newly elected President Boris Yeltsin went much further than Gorbachev ever dared. He struck a wrecking ball to the command economy in the hopes that market capitalism would spontaneously spring forth from the rubble. What emerged instead—an economy dominated by commodity exports and contentious clans—bore closer resemblance to tsarist feudalism.

Brash, daring, and mercenary, Tarasov was the prototype of the "New Russian" elite. But while Artyom was sidelined in London, the most valuable assets of the Soviet command economy—oil and gas, aluminum and nickel, diamonds and gold, media and finance—were grabbed up by post-communist robber barons. These pop-up billionaires sought to validate their newfound status with the time-tested trophies of the nouveaux riches, including country estates, super yachts, and artwork, especially Old Masters. But Russia's neo-aristocrats also devoured Modern and Contemporary celebrity artists—Picasso, Klimt, Monet, et al. And in a nationalist splurge they drove up the international market for early 20th century Russian avant-garde artists—Kandinsky, Chagall, Goncharova, et al. Under Boris Yeltsin, life was good for Russia's self-proclaimed oligarchs. Too good.

Russia's greedy and bellicose oligarchs could not agree on how to divvy up the country's assets. Their unwillingness to compromise led the transition economy to a ruinous crash. The 1998 financial crisis brought the curtain down on the "Wild Wild East," Russia's short-run spectacle of uninhibited gangster capitalism. From this time, postcommunist Russia would follow a more independent path, a more orderly path, a more familiar path.

If Russia's new elite wanted to recreate an Old World–styled aristocracy, it would have to do so with an Old Regime–like tsar as leader. Someone to impose order on the fratricidal oligarchs and demand tribute for their ill-gotten gains. In 1999, Boris Yeltsin relinquished the presidential throne to hand-picked successor Vladimir Putin. And just as it was in Imperial times, the coronation of a new tsar was an opportunity for exiled princelings to return home. In London, Artyom Tarasov was encouraged.

Catherine and Vladimir

A scuba diver in a black wet suit hovered over the seafloor. The visibility was excellent. He spied an unnaturally shaped dark object protruding from the sand. He swam lower to investigate, an old vase perhaps. Gently testing the grip, the diver lifted an elongated ceramic off the bottom. Back on the beach, a crowd gathered to see the diver's discovery: two antiquated wine amphorae, estimated at 2,500 years old. The salvaged artifacts were evidence of the existence of Phangoria, a Black Sea trading city of ancient lore. The historic find made headlines around the world. Here at the edge of the Taman Peninsula was tangible proof of a "Russian Atlantis." All in a day's work for Russia's Action-Hero President, Vladimir Putin.

When the amphorae were salvaged, in August 2011, Russians were already accustomed to their leader's annual summer adventure photo-op.

This year's marine archeology exploits were met with the usual mix of good humor and cheeky cynicism. Putin by this time had been in charge of Russia for more than ten years. He still carried favor with most of the citizenry. In the decade before his presidency, Russians had suffered a devastating postcommunist crisis: the collapse of the economy and impoverishment of the population, a rash of terror attacks and mafia turf wars, and a protracted power struggle that saw the country's first elected president blow up his parliament building. By contrast, Putin's tenure brought normalcy and order. There would be no liberal democracy or market capitalism; but for many Russians, political stability and economic security were enough.

When Vladimir moved into the Kremlin presidential suite, two centuries had passed since Empress Catherine had glided along the same vaulted passageways. Yet, despite the years, Russian politics had not changed all that much. Catherine and Vladimir, as it turned out, had more than a few things in common.

To begin, neither one was predestined for greatness, sharing humble origins instead. Catherine was a low-status princess, living in a frontier principality in Prussia. Vladimir grew up in a working-class household, living in a cramped communal apartment in Leningrad. Both had siblings who died young, and were raised as only children, self-reliant and imaginative. Their stark surroundings fueled resentment—and ambition. To rise above early life's constraints, Catherine and Vladimir showed perseverance and savvy. They both made the most of the opportunity when a powerful patron took a liking to them. Frederick the Great never counted on little Sophie becoming his arch-nemesis, after arranging her marriage to her Prussian-loving husband. And Boris Yeltsin did not anticipate Vladimir Putin would quash Russia's nascent democracy, after raising the inconspicuous ex-KGB agent to high office. Their confident public dispositions concealed inner insecurity—a craving for acceptance, respect, and adoration.

Once in the spotlight, both Catherine and Vladimir blossomed into larger-than-life personalities, the dominant historical figures of their time. Catherine's reign is synonymous with the early modern advent of Enlightened Autocracy, the Philosopher-Tsarina, actively cultivating the persona of Minerva of the North. Meanwhile, in the later 20th century, the modern cult of political leadership evolved from uniform-garbed military commander to

Swiss watch–wearing corporate chief executive. Putin partly conforms to this image, brandishing degrees in both law and economics. But Vladimir is also known for his postmodern alter ego as "Action-Hero," righting wrongs and delivering comeuppance. His tough-guy talents know no bounds: saving film crews from stalking tigers, tossing down opponents on the judo mat, exploring the Baltic depths in his Bond-like mini-sub, revving up the Night Wolves biker pack, netting a hat trick for the national hockey team, or just posing bare-chested against the vast Siberian wilderness.

In addition, the reigns of Catherine and Vladimir roused similar reactions from Western rivals. Both leaders wanted Russia to be recognized as an international Great Power. They stoked up Russia's fighting force and showed off its natural wealth. Their flaunting courtiers imitated the latest Western high fashions. Catherine's wedding for her son Grand Duke Paul in 1773 was no less a politically engineered extravaganza, staged to impress international audiences, than was Putin's hosting of the Sochi Winter Olympics in 2014. But in both cases, power brokers in the West disparaged Russian gambits to gain entry into their exclusive club. The foreign policy goals of 18th century Bourbon France and the 21st century United States were remarkably consistent—keep upstart Russia marginalized in Great Power affairs.

This enduring East-West conflict is sustained by more than geopolitical jousting. The culture clash between Russia and the West has been an ongoing theme in world politics since before Catherine's time. The dominant Western narrative on Russia has long been that of ruffians at the edge of civilization, with one foot in Europe and one in Asia. As Napoleon said: "Scratch a Russian and find a Tartar." This mindset explains the most striking similarity between Catherine and Vladimir, that is, the unrelenting Western animus directed toward them personally. In response to Russia's challenge to the Western status quo, Catherine and Vladimir both became targets of shrill vilification campaigns. At a time when France's Old Regime aristocracy was entering its death throes, the French elite was obsessed with Empress Catherine as murderous adulterer, crass wannabe, and faux philosophe. Likewise, in a period when Western democracy has experienced its own self-inflicted tribulations, Putin has become the convenient villain du jour as insidious usurper, Hitler incarnate, and world's number one megalomaniac. Thin-skinned and proud, both Catherine and Vladimir responded by being more defiant and, when the situation allowed, more antagonistic to their Western foes.

In one area, however, things were different for Catherine and Vladimir. Having come to power with a tenuous claim to the throne, Catherine indulged her aristocracy, enhancing privileges and easing obligations. Vladimir, however, was intent on taming the unruly new elite and reimposing state prerogative. In February 2003, Putin hosted the princely oligarchs at a meeting in Saint Catherine's Hall in the Grand Palace of the Kremlin. Here the President delivered his terms for holding on to wealth and privilege: stay out of Kremlin politics, pay taxes to the state, and perform service to society. After the meeting, one participant, oil tycoon Mikhail Khodorkovsky, Russia's richest man at the time, dismissively told the press that "the president does not understand that this is our money, not the government's." A year later, Khodorkovsky was indicted for tax evasion, dispossessed of his hydrocarbon fiefdom, and banished to a Siberian labor camp.

Vladimir had made his point. Russia's postcommunist aristocrats began looking for ways to appease the postcommunist tsar. And there was ample opportunity. The Russian state was broke, so benefactors were needed to build medical clinics, outfit sports teams, plant public gardens, and restore cultural treasures.

Salvaging the Past

It was tea time in London. Cozied into a corner table of the Ritz Palm Court in Piccadilly Square were Artyom Tarasov and Russian bank mogul Alexander Smolensky. In early 1998, Artyom was nearing his seventh year in exile. The pair were discussing how he might get back home. He had tried everything, he said, including running for president in 1996. Propping a phone to his ear, the distressed Smolensky demanded: "Who's stopping you from returning? Give me the name. I am dialing Yeltsin right now and we are removing that person from work." Artyom scoffed. Even a politically protected oligarch must not antagonize Russia's vengeful police and tax lords. Indeed, only one year later, a warrant would be issued for Smolensky's arrest, after a wild bank run wiped out his profits and cleaned out his investors. Artyom ordered more scones, and bided his time.

London was home away from home for Russia's new aristocrats. The City offered shelter to their fortunes and families. Artyom kept up acquaintances. So when Putin became president, he already had a powerful ally to help his return. Industrialist Viktor Vekselberg was among Russia's most notorious robber barons. In 2003, he paved the way for Artyom's homecoming by investing in his idea for a technology-innovation center in Moscow. Vekselberg also showed Tarasov how to ingratiate himself to the new tsar.

After Khodorkovsky's downfall, the Russian elite accepted their service obligations. One gesture that particularly pleased the president was the restoration of Russian cultural heritage. In 2003, Saint Petersburg native-son Putin directed a citywide renovation of Imperial palaces and monuments in celebration of the former capital's tercentennial. Vladimir sought to identify his battered postcommunist state with the grandeur of Catherine's Imperial state. The astute Vekselberg recognized an opportunity to gain favor. In 2004, he returned to Russia nine Fabergé Easter eggs from the front lobby of the Forbes Building in New York to the restored Shuvalov Palace in Saint Petersburg. In Catherinesque fashion, Viktor swooped in to plunder the entire collection for 100 million dollars just before the bejeweled baubles were due at auction. In 2007, Vekselberg opened his wallet again to subsidize the repatriation of the 16th-century church bells to the Danilov Monastery in Moscow. The eighteen bells, ranging from twenty pounds to thirteen tons, had spent the previous seventy-eight years in the Lowell House belfry at Harvard University.

Tarasov formed his own charitable organization, the Russian Foundation for the Rescue of Cultural and Historical Treasures. Even better, Artyom had a specific treasure in mind. Back in London, he had kept company with the Marchionesse of Milford Haven, a Romanov descendant. In 1891, following a steamy tryst on the French Riviera, smitten Russian Grand Duke Mikhail eloped with Princess Sophie Merenberg, granddaughter of national bard Alexander Pushkin. The marriage scandalized the grand duke's parents, as Sophie was not of matching noble pedigree. Mikhail's uncle, Tsar Alexander III, punished his nephew, banishing him from the realm and stripping him of all entitlements. The exiles-in-love settled in London, with the blessing of great aunt Queen Victoria. The couple's granddaughter became Tarasov's acquaintance. Artyom knew that the Marchionesse possessed a cultural treasure, which might be for sale.

The Romanov "Small Crown" was a delicate ruby and diamond encrusted coronet, made by Imperial Russia's finest jeweler, the House of Bolin, at the order of Grand Duke Mikhail as a wedding gift for his precious Sophie. More tiara than crown, the ornamental headgear was no match for Empress Catherine's 4,936-diamond, nine-pound, velvet-lined coronation cap. But it was still a good story, which Artyom parlayed into a public relations boon. In January 2004, Tarasov escorted the Romanov "Small Crown" back to Russia with as much fanfare as he could muster. Meanwhile, he solicited potential patrons, until he found one willing to put up five million dollars to return the historic tiara to Russia forever.

Artyom savored the role of cultural guardian angel. He looked around for a new project, and found one: Why was no one in Russia trying to reclaim Catherine the Great's masterpiece paintings from the *Vrouw Maria* shipwreck? Artyom brimmed with ideas and energy, but this reclamation project would need more than he could provide. He went to work assembling a team that possessed capital, clout, and expertise.

It takes a billionaire to raise a shipwreck. Poor Tarasov, he was only a millionaire. Fortunately, Artyom had friends in higher income brackets. He pitched his *Vrouw Maria* idea to forty-year-old wunderkind investor Mikhail Slipenchuk. When there was still a Soviet Union, Slipenchuk studied to be a geographer; but in the early 1990s, when the socialist economy unraveled, he enrolled in a finance course. By decade's end, he led "Metropol," one of Russia's wealthiest financial-industrial groups. Slipenchuk adapted smoothly to President Putin's service demands, underwriting the restoration of old Orthodox churches and a Buddhist monastery. He never gave up his interest in geography, both as exploiter and conserver. He owned lucrative mining operations in Siberia and Africa, led a campaign to clean up Lake Baikal, and as head of the Polar Explorers' Club planted a Russian flag on the North Pole. Intrigued by the legend of the *Vrouw Maria*, Slipenchuk agreed to become the portly patron of Tarasov's team.

Artyom next allied with the affable and earnest Viktor Petrakov, head of the Federal Service for the Protection of Cultural Heritage, a government body charged with tracking down lost or stolen historic treasures. In the confusion following the Soviet collapse, tens of thousands of priceless art objects were pilfered from neglected state-run cultural institutions, including the Hermitage. Once Putin came to power, Viktor's agency was transformed into a fighting force against smugglers, forgers, and thieves. Among the cultural trophies that Viktor returned to Russia was an archive of nearly five hundred historic documents, including Catherine the Great's decree to divide up Poland, which American auction houses were peddling. Tarasov's team was now bolstered by official government representation.

The project also needed scientific credentials, but the field of marine archeology was even less developed in Russia than in Finland. Russia was a continental empire, spanning the Eurasian landmass. Its long coastline mostly abutted frozen Arctic seas. Viktor Petrakov, however, knew of a Russian marine archeologist and arranged a meeting with Tarasov. Peter Sorokin was Senior Researcher at the Institute for Material Culture in Saint Petersburg, and a pioneer of underwater cultural preservation in Russia. More importantly, Peter was personally acquainted with Finland's Maritime Museum archeologists and possessed a license to conduct scientific dives in Finnish waters. Artyom was persuaded of Sorokin's credentials and invited him to join the team.

Lastly, Artyom needed a political patron. Tarasov was fully convinced of the legitimacy of the Russian claim on Empress Catherine's masterpiece paintings. He persuaded Russian foreign minister Sergey Lavrov of this as well. The recovery of Her Imperial Majesty's lost art treasures would be a feel-good salve for postcommunist Russia's wounded pride. Salvaging the culture of the past for the politics of the present. Lavrov agreed to include the shipwreck on his list of negotiating items with the Finns. The Russian bid for the *Vrouw Maria* was underway.

The Russian Plan

In mid-November 2007, the Russians and Finns convened for another round of diplomatic talks at Rovaniemi, Finland. Located in Lapland on the edge of the Arctic Circle, the twinkling tourist town is best known as the residence of Santa Claus. Here the Russian foreign minister hoped to move negotiations "on the recovery of art works from the *Vrouw Maria*." But when Lavrov brought up the issue of a joint salvage project, he was rebuffed. There would be no early Christmas gift for the Russians.

The disappointed diplomat put on an optimistic face: "The experts agreed to continue working toward a mutually agreeable solution. I am convinced that this will be the case, considering the cultural importance of the articles that are on the sunken ship. I am sure that Russia and Finland will solve this matter to the satisfaction of both countries, and in the interest of all art lovers." Privately, the Russians were growing impatient. It was now four months since Foreign Minister Lavrov and Finnish counterpart Kanerva agreed to collaborate on the wreck in principle. But the two sides were already at an impasse over what to do in practice. For the next eighteen months, Tarasov's team pressed Finland's maritime specialists and cultural bureaucrats to consent to the Russian plan for the *Vrouw Maria*.

The Russian plan was simple: raise the wreck, extract the cargo, recover the paintings. The team contracted a wreck salvaging firm in Saint Petersburg, Baltspets, whose owner Andrei Spiegel presented a sketch to the Finns on how they would perform a pontoon-style operation with heavy-lifting cranes. "They had experience in raising several ships already," Viktor Petrakov said. Baltspets was in fact practiced at raising steel hulls and large metal objects off the Baltic seafloor, but lacked experience with wooden ships and objects of culture. Tarasov reassured, "The lifting will not be rushed, but done with scientific planning. They will use special soft ropes of artificial fibers so that the wooden sides are not harmed."

Once off the seafloor, the hull would be moved to a location where salvors could safely rummage through the hold. The Russians were not really interested in the shipwreck, just the artwork. "They were mainly looking for the treasure," said Peter Sorokin. "Does the wreck have the treasure or not?" Tarasov was convinced that the pictures were cut out of their frames, wrapped up in elk skins, then packed into barrels or lead containers, with watertight seals. "There is hope," he said, "that the paintings have not been ruined." Meanwhile, expert art restorers at the Hermitage Museum were alerted to stand by. "We are ready to take on all restoration work," said

Dr. Georgy Vilinbakhov, the museum's assistant director. "We have brilliant specialists and the most modern technology."

"The Russians were excited and wanted to do things," said Päivi Salonen at the Finnish Culture Ministry. Sporting sleek Milano suits and snake-skin cowboy boots, Tarasov and Slipenchuk presented the Russian plan with swaggering certainty. Slipenchuk brought two million euros to get the project started. Across the table sat the modest Finns—polite, reticent, unyielding. The order-loving Finns were flummoxed by the Russian entourage. "It's very complicated talking to the Russians," Sallamaria said. "You never know who they are and what is their role." Salonen agreed, "Tarasov was the main contact, but who did he represent? Was he a consultant for the government? It was not the normal way we conduct business."

The Russian plan never had a chance. Tarasov's team hastily put together a presentation for their first encounter with the Finns, but things did not go smoothly. "We had no time to meet in Russia," said Sorokin, "so we devised our strategy after we arrived in Finland." Riikka Alvik recalled that "one of the members of the Russian group brought a CD for us to view, but we could not open it because our computer did not recognize Cyrillic letters. Later we managed to open it and saw that it was a big mistake. Images of a lifted submarine or something, definitely not meant for our eyes."

After the first meeting, the Finns invited Martijn Manders from the Netherlands for backup support. The Dutch marine archeologist acted as moderator, but was unable to bridge the divide. "The Russians say they want to take up the wreck and the Finns say they want to preserve it," Martijn said, "so while there may be a lot of differences, there may have been some common ground, too. This was an opportunity because the Russians were willing to pay. If the Russians want to excavate together with the Finns, then that is great. Just be sure to set up a good archeological plan for it." But this was not how the discussions proceeded. Neither side was prepared to haggle. "Right from the starting point, there was a big gap," Martijn said. "They just could not connect."

Tarasov was forced to revise the Russian Plan. He pitched the Finns with a new concept: "Another option is to send down divers, who could remove the valuables from the *Vrouw Maria*'s hold." Viktor Petrakov expounded: "Okay, you do not want to take up the ship, then let's do it like the Egyptian pyramids. The pyramids stay in place but the objects are displayed in a museum. The ship can stay underwater, that's cheaper anyway, but the objects can be raised." Again the Finns refused to go along, this time citing the safety of the divers. Frustration mounted. "First they were afraid of hurting some crabs, then some birds, then the divers," Petrakov rolled his eyes. "If you are diving, then already you are taking a risk. Besides if you don't sometimes take risks, then you just sit at home and do nothing."

The Finns eventually laid out their conditions for cooperation. At the third meeting in November 2008, at Moscow's art showcase the Pushkin Museum, Finland's director-general of the Culture Ministry, Riitta Kaivo-soja, stated that an excavation project must be international in scope, not just Finland and Russia, and must conform to UNESCO principles for underwater cultural heritage. Afraid of being left alone with the Russians, the Finns wanted to get the Dutch involved in the project. Moreover, the Russians were told, if you want to raise the wreck, then you must preserve her in a conservation museum. You must make a long-term, high-cost commitment.

Päivi Salonen said no exact figures were discussed in the meetings. But the Finnish press first mentioned twenty-five million euros. Artyom speculated that the Russians could raise that amount, as long as Slipenchuk remained engaged. When the sides met again in Moscow, Tarasov promised the Russians could put up as much as fifty million euros for the project. But as negotiations dragged on, the Finns boosted the cost to eighty million euros. Tarasov was taken aback. He countered by proposing a million euros to finance a small surgical salvage. We could break open a small section of the hull to see if the artwork is inside; and, if it is, then commit to the big project. The Finns said no.

Artyom reached out to his Swedish rival, Kjell Edwall, to suggest a grand alliance. A billionaires' summit was arranged in Moscow to discuss the contested treasure ship. The Swedish and Russian groups reached an informal verbal agreement to cooperate raising the wreck and building the Swedish-proposed ferry museum. Viktor Petrakov was encouraged: "We believed it could become an international humanitarian project. Something like Jacques Cousteau might have done, to raise up the wreck and see if there is anything extraordinary inside." Edwall and Slipenchuk were both used to grabbing first, and asking questions later, but on this occasion the tycoons prudently avoided claiming ownership of the artwork. Petrakov explained why with a Russian folk adage: "We did not want to start dividing the pelt before killing the bear." The issue was put off to a future meeting, which never occurred.

Throughout the process, Artyom stayed upbeat. He had a habit, most annoying to the Finns, of issuing press releases that said the sides were close to agreement on raising the wreck and salvaging the cargo. In the end, however, Artyom could not crack the Finnish resolve. After two years of discussion, the slumbering wreck was still in no danger of being disturbed. "The Russian timetable to lift the *Vrouw Maria* wreck is not realistic," Päivi Salonen told the *Helsingin Sanomat*. "There is much needed scientific base work that does not just happen at the turn of a hand." It was clear to the Finns that the Russians had no interest in marine archeology. "They wanted the wreck because they needed great stories about Russian history," Sallamaria hypothesized. It seemed an accurate assessment. But the differences between the Finns and Russians ran deeper than out-of-sync schedules and ulterior motives.

"They could not communicate with one another," said Martijn Manders. "It was like two different worlds. You could see that there was not going to be a solution." A Finnish participant agreed, "We were speaking English mostly, with Tarasov doing the translating, but it still seemed like we were not talking the same language. The Russians were just totally different people. They did not understand our point of view, while their position was, 'Come on, we have the money, let's just go there and lift the damn thing.'"

Tarasov tried to assure the Finns, saying that "we want to share this cultural treasure and be good neighbors." But there was no spirit of neighborliness in the negotiations. The Russians abruptly arrived, pitched their plan, and assumed acquiescence. Instead their proposal was received with suspicion and hostility. "There was a lot of talking, a lot of words, and a lot of plans, but it was just a lot of theater," said a Finnish insider. Living memories of the Cold War remain vivid in Finland, while the heroic Winter War is enshrined in the national identity. "Everybody is afraid of Russia for some reason," shrugged Petrakov, "but there is no need to be afraid, because she is normal. To everybody, it seems that we are so huge, and that we have everything. And we do have everything. Maybe they are just jealous."

GERALD EASTER *and* MARA VORHEES

While the Finns emphatically rejected the Russian Plan, they still embarrassingly did not have one of their own. "At least one good thing came out of the Russian pressure to do something," Martijn Manders noted. "The NBA decided to put up the money for the Underwater Project. I think that these things were connected." Ten years after the wreck hunter discovered the empress's treasure ship, the world was finally going to learn the Finnish plan for the *Vrouw Maria*.

19

THE FINNISH PLAN

Moments of Indecision

t seemed a reasonable position at the time. "It is not worthwhile to conjecture on lifting the wreck before it has been studied more closely on-site," said Professor Henrik Lilius, director of the National Board of Antiquities (NBA), a month after the *Vrouw Maria's* discovery. There should be no rush to decision on "such a sensational archeological find." The professor's call for restraint came amid rampant speculation on the fate of Empress Catherine's art treasure. Marine archeology, however, was not going to upstage the landlocked priorities of the NBA. So while the Culture Ministry's specially-commissioned wreck report advocated raising the ship and salvaging the cargo for a new museum along Helsinki's West Harbor, it was Professor Lilius's opinion "to investigate the wreck in its present location" that prevailed. And for the Golden Age icon, Gerrit Dou's triptych, the first moment of decision passed.

In the same interview, Professor Lilius also mentioned that "it is hard to imagine that resources for underwater archeology will be available for the next several years." Thanks to the grant writing skills of Sallamaria Tikkanen, however, those on-site wreck investigations actually took place. For three years, the MoSS project kept the Maritime Museum busier than ever monitoring and measuring the *Vrouw Maria*, while providing the NBA with a convenient reprieve from making an excavation plan. But all good grants must come to an end. "When the 2003 field season closes," wrote Ulla Klemelä, "we believe that most of the basic documentation work on the *Vrouw Maria* is done. The collected information will then help us to make the right decisions when it comes to its future." The final MoSS Project dive on the *Vrouw Maria* took place in May 2004. Five years after discovery, the museum's on-site investigations were completed and the EU subsidy expired. The NBA said nothing. And another moment of decision on the *Vrouw Maria* came and went.

The NBA leadership's disinterest in marine archeology in general explains its indifference to the *Vrouw Maria* in particular. After the MoSS project, the Baltic Sea's most famous shipwreck lay idle on the seafloor for several years. No new research plans; no new dive projects. The NBA could not even scrape up enough money for an inspection dive on the site, although it did not scrimp on legal fees to thwart Rauno's attempts to regain access to the wreck. But the tenacity that the NBA displayed in the courtroom was not matched on the sea floor. It was more important for Finland's cultural guardians to own the *Vrouw Maria* than it was to know what was in the *Vrouw Maria*.

By 2007, time had run out on the NBA's stalling tactics. External forces were making it impossible to ignore its infamous prize. Rauno's fight for control of the wreck was in the final phase, awaiting an audience with the Court of Human Rights. Russia's foreign minister was making formal inquiries about Empress Catherine's masterpiece paintings. And Swedish billionaire Kjell Edwall was touting a fantastic vision of a floating shipwreck museum. The Finnish media was again overflowing with frothy reports of projects to raise the ship. Finland's cultural mandarins were provoked into action. They ordered the museum to write another wreck report.

When the 160-page study was completed, two years later, an international workshop was convened on Suomenlinna Island in South Harbor to discuss the Finnish Plan for the *Vrouw Maria*.

To Salvage or Not to Salvage

The "Castle of Finland" is how Suomenlinna translates to English. The Swedes built the rocky harbor island fortress that guards Helsinki in the early 18th century to counter the rising Russian challenge for supremacy of the northern Baltic. In the Russo-Swedish War in 1788, King Gustav used Suomenlinna to launch a surprise attack on his cousin Catherine in nearby Saint Petersburg, in a botched bid to win back disputed Baltic territory. More than two centuries later, in November 2009, Suomenlinna's converted gunpowder vaults and naval barracks once more played a role in fending off unwanted Russian advances, this time over a disputed Baltic treasure. A host of foreign experts were summoned to the Castle of Finland "to evaluate the alternative plans of the National Board of Antiquities for the future of the wreck."

It was not the first time that Finland's Maritime Museum availed upon their international colleagues with open-ended queries about what to do with the *Vrouw Maria*. "Every time there needs to be a decision, everybody is invited," said one participant. "And every time it is the same: 'We've been diving on the wreck, we've been doing this and doing that,' and I always think, but you already had that information." For museum staff, however, these talking sessions were valued for bolstering self-confidence in their handling of the wreck. The two-day Suomenlinna conference directly addressed the one issue that the NBA most dreaded—salvaging the *Vrouw Maria*.

Museum staff drew up three salvage options, with escalating levels of commitment and cost. A minimalist option proposed to excavate the cargo for display in a museum, leaving the wreck on the seabed. This was the least expensive salvage plan, but not the least complicated. Salvaging inside the wreck at such depths entailed risk for divers and vessel. The second option was a partial salvage of the ship and cargo. The plan entailed moving the vessel to a makeshift work area in shallow water, and then extracting the cargo. Saving the well-preserved hull could not be guaranteed. Eventually the cargo and at least a section of the hull would go on display in a museum. Finally, a total salvage plan was presented. This option called for raising the vessel with the cargo inside and moving it onto dry ground, where salvaging would take place in controlled atmospheric conditions. The cargo and ship would then be prepared for permanent display in a new museum-conservation facility.

To better understand the total salvage option, the workshop heard reports of recently raised wrecks. The first was the American Civil War vessel, the *H. L. Hunley*, credited with history's first successful act of submarine warfare. The Confederate *Hunley* sunk a Union sloop along the coast of South Carolina, before springing a leak and perishing in the depths. In 1995, American wreck hunting author Clive Cussler confirmed that the *Hunley* was under a foot of silt in Charleston Harbor. In 2000, she was raised and placed in a 75,000-gallon water tank at a marine conservation facility. The process of preserving the metal hull in a sodium-hydroxide solution was expected to last twenty years. Meanwhile, Henry VIII's vaunted warship the *HMS Mary Rose* was located off the coast of Portsmouth in 1967, beginning twelve years of underwater research. The process of raising the wreck lasted three years. Like the *Vasa*, the wooden frame needed to be sprayed with a moisturizing solution for more than a decade. A special conservation museum to house the *Mary Rose* and 20,000 wreck artifacts was built in the old Portsmouth Dockyards.

If the point of these presentations was to excite NBA officials about lifting the *Vrouw Maria*, the museum staff miscalculated. The timeline for raising a shipwreck was marked in decades, while the bottom line for funding was counted in tens of millions. Wreck raising was a never-ending expense, because wreck conserving was a never-ending process. The final cost of the *Mary Rose* conservation museum was thirty-five million pounds, paid for by Britain's National Lottery Fund, corporate sponsors, and charitable trusts. The Maritime Museum estimated that the total salvage option of raising the *Vrouw Maria*, excavating her cargo, and displaying the hull and artifacts in a new museum would take 15–20 years and cost 80–100 million euros.

The Suomenlinna workshop also presented two non-salvage scenarios. The first "hands-on" option called for a new round of research. This activist approach would produce new information about the shipwreck and seafloor environment, seek to learn more about the cargo in general and the artwork in particular, and conduct preliminary investigation of a wreck raising project. But there was no commitment to locate or extract the Golden Age paintings. The second "hands-off" option called for in situ preservation.

This austere approach proposed to leave the wreck in place and untouched. Accordingly, "no new field research will be carried out at the wreck on the initiative of the NBA." This in situ option was presented as "the minimum requirement for preserving a historically important site."

The two non-salvage scenarios represented fundamentally different approaches to marine archeology. Whereas the hands-off in situ option was focused on passive preservation of a cultural heritage, the hands-on research option was focused on active archeological investigation, getting into the site, getting ahold of artifacts, and learning something new about the past.

Following the presentations, a lively debate ensued among the workshop guests. The experts agreed that the *Vrouw Maria* was "sufficiently interesting and historically important" to justify salvaging. Several experts made "points in favor" of lifting the wreck, though with reservations. "I can say easily, 'Great ship, let's excavate,' because it is so interesting," said Martijn Manders, "but set up a good plan for doing so." The NBA, however, was not willing to commit the resources necessary for a "good plan." The experts next debated the non-salvage options. Given its remote and sheltered location, it was reckoned that the wreck would fare well with in situ preservation. Finally, after hours of bandying around the different scenarios, the guests put the question back on their hosts: What does Finland want to do with the *Vrouw Maria*?

When the talking ended, the hands-on non-salvage plan prevailed. The NBA would underwrite three years of new archeological study. By choosing this option, the NBA avoided making a commitment to salvage the wreck, but did not rule out the possibility: "It can be stated that the options of excavating or raising the wreck partly underlie the Vrouw Maria Underwater Project." The venture received a million euros in funding. After a five-year hiatus, research diving on the wreck was set to resume, and with it a new chance to reveal the mystery inside the *Vrouw Maria*.

Inside the Wreck

"When diving down to forty meters, it takes time and you begin to feel dizzy," Riikka Alvik recounted, "and you don't see anything except the water around you and the person you are diving with. It's like a long trip in an open elevator. You have this guiding light but otherwise it's nothing, only water. Then suddenly you start to see something coming at you out of the darkness, the mast tops of the *Vrouw Maria*, and it is just . . . oooh!"

An advocate of hands-on archeology, Riikka was the obvious choice to lead the field operations. She possessed the technical skill to dive in the cold depths where the *Vrouw Maria* lay, and was a veteran of the MoSS Project. "My first dive was a bit unlucky because I broke my ear," she recalled, "but despite a throbbing ache, this was something I had never seen before. Visibility was at its best. There was so much sunlight that you didn't need your lamp. It was early June and the sun was shining directly overhead. You could see so much, it was amazing. It was like being in a different world, in a fairytale. I had seen many shipwrecks in good condition, but this was different. It was like going into a time machine. It was not a shipwreck, but a complete ship. Only the people were missing."

The Underwater Project marked the first time that the museum tried to learn about the *Vrouw Maria's* hidden treasure, the masterpiece paintings. This assignment was divided, above and below the water, between two rising talents at the museum, Eero Ehanti and Rami Kokko. Riikka's young recruits represented the *Vrouw Maria* generation, who were moved by the excitement of the wreck's discovery and readjusted their academic programs to maritime studies. Rami was at university in England when the *Vrouw Maria* first made international headlines: "The media said it would be lifted. Wow, I thought, now it will be studied and recovered." Both Eero and Rami enrolled in the same special course on marine archeology and museum conservation, created at EVTEK Institute of Art and Design because of the *Vrouw Maria*.

Above the water, the fashionably hip vintage cyclist Ehanti was given the problematic task of unraveling the real story of the Golden Age treasure. Discussions of the artwork, even among specialists, were riddled with speculation and misinformation. Eero's methodical probing of old historical documents and international art specialists eventually yielded the most authoritative assessment of the wreck's cultural cargo. Below the water, the thrash metal drummer Kokko assumed the role of lead diver. Having racked up more than thirty descents, Rami boasted the most underwater visits to the *Vrouw Maria* of any museum employee (though not as many as museum volunteer Kalle Salonen).

In June 2010, Riikka led her team out to the archipelago aboard the *RV Muikku*, a research vessel hired from the Finnish Environment Institute. The *Muikku*'s hulking steel frame was stuffed with meteorological gadgets, leaving little space for the divers and their gear. The NBA lent their inflatable motor boat, the *Meri 2*, to support the museum team. The best dive conditions are in early summer, but diving in June required special permission from the National Forestry Board, which oversees the Archipelago National Park. As it turned out, midsummer in Finland is not just a time for land-based pagan revelries, it is also the season in which archipelago creatures enact their own breeding rituals. To get permission from the Forestry Board, Riikka had to promise not to disrupt the conjugal affairs of Eurasian widgeons, Velvet scoters, and any other frolicking fauna in the wreck zone.

Rami stepped off the *Muikku*'s low-lying stern into the support boat, and skimmed over the surface. Ten minutes later, the *Meri 2* bobbed above the site. Rami adjusted his mask and regulator one last time, then fell backward into the waves. "The first thing that you notice will be the erect masts at twenty-two meters," he said. "At this point the sunlight is fading and you begin to sense the darkness and surrounding pressure. An excitement takes over, the thrill of diving. You never know how it will be down on the bottom." Rami made a powerful frog kick toward the *Vrouw Maria*'s main mast and followed the beckoning beam down through the impenetrable gloom. For the forty-meter descent, he used compressed air instead of mixed gas, which meant less time to complete a task before narcosis would start to dull coordination and cognition. He hovered silently above the thick oak planks of the main deck, illuminated by a phantomish glow from his head lamp. He swam toward the dark entryway inside the *Vrouw Maria*.

There are two access points into the cargo hold from the main deck. Behind the fore mast in the bow is one hatch. Rami saw space to maneuver inside, but he was doubtful of the tight egress. "You could fit snugly into the forward cargo hold," he said, "but the hatch is quite small. You can go in, but it's a risk getting out." The team used an extension-arm trash picker to reach into the fore hold. The main cargo hatch is in the center of the deck. At two meters by two meters, it is comfortably wide for a diver with steel tanks to infiltrate. The problem is the space inside, which is blocked by stacks of crates and barrels. "There's less than a meter of open water," Rami explained. "If you get crammed in there, you could get caught. It's not a place where you would want to spend your afternoon, even though there is plenty to study."

Rami decided the best chance of finding the paintings was through the main hold. He cautiously slinked through the hatchway finding a slim pocket of free space. Rami thus became the first person inside the *Vrouw Maria* since Reynoud Lourens's crew abandoned ship in 1771. Rami hesitated in the tight space, wary of upsetting the cargo. A thick grayish layer of sediment covered the hold, making it difficult to know where to look. There was not much time. The accessible items on top, clay pipes and eyeglass lenses, were already known. Rami took hold of an uncovered wooden box underneath, reached in, and clutched something soft and coiled. Checking his watch, he quickly filled a basket with more pipes and lenses, and the mysterious rolls. "I thought it was a rope," he said, "but on the surface, we saw that it was wrapped-up tobacco leaves." Rami was more comfortable on his next few descents, managing to retrieve kegs containing indigo dye and coffee beans, as well as two pumice stones and one of the ship's sounding leads. But there was no sign of Catherine's artwork.

Rami would get one more chance. This time he delved farther into the hold and glimpsed a bold red object inside a partially opened crate. The adjoining cargo teetered as Rami gingerly nudged the crate closer and gently ran his hand through the sediment. "I could not tell how much and how deep of a sample I was getting," Rami said, "but I could feel that there was something like a fabric and something solid inside." A canvas painting in a frame? But as Rami succeeded in extracting the object from the crate, he realized it was a textile, not an artwork. Lab work eventually revealed that the red-tinted finery came from the famed cloth merchants of Leiden; the vibrantly colored dye was extracted from cochineal beetles, the same ingredient used in Rembrandt's workshop to make red paint. It was a good sign for the paintings, perhaps. But the crimson-colored Leiden fabrics were as close to a Golden Age canvas as the Underwater Project would get.

At the European Court of Human Rights

While the Maritime Museum was busy with the *Vrouw Maria* in the outer archipelago, the legal battle over the wreck shifted across the continent. "It is extremely rare to have a maritime case in the European Court of Human Rights," noted Jan Aminoff. But in February 2010, the petition of *Koivusaari et al. vs. Finland* made it to the docket of the Strasbourg magistrates. The dispute had crossed into a different legal realm. No longer a contest between maritime law and the Antiquities Act, it was now a question of Rauno's basic civil rights.

The European Convention on Human Rights was ratified in 1953, in the aftermath of World War II. The accompanying Court of Human Rights was established in 1959 in Strasbourg, along the Franco-German border. The riverfront courthouse with soaring circular chambers of translucent glass and stainless steel was an architectural gesture to the postwar ideal of a united New Europe. The Court does not retry cases or reverse decisions of national courts. Rather, it deals only with cases of abusive state encroachment on protected individual liberty.

Rauno's legal complaint was rewritten to ask whether the Finnish state "had violated Rauno's fundamental rights and, if so, should the state then be obliged to pay compensation for the losses suffered." While Jan Aminoff still served as counsel, Kjell Edwall splurged for legal reinforcements from London, experts in human rights affairs. The new petition appealed to the Convention's First Protocol and to Article Six. The First Protocol guarantees a right to property, and states: "Every natural or legal person is entitled to the peaceful enjoyment of his possessions." Article Six, meanwhile, assures the right to a fair trial. Rauno's petition argued that the Finnish legislature's retroactive revision of the Antiquities Act constituted a breach of the rule of law and abuse of state power.

An appeal to the Court is first vetted by a rapporteur judge, and either dismissed outright or sent to a Chamber of Judges for further review. If the Chamber confirms a violation of one's civil rights, then the Court will order a full hearing to resolve the dispute. But the wheels of justice turn slowly in Strasbourg. Rauno's application was filed in May 2006. After passing the initial rapporteur's screening, Application No. 20690/06 waited in the queue for a Chamber review for more than three and a half years. In February 2010, a Chamber of seven magistrates under the authority of Court President, British barrister Lord Nicolas Bratza, convened to deliberate Rauno's case.

On February 23, the Chamber reached a decision: "the Court unanimously declares the application inadmissible." Finland's largest newspaper reported the verdict: "The European Court of Human Rights has finally settled the years-long battle over the *Vrouw Maria* shipwreck in favor of the Finnish state by rejecting the complaint made by the wreck finders. According to the decision, the Finnish state did not violate Rauno Koivusaari's human rights, when it denied him salvage rights to the shipwreck and artifacts."

In dismissing the complaint, the Court said that the "applicants had failed to exhaust domestic remedies." Making appeal to all available domestic options is a procedural requirement of the Court. Rauno's Strasbourg petition was undercut by the legal strategy devised for his previous appeal to the Supreme Court. At that time, the legal team decided to drop the ownership claim, since the Supreme Court had no jurisdiction over legislative acts. But the Strasbourg judges noted that Article 106 of the Finnish Constitution guaranteed a right to property, and thus offered an additional legal test. Jan Aminoff conceded that the Court's dismissal on these grounds was legitimate. "The Court of Human Rights was not an issue for us when we were planning for the Supreme Court," he said. "We had not discussed that we could end up there." On a technicality, Rauno's legal challenge was at an end.

Simple and Convenient

The first hint that a decision had been made came in a directive to Riikka's dive team: cease all field investigations on the environmental effects of excavation. Next the divers were informed that they no longer needed to take samples of the metal bolts holding the hull together. Soon all preliminary research related to lifting the wreck off the seafloor was halted. Finally, the Maritime Museum sent word to their international colleagues that a scheduled follow-up workshop to discuss the *Vrouw Maria* was canceled. There was nothing more to discuss.

Perhaps it was the Russians that provoked the decision. In autumn 2010, Tarasov's taskforce descended on Helsinki yet again to press claim on Empress Catherine's artworks. As soon as the Russian mission departed, the fed-up Finns pondered how to stave off their incessant advances. The solution was as simple as it was convenient: the Russians can't have access to the wreck, because no one can have access to the wreck. We will leave the *Vrouw Maria* just where she is, preserving her in situ. Simple because it requires doing nothing more with the shipwreck; convenient because it accords with international convention. The Finnish Plan was declared.

The NBA had a new director-general, Juhani Kostet. An urban cartographer and historian by training, Kostet served for more than two decades in museum administration before his promotion. Juhani did not bother to wait for the completion of the Underwater Project to put the new policy into effect. Funding for the research project would continue as promised, but with a scaled-down task list. The goal now was to create a museum exhibit featuring a virtual *Vrouw Maria*, rather than excavating the real *Vrouw Maria*. After that, the wreck would sit in solitude.

In April 2011, the Finnish Plan was revealed to the world. Culture Minister Stefan Wallin dispatched a cold letter to his Moscow counterpart Alexander Avdeyev, declaring the Finnish government's decision to leave the wreck in situ and terminating all negotiations for a joint salvage project. The Ministry followed with a terse press release: "The minister of culture, Stefan Wallin, says that Finland has no plans to raise the merchant vessel the *Vrouw Maria*, which sank in the Archipelago Sea off the southwest coast over two hundred years ago, or to salvage her cargo. Instead, the Maritime Museum of Finland will curate an exhibition about the ship next year."

For those involved with the *Vrouw Maria*, the official announcement was received with disappointment, but not disbelief. In Moscow, Artyom Tarasov decried the decision: "According to international law, the cargo of the *Vrouw Maria* belongs to Russia. It must be returned to its rightful owner." Meanwhile, Rauno's Swedish patron made known his view: "The *Vrouw Maria* has remained at the bottom of the Finnish archipelago since 1999. Although technology and financial resources are available to salvage and preserve the *Vrouw Maria*, this process has been stopped by the Finnish state. The actions of the Finnish state greatly affect people all over the world, who value the preservation of historical objects. The Finnish state's attitude deprives people of the opportunity to experience these art objects and risks the loss of cultural and archeological artifacts, worth among the largest total value for a shipwreck in the world."

Predictably, the Finnish plan roused indignation from the original members of the Pro Vrouw Maria Association. Rauno and Petri had originally devised the idea of a private NGO out of fear that the Maritime Museum was incapable of embracing a grand vision for the historic wreck. Their presumption proved correct. "We found something good, and they just put it in a box and closed it," Rauno griped. "It is very wrong that we have these kinds of treasures in our waters, unbelievable things, and no one can enjoy it, no one can get excited about raising it and seeing what is inside, it would be a really big story," Petri admonished. "We have such a very special wreck," bristled Pro Vrouw Maria diver Petteri Airenne. "I don't understand why the Maritime Museum people think that we must keep it down there. Of course, there is a risk to bring it up, but you must take risks to achieve something great." Achieving something great, however, was not the goal of the Finnish plan.

The most cited reasons given for the Finnish plan were cost, risk, and science. "Raising wrecks is always expensive," Sallamaria explained. "The Vasa Museum is a great place to visit, but we estimate that it will cost a hundred million euros to raise the *Vrouw Maria*. Today we need to have ethical discussions about how to use the taxpayers' money." Unfortunately, the Finnish plan did not give serious consideration to alternative funding solutions. Most notably, the government could have negotiated a collaborative arrangement with joint financing. After all, they had wealthy Russian and Swedish backers avidly lobbying for a chance to invest in a total salvage project. But the Finns had no interest in cooperating with either Putin's proxies or Rauno's patron. To do so would have meant the unthinkable—sharing control of the project. The only outside funding the museum secured was an EU-sponsored culture grant. But Sallamaria could not replicate her early grant-writing success. She explained: "It is no longer possible for us to create new bigger projects because you need a lot of time to make the application and find the funding." Entrepreneurship was not the museum's forte.

The Finnish plan averted risk. To begin, a big excavation project could cause environmental harm to the archipelago nature park, either with heavy-lifting machinery or spilled toxic substances. Päivi Salonen in the Ministry of Culture pointed out the potential eco-bureaucratic constraints: "The environmental authorities have the law behind them, so every project planned in the archipelago needs to be studied and approved beforehand. We can't just go over them and say we're doing it anyway. We need their approval." But the Culture Ministry never bothered to seek approval. "We did not go forward with this," Salonen said, "because there wasn't a project that we were pushing." Another risk was underwater accidents, endangering the divers or damaging the vessel. "It's kind of a pile of matches under the sea," said a Culture Ministry official. But on this point, the Underwater Project final report stressed that "the structural parts are sturdy." True, it was necessary to do more research on the wooden frame and metal bolts before raising the wreck, but these were the tasks that were specifically canceled by the NBA.

Finally, the plan appealed to scientific norms of maritime preservation. "There is no need to raise the *Vrouw Maria* in order to preserve her," the Underwater Project final report concluded. "Preserving her at the site where she is located complies with the UNESCO Convention on the Protection of Underwater Cultural Heritage." But the Finnish government never ratified the UNESCO Convention, and so was not bound to its recommendations. Besides, not everyone agreed with this strict interpretation. "I think that the emphasis on UNESCO has been one of the major obstacles to the wreck," said Rami Kokko. Indeed, the Convention did not actually state that in situ preservation should take precedence over excavation. As explained by Martijn Manders: "For the Finns, the first option was to leave the wreck in situ, but it was not the only option. Maybe there is an opportunity to do an excavation on the shipwreck. You may be able to present something to the world."

Among those familiar with the Maritime Museum, yet another reason was suggested: the staff was intimidated by the challenge of a big salvage project. "It is a bureaucratic mentality," Petri Rouhiainen surmised. "If you don't do anything, then you don't make mistakes." And Kalle Salonen said, "If you don't have dreams, then nothing happens. If you don't have courage, then nothing happens." Martijn Manders agreed: "The paintings are a blessing and a curse. They are a blessing because money becomes available. But they are a curse because everybody is looking at the wreck. People are saying that you are responsible for this wreck and that it must be done right. So I think it is a case of being afraid."

The Finnish plan also exposed divisions within the Maritime Museum. Riikka Alvik was chagrined by the decision's narrow-sightedness: "The lifting of the wreck would provide a boost to marine archeology for the whole world. We could discover much about 18th century northern Baltic commerce and trade routes, sailing ships and crews, even colonialism and slavery. The indigo dyes in the wreck came from slave workers in tropical locations." Rami Kokko also questioned the appropriateness of the plan: "The in situ option might work for one site, but not another. It might work for a certain amount of time, but not forever. Nothing is preserved forever, not even the *Vrouw Maria*. Some people have said that it's just a good excuse not to do anything, which is sad." Kalle Salonen added, "It's very frustrating. We did a very good job with this project, and then they just wrapped it up and put it in the refrigerator."

Who were "they" exactly? At the Maritime Museum, chief marine archeologist Sallamaria Tikkanen was against salvaging the *Vrouw Maria*, instead favoring in situ preservation. But as Maija Fast-Matikka explained: "We are just little people here, this thing went up pretty high to the head of the Ministry of Culture. We are not the kind of people who make decisions." Meanwhile, at the Culture Ministry, Päivi Salonen said: "In Finland, we have this 'low bureaucracy.' They are our experts. So we discuss these things together and we make our opinion together." And, in the middle, was the NBA's new director Juhani Kostet, who was anything but an advocate for marine archeology. But there was not one individual who imposed the Finnish plan on everybody else, rather the plan received support from influential actors at all levels of the cultural bureaucracy. "I've seen in situ preservation prevailing all the time," said Martijn Manders. "The NBA was very reluctant to touch the site." Indeed, the Finnish plan suited foremost the NBA's culture chiefs. With this policy, they could finally be rid of all the headaches caused by Rauno's discovery.

Only a month after the Finnish plan was announced, the new director-general announced an internal reorganization, eliminating the Marine

Archeology Section of the NBA. For forty years, there had been an autonomous unit of maritime expertise within the cultural bureaucracy, which now was abolished. The Maritime Museum's underwater specialists were reassigned to a general Cultural Environment Services Department.

Marine archeology long played the role of neglected stepchild in the Finnish house of culture. Rauno once predicted to Sallamaria that finding Catherine the Great's treasure ship "would lift you out of your swamp." His prophecy came true. Following Rauno's find, the Maritime Museum enjoyed an unprecedented decade of good fortune. But this development fueled bureaucratic resentments. "It's well known that marine archaeology is expensive," mused Rami Kokko. "I'm sure that within the NBA there are plenty of people that don't like seeing tens of thousands of euros put on the *Vrouw Maria*." Meanwhile, Maija Fast-Matikka described the effect of the reorganization: "The NBA just wants us to concentrate on protecting old wrecks now, and we only have two persons to do it. Any new research must come from someplace else."

Following the NBA's bureaucratic shake-up, Maritime Museum researcher Minna Leino penned a critical opinion of these developments: "Ten years ago, the National Board of Antiquities set out to be the leading institution for maritime archeology in Finland. The Government supported the decision and allocated resources to the work of the Maritime Museum. But the will disappeared and the resources redirected. Serious research in marine archeology became unnecessary and superfluous almost overnight. This is a waste of what we have in our hands, an underwater cultural heritage with enormous potential for recovery, which should be cherished as a miracle."

For the *Vrouw Maria*, the Finnish plan was a simple and convenient strategy by which the state could guarantee monopolistic control over a priceless but contested artifact of international significance. The policy, of course, meant the willful abandonment of Empress Catherine's masterpiece paintings and Gerrit Dou's iconic triptych. It was a public admission by Finland's entrusted cultural guardians that they had no intention of trying to rescue the Golden Age relics inside the wreck. And, by consigning the *Vrouw Maria* to in situ preservation, it was an assertion that no one else could rescue her cultural treasure, either.

CATHERINE'S TREASURE SHIP ABANDONED

Leiden Homecoming

Amid the redbrick, white-trimmed quaintness of old town Leiden, about a quarter mile from Kort Rapenburg, stands the Lakenhal, former residence of the Cloth Guild. When the grand hall opened in 1641, its merchant notables were turning out the choicest woolen fabrics in northern Europe, while their Galgewater artist neighbors, the fijnschilders, were turning out the finest genre paintings of the Golden Age. As the centuries passed, the headquarters of the textile industry was eventually converted into a municipal museum, to reconnect with the town's preeminent past. It was in this role, in March 2014, that the Lakenhal hosted a homecoming for native son and leading fijnschilder, Gerrit Dou.

During the Golden Age, Gerrit Dou and Leiden were synonymous. "Within our own city walls," wrote Philips Angel, the year the Lakenhal was dedicated, "we may see the very excellent Gerrit Dou." His works decorated the front parlors of town merchants and professionals. Leiden University professor of medicine and vice-chancellor, Franciscus Sylvius, hung no fewer than eleven Dou paintings on his Rapenburg townhouse walls, including *The Quack*. Leiden burgomasters were so inspired by Gerrit's oeuvre as to commission a piece to celebrate town pride (which never came to be, for lack of funds). Over time, however, the city's feelings for the artist diminished. As Gerrit's reputation fell into art world oblivion it was nary possible to locate even one Dou painting in town. But this was about to change.

"Museum De Lakenhal pays tribute to Gerrit Dou, great master of the Dutch Golden Age, with a special private exhibition of the largest collection of Dou paintings worldwide," read the press release. The show marked the first time in more than three hundred years that such a grand gathering of Gerrit's panels was seen in his hometown. It featured fourteen Dou paintings, and five more by his students, including Frans van Mieris and nephew Domenicus van Tol. The Lakenhal exhibition also served as a coming-out party for the Leiden Collection, a newly assembled private holding of Golden Age artworks, built on the foundation of Gerrit Dou and the fijnschilders.

The Leiden Collection was the undertaking of Oxford-educated American investor Thomas Kaplan, whose uncanny predictions of the ups and downs of silver, platinum, and gold markets made him a billionaire at an early age. With this fortune, Thomas and wife Daphne christened their Golden Age gallery, in 2003, when a rare Dou became available in London. "I was astonished to learn that the works of great 17th century masters such as Gerrit Dou, Rembrandt's first pupil, came up at auction on occasion, and commanded prices far less than what I would have expected," Thomas recalled. The picture was a small enamel-like portrait of a young Dutch man painted on a silver-copper oval with Dou's signature. "One painting is an accident," Kaplan noted, "but two would be a collection." A month later he nabbed Dou's *Portrait of a Woman in Profile* from a private collector in the Netherlands. Before 2003 had ended, Kaplan scored yet another fijnschilder prize, *Death of Lucretia* by Dou's "Prince of Pupils," Frans van Mieris. The Leiden Collection was launched.

Soon Thomas was acquiring nearly an Old Master a week—Dou, van Mieris, Metsu, Steen, and, of course, Rembrandt. To maintain quality, Kaplan engaged the counsel of Dou doyen Ronni Baer and Yankee curator Arthur Wheelock. Kaplan cornered the market on 17th-century Leiden masters just before the upturn; indeed, his precious metal profits were driving the upturn. In a feat reminiscent of the insatiable Empress Catherine, Kaplan in just over a decade amassed more than two hundred and fifty paintings and drawings, the largest private collection of Dutch Old Masters in the world.

"Art is long, life is short," Thomas ruminated. "Collecting Rembrandt is not an accomplishment to be praised, it is a privilege that bestows responsibility." With that sense of duty, Thomas picked up and carried forth the standard of the Golden Age cultural revolution, "building bridges through art." Thomas began to send his painted panels abroad like evangelizing disciples to inspire the rest of the world. In 2017, the Leiden Collection kicked off a world tour on the biggest stages in Paris, Beijing, Shanghai, Moscow, Saint Petersburg, and Abu Dhabi. At Empress Catherine's Salon, the Hermitage in Saint Petersburg, where the Golden Age never went out of fashion, more than a million visitors were drawn to the show. "I was at the premiere," remembered Arthur Wheelock, "and it was so enthusiastically received. They lent works from their own collection, including the Dous, and hung them next to comparable pieces. The show was beautifully done and given the pride of the place."

Across the art world, the Golden Age is back in fashion, with Gerrit Dou back in front. On the quadricentennial of the artist's birth, in 2013, the Netherlands honored him with a commemorative postage stamp. Museums once more covet a Dou attribution. In 2011, the new curator of the Brooklyn Museum was examining the storage stock when he came across a portrait that "was so finely executed, so meticulous, that if it wasn't Dou, then it was by some other master." The panel was examined by a cast of experts, who uniformly declared it an original Dou, and a prominent public space was cleared for the piece. Meanwhile, in 2016, London's Dulwich Gallery orchestrated the reunion of two Dou paintings that had not been together for 350 years, *Woman Playing a Clavichord* and *Young Lady Playing the Virginal*. The museum noted that the two delicate genre scenes "influenced similar scenes by the most revered Dutch artist Johannes Vermeer." Dou was finally getting his due.

Gerrit's comeback was further evident in the exclusive Old Masters marketplace. In 2001, one year after the National Gallery's one-man exhibition, a Dou painting broke through the million-dollar ceiling for the first time. In fact, this picture, *The Dentist*, in quintessential candlelight motif, was sold in Cologne for more than three million dollars (now in the Kimbell Art Museum in Texas). Four years later, a Dou panel topped the four million-dollar mark, when the eerily lifelike *Sleeping Dog* came on the market (now in the Museum of Fine Arts in Boston). Commenting on the picture, Arthur Wheelock quoted an 18th-century catalogue: "Everything is so beautifully painted that it equals nature." And, in 2011, Dou crossed the five million-dollar threshold, when Sotheby's sold *Old Woman Eating Porridge* to a private collector. Still Gerrit would no doubt have been ruffled to learn that his pupil, Frans van Mieris, surpassed the five million-mark three years earlier with *Young Woman Feeding a Parrot* (procured for the Leiden Collection).

These figures indicate the art world's renewed admiration for the alluring small panels of the Leiden School. Still the Big Three of Dutch Masters have nothing to fear from the rising fortunes of the fijnschilders. A portrait by Hals fetched $10 million at a Sotheby's auction in 2011 (though later exposed as a fake!); the first Vermeer to come to auction in eighty years went for $30 million in 2004; and, Rembrandt soared into the $100 million stratosphere, in 2016, with a pair of pendant portraits co-purchased by the Louvre and Rijksmuseum.

Gerrit's Leiden homecoming at the Lakenhal enjoyed a six-month run. It drew more than 40,000 visitors, among the most successful shows that the local museum had ever staged. "The return of these meticulously painted works to Leiden, where they were made in the 17th century, was a special and rare occasion," the museum declared at the exhibition's conclusion. City and artist were happily reunited. Yet still unknown was the fate of Dou's ultimate masterpiece, the coveted triptych, *The Nursery*, captured at auction long ago by Catherine the Great.

Russians Go Home

"For the first time, representatives of the Russian state will visit the wreck of the *Vrouw Maria* in Jurmo," the *Helsingin Sanomat* reported on August 31, 2010. "Russia has informed Finland of its willingness to participate in the *Vrouw Maria* project and hopes that the wreck will be lifted from the seabed. Russia has announced that it already has private funding for the expensive excavation and conservation work."

For the Finns, there seemed no end to these get-togethers with the Russians. As an item of inter-state diplomacy, the *Vrouw Maria* had gone beyond the foreign ministries and reached the respective heads of state. Finland's president promised his Russian counterpart that his country's cultural servants would work to find a mutually agreeable solution. Thus, the NBA's bureaucrats and Maritime Museum's specialists were forced to keep up appearances of engaging in discussions. But the Finns were done talking. By now the Russians were more like houseguests who wouldn't leave.

At the beginning of September, Artyom Tarasov's team was back in Finland. The visit marked the fifth encounter in which the Russians tried to coax the Finns into a joint salvaging project. Finnish patience was exhausted. At the Culture Ministry, Päivi Salonen insisted that the trip was "only an informal meeting. We can talk about things, but this is not an official negotiation." The Finnish hosts organized a field trip for their Russian guests to the outer archipelago. The one-day excursion was devised partly as a goodwill gesture to placate Tarasov's team and partly as a tactical distraction to avoid discussing the Russian Plan. Their Dutch colleagues would join them on the cruise.

The unusual international sightseeing trip caught the media's attention: "Yesterday Russian and Dutch authorities visited the *Vrouw Maria*. The visitors were shown images taken by divers of the shipwreck at forty meters down and visited the wreck site to get acquainted with recent research work." Finnish officialdom was quick to nix any speculation about a cooperative project. Riitta Kaivosoja at the Culture Ministry told reporters: "This is only a tour. The Russians previously wanted to raise the wreck, but no actual negotiations will take place this time. There are no plans now in progress. The shipwreck and the cargo are the property of the Finnish state."

If the Russians did not already feel unwelcomed, they soon would. What was supposed to be a pleasant outing in the archipelago turned peevish. The main culprit was the weather. A chartered vessel was arranged to take the Russians to meet Riikka Alvik's research team on location. The team was prepared to show off their activities, hoping to pique

Russian interest in marine archeology. But on this day, high winds made it impossible to dive on the wreck or even to take a boat out to the site. "Of course, the weather was horrible," Riikka recalled, "so we met them in the nearest harbor and could only see the site from far away. My colleague Peter Sorokin was there, and some other people who could finance the project. They were observing and did not talk much. Their interest was in how to recover the lost paintings." Riikka showed the visitors underwater photos and robot-cam videos of the hold. The images revealed little about the cargo. "I think we made it clear," said Riikka, "that there may not be anything left." If Artyom had been hoping to catch a wee glimpse of the artwork inside the *Vrouw Maria*, he was disappointed.

Tarasov and Slipenchuk grew bored. So that the trip was not a total waste, they decided to go fishing. Artyom claimed to possess the world's largest collection of hand-tied fishing lures, while outdoor sportsman Slipenchuk was a skilled angler of Siberian sturgeon and salmon. None of the Finns had the nerve to tell the Russians that fishing was strictly forbidden in the protected nature zone. And they could only cringe when the billionaire banker hooked a large Baltic pike, which he then had gutted and cooked for a late afternoon snack. It was the highlight of Slipenchuk's day.

Despite Artyom's efforts, the Finns stuck to their vow not to hear any new proposals for salvaging the wreck. They had already laid out their conditions for cooperation: "If an excavation was conducted, then it would need to be done as a single entity; we do not separate the wreck and cargo. The safest way is to lift her and move her to a conservation lab and then to a museum. Of course, the museum will need a permanent staff for research and certain requirements to regulate environmental conditions. And the museum and lab should exist before she is lifted." By 2010, the Finnish price tag for a cooperative excavation package had reached a hundred million euros. It was an offer the Russians couldn't help but refuse. "You can dream of great things," said Viktor Petrakov, "but when you are told that the cost will be in the high tens of millions of euros, then the dream will fly away." The Russians flew home.

The Finns were relieved to see them go. Plans to form an international advisory group were abandoned "given the lack of shared research goals." The *Helsingin Sanomat*'s long favorable coverage of a Finnish-Russian joint salvaging project suddenly turned negative: "Russia is demanding the return of the cargo of the *Vrouw Maria*. Finland and Russia have been arguing about the ownership of the cargo since 2007. The Russian Cultural Heritage Foundation claims that the cargo of the wreck is part of Russia and should be returned." Somehow the *Vrouw Maria* had become ensnared in the familiar narrative of Russian bully versus feisty Finn.

Over the next several years, political events beyond the archipelago reinforced this scenario, when tensions renewed between Russia and the West. Russia was recast in its customary role as antagonist, with Putin playing the part of nemesis-in-chief. And similar to the latter years of Empress Catherine, the ex-policeman's reign at home grew more conservative and authoritarian. The chill was felt in Finnish-Russian relations, and inevitably affected attitudes toward the *Vrouw Maria*. "I think realistically that we should start working more tightly with Russia and the Netherlands," said one museum employee, "but at the moment they have so many strange things happening in Russia that I am not keen on it."

The Russian Plan to raise and salvage the *Vrouw Maria* was a personality-driven campaign, stoked by the vision and skill of Artyom Tarasov. But after the debacle in the archipelago, even the upbeat Artyom was subdued. His team disbanded. Viktor Petrakov retired from government service, and Pyotr Sorokin went back to the research lab. Mega-financier Mikhail Slipenchuk found a new project to please Tsar Vladimir, patronizing the Russian karate federation. Petrakov later rued Finnish reluctance to act on the generous Russian offer: "Slipenchuk was ready to invest back then, but time has passed. Business people do not wait ten years for something to happen."

Without a real shipwreck project to work on, Artyom lost himself in a fictional one. He composed a dreamy ghost tale about the *Vrouw Maria* tragedy for Russia's romance-reading public. Meanwhile, Tarasov's familiar Jaguar was seen less often in front of Moscow's posh restaurants. In 2014, Petrakov mused, "He is hiding somewhere. I used to see him on television at least, but lately I do not see him even there." In July 2017, two weeks after his sixty-seventh birthday, Artyom died unexpectedly from pneumonia in Moscow. Soviet Russia's "first millionaire" was buried in Troyekurovsky Cemetery, on the western edge of Moscow.

For several years, all was quiet on the eastern front. Then, in October 2016, the Russian claim on the *Vrouw Maria* was revived with the promotion of Konstantin Shopotov to the Russian Cultural Protection commission. "Raising the wreck and recovering the cargo would not have been difficult, if it were not for the legal obstacles," he asserted. Decked out in military dress uniform, festooned with ribbons and medals, Retired Rear Admiral Shopotov presented a sharp contrast to the suave businessman Tarasov in both appearance and expertise. The former Soviet nuclear submarine commander was also an accomplished naval historian and the head of an underwater archeological society. The stated mission of the society Baltic Memory is "conducting underwater archeological expeditions to search for ships that are historical and cultural monuments of the Russian Federation, the national treasures of our Fatherland!"

Were the Russians revving up for another shot at recovering Empress Catherine's lost Golden Age artworks? When this question was posed to a cultural attaché at the Russian Embassy in Helsinki, she answered: "I want to be clear. The Russian government has never initiated an official legal claim on the *Vrouw Maria*." The coy consular paused before adding "Yet."

The Wreck Hunter Returns

Rauno Koivusaari stepped with trepidation into the den of Vellamo. The unpredictable water goddess of Finnish mythology, Vellamo is known for unleashing tempests against seafarers when the mood strikes her. Vellamo is also the name of Finland's new state-of-the-art maritime museum. The award-winning, tsunami-shaped building sprawls dockside in the city of Kotka, eighty miles east of Helsinki, near the Russian border. In April 2012, the Vellamo Maritime Center hosted a special exhibition dedicated to the *Vrouw Maria*.

On the premiere evening, the fashionably late Rauno discreetly entered the rear of the packed hall, where a speech was in progress. A few heads turned in the vicinity of the late attendee, registering recognition. Whispers passed through the crowd. *Look who is here.* The speaker paused and looked up from a prepared text, as spontaneous applause broke out in the room.

It was the welcome that Rauno had long dreamt of. The wreck hunter had returned.

It seems only appropriate that a show celebrating the *Vrouw Maria* should invite her discoverer. Deep wounds heal slowly, however. For more than a decade, Rauno and the Maritime Museum were mutually estranged. Less than three years earlier, Rauno published a memoir of his exploits, which prickled museum staff for the unflattering picture it drew of them. At the same time, the Vellamo Maritime Center was christened in a splashy opening gala, to which Rauno's name was conspicuously missing from the VIP list. Rauno burned from the slight, believing, rightly, that the funding for the impressive new facility was directly related to him finding the *Vrouw Maria*. Indeed, a popular expectation was that the Vellamo Maritime Center would accommodate the raised snow-brig for all to admire, until the National Board of Antiquities quashed that idea. Now, at last, Empress Catherine's treasure ship was bringing together the wreck hunter and Maritime Museum.

"Spoils of Riches" was the Maritime Museum's public presentation of the stories of the *Vrouw Maria* and her sister wreck the *Sankt Mikael*. It contained displays of 18th-century maritime history, artifacts raised from both wrecks, and a high-tech virtual-reality dive on the shipwreck. The Dutch Embassy pulled strings to lend several relevant Dutch artworks, including Laquy's copy of the Dou triptych from the Rijksmuseum and Jan ten Compe's *View of the Mint Tower* from the Amsterdam Museum. The temporary exhibit was well received, although it was but a fraction of what Rauno had envisioned. The show closed after a seven-month run.

Since returning from Ecuador, Rauno was preoccupied with non-wreck-hunting interests. He had been at work on an underwater mechanical device, which could harness the force expended in a wave surge as a natural energy source. Rauno's wave-roller was patented, incorporated, and installed along the coast of Portugal. The invention was a success. But when asked if he would now turn his attention to the technology business, Rauno smiled, "No, I am still thinking about shipwrecks."

In May 2015, the Baltic wreck hunter once more was the subject of international headlines: "Centuries-old Shipwreck Chockful of Gold Found Off Finnish Coast." Rauno reportedly had uncovered the long-lost medieval Hanseatic trading vessel *Hanneke Wrome*. The *Titanic* of 15th-century northern Europe, the *Hanneke Wrome* was massive, luxurious, and tragic. Hailing from the German town of Lübeck, the double-castled, 130-foot-long hulk was leading a trade convoy through the upper Baltic to Tallinn, Estonia, in November 1468. The ship carried 10,000 gold guilders and 200 well-heeled passengers, including the Lord and Lady of Castle Raseborg in southern Finland. Ten miles from Tallinn, the ship sailed into a fierce autumn gale and the captain turned astern to find safe haven along the Finnish coast. But the large hulk was difficult to maneuver against the strong winds. A heaving wave sent the ship into the rocks, and she capsized. According to an eyewitness aboard an escort vessel, the *Hanneke Wrome* "fell suddenly and drowned in the blink of an eye." There were no survivors, and her cargo of gold coins was never recovered.

Rauno's hunch about the wreck site came from relentless archival digging, which uncovered convoy survivor statements in Tallinn, cargo lists in Lübeck, and recovered flotsam records in Raseborg. Rauno mustered a multinational crew of Scandinavians and South Americans to search for the wreck for almost a year before the find. But the splintered *Hanneke Wrome* was not easy to identify. Rauno reported "We've found three large sections made of incredibly wide oak planks, an inch and a half thick. There is an anchor exactly like the type used on Hanseatic ships. When it hit the rocks, the hull smashed like a wine bottle against a table. It must have been a violent storm." The gold coins, however, were elusive. Rauno speculated about the lost treasure: "I suppose the gold could still be there, and possibly some silver. No matter, there is going to be something sweet on the bottom. It will still be a good archeological find."

This time Rauno and the Maritime Museum worked as a team. Rauno was reunited with two former museum friends on the project. "The discovery as an archeological site will be most significant," Maija Fast-Matikka told reporters, "especially if it is a medieval cog." And Riikka Alvik was encouraged about the discovery. "The long oak wood samples look promising. I hope they turn out to be medieval. Then we can start a larger research project." But the endeavor never got underway. Laboratory analysis of the oak fragments showed that Rauno's wreck was only 350 years old, not 550 years old. After the big publicity splash, it was not the ship they were looking for. But this did not stop the Finnish Broadcasting Company from going forward with a six-part historical-adventure television series about the *Hanneke Wrome* tragedy.

Rauno was unfazed by the finding. Disappointment goes with the profession, as does steadfast optimism. "I have been tracking down wrecks for three decades. In my bookshelf, I have tons of folders and notebooks containing information that I have collected on shipwrecks," Koivusaari said. "The most interesting of these I will continue to investigate. I don't want to get bored." Besides, Rauno did not really have anything more to prove. The wreck hunter's name would forever be linked to the most fabled of Baltic shipwrecks, the *Vrouw Maria*.

Treasure Ship Abandoned

"I still support lifting the *Vrouw Maria*," said Pekka Honkanen, twenty years after he was commissioned to write the first wreck plan for the Culture Ministry. "The story is so fascinating that it continues to come back to life." If the National Board of Antiquities hoped that the Finnish Plan would quell interest in the *Vrouw Maria*, it was wrong. For more than a decade, Catherine the Great's treasure ship was a topic of wonder and expectation in Finnish media. Popular musing on the wreck did not cease after the in situ declaration. The NBA might have wanted to forget the *Vrouw Maria*, but others still found inspiration in the Baltic legend.

"A *Vrouw Maria* Museum to be Established," sang the teasing *Helsingin Sanomat* headline in March 2012. Less than a year after the Finnish Plan was proclaimed, Finland's largest daily restarted the discussion of a *Vasa*-style museum for the wreck. This opinion was sparked by Helsinki city officials, who said they could borrow as much as 140 million euros to construct a new museum facility along the waterfront to entice the Guggenheim Foundation. Guggenheim means tourists, and tourists mean revenue. Applying this fiscal logic, the editorial suggested an alternative attraction: "Let's take a look at Stockholm. Over the past twenty-one years, the Vasa Museum drew an average of 8.5 million visitors per year, 80 percent of whom were foreign. In the waters beyond Nauvo, we have our own

18th-century prize, the *Vrouw Maria*, filled with even greater treasures inside. It would be a terrific project to watch the historic process from the lifting of the wreck to the final conservation. And we could have a brilliant architectural competition for the building."

More public lobbying for a shipwreck museum was conducted in the national press. An impassioned pitch for an aquarium-style museum was made in March 2015. The concept called for both the *Vrouw Maria* and the *Sankt Mikael* to be displayed: "These treasure ships have slept on the seabed for almost three hundred years. At the time they were found, there was talk about lifting them, like the *Vasa* shipwreck, but museum staff could only scratch their heads helplessly. It was easier just to leave the wrecks in place. But now they are no joy for anyone." The editorial proposed "a brilliant idea—raising the treasure ships, moving them to an empty Helsinki dock, and building giant seawater aquariums for them. It will be a living museum where marine archeologists can dive on the wrecks and search the cargo, and the public can follow the diving and conservation work. The Treasure Ship Aquarium could be part of a multidimensional Baltic Maritime Center that is now missing from our capital."

In early 2017, the idea of a *Vrouw Maria* museum reappeared again. This time the discussion was initiated not by the media, but by the Helsinki City Council. After the city's Guggenheim negotiations came to naught, maritime buffs seized the opportunity. In February, Helsinki City Councilor Terhi Koulumies, along with seventeen other councilors, proposed "to investigate if the City of Helsinki could promote the lifting of the *Vrouw Maria* from the sea and the building of a shipwreck museum next to Market Square, on the site formerly designated for the Guggenheim." The proposal, according to Councilor Koulumies, was prompted by popular demand. "The initiative comes from citizens and enthusiasts," she said. "They contacted me. It will be expensive, but we will see if we can find partners to share the costs." And just like that, hopes were rekindled for raising Catherine's treasure ship and making it the centerpiece of the Helsinki harbor front.

This challenge could not be ignored. Less than a week after the *Vrouw Maria* was added to the local legislative agenda, NBA director-general Juhani Kostet responded, saying that "such a project will not be implemented in the near future." Juhani then recited the usual list of reasons for doing nothing with the wreck. "The best place for her is under the sea," Kostet said. "There the ship will be best preserved and we can research the wreck, if ever there is some money available." Terhi Koulumies was startled by the culture chief's swift rebuff. "I do not think we should be imposing limits on our inquiries," Terhi said. "The proposal only seeks to find out how expensive the project would be and if there are parties interested in financing it. It is the elected official's job to follow up on the good ideas of the city's residents."

In principle, Finland's cultural bureaucrats welcomed proposals for new research and salvage projects on the *Vrouw Maria*; but in practice, they swatted away those whom they suspected were really serious about it, as City Councilor Koulumies learned. By the time the *Vrouw Maria* initiative came before the entire City Council for consideration, the NBA had asserted its position and prerogative. The City Council deferred. After a brief discussion about the merits of the proposal, it was resolved: "If the state decides to establish and locate a *Vrouw Maria* Museum in Helsinki, then the city will welcome the project and look for a suitable seaside site. However, the City of Helsinki is not the responsible body for operating and financing a museum. Thus, the Council will not take an active role in investigating the conditions for raising the wreck."

It wasn't until 2019—twenty years after the *Vrouw Mara* was found—that Finnish cultural officials took further steps on the fabled ship. The newest project involved a partnership with Badewanne, a nonprofit group of volunteer divers who specialize in documenting Baltic wrecks. The goal was to create a new, ultrarealistic three-dimensional model of the *Vrouw Maria*. Modeling technology had improved dramatically over the past decade, thanks to video, photography, and photogrammetry software, so the new model would be much improved from the virtual simulation of 2012. The project was an attempt to make the *Vrouw Maria* more accessible to the public, while preserving her in situ.

Ideally, the model would mean that "people will be able to appreciate the ship in all its glory from above the water." The research would not offer new information about the wreck or her cargo; it would just offer a clearer picture of what was already known. As explained by Badewanne diver Juha Flinkman: "The main advantage of this model is that it is an effective way of showing how the *Vrouw Maria* looks in her present state. It can be used both in printed publications, and as a computer-generated image that can be rotated and viewed from different angles." Flinkman did not anticipate any new insights gained from the project, but added that, "for the general audience, the model will be a blast." The interactive model was slated to go on display in 2020 at a new marine archeology museum being built next to the Vasa Museum in Stockholm.

And so the NBA conducted another *Vrouw Maria* project that would not reveal the mystery of her prized cargo. Even more confounding, this virtual model would be exhibited not in Helsinki, not in Kotka, but in Stockholm. Once again, the initiative and the outcome highlighted the NBA's ambivalence toward Finland's underwater cultural heritage. The *Vrouw Maria*'s unfinished story reflects a deeper incongruity of national culture.

Who raises shipwrecks? The Swedes raised the warship *Vasa* and the English raised Henry VIII's flagship *Mary Rose*, to serve as living proof of a proud imperial past. The United States raised the huge gun turret of the Civil War iron-clad *Monitor*, and then conducted a solemn final tribute at the hallowed burial ground of Arlington National Cemetery for the two skeletons found inside. And the Dutch raised a 600-year-old, 60-foot-long Hanseatic trading cog from the river IJssel, to be conserved and displayed for the public. Seafaring nations and conquering empires raise shipwrecks. The stories of these consecrated marine artifacts complement prevailing national legends. The narratives help confer a collective sense of identity, connecting individual citizens to the national community. We are an adventurous people, a brave and triumphant people. But the *Vrouw Maria* is a different sort of shipwreck; and the Finns have a different sort of history.

Only a month after the *Vrouw Maria* was located in the archipelago, NBA director Henrik Lilius published a long piece in the *Helsingin Sanomat*, seeking to dampen popular expectations about the sensational discovery. "The *Vrouw Maria* has launched a debate about the role of marine archeology in our country," the professor acknowledged, but it would not change existing priorities. "The *Vrouw Maria*'s treasure trove inevitably raises another problem," he said. "Ownership of the wreck is the property of the Finnish state according to our legislation. But are the *Vrouw Maria* and her valuables really Finnish cultural property in the true sense of the word? The ship sailed through Finnish territorial waters, so it is part of our maritime history, but its cargo was never intended for import to Finland. This has to be kept in mind when exploring funding models."

The *Vrouw Maria* may have captured Finnish public imagination, but it did not coincide with Finnish national narratives. The director's statement effectively disassociated the *Vrouw Maria* from Finland's past. Yet the NBA would spend the next decade in court asserting that the *Vrouw Maria* and her cargo were vestiges of Finnish national culture. This striking contradiction runs through the *Vrouw Maria*'s story from the moment of her discovery. It is ours, but it is not ours. It is part of Finnish cultural heritage, yet it is not.

Indeed, Professor Lilius was right: the *Vrouw Maria*'s story is not a particularly Finnish tale. It is an international story. A Danish captain, a Dutch ship, a Russian consignment, a Swedish salvage, a Finnish discoverer. The *Vrouw Maria*'s story is captivating precisely because it is not one country's story, but a continent's story, a civilization's story.

The *Vrouw Maria* is arguably the most extraordinary shipwreck discovery of modern times—a peerless cultural artifact of Enlightenment Europe. The perfectly preserved snow-brig is the early modern means of conveying both skillfully crafted goods and socially transforming ideas. The Dutch Golden Age cargo is an artistic expression of the social values that infused the Enlightenment, espousing the inherent self-worth and potential of every individual, regardless of class or creed. The ship was destined for the court of an epoch-defining monarch whose name has become synonymous with progress and enlightenment, if not democracy. The wreck is a one-of-a-kind cultural relic that celebrates humanity in its most optimistic pose.

But who will salvage the *Vrouw Maria*? As legal guardian, only the NBA can take the lead to excavate the historic wreck. To date, Finland's cultural custodians have been loath to assume the task. When Professor Lilius questioned whether the *Vrouw Maria* was part of the Finnish experience, he was articulating a narrow and self-limiting view of the nation. But the NBA is not the bailiwick of one boss, nor one nationalist narrative. It is a wonderfully rich institution of diverse talent and perspective. And the story of the Finns, like any nation, is not a solitary tale, but a cross-cultural European story. "We should be proud that the *Vrouw Maria* is in our territorial waters," said Eero Ehanti. "It represents our common European heritage and it is our privilege to have this wreck."

Sitting in the main library at the NBA, Riikka Alvik cradled her knees and rocked back in an armchair. She was thinking aloud about the wreck: "The same year the *Vrouw Maria* sank, Casanova was looking at Pompeii. He was a tourist. It is so wonderful that people were traveling. It is amazing how international it all was, how global the Baltic Sea was. Some said the *Vrouw Maria* is not our history, but I think it is definitely our history. The Gulf of Finland was this big highway going to Russia. Merchants stopped here, salvages were based here, it was the lifestyle of the archipelago people. To raise the *Vrouw Maria* would not just be putting a shipwreck in a museum, but recreating this fascinating world all around her, with some of the most interesting characters in history. They are long dead of course, but they still live in this story. And in the center would be this tiny, quite ordinary merchant ship."

The *Vrouw Maria* is not the symbol of one individual nation or the bloodstained glories of war. It is a symbol of a larger transnational Europe and the peaceable triumphs of commerce and culture. In a time of resurgent nationalist chauvinism, this historic maritime relic revitalizes the unifying narrative of a common European home. The final pages of the *Vrouw Maria*'s remarkable story are still to be written. It is up to her Finnish keepers to allow the saga to be completed. Not as an object of exclusive nationalist gratification, but as a premier cultural artifact of Enlightenment Europe.

In the meantime, Catherine the Great's treasure ship lies abandoned on the Baltic seafloor, a lady in waiting. While Gerrit Dou's oak-paneled triptych, *The Nursery*, once the most coveted and beloved piece of art produced in the Dutch Golden Age, remains cloistered in chilling darkness. This inspirational artifact is too valuable to be left to slow and silent deterioration under the sea. The wonder of the *Vrouw Maria* is not if, but when her long-delayed voyage will reach its end, and the mystery of her extraordinary cultural treasure will at last be revealed.

Epilogue
THE TREASURE

L et us not delude ourselves about paintings that have spent six months in the water," cautioned Catherine's enlightened envoy Dmitry Golitsyn. In April 1772, the archipelago's winter ice cover broke and an intensive rescue operation for the *Vrouw Maria* got underway. In The Hague, Dmitry anxiously awaited tidings from the searchers: "Still, a glimmer of hope remains with me."

The empress proceeded on the assumption that the paintings could be salvaged and repaired. As a flotilla of Swedish wreck salvors took to the sea, a team of Russian art restorers traveled to Finland. They remained lodged in Turku for the entire searching season, at the ready for the moment the ship was located. Her Majesty dispatched Major Thiers to oversee the recovery efforts and to pressure the local governor, Baron Rappe. "I have spoken to Monsieur Count General Ehrensvärd, as he himself is a skilled painter," the governor reported to the major, "in order to know how to proceed with the damaged paintings." In a letter to Governor Rappe, the Russian Foreign Minister Nikita Panin was optimistic: "The painters and connoisseurs, who study all things related to art, reassure us about the survival of the paintings . . ." And so the commotion continued for more than a year, as politicians and painters fretted about how to restore the artwork, and fishermen and salvors hunted in vain for something to restore. All galvanized by a "glimmer of hope."

But what really were the chances that Empress Catherine's masterpiece treasures could survive the wreck of the *Vrouw Maria*? Two and a half centuries later, the question is still pertinent. But until the wreck is salvaged and its contents scrutinized, it is impossible to know the answer. The ship itself appears in remarkably good condition, its sturdy oak hull preserved by the Baltic's frigid, brackish, worm-free waters. This has only encouraged speculation about what might be found inside. Treasure hunters, marine archeologists, art historians, financial investors, and adventure-story lovers continue to contemplate the fate of the precious cargo.

The most optimistic conjecture insists the paintings would survive the drowning as long as they were packaged properly. According to this argument, it was common practice in the 18th century to remove valuable paintings from their frames, roll them up, and store them in wax-sealed waterproof lead tubes. Such careful packaging protected valuable artworks on sea journeys, should the worst occur, even underwater. The *Vrouw Maria*'s Swedish and Russian suitors suggested that her masterpieces were packed precisely this way, fueling fantasies of salvaging priceless canvases in pristine condition. In 2008, Boris Sapunov, chief research officer at the Hermitage Museum, surmised: "If the packaging was unreliable, Catherine II would not have spent two years trying to retrieve the lost items. But if everything was packaged as the sources describe and a constant temperature was maintained in the containers, then the wax will have kept out the cold water." As recently as 2016, Rear Admiral Konstantin Shopotov affirmed: "If the paintings are still there, they are packed in tubes, and we can assume their complete safety."

Unfortunately, the "sources" referenced by Sapunov and Shopotov are unknown to other scholars. Certainly Dmitry Golitsyn, who personally oversaw the packing and shipping of the artwork, did not seem confident that the paintings would be safe from seawater. The ambassador's correspondence makes no mention of lead tubes, nor any other protective measures. The only confirmed account of the packaging pertained to Golitsyn's own pictures, which were boxed in straw-filled crates and stored in the captain's quarters. Indeed, the curator for Dutch art at the Hermitage, Irina Soko-lova, offered a more tentative opinion than her optimistic colleague: "I am an expert on painting, not packing and shipping, so I am rather poorly informed about how this was done in the 18th century. But judging by the documents, the paintings were packed in hay and wooden boxes. If so, I doubt that the paintings could have been preserved."

Other pessimistic opinions contend that Empress Catherine's art trea-sures have most likely been destroyed. These assessments are based on assumptions about the long-term effects of seawater on the supports and materials used in the paintings. They are doubtful, but not definitive.

One assumption is that canvas corrodes quickly in Baltic waters, the evidence being the general absence of sail cloth found in the graveyard of wrecks. And yet, during the Vrouw Maria Underwater Project, divers retrieved samples of dyed red fabric, its fibers still intact, its color fresh and bright. "Considering the paintings, you might have a well-preserved canvas," speculates conservator and marine archeologist Rami Kokko, who brought up the cloth sample. "You might even have some of the painting still remaining, because now we know how even the most delicate materials are preserved. So why not?" Finnish antiquarian Wenzel Hagelstam points out that canvas was actually not the most common material for 17th-century artwork. "In those days, paintings were mostly done on an oak surface. The paint and the panel could very well endure the elements." Indeed, five of the paintings onboard the *Vrouw Maria* are known to be on oak panels, including Dou's treasured triptych.

David Bull, a New York art restorer with more than six decades of experience in the business, disagrees. "The wood itself would expand and contract, but the paint, which is very brittle, would not be able to move with the fluctuations of the panel," stated Bull. "If there is paint attached to the panel it's going to break away." Once again, Rami Kokko provides contrary evidence. In the Underwater Project, he took samples of both pine and oak from different parts of the boat to analyze the wood's condition. "The pine wood appears to be almost as good as fresh pine. There's hardly any shrinkage or cracking of the wood, even without any conservation. This is because of the biology and chemistry of the Baltic water—cold, low salinity—it's as if it has been in the refrigerator for 230 years. And oak is even more resistant to rotting and degradation." So it is not a foregone conclusion that the oak panels cannot hold paint.

Besides the supports, there is concern about the binders and pigments used to make the paints. Hagelstam points out that "binders do not do well with water," referring to the wax, gum, or oil that is used to adhere the pigments. Gerrit Dou likely used linseed oil as a binder, often thickening it with egg yolk or thinning it with urine. If the binder is washed away, what happens to the pigment? Riikka Alvik suggests that the pigments would likely be separated from the supports. "If we can find the box where the paintings are, it should be opened in a laboratory, because the pigments would be floating everywhere."

A related question is the grounding, or primer, that is often applied to a panel prior to painting. This is the warm glue that Gerrit Dou melted down from rabbit skin. In 1772, Governor Rappe in Turku apprised the Russians of this potential peril. "In times past, artists would rub a canvas with a kind of paste before beginning to paint, in which case the seawater could have entirely dissolved the paste and the colors would be completely detached. But if the varnish and color were applied on the canvas without this paste, the painting could be conserved easily, considering that the sea-water on our coast is not so saline." Contemporary spectroscopic analysis confirms Rappe's observation that it was common for Golden Age artists to apply a grounding to the support, before applying the layers of paint. But whether it was used for these particular paintings is unknown; and indeed, the effect of seawater has not actually been investigated.

Unfortunately, there is simply no precedent for artwork salvaged from a shipwreck. One might look instead to other wooden objects that were submerged for centuries in Scandinavian waters, which were eventually raised with color and images still discernable to the naked eye. In 1903, a farmer in Vestfold, Norway uncovered an ancient Viking burial mound, containing among other artifacts, the remains of a ship. The so-called Oseberg Ship, dating to 820 C.E., was remarkably well preserved by the ground water that engulfed it for centuries. After excavation, the vessel underwent a twenty-one-year drying-out process and today is considered one of the world's finest examples of a conserved Viking ship. Most notably, the pine oars found with the craft still show traces of the original painted decorations. Next door in

Sweden, the mighty *Vasa* displayed traces of pigment on her ornamental carvings, when she was salvaged after 333 years under the Baltic Sea. The *Vasa*'s head conservator, Emma Hocker, noted that the sculptures with the most remaining pigment were the ones that had fallen off the ship and were resting on the sea floor, covered in silt. Considering the fate of an oak-panel painting, Hocker inferred, "it depends how well it's been covered up. If it was covered up rapidly with silt and if the type of silt was not too erosive, it improves the chance that it could survive." Perhaps, it is notable that Rami Kokko found the *Vrouw Maria*'s cargo smothered under a thick layer of silt.

"Never tested. Nobody knows," shrugged Riikka Alvik, when asked if paint would adhere to wood panels after two centuries underwater. "Most likely the non-organic paints still exist but are they still visible as a picture?" The Finnish marine archeologist was skeptical, but added, "Something always absorbs into the wood or canvas. Everything usually leaves some kind of trace." But will this trace be visible to the naked eye, discernible with the aid of infrared and X-ray technology, or restorable to some semblance of the original image?

The two extreme opinions about the *Vrouw Maria* treasures—the paintings survived in near pristine form or the paintings are utterly destroyed—seem the least likely outcomes. Most certainly, some vestige of the artwork still exists. At a minimum, the oak panels, including Gerrit Dou's triptych, are somewhere in the hold, and probably the canvases as well, given the remarkable condition of the fabric that was already salvaged. But it is not really useful to think about the *Vrouw Maria*'s precious cargo in terms of beautiful Baroque masterpieces ready to hang on a wall. The paintings are severely damaged, perhaps irreparably so. They are unlikely to be restorable as museum-quality works of art. Regardless, the paintings—even in a ruined state—will still be conservable as archeological artifacts of extraordinary historic significance.

The most affecting cultural relics are rarely in mint condition, from crumbling Roman temple ruins to dismembered Greek statues divine, from the cuneiform shards of a Sumerian vase to the cosmic fragments of a Mayan calendar. Here in the Finnish archipelago are the remains of the most revered paintings from the cultural revolution that was the Dutch Golden Age. No less than da Vinci's *Mona Lisa*, Gerrit Dou's *The Nursery* was a transcendent artwork, an iconic rendering of a life well-lived through nature, learning, and purpose. Even in a damaged state, the oak-panel trip-tych remains an artifact that embodies the greatest achievements of early Modern Europe.

That's to say nothing of the ship itself and other cargo aboard. It was a Dutch ship en route to Russia, transporting an inestimable cache of goods from around the globe. It remains a singular specimen of an 18th century snow-brig from the Age of Sail. "These ships," noted Riikka Alvik, "were masterpieces of the technology of the time." And, unlike the paintings, we know the *Vrouw Maria* is exceptionally well preserved on the Baltic seafloor.

In spring of 1772, Prince Dmitry Golitsyn held out a "glimmer of hope" for the recovery of the artistic treasures aboard the *Vrouw Maria*. Two hundred and fifty years later, the lost treasure ship has been found. But a decision to raise or excavate the *Vrouw Maria* should not be based on the presumed state of the paintings. The treasure has been transformed. No matter their state, the *Vrouw Maria* and her masterpiece cargo today represent incomparable cultural relics of Enlightenment Europe. The artworks and artifacts that we choose to celebrate are the ones that tell the stories that are most poignant for where we come from, who we are, and where we want to go. At this time, what could be more important for Europe—and the world—than a story that rises above exclusive nation-alist creeds and reconnects to the transcendent humanistic values at the foundation of our modern society? This is the *Vrouw Maria*'s cultural treasure, and there still exists a "glimmer of hope" that it can be salvaged for the enrichment of all.

GLOSSARY

Åbo Swedish name for Turku, the de facto capital of the province of Finland under Swedish rule.

Antiquities Act Enacted in 1963, a Finnish law that protects shipwrecks and contents that are more than one hundred years old, and grants responsibility and ownership to the National Board of Antiquities.

Archipelago Maritime Society A Finnish diving club that undertook an unsuccessful search for the *Vrouw Maria* in 1998.

Baltic Eye Support vessel employed by the Pro Vrouw Maria Association for the search for the *Vrouw Maria* and other expeditions.

Culture Ministry Formally the Ministry of Education and Culture, the Finnish ministry that oversaw the National Board of Antiquities and later the Finnish Heritage Agency.

Encyclopédie A general encyclopedia published in 18th-century France, considered to represent the ideas of the Enlightenment. Edited by Denis Diderot and written by various contributors known as *Encyclopédistes*.

fijnschilder School of Dutch Golden Age ultrarealist artists from Leiden, literally "fine painting." Founded by Gerrit Dou.

fluke On the arm of an anchor, the triangular plate that catches on the sea floor.

fluyt A Dutch sailing vessel used to transport cargo in the 17th and 18th centuries.

Galgewater A part of the Rhine that runs through Leiden, also a nearby street.

genre painting Popular during the Dutch Golden Age, a style of painting that depicts domestic scenarios and other scenes from everyday life.

Helsingin Sanomat Largest daily newspaper in Finland.

in situ preservation The preservation of archeological relics and sites by leaving them in place, a concept that gained traction in archeology circles in the late 20th century.

kedge A light secondary anchor.

GLOSSARY

Kronborg A 16th-century Danish castle in the town of Elsinore (Helsingør in Danish), overlooking Øresund strait between Denmark and Sweden. Site of Elsinore castle in *Hamlet*.

Maritime Museum of Finland (MMF) Established in the 1960s on Hylkysaari island in Helsinki to study and display marine archeology, under the auspices of the National Board of Antiquities. Moved in 2008 to Vellamo Maritime Center in Kotka.

MoSS Project An EU-sponsored project from 2001 to 2004 that monitored four northern European shipwrecks, including the *Vrouw Maria*.

National Board of Antiquities (NBA) Finnish agency formed in 1972 (successor to the Archeological Commission), responsible for preserving and studying archeological sites. Operates under the auspices of the Ministry of Education and Culture. Later known as the Finnish Heritage Agency (Museovirasto).

Öresund (Swedish) **Øresund** (Danish) A strait marking the border between Denmark and Sweden, also known as the Sound.

Pro Vrouw Maria Association Private nonprofit association created to search for, research, and salvage the Vrouw Maria wreck.

Salvage Act A principle of maritime law that entitles a salvor to keep the rescued ship or cargo or to claim a reward of equal value, also "Finders Keepers."

side-scan sonar An echo-locating device that is dragged behind a boat to find large objects underwater.

snow-brig A two-masted, square-rigged sailing vessel, popular in the Baltic in the 18th century, also *snow*.

State Archeological Commission Finnish organization formed under Russian rule in 1884 to preserve Finnish historical monuments. Precursor to the National Board of Antiquities and the Finnish Heritage Agency.

Teredo Boat belonging to Teredo Navalis Society and loaned to Pro Vrouw Maria Association for the search for the Vrouw Maria.

Teredo Navalis Society A diving club based in Helsinki and named after the eponymous shipworm. Members often volunteered and worked closely with the Maritime Museum of Finland.

UNESCO Convention on Underwater Cultural Heritage A 2001 convention that established a set of norms for protecting shipwrecks and other underwater archeological sites, advocating in situ preservation as the first option to consider.

Vrouw Maria Underwater Project A project of the National Board of Antiquities from 2009 to 2012 to study the wreck and cargo and to examine the options for preserving the wreck.

NOTE ON CURRENCIES

It is nearly impossible to compare historic prices to modern prices, especially across eight different currencies and four different centuries. The options for historical currency conversions are imperfect at best, and do not account for differences in standards of living and other critical factors. For this reason, we have left prices in their original currency.

écu A unit of French currency in use from the 13th century until the French Revolution.

Euro (€) Official currency of most member countries of the European Union, adopted by Finland in 1999. In 2010, €1 = $1.35 according to www.xe.com.

florin (fl) Dutch unit of currency from the 17th century until 2002, also guilder.

guilder (fl) Dutch unit of currency from the 17th century until 2002, also florin.

livre French unit of currency from the 8th century until the French Revolution.

markka (mk) Finnish currency from 1860 to 2002.

pound (£) British currency used since the 12th century.

rigsdaler, riksdaler Units of currency used in Sweden and Norway-Denmark respectively in the 17th to 19th centuries, also *daler*.

ENDNOTES

PROLOGUE: THE WRECK

p. xi On Castle Kronborg, Elsinore, and the Sound Dues, Degn (2018), Lauring (1968).

pp. xi–xiv Description of Baltic Sea journey, Palmer (2006).

p. xii The *Vrouw Maria*'s cargo list and Customs House receipt were uncovered by pioneering Baltic maritime historian Christian Ahlström, (1979, 1997, 2006).

pp. xii, xiv The most comprehensive and eloquent source on the *Vrouw Maria*'s ill-fated voyage is the essay by Eero Ehanti in NBA (2012).

pp. xv–xviii Details of the wreck from the captain's Declaration, in Swedish National Archives, translated copy provided by E. Ehanti.

1: REMBRANDT'S APPRENTICE

The New Student

pp. 3, 5 On 17th century Leiden, Schama (1997), North (1997), Israel (1998).

p. 3 The home of Jansz Douwe at no. 12 Kort Rapenburg stands today. The site is identified with a historic marker, placed on the tercentennial of Gerrit's birth in 1913.

p. 3 Description of young Rembrandt: painting *Self-Portrait*, 1629, (Boston: Isabella Stewart Gardner Museum).

pp. 4, 5 Dou early biography and family, Martin (1902), Baer (1990).

pp. 4, 5 Rembrandt in Leiden, Chong (2000).

p. 5 Rembrandt's apprentice fee, Slive (1953), 92.

In the Master's Studio

pp. 6–9 Rembrandt's studio practices, teaching style, and painting materials, Alpers (1988), van de Wetering (1997), Chong (2000), Rembrandthuis (2013).

p. 6 Description of studio, Rembrandt's painting *Artist in His Studio*, circa 1626–28 (Boston: Museum of Fine Arts). Speculation exists that the "artist" in this painting is young apprentice Dou. Martin (1902), 39.

A Visitor from the Royal Court

pp. 9, 10 Huygens and art collecting, Alpers (1983), Dekker (2013).

p. 10 Huygens on Rembrandt and Lievens, Huygens (1629–31).

pp. 10, 11 Rembrandt correspondence with Huygens, (1639).

p. 11 Price of commission, North (1997), 83.

p. 12 Kerr quote, "Rembrandt van Rijn," http://www.rembrandtpainting.net/rembrandt_life_and_work.htm.

ENDNOTES

The Mystery of *Anna and the Blind Tobit*
p. 13   On *Blind Tobit Greeting His Son*, Perlove et al. (2009).

pp. 13, 14   Attribution controversy over *Anna and the Blind Tobit*, Rose-de Viejo (2002), Ford (2018).

pp. 14, 15   Additional attribution controversies, Chong (2000).

2: THE PRINCE'S BRIDE
Unexpected Invitation
pp. 16–18   Childhood and family, Alexander (1989), Rounding (2006), Massie (2011).

King of Prussia
pp. 18–21   Frederick the Great, young Catherine, Prussian intrigue, Alexander (1989), Rounding (2006), Massie (2011).

Secret Journey
pp. 21–24   Details of overland journey to Russia, Alexander (1989), Rounding (2006), Massie (2011).

Audition for an Empress
pp. 24–27   At the court of Empress Elizabeth, *Memoirs* (2006), Massie (2011).

3: FROM PUPIL TO MASTER
On His Own
p. 29   The Galgewater studio, Martin (1902), 57, Baer (2000), 33.

p. 29   Interior of Galgewater studio and props featured in Dou paintings. See, for example, *The Young Mother*,1658, (The Hague: Mauritshuis).

p. 30   Dou's early reputation, Baer (1990), 5.

p. 30   Sandrart on Dou's work style, Martin (1902), 49.

The Guild of Saint Luke
p. 30   The Guilds of St. Luke, Montias, (1977).

p. 31   Philips Angel on Dou, Angel, (1996 [1641]).

p. 31   Jan Orlers on Dou, Sluijter (2000), 204.

pp. 31, 33   Dou's spreading fame, Martin (1902), 45.

p. 32   Pieter Spiering and Queen Christina, Gaskell (1982), Alpers (1988), 94, Baer (1990), 44, n. 37.

p. 33   Leiden artists' appeal for guild, Sluijter (2000), 207.

The Leiden School
pp. 33, 34   Typical breakfast, Anderson (2013), 170.

pp. 34–36   Dou's work routine and painting technique, Martin (1902), 84–86, Baer (1990), Boersma (2000).

p. 36   Dou's students and followers, Martin (1902), 86–89, Baer (2000), 32.

Golden Age Superstar
pp. 36–39   Details of de Bye show, Martin (1902), 66–71, 145–147.

p. 37   Provenance of "Dropsical Woman," Champlin et al. (1913), 426.

p. 39   Leiden burgomasters offer to Dou, Martin (1902), 72, 73.

p. 40   Rise in popularity of genre painting in 17th century, North (1997), 99.

ENDNOTES

pp. 40–42   Dou becomes international celebrity artist, Martin (1902), 58–63, Cust (1917), Baer (2000), 30, 31, Bakker (2017).

The Nursery
pp. 42–44   Dou's intended meaning of the panels of *The Nursery*, Emmens (1997).
p. 44   Provenance of *The Nursery*, Korevaar (2011).
pp. 44, 45   Steen's tavern and van Mieris, Chapman (1993).

4: FROM FRÄULEIN TO EMPRESS
Transvestite Tsarina
pp. 46–48   Naumov (1996), *Memoirs* (2006), Rounding (2006), *Zapiski* (2010).

The Wedding
pp. 49–51   Naumov (1996), *Memoirs* (2006), Rounding (2006), *Zapiski* (2010), Massie (2011).

Love and Marriage
pp. 51–55   Kamensky (1992), *Memoirs* (2006), Rounding (2006), *Zapiski* (2010), Massie (2011).

Dangerous Liaisons
pp. 55–57   Kamensky (1992), *Memoirs* (2006), Rounding (2006), *Zapiski* (2010), Massie (2011).

Matushka, the Time Has Come
pp. 58–60   Kamensky (1992), *Memoirs* (2006), *Zapiski* (2010), Massie (2011).

5: TEMPLE OF ARTS
The Wine Merchant
pp. 61–63   Jan Braamcamp and family background, Bille (1961), vol 1.
p. 61   Braamcamp children in Achterburgwal home shop, Bille (1961), vol. I, 9.
p. 62   The Dutch and global wine trade, Estreicher (2006), 69–71.

Rise of the House of Braamcamp
p. 63   Description of lawyer, after painting of Adriaen van Ostade, *Lawyer in His Study*, c. 1680 (Rotterdam: Museum Boijmans).
pp. 63–65   Gerrit Braamcamp and family business, Bille (1961).

Golden Age Connoisseur
pp. 65, 66   Tischbein on good Dutch collection, Priem (1997), 127.
p. 66   Braamcamp's art advisors and dealers, Bille (1961).
p. 67   First purchase of Willem van Mieris, Bille (1961), vol 2, 33, 34.
pp. 67–69   Collecting Old Masters, Bille (1961), 222.

Temple of Arts
pp. 70, 71   On the Sweedenrijk mansion, Bronkhorst (2018), 291–301.
pp. 71–73   Description of rooms and displayed paintings, Bille (1961).

ENDNOTES

The Nursery Comes Home
pp. 73, 74   Rooleeuw collection and sale to van Hoek, Korevaar (2011), 138.

pp. 74, 75   Van Hoek's art collection, Jonkheere (2008), 118, fn. 253.

p. 76   Bernard family sale to Braamcamp, Bille (1961), 41, 42.

6: THE TSARINA'S SALON
A Player Is Born
pp. 78, 79   Frederick and Catherine as enlightened despots, Massie (2011), Mitford (2013).

pp. 79–81   Gotzkowsky purchase, Jacques (2016), 28–31.

French Connection
pp. 81, 82   Description of Madame Geoffrin's salon, from ensemble portrait painting by Lemmonier *Reading of Voltaire in Salon of Madame Geoffrin* (Malmaison, 1812).

p. 83   On Dmitry Golitsyn, Tsverava (1985).

p. 84   Diderot and Catherine, Zaretsky (2019).

Urge to Splurge
pp. 85, 86   Diderot as Catherine's art agent, Zaretsky (2019), Jacques (2016).

pp. 86–88   On Catherine's purchases, Levinson-Lessing (1985), Neverov et al. (1997), Jacques (2016).

Twilight of Aristocracy
p. 88   On 18th-century French aristocracy, Chaussinand-Nogaret (1985).

pp. 90, 91   Walpole collection controversy, Touy (2013), Jacques (2016).

pp. 91, 92   Grimm correspondence with Catherine, Grot (1880).

Minerva's Playhouse
p. 93   Catherine as Russian Minerva, Dianina (2004).

pp. 94, 95   The construction, art collection, and rules of Catherine's Hermitage, Norman (1997), Massie (2011), Jacques (2016).

7: SALE OF THE CENTURY
The Controversy
p. 96   Braamcamp's death, Raye (1935), ch. 37; Bille (1961), vol. I, 220.

p. 97   Trends in 18th century Dutch art market, Bille (1961), Korthals Altes (2000), Jonckheere (2008).

p. 98   Van Gool and Hoet quotes, Korthals Altes (2000), 258, 259, 268, 269.

pp. 98, 99   Organization of Braamcamp auction, Bille (1961), vol. I, 225.

On Her Majesty's Secret Service
p. 99   Voltaire letter to Catherine, *Documents* (1931), 121–123.

pp. 99, 100   Correspondence between D. A. Golitsyn and A. M. Golitsyn, RGADA (fond: 1263).

p. 101   Golitsyn's agents, Bille (1961), vol. 1, 170.

Lot No. 53
p. 102   Catherine's rivals and their agents, Bille (1961), vol. I, 170.

pp. 102–105   Details of buyers and prices, van der Schley (1771), Bille (1961), vol II.

ENDNOTES

p. 104   Sale of *The Nursery*, van der Schley (1771), 21.

p. 105   Tronchin's letters to Golitsyn, Tronchin (1895), 314–320.

p. 105   Correspondence between D. A. Golitsyn and A. M. Golitsyn, RGADA (fond: 1263).

Sale of the Century

p. 106   Braamcamp auction totals, van der Schley (1771), Bille (1961), vol II.

p. 107   Ploos van Amstel purchase, Korevaar (2011), 140.

pp. 107, 108   Braamcamp inheritance, Bille (1961), vol. 1.

p. 108   Sale of 462 Herengracht, Raye (1935), ch. 37.

Dam Square

p. 109   Description of Dam Square, from painting by Jan Ekels, *View of the Dam in Amsterdam* (Amsterdam Rijksmuseum).

p. 109   Lodewijk Hovy and Dutch merchants in Russia, Veluwenkamp (1995).

p. 110   Merchants investing in the *Vrouw Maria* voyage, Gelderblom (2003).

8: CATHERINE'S TREASURE SHIP LOST
Turku 1771

p. 112   Correspondence between D. A. Golitsyn and A. M. Golitsyn, RGADA (fond 1263).

p. 113   On Turku/Åbo, Klinge (1983).

pp. 113, 114   Lourens arrives in Turku, Delgado (2004), ch. 7.

Art of Diplomacy

pp. 114, 115   Relations between Catherine II and Gustav III, and the Swedish court, Olausson et al. (1999).

pp. 115, 116   Panin and Catherine's diplomatic corps, Ransel (1975).

pp. 116, 117   Golitsyn letter to Tronchin, Tronchin (1895).

Science of Salvaging

pp. 117–119   On preindustrial wreck salvaging, Blot (1995), Ratcliffe (2011).

pp. 117, 118   On Swedish Crown salvaging, Ahlström (1997).

Business of Shipwrecks

p. 119   Correspondence between A. Golitsyn and A. M. Golitsyn, RGADA (fond 1263).

pp. 120, 121   Inventory of salvaged cargo, Delgado (2004), 97, Ahlström (1978), 66, NBA (2012), 98.

p. 121   News of the wreck in Amsterdam and reaction of investors, Gelderblom (2003), 112.

p. 122   Captain Lourens after the wreck, Pickford (2006).

Treasure Ship Lost

p. 123   Correspondence between A. M. Golitsyn and D. A. Golitsyn, RGADA (fond 1263).

p. 123   Catherine's reward and Swedish salvage efforts, Alhström (1978), 67, 68, Pickford (2006), 114, 115.

p. 123   Panin quote, Gelderblom (2003), 114.

pp. 124, 125   Golitsyn letter to Tronchin, Tronchin (1895), 318.

p. 126   Correspondence between A. Golitsyn and A. M. Golitsyn, RGADA (fond 1263).

9: AGE OF REVOLUTION
Eclipse of an Artist
pp. 129, 130   Death of Dou, Martin (1902), 75.

p. 130   Dou's reputation after death, Martin (1902), 96, 97, Wheelock (2000), 15.

p. 131   Hawthorne quote, Hawthorne (1881), vol. II (August 2).

p. 132   Thoré-Bürger quote, Nochlin (1989), 1.

p. 132   On the Rembrandt myth, McQueen (2000/2001).

p. 133   Thoré-Bürger on Dou, Wheelock (2000), 16.

pp. 134–136   Catalogue notes from Hudson-Fulton Dutch Art Exhibition, Valentiner (1910).

p. 135   Ludwig Justi quotes, *New York Times,* (January 23, 1910).

p. 135   Kenyon Cox quote, Wheelock (2000), 23, fn. 8.

p. 136   *Dropsical Woman* at the Louvre, Foucart (1970).

Death of an Empress
p. 137   On Pugachev Rebellion, Madariaga (1981), Alexander (1989).

p. 138   Voltaire and Catherine's invitation, Wolff (1994).

pp. 138–140   Diderot journeys to Saint Petersburg, Curran (2019), ch. 11.

pp. 140, 141   Death of Empress Catherine, Massie (2011), ch. 73; Jacques (2016), 359, 360.

pp. 141, 142   On Alexander, Napoleon, and Josephine, Lieven (2010).

p. 142   Alexander acquires paintings from Josephine, Sokolova (1988).

p. 143   Description of Tsar Alexander in Porvoo Cathedral, from the painting by Emmanuel Thelning "Opening of the Diet of Porvoo," 1812, (Diocesan Office of Porvoo).

pp. 143, 144   On rise of Finnish nationalism and independence in Russian Revolution, Jussila (1999), Kirby (2006).

10: GRAVEYARD OF WRECKS
Borstö Island, 1953
pp. 145–148   Andersson brothers, Nils Cleve, and Borstö wreck, Nurmio-Lahdenmäki (2006), 13–15.

Graveyard of Wrecks
p. 148   Poem by Henry David Thoreau, "Though All the Fates."

pp. 148, 149   Baltic seawater conditions and shipworm, Kautsky et al. (2003).

p. 149   The "Baltic Anomaly," *Daily Mirror,* (April 26, 2016).

pp. 149, 150   The "Champagne Schooner," Reuters, (June 3, 2011).

p. 150   Sinking of *Wilhelm Gustloff,* Prince (2013).

pp. 150–152   Anders Franzén and the *Vasa,* Franzén (1974).

Mystery Ship
pp. 153, 154   Swedish divers and exploration of Borstö wreck, Nurmio-Lahdenmäki (2006), 54–83.

p. 155   The Antiquities Act, NBA, and underwater heritage in Finland, Fast-Matikka (2006); Nurmio-Lahdenmäki (2006), 40.

The Scion and the Sea
pp. 156, 157   Interview, Ahlström.

p. 158   Archival research on Borstö wreck, Ahlström (2006).

ENDNOTES

Final Voyage of the *Sankt Mikael*
pp. 159, 160   Details of voyage, Nurmio-Lahdenmäki (2006).
p. 161   Finding key document on the *Vrouw Maria*, Ahlström (2006), 108.

11: THE WRECK HUNTER
Leningrad, 1985
pp. 163, 164   On late Soviet Leningrad, Miles (2018).
pp. 165, 166   Anecdote of Koivusaari in Leningrad, Saure (2009), 24–34.

An Exceptional Finn
pp. 166–168   Interview, Koivusaari; Saure (2009), 12–23.

An Obsession Is Born
p. 169   Interest in the *Titanic*, interview, Koivusaari; Saure (2009), 37, 38.
p. 170   Becoming a diver, Saure (2009), 37–78.
p. 171   On side-scan sonar, Kennedy (2005).
p. 171   Acquisition of side-scan sonar and diving business, interviews, Ilola, Koivusaari; Saure (2009), 76–78.

Shipwreck Fever
p. 172   Calypso diving club and the *Carolina Fredrika*, Saure (2009), 154–159.
pp. 172, 173 On shipwreck fever, Saure (2009), 43, 44.
pp. 172, 173 Koivusaari quote on finding wrecks, Saure (2009), 182.
p. 174   Quote, ". . . like *Flying Dutchman*," interview, Rouhiainen.
pp. 174, 175 On 1998 search for the *Vrouw Maria*, interviews, Talvela, Koivusaari, Rouhiainen; Saure (2009), 84–89.

12: GOLDEN AGE SECRETS REVEALED
Decoding Dau
p. 178   Heckscher on Panofsky, *Dictionary of Art Historians*, http://arthistorians.info/panofskye.
p. 179   Emmens on Panofsky, Emmens et al. (1967–68).
p. 179   Quote, "I lose myself . . ." Bruyn (1971).
p. 180   Quote, "A disastrous book. . ." Fuchs (1970).
p. 180   Emmens and poetry, Freedburg (1983), 144.
pp. 180–182   Emmens on Dou, Emmens (1997), Reznicek (1972), Hecht (2002).
pp. 182, 183 Death of Emmens, Bruyn (1971), Reznicek (1972).
p. 183   Emmens's impact on historiography, Freedburg (1983), Hecht (2002).
p. 183   On 1976 Rijksmuseum show, De Jongh (1976), 88.

Making a Map
p. 184   Anecdote in bed, interview, Koivusaari.
pp. 186–188   Unraveling clues from old maps, interview, Koivusaari, Saure (2009), 94–96.
p. 190   Making plan for the *Vrouw Maria*, interviews, Rouhiainen, Koivusaari, Saure (2009), 88, 89.
p. 191   Creating Pro Vrouw Maria Association, interviews, Koivusaari-2, Rouhiainen, Kalonen, Airenne, Ilola.
p. 192   Finding last clue in Amsterdam archive, interview, Martikainen, Saure (2009), 90.

13: RESTORING A MASTER
Bourgeois Baron

p. 193   Exhibition press release, National Gallery of Art/NGA (April 11, 2000), https://www
              .nga.gov/press/exh/0140.html.

pp. 194–196   Andrew Mellon and National Gallery, Cannadine (2006).

pp. 195, 196 Soviet selling Old Masters, Williams (1979), 162, 169, Semyonova (2013).

Yankee Curator

p. 197   Interview, Wheelock, *The Georgetowner* (April 27, 2000), http://www.wheelock
              genealogy.com/.

p. 198   NGA, Dutch Art, and remodeling, interview, Wheelock.

p. 198   On NGA Vermeer Show, Wheelock (1995).

pp. 198, 199 Proposing Dou show, interview, Wheelock.

A Gathering of Dous

pp. 199–202   Organizing the show, interview, Wheelock.

p. 201   Cheltenham curator Paul McKee escorting Dou painting, *Gloucester Echo* (April 1,
              2000).

Master Painter in the Age of Rembrandt

p. 202   Press reviews, *Washington Times* (April 15, 2000), *Washington Post* (April 16, 2000),
              New York Times (April 25, 2000), *Wall Street Journal* (May 25, 2000).

pp. 202, 203 NGA director quote, NGA archive.

p. 204   European press reviews, *Financial Times Europe* (September 9, 2000), *Bisdomblad*
              (December 22, 2000).

pp. 204, 205 Cumming's review, *The Guardian,* (September 3, 2000).

p. 205   Spurling's review, *Spectator,* (September 16, 2000).

p. 205   Gaskell's review, *Historians of Netherlandish Art-Newsletter,* (May 2000).

14: CATHERINE'S TREASURE SHIP FOUND
Meeting at the Museum

pp. 206–209   Details of meeting, interviews, Koivusaari, Martikainen, Rouhiainen.

Getting Organized

pp. 209–212   Organizing expedition, interviews, Koivusaari, Martikainen, Rouhiainen, K. Salonen.

Midsummer

p. 213   Final preparations and voyage, interview, Koivusaari; Saure (2009), 91, 92.

p. 214   On expedition send-off, Saure (2009), 91, 92, 109, *Helsingin Sanomat,* (June 28,
              1999).

p. 215   Arrival at Jurmo, interviews, Koivusaari, Martikainen, Rouhiainen.

pp. 215, 216 Description of the *Teredo* and crew, from documentary video footage by
              Mikael Martikainen.

Treasure Ship Found

pp. 216–218   Search operation and discovery, interview, Koivusaari, Rouhiainen, Martiainen;
              Saure (2009), 96, 97.

pp. 218, 219 Description of wreck by divers, interview, K. Salonen; Saure (2009), 98, 99.

p. 219 Pulkinen quote, *Helsingin Sanomat*, (July 2, 1999).

p. 220 Ahlström's arrival, interviews, Koivusaari, Ahlström; Saure (2009), 99–101.

Three Parties

p. 220 Opening quote, *Ilta Sanomat*, (July 1, 1999).

pp. 221, 222 Crew celebrations and media frenzy, interviews, Koivusaari, Ahlström, K. Salonen, Rouhiainen, Airenne.

p. 222 Rival dive team is rebuffed, interviews, Talvela, Koivusaari, Saure (2009), 106.

p. 222 Mysterious Russian phone call, *Ilta Sanomat*, (July 6, 1999).

pp. 223, 224 On research activities, interview, K. Salonen; Saure (2009), 102, 103.

pp. 224, 225 Maija Fast-Matikka visits the *Teredo*, interviews, Koivusaari, Fast-Matikka, Arienne, Saure (2009), 105, 106.

p. 225 Quote—"Nightmare on Elm Street . . ." interview, Rouhiainen, Saure (2009), 109.

15: FINDERS KEEPERS
On Holiday

p. 230 Quote, "We have seen . . ." AP, (June 30, 1999).

p. 230 Quote, "The wreck legally . . ." *Helsingin Sanomat*, (July 2, 1999).

p. 230 Dive research summary and return trip, Saure (2009), 108–112.

p. 231 Encounter at museum, interview, Koivusaari; Saure (2009), 109, 110.

pp. 232, 233 Trademark dispute, Interviews—Koivusaari, Rouhiainen, Martikainen, Alvik, Saure (2009), 110, 111.

No Diving Allowed

p. 233 Quote, "If it is . . ." *Helsingin Sanomat*, (July 1, 1999).

p. 233 Quote, "There are insanely . . ." *Ilta Sanomat*, (July 1, 1999).

p. 234 Fear of looting, *Ilta Sanomat*, (July 3, 1999).

pp. 234, 235 Lack of resources, *Helsingin Sanomat*, (August 1 and 10, 1999).

p. 235 Making a wreck plan, *Helsingin Sanomat*, (July 2, 1999), *Ilta Sanomat* (July 3, 1999).

pp. 235, 236 Proposal for museum and Pro Vrouw Maria to work together, interviews, Fast-Matikka, Martikainen.

p. 236 Disagreement within NBA, interview, Honkanen; *Helsingin Sanomat*, (August 1 and 10, 1999).

p. 237 Interest in marine archeology, *Helsingin Sanomat*, (November 22, 1999).

p. 237 Pro Vrow Maria application rejected, interviews, Koivusaari, Martikainen.

War of Laws

pp. 238, 239 Pro Vrouw Maria team's reaction to lawsuit, interviews, Rouhiainen, K. Salonen, Martikainen.

p. 239 On Kähäri and lawsuit, *Helsingin Sanomat*, (May 17, 2000; January 5, 2000).

p. 239 NBA reaction to lawsuit, interviews, Tikkanen, Honkanen; *Helsingin Sanomat*, (May 17, 2000; July 4, 2000).

pp. 239, 240 Meeting with NBA lawyers, interview, Koivusaari.

pp. 240, 241 Effects of lawsuit, interviews, Koivusaari, Alvik, Fast-Matikka.

p. 241 Museum 2000 expedition, Teredo Navalis Society, http://www.teredo.net/projekteja/vrouw-maria-1999-2007/.

The Silver Brig

pp. 243, 244 On the *De Catherina* and 2000 search, interview, Koivusaari, Saure, (2009), 171–182.

p. 244 Press coverage, *Helsingin Sanomat*, (July 2 and 11, 2000).

p. 244 NBA reaction, *Helsingin Sanomat*, (July 12, 2000).

p. 245 Rauno quotes regarding dispute, *Helsingin Sanomat*, (July 14 and 19, 2000).

p. 245 Not guilty finding, *Helsingin Sanomat*, (October17, 2002; April 17, 2003).

At the Maritime Court

p. 246 Quote—"The *Vrouw Maria* is . . ." Kaleva, (May 29, 2002), http://www.kaleva.fi /uutiset/juttu/233169/?m=juttu&j=233169&jo=juttu.

p. 246 Maritime Court decision, ECHR, (2010).

16: THE DUTCH RETREAT
We Have Found Your Ship

p. 247 Quote—"When the ship . . ." interview, Alvik.

p. 247 UN Law of Sea quote, UNCLOS III, arts. 149, 303 (1983).

p. 248 Quote—"The Netherlands was . . ." interview, Fast-Matikka.

p. 248 Quote—"We invited him . . ." interview, Tikkanen.

Protecting the Treasures of the Deep

p. 249 Quote—"Much of what . . ." Manders (2017), 15–18.

pp. 249, 250 On commercial salvors and in situ preservation, interview, Manders.

p. 251 On the *Rooswijk* shipwreck, *Current World Archeology*, no. 86, December 5, 2017, *De Rooswijk*, https://www.youtube.com/watch?time_continue=8&v=OqtKCYHvVus.

The Dutch Claim

pp. 252–254 Manders quotes, interview, Manders.

p. 252 Salonen quote, interview, P. Salonen.

A Salvaged Treasure Goes Home

p. 254 Golitsyn letter to Hovy, RGADA (fond 1263).

p. 255 On painting *Jephtah and His Daughter*, Sokolova (1988), Bille (1961) vol. 2, 107.

p. 255 Turku auction inventory, Delgado (2004), 97.

p. 256 On Golitsyn and ten Compe's *The Mint*, Bille (1961), vol. II, 12, 94, Ehanti (2011) 8, 9.

pp. 256, 257 Provenance of *The Mint* and Schouten's watercolor, correspondence, Tom van der Molen, curator, Amsterdam Museum.

17: THE SWEDISH PATRON
At the District Court

p. 258 Diver J. Rajala quote, *Helsingin Sanomat*, (April 7, 2001).

p. 259 Wetterstein and Heltunnen quotes, *Helsingin Sanomat*, (September 26, 2000).

p. 259 NBA legal strategy, Aminoff, (2008).

pp. 259, 260 Trial summary and prospects for appeal, interview, Aminoff, Martikainen.

Adventures in Treasure Land

p. 261 Swedish press quote, *Götenborgs-Posten*, (November 24, 2011).

p. 261   Edwall quote, interview, Edwall.

p. 262   Edwall's Incan adventures, Edwall, (1995).

pp. 263–265   Ecuador, *La Capitana*, McClung, interviews, Koivusaari, Mansilla-Koivusaari; Saure (2009), 207–226.

p. 265   Edwall and the *Vrouw Maria*, interviews, Koivusaari, Edwall, Arvas.

At the Court of Appeals

p. 266   At the Appeals Court, *Helsingin Sanomat*, (August 26, 2004).

p. 266   Quote—"It was quite . . ." interview, Martikainen.

p. 267   Appeals Court decision, ECHR, (2010).

p. 267   Decision's ambiguity, Aminoff, (2008), 121, 125.

The Swedish Plan

p. 268   Edwall quote, "You know the triptych . . ." interview, Edwall.

p. 269   Design of floating museum, interviews, Edwall, Arvas, 'Vrouw Maria Maritime Museum' website designed by Arvas, http://www.vrouwmaria.com/.

p. 269   Reaction to plan, interviews, Alvik, Kokko.

At the Supreme Court

p. 270   MoSS Project report, NBA (2004).

p. 271   Quote, "was dead beforehand . . ." interview, Aminoff.

p. 271   Supreme Court decision, ECHR, (2010).

18: THE RUSSIAN ADVANCE

Moscow, 2007

p. 272   Lavrov announcement, Interfax, (July 5, 2007).

p. 273   Quotes by Kanerva and NBA, *Helsingin Sanomat*, (July 6 and 23, 2007).

p. 273   On abandonment, Lipka, (1970).

pp. 273, 274   *Vrouw Maria* abandonment, interviews, Manders, Edwall, Alvik.

Russia's First Millionaire

p. 274   Law on Coops, *Pravda*, (June 8, 1988).

pp. 275, 276   Tarasov on becoming a millionaire and exile in London, Tarasov (2004), interview published in *Russia Beyond* (July 29, 2017), https://www.rbth.com/business/2017/07/29/how-some-russian-oligarchs-got-unbelievably-rich-in-unbelievable-ways_812844.

Catherine and Vladimir

p. 277   Putin and Russian Atlantis, *RT*, (August 10, 2011), *Guardian*, (August 12, 2011).

pp. 278, 279   Putin's cult of personality, Easter, (2008).

p. 280   Putin meets oligarchs, *Kommersant*, (February 20, 2003).

Salvaging the Past

p. 280   Anecdote at Palm Court, *Vechnost Obektiv*, (April 16, 2014).

p. 281   Vekselberg, Fabergé eggs, Danilov bells, *New York Times*, (February 4, 2004), *Guardian*, (September 7, 2007).

p. 282   Romanov small crown, Tarasov (2004), AP video, https://www.youtube.com/watch?v=lUDCdT9zz4Y.

p. 282   On Slipenchuk and Metropol: *Russkii Telegraf* website, https://rutelegraf.com/en/lichnoe-delo/mixail-slipenchuk.

p. 283   Tarasov's team, interviews, Petrakov, Sorokin.

The Russian Plan

p. 284   Lavrov quote, Russian Foreign Ministry press release, (November 16, 2007).

p. 284   On Russian salvage and restoration plan, interviews, Petrakov, Alvik, Sorokin; Tarasov in *Telegraph*, (November 18, 2008) and RT, (November 19, 2008).

p. 285   Finnish reaction, interviews, P. Salonen; Tikkanen, Alvik.

pp. 285, 288 Manders quotes, interview, Manders.

pp. 285, 286 Revised plan, Tarasov interview in RT, (November 19, 2008); interview, Petrakov.

p. 286   Conditions for cooperation, NBA (2014), 52; interview, P. Salonen.

pp. 286, 287 On Swedish-Russian cooperation, interviews, Edwall, Petrakov.

p. 287   Miscommunication and divergent interests, interviews, Manders, P. Salonen, Tikkanen, Alvik, Ehanti.

p. 287   Russian reaction, interview, Petrakov.

19: THE FINNISH PLAN
Moments of Indecision

p. 289   Lilius quote, *Helsingin Sanomat*, (August 1, 1999).

p. 290   Klemelä quote, MoSS Newsletter, (no. 1; 2003).

p. 290   Museum report, NBA, (2007).

To Salvage or Not to Salvage

p. 291   Suomenlinna conference, NBA (2014), 53; interview, Manders.

p. 292   Cost of the *Mary Rose*, BBC News, (May 30, 2013).

p. 293   Quote on in situ option, NBA, (2014), 76.

p. 293   Quote—"I can say . . ." interview, Manders.

p. 293   Choosing an option, NBA (2014), 6, 8.

Inside the Wreck

pp. 293–296 Interviews, Alvik, Kokko, Ehanti; NBA, (2014).

At the Court of Human Rights

p. 297   Quote, "It is extremely . . ." interview, Aminoff.

p. 298   Court decision, ECHR, (2010).

p. 298   Newspaper quote, *Helsingin Sanomat*, (March 13, 2010).

Simple and Convenient

p. 298   Directives to dive team, NBA, (2014), 17, 18.

p. 299   Culture Ministry press release, YLE, (April 14, 2011).

pp. 299, 300 Reaction to announcement, interviews, Koivusaari, Rouhiainen, Airenne, Edwall; Tarasov quote in *Helsingin Sanomat*, (September 8, 2010).

pp. 300, 301 Defense of *in situ* option, interviews, Tikkanen, P. Salonen, Paasilehto; NBA (2014), 8, 37–39.

p. 301   On UNESCO convention, interviews, Kokko, Manders.

p. 301   Intimidation factor, interviews, Rouhiainen, K. Salonen, Manders.

pp. 301, 302 Within-museum criticism, interviews, Kokko, K. Salonen; Alvik quote, *Helsingin Sanomat*, (October 24, 2011).

p. 302 Decision-making process, interviews, Fast-Matikka, P. Salonen, Manders.

pp. 302, 303 Abolishing Marine Archeology section, interviews, Kokko, Fast-Matikka; NBA, (2014), 56.

p. 303 Leino editorial, *Helsingin Sanomat*, (June 28, 2011).

20: CATHERINE'S TREASURE SHIP ABANDONED
Leiden Homecoming

p. 304 Angel quote, Martin (1902), 43.

p. 305 Dou's popularity in Leiden, Sluijter, (2019).

p. 305 Lakenhal show press release and attendance, https://www.lakenhal.nl/en/story/gerrit-dou-the-leiden-collection-from-new-york.

pp. 305, 306 Thomas Kaplan and the Leiden Collection, Kaplan (2010); interview, Wheelock.

p. 306 Quote, ". . . was so finely executed . . ." *New York Times*, (March 25, 2011).

p. 306 Quote, ". . . influenced similar scenes . . ." *The Guardian*, (July 3, 2016).

p. 307 On *Sleeping Dog*, *Wall Street Journal*, (October 19, 2018).

Russians Go Home

p. 307 Russians visit archipelago, *Helsingin Sanomat*, (August 31, 2010).

pp. 307–309 Finnish reaction, interviews, Alvik, P. Salonen; *Helsingin Sanomat* (August 31, 2010).

p. 309 Russian reaction, interviews, Alvik, Petrakov.

p. 309 Finnish-Russian discussions ended, NBA, (2014), 52.

pp. 309, 310 Negative press coverage, *Helsingin Sanomat*, (September 8, 2010).

p. 310 Tarasov's team disbands, interview, Petrakov.

p. 311 Konstantin Shopotov, Baltic Memory, Russian Embassy/Helsinki, TASS, (October 13, 2016); interview, Terpilovaskaya.

The Wreck Hunter Returns

pp. 311, 312 *Spoils of Riches* show, interview, Koivusaari; NBA, (2012).

pp. 312, 313 On *Hanneke Wrome* and Rauno's discovery, Saure (2009), 72, *Helsingin Sanomat* (May 1, 2015), *HuffPost*, https://www.huffpost.com/entry/shipwreck-treasure-finnish-coast_n_7224232.

p. 313 Museum staff quotes, *Helsingin Sanomat*, (May 1, 2015, November 17, 2015).

p. 314 Quote, "I have been tracking . . ." interview, Koivusaari.

Treasure Ship Abandoned

p. 314 Quote, "I still support . . ." interview, Honkanen.

pp. 314, 315 Public appeals for shipwreck museum, *Helsingin Sanomat*, (March 3, 2012, March 4, 2015).

pp. 315, 316 City Council initiative and reaction: Päätökset, (March 28, 2017; September 11, 2017), *Helsingin Uutiset*, (February 22, 2017), *Helsingin Sanomat*, (February 22, 2017); interview, Edwall.

p. 316 Quote, "people will be able . . ." SuuntoDive, (June 13, 2019).

p. 316 Quote, "The main advantage . . ." interview, Flinkman.

pp. 317, 318 Lilius quote, *Helsingin Sanomat*, (August 1, 1999).

p. 319 *Vrouw Maria* as international symbol, interviews, Ehanti, Alvik.

ENDNOTES

EPILOGUE: THE TREASURE

p. 321   Golitsyn quote, Tronchin, (1895), 318, 319.

pp. 321, 324 Governor Rappe on restoration, Ehanti, (2012), 68.

p. 321   Panin quote, Gelderblom, (2003), 114.

pp. 322, 323 Sapunov, Sokolova, and Shopotov quotes, *Itogi*, (July 21, 2008), TASS, (October 13, 2016).

p. 323   Seawater effects on supports and materials, interviews, Manders, Kokko, Bull, Alvik; Hagelstam in *Ilta Sanomat*, (July 1, 1999).

pp. 324, 325 The *Vasa* and Viking ship examples, interview, Hocker, Viking Ship Museum (Oslo), https://www.khm.uio.no/english/visit-us/viking-ship-museum/exhibitions/oseberg/oseberg-found.html.

pp. 325, 326 Quote, "These ships . . ." interview, Alvik.

BIBLIOGRAPHY

Ahlström, Christian. "Documentary Research on the Baltic: Three Case Studies." *International Journal of Nautical Archeology and Underwater Research.* Vol. 7; no. 1, 1978.

Ahlström, Christian. *Sjunkna Skepp.* Stockholm: Natur och kultur, 1979.

Ahlström, Christian. *Looking for Leads.* Helsinki: Finnish Academy of Science and Letters, 1997.

Ahlström, Christian. "Identification through Archival Source and Finds." in Nurmio-Lahdenmäki (2006).

Alexander, John. *Catherine the Great: The Life and Legend.* New York: Oxford University Press, 1989.

Alpers, Svetlana. *The Art of Describing: Dutch Art in the Seventeenth Century.* Chicago: University of Chicago Press, 1983.

Alpers, Svetlana. *Rembrandt's Enterprise: The Studio and the Market.* Chicago: University of Chicago Press, 1988.

Aminoff, Jan. "Historic Wrecks and Salvage under Finnish Law: Recent Developments." In *Shipwrecks in International and National Law.* Eds. Rak and Wetterstein. Turku: Institute of Maritime Law, 2008.

Anderson, Betsy. *Breakfast: A History.* Lanham, Md.: Rowman & Littlefield, 2013.

Angel, Philips. "In Praise of Painting." Trans. Michael Hoyle. *Simiolus.* Vol. 24, nos. 2, 3, 1996 [1641].

Baer, Ronni. *The Paintings of Gerrit Dou, 1613–1675.* PhD Thesis: New York University, 1990

Baer, Ronni. "The Life and Art of Gerrit Dou." In *Gerrit Dou, 1613–1675.* Ed. Arthur Wheelock. Washington, DC: National Gallery of Art, 2000.

Bakker, Piet. "Gerrit Dou and His Collectors in the Golden Age." *Leiden Collection Catalogue.* Ed. Arthur Wheelock Jr, Ed. Online archive, 2017. https://www.theleidencollection.com/essays /gerrit-dou-and-his-collectors-in-the-golden-age/

Bille, Clara. *De Tempel der Kunst of het Kabinet van den Heer* Braamcamp. Vol. I, Braamcamp biography; Vol. II, auction catalogue. Amsterdam: De Bussy, 1961.

Blot, Jean-Yves. *Underwater Archeology.* New York: Abrams, 1995.

Boersma, Annetje (2000), "Dou's Painting Technique: An Examination of Two Paintings," In *Gerrit Dou, 1613–1675.* Ed. Arthur Wheelock. Washington, DC: National Gallery of Art, 2000.

Bronkhorst, Arjan, ed. *Amsterdam Canal Houses.* Amsterdam: Lectura Cultura, 2018.

Bruyn, J. "In Memoriam—J. A. Emmens." *Similolus.* Vol. 5, nos. 1, 2, 1971.

Cannadine, David. *Mellon: An American Life.* New York: Knopf, 2006.

Catherine II. *Documents of Catherine the Great: Correspondence with Voltaire.* Ed. W. F. Reddaway. Cambridge, UK: Cambridge University Press, 1931.

Catherine II. *Memoirs of Catherine the Great.* Trans. M. Cruse and H. Hoogenboom. New York: Modern Library, 2006.

BIBLIOGRAPHY

Catherine II. *Записки Екатерини II.* Moscow: Azbuka-Klassika, 2010.

Champlin, John D., and Charles Perkins. *Cyclopedia of Painters and Paintings.* Vol. I. New York: Charles Scribner's Sons, 1913.

Chapman, H. Perry. "Persona and Myth in Houbraken's Life of Jan Steen," *The Art Bulletin.* Vol. 75, no. 1, 1993.

Chaussinand-Nogaret, Guy. *French Nobility in the Eighteenth Century.* Cambridge, UK: Cambridge University Press, 1985.

Chong, Alan, ed. *Rembrandt Creates Rembrandt: Art and Ambition in Leiden, 1629–1631.* Zwolle: Waanders: 2000.

Curran, Andrew. *Diderot and the Art of Thinking Freely.* New York: Other Press, 2019.

Cust, Lionel. "Notes on Pictures in the Royal Collections: On Some Paintings by Gerard Dou." *Burlington Magazine.* Vol. 30, 1917.

Delgado, James. *Adventures of a Sea Hunter: In Search of Famous Wrecks.* Vancouver: Douglas & McIntyre, 2004.

Dianina, Katia. "Art and Authority: The Hermitage of Catherine the Great." *Russian Review.* Vol. 63, no. 4, 2004.

Dekker, Rudolf. *Family, Culture and Society in the Diary of Constantijn Huygens Jr.* Leiden: Brill, 2013.

Deep Sea Detectives. *Lost Treasure Ship Found!* DVD: History Channel, 2003.

Degn, Ole, ed. *The Sound Toll at Elsinore: Politics, Shipping, and the Collection of Duties, 1429–1857.* Copenhagen: Museum Tusculanum Press, 2018.

Easter, Gerald. "The Russian State in the Time of Putin." *Post-Soviet Affairs.* Vol. 24, no. 3, 2008.

Edwall, Kjell. *På Vag Mot Inkaskatten.* Stockholm: Raben Prisma, 1995.

Ehanti, Eero. "Lost at Sea." In National Board of Antiquities, 2012.

Ehanti, Eero. "*Vrouw Maria* and the Braamcamp Paintings." In CODART *Courant.* (Spring 2011).

Emmens, J. A. "A Seventeenth-Century Theory of Art: Nature and Practice," in Wayne Franits, Ed. *Looking at Seventeenth-Century Dutch Art.* Cambridge, UK: Cambridge University Press, 1997.

Emmens, Jan, and Gary Schwartz. "Erwin Panofsky as a Humanist," *Simiolus.* Vol. 2, no. 3, 1967/68.

Estreicher, Stefan. *Wine: From Neolith to the 21st Century.* New York: Algora, 2006.

European Court of Human Rights/ECHR (2010), Chamber Decision of Case of Koivusaari et al. vs. Finland. Application no. 20690/06; February 23. http://echr.ketse.com/doc/20690.06-en -20100223/view/.

Fast-Matikka, Maija. "Finland" in *The Protection of Underwater Cultural Heritage,* Sarah Dromgoole, Ed. Leiden: Martinus Nijhoff, 2006.

Ford, Charles. *Lives of Rembrandt.* Los Angeles: Getty Museum, 2008.

Foucart, Jacques. *La Siècle de Rembrandt.* Paris: Musée du Petit Palais, 1970.

Franits, Wayne, ed. *Looking at Seventeenth-Century Dutch Art.* Cambridge, UK: Cambridge University Press, 1997.

Franzén, Anders. *The Warship Vasa: Deep Diving and Marine Archeology in Stockholm.* Stockholm: Nordstedt, 1974.

Freedburg, David. "*Verzameld Werk* by J. A. Emmens." *Simiolus.* Vol. 13, review essay, 1983.

Fuchs, R. H. "Reconstructing Rembrandt's Ideas about Art," *Simiolus.* Vol. 4, no. 1, 1970.

Gaskell, Ivan. "Gerrit Dou, His Patrons, and the Art of Painting," *Oxford Art Journal.* Vol. 5, no. 1, 1982.

Gelderblom, Oscar. "Coping with the Perils of the Sea: The Last Voyage of *Vrouw Maria*." *International Journal of Maritime History*. Vol. 15, no. 2, 2003.

Grot, J., Ed. *Письма Гримм к Императрице Екатерине II*. St. Petersburg: Типография императорской академии наук, 1880.

Hawthorne, Nathaniel. *Passages from the English Note-Books*. Boston: Houghton Mifflin, 1881.

Hecht, Peter. "Art Beats Nature, and Painting Does So Best of All." *Simiolus*. Vol. 29, nos. 2/3, 2002.

Ho, Angela, "Gerrit Dou's Enchanting Trompe-l'oeil." *Journal of Historians of Netherlandish Art*. Vol. 7, no. 1, 2015.

Huygens, Constantijn (1629–1631). Excerpts from *Autobiography of Constantijn Huygens*. Ed. and trans. Benjamin Binstock. *Art Humanities Primary Source Readings*, no. 29. https://arthum .college.columbia.edu/sites/default/files/PDFs/arthum_rembrandt_reader.pdf.

Huygens, Constantijn. Excerpts from *Rembrandt's Letters* (1639). Art Humanities Primary Source Readings. No. 30. Ed. and trans. Benjamin Binstock. https://arthum.college.columbia.edu /sites/default/files/PDFs/arthum_rembrandt_reader.pdf.

Israel, Jonathan. *The Dutch Republic*. Oxford, UK: Oxford University Press, 1998.

Jacques, Susan. *The Empress of Art: Catherine the Great and the Transformation of Russia*. New York: Pegasus Books, 2016.

Jonckheere, Koenraad. *The Auction of King William's Paintings*. Amsterdam: John Benjamins, 2008.

Jongh, Eddy de. *Tot lering en vermaak: betekenissen van Hollandse genrevoorstellingen uit de zeventiende eeuw*. Amsterdam: Rijksmuseum, 1976.

Jussila, Osmo et al. *From Grand Duchy to Modern State: A Political History of Finland Since 1809*. London: Hurst, 1999.

Kamensky, *А. В. Под Сению Екатеринии*. St. Petersburg: Lenizdat, 1992.

Kaplan, Thomas. "A Portrait in Oil," *The Leiden Collection*. 2019. https://www.theleidencollection .com/a-portrait-in-oil/.

Kautsky, Lena, and Robert Kautsky. "The Baltic Sea in a Geological and Biological Perspective." In *Treasures of the Baltic Sea*. Stockholm: Swedish Maritime Museum, 2003.

Kennedy, Pagan and J. Kim Vandiver. "Harold Eugene Edgerton, 1903–1990." *Biographical Memoirs: National Academy of Sciences*. Vol. 86, 2005.

Kinder, Gary. *Ship of Gold in the Deep Blue Sea*. New York: Grove Press, 1998.

Kirby, David. *A Concise History of Finland*. Cambridge, UK: Cambridge University Press, 2006.

Klinge, Matte. *Ancient Powers of the Baltic Sea*. Helsinki: Otava, 1983.

Korevaar, Gerbrand. "Willem Joseph Laquy Copies Gerrit Dou." *Rijksmuseum Bulletin*. Vol. 59, 2011.

Korthals Altes, Everhard. "The Eighteenth-Century Gentleman Dealer Willem Lormier and the International Dispersal of Seventeenth-Century Dutch Paintings." *Simiolus*. Vol. 28, no. 4, 2000.

Lauring, Palle. *A History of the Kingdom of Denmark*. Copenhagen: Host, 1968.

Levinson-Lessing, V. F. *История картиной галерея Эрмитажа, 1764–1917*. Leningrad: Isskustvo, 1985.

Lieven, Dominic. *Russia Against Napoleon*. New York: Viking, 2010.

Lipka, L. J. "Abandoned Property at Sea: Who Owns the Salvage Finds." *William & Mary Law Review*. Vol. 12, no. 1, 1970.

Madariaga, Isabel de. *Russia in the Age of Catherine the Great*. New Haven, Conn.: Yale University Press, 1981.

Manders, Martijn. "Preserving a Layered History of the Western Wadden Sea." Leiden University: Doctoral Thesis, 2017.

Martin, Wilhelm. *Gerard Dou.* Trans. Clara Bell. London: George Bell, 1902.

Massie, Robert. *Catherine the Great.* New York: Random House, 2011.

McQueen, Alison. "Reinventing the Biography, Creating the Myth: Rembrandt in Nineteenth-Century France." *Simiolus.* Vol. 28, no. 3, 2000/2001.

Miles, Jonathan. *St. Petersburg: Madness, Murder, and Art on the Banks of the Neva.* New York: Pegasus Books, 2018.

Mitford, Nancy. *Frederick the Great.* New York: New York Review of Books Classics, 2013.

Montias, John. "The Guild of St. Luke in 17th-Century Delft and the Economic Status of Artists and Artisans," *Similous.* Vol. 9, no. 2, 1977.

National Board of Antiquities/NBA. *MoSS Project: Final Report.* Helsinki: NBA, 2004. moss.nba .fi/download/final_report.pdf.

NBA. *Selvitys Tutkimuksista, Tuloksista ja Tulevaisuuden eri Vaihtoehdoista.* Helsinki: Maritime Museum, 2007.

NBA. *Lost at Sea, Rediscovered.* Kotka: Maritime Museum of Finland, 2012.

NBA. *Vrouw Maria Underwater Project: Final Report.* Helsinki: NBA, 2014.

Naumov, V. P. "Empress Elizabeth I, 1741–1762." In *Emperors and Empresses of Russia.* D. Raleigh and A. Iskenderov, Eds. Armonk, N.Y.: M. E. Sharpe, 2014.

Neverov, Oleg, and Mikhail Piotrovsky. *The Hermitage: Essays on the History of the Collection.* St. Petersburg: Slavia, 1997.

Nochlin, Linda. *Politics of Vision: Essays on Nineteenth-Century Art and Society.* Boulder, Colo.: Westview Press, 1989.

Norman, Geraldine. *The Hermitage: Biography of a Great Museum.* London: Pimlico, 1997.

Nurmio-Lahdenmäki, Anna, ed. *St. Michel, 1747.* Helsinki: Fingrid Oyj, 2006.

North, Michael. *Art and Commerce in the Dutch Golden Age.* New Haven, Conn.: Yale University Press, 1997.

Olausson, Magnus, and G. Vilenbakhov, eds. *Catherine the Great and Gustav III.* Stockholm: Nationalmuseum, 1999.

Palmer, Alan. *The Baltic: A New History of the Region and Its People.* New York: Abrams, 2006.

Perlove, Shelley, and Larry Silver. *Rembrandt's Faith: Church and Temple in the Dutch Golden Age.* University Park, Penn.: Penn State University Press, 2009.

Pickford, Nigel. *Lost Treasure Ships of the Northern Seas.* London: Chatham, 2006.

Powers, Dennis. *Treasure Ship: The Legend and Legacy of the S. S. Brother Jonathan.* New York: Citadel, 2006.

Priem, Ruud. "The Most Excellent Collection of Lucretia Johanna van Winter." *Simiolus.* Vol. 25, no. 2/3, 1997.

Prince, Cathryn. *Death in the Baltic.* New York: Palgrave Macmillan, 2013.

Ransel, David. *Politics of Catherinian Russia: The Panin Party.* New Haven, Conn.: Yale University Press, 1975.

Ratcliffe, John. "Bells, Barrels, Bullion: Diving and Salvage in the Atlantic World, 1500–1800." *Nautical Research Journal.* Vol. 56, no. 1, 2011.

Raye, Jacob Bicker. *The Diary of Jacob Bicker Raye.* Amsterdam: HJ Paris, 1935.

Rembrandt van Rijn: Biography and Chronology. http://www.rembrandtpainting.net/rembrandt_life_ and_work.htm.

Rembrandthuis. "Rembrandt's Painting Materials." Amsterdam: Rembrandt House Museum, 2013.

Reznicek, E.K.J. "Jan Emmens." *Burlington Magazine.* Vol. 114, 1972.

Rose-de Viejo, Isadora. "On the Madrid Provenance of *Anna and the Blind Tobit.*" *Burlington Magazine.* Vol. 144, 2002.

Rounding, Virginia. *Catherine the Great: Love, Sex, Power.* New York: St. Martin's Press, 2006.

Saure, Heikki. *Aarrelaivojen Jäljillä: Rauno Koivusaaren Meriseikkailuja.* Helsinki: Otava, 2009.

Schama, Simon. *The Embarrassment of Riches: An Interpretation of Culture in the Dutch Golden Age.* New York: Vintage, 1997.

Semyonova, Natalya, and Nicolas Iljine, eds. *Selling Russia's Treasures.* New York: Abbeville, 2013.

Slive, Seymour. *Rembrandt and His Critics.* The Hague: Martiinus Nijhoff, 1953.

Sluijter, Eric Jan. *Seductress of Sight: Studies of Dutch Art in the Golden Age.* Zwolle: Waanders, 2000.

Sluijter, Eric Jan. "Gerrit Dou and the Art of Deception." Boston: Museum of Fine Arts public lecture video source, 2019. https://www.youtube.com/watch?v=W3OBSs6aelI.

Sokolova, Irina. *Dutch and Flemish Paintings from the Hermitage.* New York: Abrams, 1988.

SuuntoDive. "The Baltic Unveils Treasures with the Help of Suunto Divers." https://www.suunto .com/en-us/sports/News-Articles-container-page/the-baltic-unveils-treasured-secrets-with-the -help-of-suunto-divers/; 2019.

Tarasov, Artyom. *Миллионер.* Moscow: Vargius, 2004.

Tarasov, Artyom. *Тайны Фрау Марии.* Moscow: Astrel, 2010.

Touy, Thomas. "Houghton Revisited: The Walpole Masterpieces from Catherine the Great's Hermitage." *British Art Journal.* Vol. 14, no. 1, 2013.

Tronchin, Henry. *Le Counseiller Francois Tronchin et Ses Amis.* Paris, 1895.

Tsverava, G. K. *Дмитрии Алексеевич Голитсын, 1734–1803.* Leningrad: Nauka, 1985.

Valentiner, W. A. *Catalogue of a Collection of Paintings by Dutch Masters of the Seventeenth Century.* New York: Metropolitan Museum of Art, 1910.

van de Wetering, Ernst. *Rembrandt: The Painter at Work.* Amsterdam: Amsterdam University Press, 1997.

van der Schley, Phillipus, et al. *Catalogus van het Uitmuntend Kabinet Schilderyen door den Heere Gerret Braamcamp.* Amsterdam, 1771.

Veluwenkamp, Jan Willem. "Dutch Merchants in St. Petersburg in the Eighteenth Century." *Tijdschrift voor Skandinavistiek.* Vol. 16, 1995.

Wheelock Jr., Arthur, ed. *Johannes Vermeer.* Washington, DC: National Gallery of Art, 1995.

Wheelock Jr., Arthur, ed. *Gerrit Dou, 1613–1675.* Washington, DC: National Gallery of Art, 2000.

Waibor, Adriaan. *Gabriel Metsu, 1629–1667.* New Haven, Conn.: Yale University Press, 2012.

Williams, Robert. "The Quiet Trade: Russian Art and American Money." *Wilson Quarterly.* Vol. 3, no. 1, 1979.

Wolff, Larry. *Inventing Eastern Europe.* Stanford, Calif.: Stanford University Press, 1994.

Zaretsky, Robert. *Diderot and Catherine: The Empress, the Philosopher, and the Fate of the Enlightenment.* Cambridge, Mass.: Harvard University Press, 2019.

BIBLIOGRAPHY

Newspapers/News Services

Associated Press (USA)

BBC (UK)

Bisdomblad (Netherlands)

Daily Mirror (UK)

Financial Times Europe (UK)

Gloucester Echo (UK)

Helsingin Sanomat (Finland)

Helsingin Uutiset (Finland)

HuffPost (USA)

Ilta Sanomat (Finland)

Interfax (Russia)

Itogi (Russia)

Kaleva (Finland)

Kommersant (Russia)

New York Times (USA)

Päätökset (Finland)

Pravda (Russia)

Reuters (UK)

RT (Russia)

Russia Beyond (Russia)

Spectator (UK)

TASS (Russia)

Vechnost' obektiv (Russia)

Wall Street Journal (USA)

Washington Post (USA)

Washington Times (USA)

YLE (Finland)

Archives, Libraries, and Museums

Amsterdam City Archives, Amsterdam.

Amsterdam Museum, Amsterdam.

Archive of the Ministry of Foreign Affairs of the Russian Federation (Архивы МИД России), Department of Historical Documents, Moscow.

Bapst Art Library, Boston College, Boston, MA.

European Court of Human Rights Library (www.echr.coe.int).

Finnish Heritage Agency (formerly National Board of Antiquities), Helsinki.

Harvard University Fine Arts Library, Littauer Center, Cambridge, MA.

National Archives of Finland (Kansalliskarkisto), Helsinki.

National Archives of Sweden (Riksarkivet) Stockholm.

National Gallery of Art, Washington DC.

Rijksmuseum, Amsterdam.

Russian State Archive of Old Acts (Российский Государственный Архив Древник Актов, РГАДА), Moscow.

Russian State Library (Российская государственная библиотека), Moscow.

Interviews

Aarts, Marina (2019, June 6) Telephone interview from Amsterdam.

Ahlström, Christian (2013, August 6) Personal interview in Helsinki.

Airenne, Petteri (2014, June 12) Personal interview in Kirkkonummi, Finland.

Alvik, Riikka (2013, August 22) Personal interview in Helsinki.

Alvik, Riikka (2014, June 4) Personal interview in Helsinki.

Alvik, Riikka (2019, March 28) Email interview.

Aminoff, Jan (2013, August 15) Personal interview in Kirkkonummi, Finland.

Arvas, Fredrik (2019, May 6) Telephone interview from Stockholm.

Baer, Ronni (2014, March 29) Personal interview in Boston, MA.

Bull, David (2019, June 12) Telephone interview from New York, NY.

Edwall, Kjell (2019, April 23) Telephone interview from Monte Carlo, Monaco.

Ehanti, Eero (2013, July 31 and August 8) Personal interviews in Helsinki.

Ehanti, Eero (2014, June 12) Personal interview in Helsinki.

Ehanti, Eero (2017, June 28) Personal interview in Helsinki.

Fast-Matikka, Maija (2013, July 31) Personal interview in Helsinki.

Flinkman, Juha (2019, September 17) Email interview.

Hocker, Emma (2013, August 20) Personal interview in Stockholm.

Honkanen, Pekka (2019, August 6) Telephone interview from Finland.

Ilola, Ari (2014, June 9) Personal interview in Kirkkonummi, Finland.

Koivusaari, Rauno (2013, August 7 and August 13) Personal interviews in Koria, Finland.

Kokko, Rami (2013, August 25) Personal interview in Helsinki.

Kokko, Rami (2014, June 12) Personal interview in Helsinki.

Korthals Altes, Everhard (2014, March 4) Personal interview in Amsterdam.

Manders, Martijn (2014, March 6) Personal interview in Leiden, Netherlands.

Mansilla-Koivusaari, Giselle (2013, August 13) Personal interview in Koria, Finland.

Martikainen, Mikael (2013, August 28) Personal interview in Espoo, Finland.

Martikainen, Mikael (2014, June 5) Personal interview in Espoo, Finland.

Paasilehto, Satu (2013, August 16) Personal interview in Helsinki.

Petrakov, Viktor (2014, May 19) Personal interview in Moscow.

Priem, Ruud (2014, March 4) Personal interview in Amsterdam.

Rouhiainen, Petri (2013, August 14) Personal interview in Kirkkonummi, Finland.

Salonen, Kalle (2014, June 6) Personal interview in Kirkkonummi, Finland.

Salonen, Päivi (2013, August 16) Personal interview in Helsinki.

Sokolova, Irina (2014, May 21) Personal interview in St Petersburg.

Sorokin, Pyotr (2014, May 21) Personal interview in St Petersburg.

Talvela, Erkki (2014, June 11) Personal interview in Helsinki.

Terpilovskaya, Olga (2013, August 14) Personal interview in Helsinki.

Tikkanen, Sallamaria (2013, July 31) Personal interview in Helsinki.

Virtanen, Kalle (2014, June 28) Personal interview in Helsinki.

Wheelock, Arthur (2019, April 17) Personal interview in Washington, DC.

ACKNOWLEDGMENTS

The saga of the *Vrouw Maria* spans the globe, and so too did our efforts to document her journey. We received valuable insights, information, and assistance from all corners of Europe and the US. Our expert advisors on art history and conservation included Marina Aarts, Everhard Korthals Altes, and Ruud Priem in Amsterdam, David Bull in New York, Antoine Wilmering at the Getty Museum in Los Angeles, Tom van der Molen at the Amsterdam Museum, Céline Dauvergne at the Musée de Louvre in Paris, Irina Sokolova at the State Hermitage Museum in St Petersburg, Ronni Baer at the Museum of Fine Arts in Boston, Arthur Wheelock at the National Gallery of Art in Washington DC, and Lara Yeager-Crasselt at the Leiden Collection in New York. Thomas Kaplan was also more than willing to share his story as a collector and his love of Golden Age art. Martijn Manders in Leiden was a font of wisdom about the politics and practices of maritime archeology. In Sweden, Emma Hocker provided valuable insights on the conservation of the *Vasa,* while Kjell Edwall and Fredrik Arvas shared their vision of a *Vrouw Maria* museum. In Russia, Leonid Ragozin and Asiya Suleymanova helped with interviews and contacts, while Pyotr Sorokin and Viktor Petrakov spoke about their participation in the Russian delegation.

Further, many folks in Finland freely offered their personal reminiscence and professional expertise, especially: Christian Ahlström, Petteri Airenne, Riikka Alvik, Jan Aminoff, Juha Flinkman, Pekka Honkanen, Ari Ilola, Minna Koivikko, Giselle Koivusaari, Rami Kokko, Maija Mattika, Satu Paasilehtu, Petri Rouhiainen, Kalle Salonen, Päivi Salonen, Erkki Talvela, Olga Terpilovskaya, Sallamaria Tikkanen, and Kalle Virtanen. Mikael Martikainen shared his video footage and personal accounts of the expedition to find the *Vrouw Maria*, while Rauno Koivusaari spent hours regaling us with tales of his adventures at sea and showing us his scrapbooks. We would have understood much less without the assistance of Riku Rinta-Seppälä on translation. Eero Ehanti has been our champion since the day we met him, and we always appreciate his excellent insights, unrelenting enthusiasm and incomparable headwear. All of this input was invaluable for piecing together the story of the *Vrouw Maria*. Any errors are our own.

We are grateful for the ardent support of Jill Marr, baseball mom, wine lover and agent extraordinaire at Sandra Dijkstra Agency, as well as Jessica Case, our enthusiastic Russophile editor at Pegasus Books. Boston College supported us with a Faculty Fellowship and travel grant. Riikka Alvik, Lauren Hammer, Jane Kendrick, Martijn Manders, Mikael Martikainen, and Tony Wheeler gave valuable feedback on drafts of the manuscript. Kathleen Easter, Claire Moodie, Tuomas and Tiia Ojala, and Marty Vorhees helped out in unexpected but invaluable ways. Roy and Ruth Vorhees played a critical role in bringing this book to life by accompanying us on our travels, entertaining our children, and always believing in us. Speaking of our children, Van and Shay tagged along on many research trips and tolerated our many hours in front of computers. They have witnessed every step of the creation of this book; may they be inspired to continue to travel the world, discover its many treasures, and share their stories.

Finally, we are forever thankful for our first introduction to Finland back in 1988—a trip that was sponsored by Youth for Understanding (YFU) and the Finnish-US Senate Youth Exchange (FUSSYE). Ever since, we have been welcomed into the hearts and homes of Outi and Kauko Ojala, who are the truest example of Finnish hospitality, rivaling even the Moomins in their love of laughter and generosity of spirit. Never enough *kiitos* and *kippis*.

INDEX

INDEX

INDEX

INDEX

INDEX

INDEX